THE MASTER

HIS LIFE AND TEACHINGS

THE MASTER

KNOWN UNTO THE WORLD AS
JESUS THE CHRIST

HIS LIFE AND TEACHINGS

BEING RECOVERIES BY THE WRITER THROUGH
ILLUMINATIONS, VISIONS AND EXPERIENCES
WHEREIN ARE SET FORTH THE INNER MEANINGS
OF THE MASTER'S TEACHINGS, AND THE NATURE
OF HIS JESUSHOOD AND CHRISTHOOD.

J. TODD FERRIER

THE ORDER OF THE CROSS
10 DE VERE GARDENS, KENSINGTON, LONDON W.8

First Published in 1913
Second Edition, 1925
Reprinted 1953
Reprinted 1980

ISBN 900235 02 6

PRINTED IN GREAT BRITAIN BY
LOWE AND BRYDONE PRINTERS LTD, THETFORD, NORFOLK

DEDICATION

To the Name and Memory of the BELOVED ONE through whom the beautiful manifestation of Christhood was given and the mysterious Sin-offering accomplished, concerning which remarkable events the following Illuminations and Recoveries came to me :—

To AMY, helpmeet and companion, the sharer of the loneliness and awful sorrow which were my portion during the years in which the Recoveries were made and the Illuminations received ;

To ROBERT HOWELL PERKS, M.D., F.R.C.S., my friend in tribulation and brother in ministry, whose confidence in the heavenly nature and source of the Teachings herein set forth (with many others yet to be given to the world) has often comforted me amid conditions the most trying and painful ;

And to all Souls who are able to receive the message, and who would know the blessedness of the realization of the holy estates of Jesushood and Christhood, and understand the profound mystery of the Sin-offering, this endeavour to restore the sublime vision given through the Life and Teachings of the beloved Master, is affectionately dedicated.

PREFACE

In presenting this volume to the religious public as a contribution to the theological problems of our time, especially the difficult question of the reality of the beloved Master who is known as Jesus the Christ, the writer would have it understood that he lays no claim to such scholastic attainments as have been revealed in the works of recent writers on the Historical Jesus ; nor does he desire that this volume should be regarded as a contribution of that order. Whilst criticism of the traditional sources and interpretations has been found necessary in the new statement of spiritual facts, it should be borne in mind that the chief object of the work is essentially spiritual. The appeal in the Teachings is, as it was in the days of the Manifestation, direct to the Soul, and not to the Traditions of the Elders, however venerable. For this reason he feels that the teachings will not command the interest and approbation of those who are accustomed to follow the purely traditional methods of research and interpretation ; but he has reason for believing that there are many Souls awaiting such a message, who will gladly welcome a true vision of the Master, and what He meant by Jesushood, Christhood, and a Lord-consciousness.

J. TODD FERRIER.

" Roselle," Paignton.

PITY   COMPASSION   LOVE

SELF-ABANDONMENT

REDEMPTION

The Order of the Cross

SPIRITUAL
AIMS AND IDEALS

THE Order is an informal Brotherhood and Fellowship, having for
its service in life the cultivation of
the Spirit of Love towards all Souls:
Helping the weak and defending the
defenceless and oppressed; Abstaining
from hurting the creatures, eschewing
bloodshed and flesh eating, and living
upon the pure foods so abundantly
provided by nature; Walking in the
Mystic Way of Life, whose Path leads
to the realization of the Christhood;
And sending forth the Mystic Teachings
unto all who may be able to receive
them — those sacred interpretations
of the Soul, the Christhood, and
the Divine Love and Wisdom, for
which the Order of the Cross stands.

SELF-SACRIFICE

SELF-DENIAL

REGENERATION

ILLUMINATION

SERVICE   DEVOTION   PURITY

Contents

PART I.

Did the Master Live as a Man?

*Being an answer to the present-day
inquiry such as the historical
records have failed to furnish, and transcending
any historical or
traditional
evidence.*

A

HISTORY REPEATS ITSELF

WAS there ever such a manifestation of Christhood as the Western World believes to have been made nineteen centuries ago ?

Did Jesus live as a man upon the outer spheres of this world ; and if so, was He the one through whom the Christhood was made manifest ?

If Jesus did live some nineteen centuries ago, and if He became the vehicle of the Christhood manifestation, where may we find certain evidence of that fact in view of the contradictory positions taken up by the several schools of thought within the Churches, and the untenable positions which were held by those schools who implicitly trusted the four Gospels wherein the life of the Master is supposed to be truly set forth, but which have been shown to contain the most irreconcilable statements ?

Or is the presentation in the four Gospel Records not to be taken literally, nor to be understood in a personal sense, nor to be interpreted in relation to any one incarnate life ; but rather to be viewed as the idealization of the life of every man, that life unto the attainment of which all Souls yearn ? Is it the dream-vision of the sublime " life in fulness " that breaks in the appointed time upon every one to thrust him or her forward to the attainment, by realization, of perfect Being ?

Such are some of the questions of the hour, and they are questions which are momentous in nature, and whose answers should be found. They are questions whose right answers *must* be found if historic Christianity is to play its true part in the new age which is now breaking upon the world. The time is past when earnest seekers after the truth can be satisfied by an appeal to any external authority. The claims put forth by the various Orthodox Schools on behalf of the four Gospel Records, have been found wanting. Hence the distrust with which many most earnest, thoughtful, and cultured men and women regard the accredited sources of information concerning the Life and Teachings of the blessed Master. To them the New Testament Records seem to contain the most remarkable contradictions in their narratives ; and many statements concerning the Christ's conduct, which, in the very nature of things, and assuming the fact that the Master was born into this world as a man, were impossible. And we cannot but regard this new awakening of the spirit of earnest inquiry, and all the questions concerning the reality of the Christhood manifestation, as the rehabilitation of that Soul inquiry during the early centuries of this Era which, for lack of true guidance and illumination, issued in the positions taken up by the Docetæ and the true Gnostics. History repeats itself. And it may be that many scholars, not discerning the meaning of the renewed inquiry, nor understanding the spirit moving behind and through the questioners, will behold nothing more in these things than the revival of the ancient gnostic heresies. For that is how many men will be led to view the new awakening, and to speak and write of it—men great and noble in their way, but who are so bound with the chains of literalism that they cannot get away from the physical and historical and, therefore, low lying valleys, and are unable to ascend to those heights where the vision is truly spiritual, rarefied and beautiful, and full of a certainty transcending any outward evidence of truth.

The Higher Criticism

From an historical standpoint, the Higher Criticism has been a great success, though from a spiritual point of view the same cannot be said of it. Indeed spiritually it has been an entire failure, for it has never been *a true* Higher Criticism. It has never attempted to find, in any degree whatever, the true spiritual significance lying beneath and beyond the things recorded, but has contented itself with arranging the writings according to data, and treating the contents of these in a purely verbal and historical way. As an honest endeavour on the part of many of the most cultured scholars, it has never reached those spiritual altitudes which should be found and scaled by a true Higher Criticism, nor shown that it had any power or even desire to do so. It has failed lamentably in that it could not penetrate the outward veil to find the treasure behind it. It has taken away without giving ; it has destroyed without building up. It has taken away so much as untrustworthy, and left thoughtful and enquiring men and women who trusted the Records, to grope in the darkness. It has razed the foundations upon which so many had built, and has caused their superstructures to be thrown down ; but it has left those who have thus suffered loss, amid the ruins it has made, being unable to reveal to them the only true and sure foundation on which to build faith and life.

WHAT IT HAS DONE OF GOOD

Yet we must acknowledge that one great good has issued from its destructive work. It is this : it has awakened many from their false security. It has sent a wave of disturbing influences right over the sea of thought within the Churches, compelling many to change their moorings and seek an anchorage where belief cannot be shaken and driven away from its sure and certain hold of truth. And thus a great work has been done by it. For it has prepared the way for the breaking of the spiritual vision upon all true mystic Souls through constraining them, by means of its conclusions, to seek for another view than that usually held by the various Theological Schools concerning the life of Jesus and the nature of the Christ, the real Teachings concerning the life unto which He called all Souls, and the work which He said He had come to accomplish. If its methods have been ultra-rationalistic, and its more apparent results just such as have brought joy to the heart of the rationalist, yet assuredly good has grown out of its work for the mystic Souls ;

for these have been driven to the spiritual realm or Kingdom of the Soul, to there seek for the true and inner meaning of the Life and Teachings of the Master. Though for these hungering Souls the work of the Higher Criticism has not discovered the real wealth buried beneath the mass of apparent history found in the present gospels, yet the taking away of so much of the debris has contributed in no small degree to the possibility of the true portraiture of the Master being restored to the whole western world. For it is absolutely essential to that much to be desired realization, that those who are the accredited scholars within the schools should remove the false glamour that has surrounded the Gospel Histories, and, consequently, the mistaken trust that has been so fully and unquestionably reposed in them as true records of the Life lived by the beloved Master, the Teachings which He gave in public and private, the Works which He wrought, and the purpose of the Manifestation. The careful examination and sifting of the subject-matter found in the narratives has removed some barriers that once were deemed insuperable. Imaginary obstacles have passed away. But the true spiritual realm has not been reached through the casting of the materials into the crucible, rich as these are ; nor has the true solvent been found by the Higher Criticism whereby the profound problems arising out of the Christhood history can be solved. For the spiritual realm cannot be reached by seeking along the merely historical plane ; nor can the true solvent be found by any such methods as those adopted by the Higher Criticism. These are both of the Kingdom of the Soul, and they must be sought for and found by man within the inner sanctuary of his own being.

HOW THE MYSTICS WERE MISLED

The true mystics have never been satisfied with the Gospel Records as mere histories. This they have made obvious in their writings, from the post-Apostolic Fathers until our own time. They have always felt the necessity for other than a literal reading of these Records, and have striven after the spiritual meanings hidden within the letter. Though they were unable to discern the innermost meanings in the teachings associated with the life of the Master, yet they recognized in them allegories of profound Soul verities. And it is this same attitude of earnest seeking and spiritual inquiry which we find in our midst to-day. The Higher Criticism has helped these Souls on the historical plane by confirming their own inner feelings concerning the Records, that these could not be accepted literally as a true portraiture of the Christ ; and so, in seeking for the true picture of the Christhood, we have a revival of early gnosticism in its various phases, and even a re-affirmation of the position taken up by the Docetæ.

Nor is it surprising that there should be found those who question whether there ever was such a thing as a Divine Manifestation ; whether the holy estate of Christhood was revealed through any one life ; whether indeed any man lived such a life as the Jesus-life. For the Records themselves, with their astounding contradictions and impossible situations as literal events, give no sure and certain evidence of the fact that the one whom we speak of as the Master really did live, and that in His life He was *Jesus, the Christ, and the Lord.* For many of the events recorded are in direct opposition to the beautiful meaning of these terms, as will be presently shown. Some of the situations in which the Master is found, would have been betrayals of the life of purity, illumination, and divine direction signified by them. For instance, there could have been no Jesus-life in a man who drank wine and ate the flesh of the creatures. There could not have been Christhood in one who poured out such scathing woes upon individuals who differed from him. Nor could there have been the consciousness of the Divine Presence within the Soul so as to make him one with that Presence in the whole purpose and glory of life, in any one who called himself the " Bread of Life," the " True Vine," the " Light of the World," the " Water of Life," the " Door into the Sheepfold," the " Good Shepherd," the " Son of Man," and other like titles. For the very consciousness of the Divine Presence within him would have led him always to speak of these titles as belonging wholly to the Divine (which indeed the blessed Master always did, though the writers of the Records gave them a personal turn, and made it appear as if the Master applied them to Himself).

But though the mystic Souls have rejected the Gospel Records as literal statements of historic narrative, and have sought for the spiritual meanings that they felt were to be found within the narratives, yet they have not been able to arrive at the true and full vision of the Christ-life that was made manifest through the blessed Master, owing to the difficulties arising out of the wrong presentation in the Records. They have beheld something of the innate light showing itself within the narratives, but could not discern the glorious meaning of a Christhood because of the false things worked up into these. Glints and gleamings of some sublime life have they gathered out of these narratives ; but the Radiant Image they have been unable to behold for the now obvious reason that it is so greatly obscured by portraitures which were not true of the Master. *For, to behold that wonderful vision of the Radiant Image would be to behold the true meaning of the Jesus-life, the significance of a Christhood, and the wealth of realization indicated in the Vision of the Lord.* And it is the restoration of that vision to the mystic Souls which we have endeavoured to present, so that the Master as He was may be beheld once more, the Jesus-life understood, the Christhood-life realized, and the sublime Vision of the Lord attained.

B

QUESTIONS OF MOMENT

IF the Master did not live upon the earth as man in the state of the Jesus-life, and as the vehicle of the Christhood manifestation, whence came the wonderful Teachings ascribed to Him ? Supposing there was no incarnate life known as the Master, how did these profound and sublime Teachings come, and who were the recipients of them ? Though the radiance of the image of Christhood is veiled in the Gospel Records, and though the very form is marred in outline, yet the image is discernible. It is seen, though very imperfectly. It is even felt by the Soul ; for in a remarkable way it draws Souls towards itself. Though the glory be veiled and the image marred, its magnetic power is still operative. How was this radiant image, so full of divine attraction even in its veiled and marred presentation, impressed upon the minds of those who wrote of it ? Whence could such an image be born or fashioned within the Soul ? It is acknowledged to be most transcendent, and that even by those who have not had any opportunity of beholding it in its full purity, beauty and glory. Unto whom then was such a conception of life given ?

All that is implied in these questions does not appear to have seriously weighed with those who reject the assumption that the Master did actually live upon the earth as a man. Even the position taken up by modern Docetism, though it has something to recommend it, does not lessen the difficulties of the situation created by the discovery that within the writings of the four Evangelists the radiant image may be traced, though it is in a veiled and marred condition. For, if the Teachings were discovered by some Souls in their search for the Divine Life, where did they discover them ? And if they were communicated unto them because they were ready to receive them, how were they communicated ? Upon what plane of experience did they receive these most wonderful Teachings concerning the

11

Christhood ? Indeed, if no real body of manifestation was shown to them, and the various states of the Jesus-life, the Christ-life, and the Vision of the Lord, illustrated by means of it, how came it to pass that they were able to understand the meaning of the Teachings communicated to them ? And if they really beheld a body of manifestation, where did they behold it ?

The demands upon the credulity of the mind which either of these two theories of the Divine Revelation implied in the Teachings concerning the Christhood, are even greater than those made by a rightly interpreted historical life through whom the Manifestation was made and the Teachings given. For, to have been able to receive with the understanding the wonderful Teachings wherein the beautiful, radiant, Divine Image was originally revealed, would have meant that those who were so blessed in their experience and honoured of the Heavens, were themselves in a state of Christhood :—that is, that they were in a spiritual state which enabled them to function upon the higher spiritual spheres and receive from them, even in a fuller sense than the best prophets ever received, the sublime Teachings. Or if these Teachings were given through such a body of manifestation as we can only designate a " phantom " or ethereal order, and the various states illustrated through that body, then those who were the recipients of such a vision, or rather, series of visions, must have known at some time of their history what a Christhood was, otherwise how were they able to recognize the manifestation as that of Christhood ? What could they have understood of the Nature, the Attributes, the Office, and the Purpose of a Christhood, supposing they had never known anything of such an estate within themselves ?

How Divine Revelation Comes

In the process of Divine Revelation, only those things which the Soul hath known of old time may be again unveiled or revealed to her. What she hath not known would not be understood by her when presented. And herein lieth the mystery of *real intuition* or the inborn knowledge of spiritual and divine things. And herein also is to be found the meaning of the inherent mysticism of a high order so manifest in some Souls, and in less intense degree in others. *True Revelation is by means of Soul recovery.* And it is accomplished through the indwelling Paraclete, the Divine Remembrancer, who brings to the Soul the remembrance of *all* things which have been known unto it of old time. But such a state of experience for any one implies a Christhood. For Christhood is a condition of the innermost life, *a state of the Soul ;* and it is a state of *illumination.* It is a spiritual experience in which the Lamp of the Soul is kindled from the Divine Spirit. In that state the whole Sanctuary of the innermost Being is lit up, everything of the past is revealed to the Soul, and all things appear in their true relationship. But such an exalted state of experience also implies, in the very nature of things, the attainment of the Jesus-life ; for the realization of Christhood is the crown of the Jesus-life. It is that state of perfect interior illumination as the result of the attainment of Jesushood or the life of purity and love.

If, therefore, the wonderful vision which is found veiled and marred in the Gospel Records, was beheld by those who first communicated the Revelation of the radiant image of the divine Christhood, with all the wealth of individual and planetary history implied in the wonderful Teachings, they must have been not only in that state of experience which we have spoken of as Jesus-hood, the life of beautiful purity and spiritual love ; but they must also have been in the state of Christhood, and so able to receive such a sublime vision from the Divine Spirit within them, and to understand its profound significance. *Who is prepared to accept this solution of the Christ problem ?* To accept it would not lessen the difficulties concerning the Manifestation ; it would increase them.

13

THE PURPOSE OF THE MANIFESTATION

But let us turn to another side of the question and see whether in it the true answer may be found. As Revelation is by means of Soul recovery through the restoration of the innermost life to a state of consciousness in which the Divine Presence or Paraclete is realized in such fullness that the Soul is able to see in the light of that Presence, it is evident that few have reached that state at any time. And so Souls have had to be spiritually educated through the objective world. Religious symbolism has had a great and beautiful purpose, when rightly understood and interpreted. It has been a means of education. The Soul had to learn the meaning of spiritual things through the visualization of them. Even those who had once known the inner meaning of the truths visualized, but who had lost them after what is understood as " The Fall," had to have their own inherent knowledge recovered for them by means of the language of symbols. And when any one rose up out of the sensuous conditions around him and found himself able to look upon the Angelic World and receive teaching from those Heavens, the teaching was given in the language of symbols. It was in that language that so many of the prophetic visions were received.

But in the case of the recovery of the Soul to the consciousness and realization of Christhood, something more than symbol was required. It became necessary for the Jesus or pure life to be once more interpreted to the world, and the meaning of a Christhood made manifest ; for the meaning of Christhood had been lost even amongst those who belonged to the Schools of the Prophets. The memory of what was implied in the beautiful estate slept within those who once had known the experience. The effect of the materialization of all the sacred Mysteries, and the profound impersonal spiritual meanings contained in the realization of Christhood, was, to throw a veil over the inner vision and prevent the meanings from being truly understood.

This was one reason why Souls could not behold the vision again, nor reach up to it.

But there were also other reasons, and one very special reason, why it was found to be so difficult to return into the consciousness of the Soul's ancient heritage. It was the state of the Astral Kingdom. The Astral Kingdom is the elemental world whose circulus embraces the Earth and acts as the middle kingdom between the physical spheres and the Heavens. It is " the middle wall " or " partition " referred to in the Epistolary Letters. It is that world wherein all " the graven images " were written, " the handwritings " which were against us, and which had to be blotted out before Redemption could be accomplished in its fullness for the world. And it was on account of the condition of that elemental kingdom that so few rose in spiritual estate even to the Jesus-life ; for it oppressed them, and afflicted them with its evil influences. It prevented the Angelic Heavens from approaching most Souls, and perverted the beautiful messages from the Divine Love which were sent down.

It was therefore an absolute necessity in the work of the Divine Love for the accomplishment of the Redemption of all Souls, that the conditions of that kingdom should be changed ; that the " graven images " which were as " handwritings " against us, should be blotted out ; that the elements of that kingdom should be so purified that they would no longer afflict the Soul nor hinder its heavenward march. And it was that work which constituted the tragic Sin-offering, and which took place after the Divine Manifestation. It was the work which the Christ-Soul whom we have to speak of as the Master, went away to accomplish.

THE THREEFOLD DIVINE PURPOSE

The coming of the Christ into " this cosmos " or order of things, had, therefore, a threefold purpose. He was made manifest in order that " the works of the devil " might be overthrown—that is, that the effects of the negativing and destroying elemental powers of the Astral Kingdom might be overcome. He came to do the works of the Father, to make Him manifest, to declare and interpret His Love, to reveal His glorious Wisdom which had been hidden for untold ages, to seek out unto the finding of " the lost sheep of the House of Israel " (those Souls who once knew the Christhood and its ministry), and to give Himself as " a ransom " for the world.

Of such a nature was the sublime manifestation given through the Master. It was first of all an embodiment of the Jesus state —that experience of life in which every way is pure, every purpose noble, and the love is all-embracing and universal in its sympathies and expressions.

Then it was an interpretation, and so a revelation, of the meaning of Christhood—that beautiful experience in which the innermost life is truly and fully illumined from the Divine Spirit, and is able to understand and interpret the Divine Wisdom ; the attainment by such an one of that inherent power by means of which he or she can rise above all elemental influences, and reach the most transcendent experiences in what may be spoken of as the Divine Vision.

And then it was the manifestation and interpretation of the purpose of the Eternal and ever Blessed One towards all His children, even the very least, even all those who were afar off in their spiritual state, that they should be delivered from their bondage and saved from all their enemies, even from the influences of the elemental world, and that they should be brought up into the wonderful spiritual state of the Jesus-life, and know the joy which the full redemption brings.

C

HOW HIS COMING WAS OBSCURED

WE recognize how imperfect the evidence is of a historical order that He whom we speak of as the Master did live as a man. The Gospels cannot be trusted as sure evidence, for they are in many ways self-contradictory. They have been appealed to by the schools all through the centuries ; but in vain. As far as they are concerned, no true solution of the question has been given, nor have they enabled any one to behold the blessed Master *as He was*. The true meaning of Christhood has remained hidden. They called the Master, Jesus ; but they knew not the meaning of the term, and in what sense He was Jesus. They named Him the Christ ; yet in the presentation of that Christhood they betrayed all that is implied in the sacred term. They gave Him the title of Lord, bringing down the Divine Name to the mere personal life ; and thus they confused things that were essentially different, and veiled the divine vision.

For in the Records these beautiful terms are not interpreted by and through the Master, but are all related to Himself personally. His coming into this cosmos is so much misrepresented that no one can learn from the evangelists the nature and manner of His coming, with the result that it is shrouded in an atmosphere of unreality. The very stories by which His coming was surrounded and supposed to be explained—stories which have given rise to so much conflict—stories supposed to foretell His birth and the nature of it, and the accompanying of it with the most astounding phenomena in the Heavens— had naught to do with the birth of the man into the outer spheres, but were all spiritual in their nature and divine in their innermost meanings. They were so used that they obscured the true humanity of the life born. Nor could the nature of

17

His birth be clearly discerned. And through this wrong use of them, all the wealth of spiritual history hidden in these stories also became lost to the Soul. Indeed, from His birth until He passed away at the conclusion of the Divine Manifestation when the Christhood was withdrawn in order that the Sin-offering could be begun, the Master's life, ministry and teachings were obscured, misrepresented, and thus made to fail in their beautiful purpose. So effectually indeed did the writers of the Records accomplish the obscuration of the Christ-vision given through the Master, that no one has ever discerned the true image within them. The Jesus they portray does not live the Jesus-life ; He eats flesh and drinks wine. Of Him did they write that, so accentuated was eating and drinking in His life, the people said, " Behold a gluttonous man and a wine-bibber." The Christ they draw is not the image of the Radiant One : it is too Jewish ; it savours of the Jewish conception of the Divine Father. The outbursts of indignation, the harsh judgments against individuals, the personal claims attributed to Him, His acceptance of the homage of men and women, His claim to be the Lord, were not true features of a Divine Christ-hood.

For such a Christhood is, in the very nature of things, as inpersonal even as the Divine Father. It is pure in every thought and patient under the most severe ordeal, even as the Divine Love has always been. It is most lowly in spirit, ever meek and gentle, refusing the homage of men, and directing all Souls to worship the Eternal Father only. The writers of the Gospels did not understand the true meaning of Christhood ; they have therefore most grievously misrepresented it and done dishonour unto Him who made it manifest. For the Christhood of the blessed Master was the true revelation of the Radiant One. It was the perfect interpretation of the Divine Love and the Divine Wisdom through the Jesus-life. And had that manifestation of the Divine Love and the interpretation of the Divine

18

Wisdom been truthfully set forth in the Gospels, the history of Christianity would have been one woven in Love, and not in the blood of the saints ; it would have been one written in letters illumined with the Light of the Divine Wisdom, and not in those of darkness, persecution and anguish. The Radiant Image would have been beheld by all who truly sought the vision, and the Jesus-life would have been understood and lived by them. There would have been no doubt left in the Records regarding the reality of His appearing, nor of the nature of Christhood, nor of the sublime purpose of the Divine Manifestation through Him ; for He would have been seen as He was, and understood in the wonderful work He had to accomplish.

And now we have to speak of Him as He was, and how the vision and knowledge of it has come to us. In doing so we know we shall tread on difficult ground, and lay ourselves open to being both misunderstood and misrepresented. We therefore do it with feelings of great diffidence, and only because it is laid upon us to tell what we know. We are constrained and led by powers other than those of men, or of the world, to interpret the Life and Teachings of the beloved Master in a manner consonant with the Divine Manifestation which was made through Him. A great burden has been laid upon us, even that of *the recovery*, by experiences hereafter indicated, of the long lost vision of that Christhood which was so wonderfully made manifest through the Master, and also the profound Teachings which He gave to the inner group of the disciples. In vision we have beheld Him under manifold experiences, from the days of His childhood up to the tragic Gethsemane, and afterwards.

D

THE VISIONS BEHELD

THE New Interpretations of the Life, Teachings and Purpose of the sublime manifestation through the Master, which we have been led to give in the various unfoldments that will be found in this volume, have all come to the writer as the result of experiences of the most strange and even profound nature through which he has been made to pass. All the conditions suggested by the narratives, and the experiences indicated in the Logia, even where the experiences were of a deep and tragic nature, have been passed through by him. The remarkable Life of the blessed Master ; who He was ; who it was who over-shadowed Him ; His home in childhood ; His training in youth ; His manhood ; how He lived and served : —the wonderful manifestation of the Divine Love which was beheld in his life, and of the Divine Wisdom recognized in His Teachings :—the overwhelming mysteries associated with the Sin-offering accomplished by Him—these have been given to him in visions, Illuminations and momentous Realizations. They have come to him in hours when the conditions within and around him were such that he has felt as if he were no longer a denizen of this world, and that the world's activities were all hushed, as if they must be silent in the presence of the new conditions born from the approach of the Divine Presence. They have come in the night season, in the morning, and even in the noon-day, amid the great silence which was imposed upon his life. To describe adequately the experiences as they were passed through, is impossible. The things seen, heard and felt by him, could not be described. Many of them cannot even be spoken. But he has been conscious of passing, as it were, far out of the spheres of the Earth ; of being lifted up into the Angelic Heavens after the manner in which it is said the ancient Seers were carried up of the Spirit. Visions of the most transcendent nature have broken upon him in those hours. These

20

were concerning the past history of this Planet ; its real Golden Age and its terrible Fall ; the Mystery of its varied Races, Creature and Human ; the true nature and evolution of the Human Soul ; the Mystery of the Redemption and the age of the Regeneration ; the ministry of the Divine Love and Wisdom unto the Planet and its Races in the long ages of its history ; the wonderful purpose of the Divine Love and Wisdom concerning the Restoration of the Earth and all her Souls to their pristine glory ; the glorious Manifestation of that purpose revealed and interpreted through the Life and Teachings of the Master, from the meaning of the Jesus-life and the Christhood estate to the accomplishment of that profound work known now as the Sin-offering.

EXPERIENCES PASSED THROUGH

Such events as he has been permitted to record concerning the Master during the Manifestation through Him, and the Sin-offering after the Manifestation, he has not only witnessed as one might witness a series of dioramic scenes, *but he has had to feel them as if the actions had some relation to himself*, and he has felt them sometimes so intensely as to be quite overwhelmed. All the joys and the sorrows; the hopes and the discouragements; glory ineffable, and darkness of Soul indescribable ; the joyance of great hope, and the saddening effect of the most terrible disappointments ; the sublimity of the Beatific Vision, and the unspeakable horror of those things which are generated in the Hells of the world ; the wonderful blessedness of the Jesus-life and the Christ-consciousness, and the fearful nature of the burden of the Sin-offering ; the pain and sorrow of the Master as He moved through the awful conditions of Jewry, and the still more poignant pain and sorrow, anguish and agony of the Gethsemane Vision ;—these have all been experienced by him in the wonderful recovery of the knowledge of the Master as He was, and the work which He was sent from the Father to do. And had it not been that the very Heavens were bowed down in beautiful ministry unto him, he could not have borne the burden, so terrible was it in nature, and so great was the poignancy of the Soul-anguish.

That the blessed Master lived as man, the writer has the assurance from that unfailing source whence all things are truly known. And the nature of the disaster that befell the beautiful spiritual states which He interpreted as the Jesus-life and the Christhood consciousness, with the luminous Teachings which He gave, he also knows from the same sure source. The traditional sources do not recognize that source as sure because it does not belong to the outward phenomenal world. Yet the Schools will have to recognize it. Indeed the remarkable and gracious spiritual movements in the world to-day resulting from the new Soul-awakening, are hastening the hour. The withering breath of criticism sent forth by the advanced scholars, is doing much to remove any surety from the traditional sources and methods which may be in the minds of those who have so implicitly trusted them ; whilst *the Holy Breath of the Divine Spirit within the Soul* is constraining truly spiritual men and women to seek for guidance from that world whence all that is best within them has come. *For that world is a stupendous reality.*

The Master

*Being the true picture of Him as
He was in His Life, private
and public ; and of the nature
of His Teachings to the
inner group of disciples,
and to the whole
world, given in
Parable and
Allegory.*

A

THE ADVENT OF THE MASTER

TO draw a perfect picture of any one is not an easy task. The artist and the biographer know this. So easy is it to fail to get the true expression, the features as they reveal themselves in repose and under the deepest feeling. And of the Master is this specially true. In presenting a picture of Him as He was, the difficulties are great.

First of all, there is the knowledge that He was not just as other men are ; that He stood alone. As he has written of Him, the writer has felt how inadequate any portrayal of His most wonderful Life must be. It was so unlike the life lived by men and women, for it was transcendent in its blessed realizations and beautiful manifestations ; whilst in the later years it was most sad, for He was called upon to pass through the most mysterious sorrows and profound anguish. His Life was so wonderful that it is not too much to write of it that it was the very glory of God in sublime manifestation ; and the very pleroma of all human sorrow and anguish. Well may we write of Him, that, in His Life, He was the express likeness of the Father. Yet when we turn to the closing years of that Life, how may we make obvious the meaning of the awful mysterious sorrow and anguish which wore Him down and found vent in the unspeakable agony of the Gethsemane cry ? Verily, He stood alone !

Then there is this difficulty, that those who are interested in any portraiture of Him that might be presented, have been taught certain things concerning Him which are foreign to a true picture of the life He lived and the work He did ; and in the mind of all who have received these teachings there is a bias against the embodiment of Him as He was, a bias so accentuated through the influences of all the ages of the Christian Era, that it is most difficult to overcome.

25

And then there is that almost insuperable difficulty of the Gospel Records, the sources of these false lineaments, to criticize which seems sacrilegious to many, and arouses in these latter such a state of opposition that it becomes almost impossible for them to even give a hearing to any other view of these Records than what is acknowledged to be traditional.

But unto all who are in that blessed state of Soul-desire when Truth is sought out at all cost, and everything of this world is accounted as nothing in comparison with its possession, we will endeavour to give a very brief outline of the conditions amid which the Master came, the wonderful Life He made manifest, the still more wonderful Teachings given by Him to the inner group of disciples, together with the meaning of His deep mysterious anguish and sorrow, and their relation to the accomplishment of the tragic Sin-offering.

THE STATE OF JEWRY

When the Master came into this world the spiritual conditions were very bad. Jewry was only a religion in name. Spiritual impoverishment had become the natural state of the people. The " balm of Gilead " had been long lost—the knowledge and power of a divine healing for all Life. Within the elaborate priesthood of Jewry there was no true physician found who could diagnose the hurt of the people, and bring to them the divine healing and comfort. Bald ceremonial and lifeless traditions were accounted true religion. *It was a religion without the Spirit.* Within the Synagogues the light to guide the Soul was as the darkness, for a naked literalism had blinded the Intuition. The Temple in Jerusalem which was looked upon as the abode of the Divine Presence, and regarded with feelings the most sacred, was simply a magnificent abattoir. Its threshold was the scene of the most astounding cruelties, and its Altars may truly be said to have " run blood " continually. The outer courts were as shambles, and the priestly courts were scenes of death. The creatures were sacrificed as a most solemn religious function, one which was supposed to be acceptable to the Divine Love, and the ritual by means of which the healing of the people could alone be accomplished. The whole religious atmosphere was heavy ; indeed it could not be otherwise. The spiritual density of the conditions was appalling. No Divine Cloud rested upon the Sanctuary. Instead of that holy and significant sign of the Presence of the Eternal One within the sanctuary of the Soul, there was a cloud belt environing and overhanging the holy city, literally and spiritually. It was the blood of the slaughtered creatures. Jerusalem was a city of tragedies, the more tragic because they were done in the name of the holy and ever Blessed One, and on behalf of the spiritual welfare of the people. The leaders and teachers of the people lived in that cloud ; it was their natural element. They looked at everything through it, yet saw not that it miraged all things. Its depressing conditions were unfelt by them ; they were unconscious of the hurt which its evil elements brought.

THE MATERIALIZATION OF HEBREW MYSTERIES

Jewry was an amazing illustration of the inversion of everything that was of the Soul, and the perversion of everything divine. All the sacred Mysteries handed down from the ancient Hebrews, had been materialized. Terms expressive of the most beautiful experiences in the growth and unfoldment of the Soul, were applied to persons, situations, rivers, places, uplands and mountains. The history of the Soul going away from the land of the Divine Life, was converted into that of a man upon these outer spheres.[1] The story of the Soul in spiritual bondage was changed into a history of the Jews in Egypt. The deliverance

---

[1]Whereas the true history on which that story was built was Planetary. Abraham was not a man, but the representation of the divine estate of the Soul whom we are accustomed to think of as the Planet And the going down of Abraham into Egypt was the descent of the whole spiritual system of this world, into the conditions of life which the term Egypt represented in the ancient times. And likewise was the offering up of Isaac a profound spiritual and soullic event.

of the Soul from the powers that oppress and degrade it, was made to relate to a supposed miraculous deliverance of the Jews from the thraldom of life under one of the Pharaohs. The journeyings of the Soul in " the wilderness of sin," its bitter experiences, disappointments and afflictions, were made use of to build up a false history of the Jews crowded with wonderful events and miraculous interpositions on the part of the Divine. The Mysteries of Mount Sinai and Mount Horeb, whose meanings were purely soullic, and concerning the divine purpose, the Priesthoods took and turned into outward things. The teachings relating to the Tabernacle and the Temple— teachings wholly spiritual and essentially inward, and both retrospective and prospective—were all converted into objective and material things. The Tabernacle in the wilderness and the Temple in the land of promise, were materialized into meanings which associated them with mere earthly houses for priestly ceremonial. The sacred Ark of the Divine Presence within the sanctuary of every Soul, became in their hands a small tabernacle fashioned by them and carried from place to place on great occasions as the very Ark of the Divine Presence. The most sacred history of the Planet's spiritual household, and the stages or stations of the Soul's true evolution implied in " the twelve sons of Jacob " and " the twelve tribes," they exploited of all their wonderful significances, and applied to twelve men, twelve communities born from these men, and the twelve portions of the land of Palestine apportioned to each community. They took the teachings concerning the Christhood estate which were known to the Hebrews, and brought all of them down in their meanings, as may be discovered in the mutilated fragments scattered throughout the writings of the Old Testament, especially in the Prophetic Books. The doctrine of the coming Sin-offering which had been communicated unto the ancient Seers of the *true* Hebrew Communities, and which may be found amid the wreckage of the once compact teachings of this ancient people, now strewn throughout the Hagiographa or Sacred Poetical Books, and the Prophets, the various Priest-hoods changed into the awful system of bloody sacrifices which prevailed throughout the history of Jewry—a system that dethroned the Divine Love, betrayed the Divine Wisdom, and degraded the things that were once so sublime to make of them in their representation, things terribly sensuous and cruel.

They thus converted the most profound Soul-histories into the outward history of themselves as a peculiar people and nation, using all the sacred terms which were related in an empirical sense to those histories, to designate the mountains and hills, rivers, districts, cities and villages of their land, until all the Mysteries, the marvellous heritage once possessed by the Hebrews, became lost to the Soul. Like the most sacred planetary spiritual essences whose generative, fructifying and nourishing powers depend upon their purity and volatility, and whose service in the Planet's economy is nullified when they are crystallized ; so was it with the heavenly treasures which fell into the hands of the materializing priests of Jewry. They were shut up in material forms, crystallized into the rites by which Jewry has been known, deprived of their power to nourish the Soul, robbed of their fructifying energy to such an extent that Jewry became a dead religion, a religion without the Light of the Spirit, and, therefore, a religion incapable of giving birth to Christhood, and which did not even bring forth the Jesus-life—*i.e.*, a life of purity and love.

DID JEWRY PRODUCE THE MASTER ?

The Master was not born of Jewry, notwithstanding all that has been written to prove that He was. There was *no room in the Inn* of Jewry for so blessed an event. And this would have been evident in any true portraiture of Him. To all who once behold the true picture, the Jewish elements which marred and falsified that picture, are obvious. So far from producing Him, Jewry became an ever-increasing and painful burden to His spirit as the consciousness of the divine purity, goodness, and love grew within Him. He shrank from contact with the conditions generated by the awful system.

Though the Master came into this world at such a time, and into a land whose conditions were so impure, yet He was born of pure parents. For they were not of Jewry. They were of the line of the Prophets. The true Prophets were not Jews ; they were the remnant of the ancient Hebrews. The pure spiritual prophetic teachings and the teachings of the priesthood were at variance. Throughout the Old Testament they are two distinct and irreconcilable religions. *The Prophets represent the divine voice within the Soul ; the Priests represent the hierarchical, sacerdotal, ceremonial, materializing influences which obscure and destroy the holiest of spiritual histories, and drown and silence the divine voice within.* Surely students of Old Testament history cannot fail to see this, it is so obvious.

The parents of the Master were *living Souls :* they were alive to every pure and spiritual good. Between them and the Jewish priesthood there was nothing in common. No part did they take in the Temple services, though from the Gospel Records it would appear as if they had done so. They were of the purest community of the Essenes. No creature was sacrificed by them in religious rite, nor yet for food or clothing ; for they knew that the only true sacrifice was spiritual, and that to eat any creature who had looked with living conscious eye upon life, was evil, a great wrong done to the creature and the Soul. Nor did they drink of any fermented cup, knowing well that the perfect equilibrium of the body could not be retained if evil elements were introduced. The pure fruits of the Earth constituted their dietary. They lived purely ; and in all their ways they were pure.

THE CHILDHOOD OF THE MASTER

From His Parents the Master, therefore, inherited a pure

body. It was a vehicle suited to the Life He had to make manifest. It was obedient to all the upwardness of His Being. In it were no elements to disturb the balance of His life. The fires of desire were not present even in latent form. All the functions of the vehicle were performed in harmony with the central will. And in order that it might always be so, the home was kept pure. The atmosphere of it was sacredly guarded against the influences of the evil conditions surrounding Jewry. It was sweet with the purity and goodness of Angelic Love. The daily meals were pure and simple. Nothing but fit nourishment ever passed their lips. The defilement caused by the partaking of flesh-foods was unknown. No emblems of cruelty did the Master ever behold upon the threshold ; the shadows of death were not there. The monstrous wickedness of Jewry was to them all a most fearful abhorrence. All the signs and emblems within the home were those of Divine Charity. The gates of life were the avenues of love. Every sense was attuned to the Divine Will ; the influence of all was harmonious. The pure fruits of the Earth by which they nourished themselves, were unto them emblems of beautiful thoughts and signs of the graciousness of the Father unto all His children. Within the home the conditions were truly heavenly. In no mere imaginary way, but in a true poetic and empirical sense, Angels trod its threshold. The Divine Presence was there, for it was a Sanctuary. The Divine Love flooded it with His Radiance. The child grew in grace and in stature, nourished in body, mind and heart upon everything pure, beautiful and spiritual.

It was in such an atmosphere that the Master spent His childhood and early youth, growing in the grace of the Divine Love, opening out ever more and more to the inflowing Light of the Divine Wisdom. In all His ways He was beautiful. His Life bathed in the beautiful Divine Life-stream, whose waters filled His whole Being as the waters of the ocean fill every

31

part where they flow, even every nook and crevice of the rock-bound coast. It may be said that upon His brow there ever rested the crown of the Angelic Life. He was sphered in the Angelic World ; and, as a result, there was within Him the rapidly unfolding consciousness of all that that blessed Life meant. He always felt the influences of that world upon Him, and gladly responded to them. Communion with that world was His delight as He drank in the knowledge which came to Him from those heavenly visitants who were His constant companions. Unto His vision the Heavens were open, and life upon them was His native air. It was thus that He unfolded until the fulness of manhood was reached, and with it that fuller consciousness of the work for which He had come into this cosmos.

B

THE MISSION OF THE MASTER

The Mission of the Master has been regarded as the proclamation that the Kingdom of Heaven was at hand ; the founding of that Kingdom upon the Earth in the form of a Church ; and then the giving of Himself to die on the Roman Cross in a sacrificial capacity in order to accomplish a Redemption for the World which was objective to and apart from all Souls, and thereby to obtain for the Human Race the Forgiveness of Sin on the part of the Divine. With a view to the realization of the founding of this Kingdom, the Twelve are said to have been chosen and trained ; and around this idea are made to gather most of the Teachings which were said to have been given unto the multitudes and the Twelve.

In this matter the teachers in the Churches have followed the erroneous presentation of these Teachings as they appear in the Gospel Records. For in these documents the Divine Kingdom upon the Earth is apparently one of the dominant notes. And it may be heard reverberating all through the Gospel history, from the wonderful Birth-stories unto the Ascension, and beyond these most marvellous spiritual events which have been related to the Master's outward history, right down into the Epistolary Letters. Indeed the phenomena surrounding and accompanying it from its inception, were of a super-natural order. Marvellous signs and wonders ushered it in, beginning with the miraculous birth of the Master, and continuing through His public ministry until His equally miraculous resurrection and ascension.

These phenomena have played their part in the historic development known as Christianity,[1] notwithstanding the fact that there is such an air of unreality about them all when viewed as objective events. They are lacking in the essentials of a true humaneness. The appearance of the Angels to Elizabeth and Zacharius, to Mary and Joseph ; the Angelic vision of the Shepherds in the plains of Bethlehem ; the celestial vision of the Star by the Magi, and the movements of the Star in leading these kings of astrological science to and from Bethlehem ; the vision of the Dove, and the Voice from out the Cloud at the Baptism by John ; the events associated with the Temptations in the Wilderness ; the phenomena of the Transfiguration ; the Feeding of the Multitudes upon five barley loaves and two small fishes ; the miraculous works associated with the Sea of Galilee ; the astounding stellar incidents accompanying the crucifixion, and the equally amazing events in the train of the resurrection ; and then the finale when the Master is said to have disappeared in the clouds—all these and many other events of a like order are supposed to have taken place as recorded, surrounding the Master with a super-naturalism which

---

[1] We have thus to qualify the term here ; for, as must be most evident to every sincere student of the history, *Historical Christianity* has not been Christianity at all ; it has not been in any true sense the Religion of the Jesus-life and the Christhood Consciousness, and, as such, the embodiment of the Life and Teachings of the Master.

belonged to the teachings of Jewry, destroying the true nature of His sublime Christhood, giving a false view of the Divine Manifestation through Him, causing His Life and Teachings to be sadly misunderstood, His beautiful mission to be entirely misrepresented, and the Kingdom of God to be so materialized that those who have earnestly sought for it have been unable to understand its true nature, and have been misdirected as to *where* and *how* it could be found.

THE KINGDOM OF THE HEAVENS

To understand what the mission of the Master was, is also to see how far the Churches have been misled, and what was the nature of the disaster which befell His Teachings. He did not appear on the Earth to found a new kingdom; He came to restore the Life of the Kingdom of the Heavens unto the Soul. He came unto the fulfilling of the divine laws of Life, not to supersede them. The " jots and tittles " of the Law which had to find fulfilment, were not those of the priestly and ceremonial traditions, but those of the Divine Love—*mercy, purity, compassion and pity*. The Kingdom He proclaimed was in being, and men wote not of it. Its Gates had been practically closed to most Souls owing to the conditions set up by the religious and social life of Jewry, and the like conditions in all the other Great Religions; for in all of them there was wrought, by means of the Priesthood Orders, the materialization of all the holy Mysteries of God and the Soul. The Kingdom of God was at hand; and it was now possible to find it. That was His message. But the Kingdom was *within* the Soul. And the way unto the full realization of it was by means of the Kingdom of the Heavens, the Life of that Kingdom finding embodiment in the ways of life. The Kingdom of the Heavens was near for all who were prepared to enter into its sacred ways. Once more the Angelic World had become a reality. Once more were the Heavens to be opened unto the Soul, and the vision of the Angels ascending and descending to be restored; for though these Heavens had been shut up so long that no spiritual rain had fallen for many ages, now were they to be brought very near unto all Souls that the blessings of the Most High might not only be poured out as in former ages, but realized unto glorious fulness.

We are not unaware of this fact, that it is most difficult to impress men and women with the reality of the Angelic World. Beyond what is expressed in some form of belief, and which so often has no reality to those who assent to it, even those within the Churches who ought to know the reality from experience, are not only in complete ignorance of it, but reject any message purporting to come from that realm ; and this, too, though the message may bear within itself the seal of the Divine Spirit. The empiricism in which the Churches believe does not yet embrace such a blessed experience. It is not too much to say that it is scarcely believed in. Certainly the attitude of the Churches as a whole, and in particular their teachers and scholars, is to nullify any belief they may formally give their assent to. Patriarchs, Seers, Prophets and Apostles of past ages *may* have risen up into that Kingdom to hear, see, behold and receive of its wonderful life and ministry ; but that such things are also possible to-day they deny, and reveal this spirit of negation by their incredulity and cynicism. It cannot be maintained with any degree of fairness that the scholars and teachers of the Churches have been open to seriously, and from the heart, consider any teachings which have been received from the Angelic World. For they all judge, in varying degrees according to their ecclesiastical and theological standpoint, after " the traditions of the elders." What happened in the days of the blessed Christhood Manifestation takes place to-day. The Churches are in bondage to the traditions of their elders. Their chief priests and scribes are, truly, reluctant to consider the claims of any teachings which essentially differ in things fundamental, and which cannot claim to have come in the traditional way. And yet the intrinsic value of any teachings surely lies in their spiritual power as vehicles through which to arrive at the full realization of Life in the Divine—Life in the innermost where all is lit up with the Light of the Divine Wisdom ; and Life in the outermost where every sphere is purified, so that *all* life's ways reflect the glory of the Divine Love. For those teachings which are of God, and come to us through the Angelic World, contain within themselves such power of light, and always make for the *true* redemption of the individual and the race.

THE ANGELIC WORLD A REALITY

Now, the Angelic Kingdom is a glorious reality. Of this we may write with certitude. Empirically we know it. We have felt its presence ; we have breathed its atmosphere ; we have beheld its blessed ministry unto this World ; we have heard and seen upon its threshold. And we know that it is not only possible to receive from it messages concerning the Soul, and even the Divine Love and Wisdom, but that Souls who have entered upon the Life of the Kingdom, are in these days receiving such communications from it. Many are they who have at last found the Jesus-life and entered into some measure of the blessed realizations which follow that life, even the consciousness of the nearness of the Angelic World, yea, of its very fellowship. Nay, there are some who have transcended even that beautiful state to enter into a yet deeper consciousness of that World so as to live in its very atmosphere, hear its sublime harmonies, and behold its glorious visions.

And what these Souls are experiencing is just what should have been experienced throughout the history of Christianity, and what would have taken place with an ever-increasing fulness of realization, but for the false direction given to the new religious movement through the Pauline Epistles and the received Gospel Records. For it was the coming of the kingdom of love, light and spiritual liberty into the lives of all who were able to receive it, which the Master meant, and towards which *His own Life pointed the way*. For " the kingdom " was one whose Nature was spiritual and inward, whose Laws were those of the Divine Love applied to all of life's actions, whose Life was made manifest in purity, compassion and pity. The foundation was within the realm of the Soul ; the manifestation was given within the realm of the objective life. The operation of the Laws of the Kingdom was secret, but the evidence of their activity was obvious. The Life of the Kingdom was hidden from the gaze of the vulgar mind, like the mysterious life-essence of all things ; but the Life was made manifest in the heavenly conditions that grew around the individual, and in the bloom and fruits expressed in thought and action. It was always seeking, like the merchant dealing in goodly pearls, to find " the pearl of great price " in the hidden depths of the Soul— the pearl of the Divine Image, to be brought up and revealed in the glory of Christhood. It was ever as one on a voyage of discovery, finding " the treasure " of the Divine Image within the Soul buried in the field of the life of this world, and giving up all this world's powers in order to possess it in the recovered consciousness of the indwelling Divine Presence. It was as one who, having lost a valuable coin, seeks it until it is found ; for the coin with the king's superscription upon it, lost amid the dust of materialism, is none other than the valuable life upon which the Divine Image was impressed, which is once more found by *the woman element in man* when illumined with the Light of the Divine Presence within—*the Intuition*.

THE KINGDOM WAS OF THE SOUL

The Kingdom was, therefore, wholly spiritual and inward, having no outward manifestations other than the life which was the interpretation of the Laws of the Divine Love. It was absolutely non-ecclesiastical. Mere priesthoods and scholastic centres could not build it up. Indeed, the work of these latter seems always to have been to veil the true Kingdom by means of their ceremonials and traditions. Jewry did not know it ; obviously it was beyond the understanding of the priesthood and leaders. It was not contained within all its sacrificial ritual and elaborate ceremonial. There could have been no more striking contrast presented than that Kingdom of the Heavens and Jewry ; and it found little real response in the midst of such a lifeless religion. To the priests, scribes and pharisees who represented Jewry, the Life of the Kingdom of the Heavens was a constant rebuke. They did not like it. Its ways as illustrated in the Life of the Master, they condemned The. sacrificial system was vital to them, for it was in harmony with their conception of the one they worshipped in place of the Eternal and ever Blessed One—a god who was local in his dwelling, tribal in his love, and fearful in his anger and judgments. Jewry was indeed barren soil for the seed to fall into. For the new Kingdom which was *not* of this world, enforced upon all who entered into its realms, the living of the Angelic Life in so far as it was possible to realize it in these outer spheres under the conditions which prevailed. And that Life transcended Jewry even as the heavens transcend the physical planes of the Earth. Its atmosphere was rarefied like that upon the great altitudes in which only those who have prepared themselves can live ; and it was thus in remarkable contrast to the dense, heavy, stifling atmosphere of Jewry. The footsteps of all those who sought to enter it had to be as those who climb the heights ; every weight and encumbrance must needs be left behind. The path to be trod by such Souls was narrow, and had no room upon it for the social and national traditional paraphernalia ; and it was so steep that they had to unburden themselves of all things that were not essential to their progress. The sacrificial system of Jewry had to be repudiated in the most unreserved manner ; and the barbarous habits and customs which it taught and embodied, had to be put away for ever.

How the Master Revealed the Kingdom

We have now to show how the Master revealed the Kingdom of the Heavens, and in doing this we are led to expound the titles which were given to Him. He has come to be designated in history as Jesus Christ the Lord, as if these had been His personal and family names. So long have these titles been applied to Him as names, that their association with Him in a family and personal sense has become traditional. But though through all the Era these titles have been given to Him in a personal sense, yet the application of them to Him in such manner was the outcome of a great and grave mistake. Indeed, so grave was the mistake that the results have been momentous upon the history of Christianity. For the new religious development became a belief in the history and work of one person, rather than the beautiful unfoldment of the Jesus-consciousness, and then the Christ-consciousness, of the Soul. Titles entirely impersonal in their meaning, and purely spiritual in their significations, and which were related to inward states of Soul-consciousness, and so of Soul-realizations, were associated with the personal life. This disastrous mistake was made by those who wrote the Gospel Records ; for they knew not the name of the Master, nor the beautiful meaning of the three titles they made use of in a personal sense. In the original Gospel written by the *real* St. Matthew, and in the Logia of St. John, these sacred titles were not associated with the Master as personal names, but only in relation to the states that they represented, and which He so beautifully interpreted and made manifest.

Our readers will therefore have to divest themselves of the familiar traditional use of these terms, in order to understand them in their representative capacity. That they were impersonal titles is obvious when their inner meaning is known. It is quite true that He was Jesus, The Christ, and as The Lord ; but only in *the realization of the states of being* of which these terms spake.

The interpretation of these terms and their relation to the Life of the Kingdom of the Heavens, will make this self-evident.

C

THE JESUS-CONSCIOUSNESS

In the threefold manifestation given through the Master, the Jesus-life came first. It had to be interpreted through the personal life. The nature of the Jesus-life was just what the term implied. It meant the state of salvation from the dominance of the sense-life. He was to be called Jesus because He would save the people from their sins, *i.e.*, from the false and evil ways of living. He was therefore Jesus in His own ways. His life was absolutely pure and good, full of love, compassion and pity ; and therein it made manifest the estate of the Jesus-life, and thus interpreted what it meant for any one to be redeemed from bondage to the sense-life. *The Jesus-life was the Redeemed Life.* In revealing to men and women the nature of the Redeemed Life, and calling them to follow it unto fulness of realization, He acted as the Saviour of Life. There was no Redemption to be found in any other way than that of following the path which led on to the perfect fulfilment of the Laws of the Divine Love. Not knowing the nature and purpose of the Sin-offering because of the unfortunate misrepresentation in the Gospel and Epistolary Records of that stupendous work, the Churches have always confounded it with the Redemption and the Atonement, and made of these latter something objective to the individual life, and accomplished for all Souls apart from any consent or action on their part ; although the Churches have believed that *the efficacy of it* all was dependent upon a belief by the individual, in the fact. But the Sin-offering was of a different order, as will be shown presently in some of the Unfoldments. Whilst the relationship between the Sin-offering, the Redemption and the Atonement is intimate, yet they are quite distinct. And the evidence of this is not only to be found in the distinctive

Teachings of the Master, but in the history of the new religious movement. *The accomplishing of the Sin-offering as it was propounded by the Schools, did not help the Western World to arrive at the realization of the Redeemed Life.* That World has not yet found its Redemption from sense-dominion ; so it is yet far from the blessed realizations entered into when the Atonement is fully accomplished.

It is not here necessary to dwell upon the historic development of Christianity in either the intellectual or ecclesiastical domain ; for that must be known to all earnest students of that history as anything but one of goodness, light and love. If this be doubted, then let the ages speak ; and let the vision of the oppressed, the persecuted, the martyred Souls who sought the highest within them, rise up before the doubters and tell them what the Churches did in the name of the Holy One, unto the Saints. Enough for our present purpose to remind the reader that *The Redemption* as the Master taught it, has never been understood in the West ; and the Redeemed Life as interpreted by the Master in His own Life, has never been even known. For had the Redeemed Life been followed and attained by the West, the Redemption would have been accomplished long ages ago.

The Way to the Jesus-Life

In the Teachings of the Master the path to the realization of the Jesus-life was marked by *self-denial*. It was the first cross which had to be borne by every one who entered upon the path. There was no other way into the Kingdom of the Heavens. The Jesus-life had to be won. The Kingdom could only be entered by means of the narrow door of the Jesus-life ; and to reach it the straitened way had to be trod. The tendency of the Soul to seek for the fulfilment of life through the senses had to be checked by obedience to the voice of the innermost Life— the Divine whose dwelling was in the secret place. The Will of the Father who loved all Souls, human and creature, had to be done on the Earth-spheres, even as that Will was done in the Kingdom of the Heavens. And the Earth-spheres included the activities of the outward life, such as eating, drinking, desiring, feeling, purposing and serving. It was in these things that the cross had to be borne, that cross of self-denial which afterwards was to issue in the fuller cross of self-sacrifice. No one could be a disciple of the Jesus-life who was not prepared to follow that path unto the perfect realization of the redeemed state. The request " We would see Jesus," had to find fulfilment in the Jesus state.

THE JESUS-LIFE NOT RECOGNIZED AND LIVED

In looking back through the ages of this Era, and in seeing how the Life and Teachings of the Master have been interpreted, we cannot but wonder how such a state of things as these ages reveal could ever have been associated with the doctrine of an accomplished Redemption. For, with the exception of a few of the higher Mystics who sensed something of the truth, the Churches have never lived the Jesus-life. The people have not known it ; the leaders and teachers have not taught it. Those who felt after it had practically to retire into the cloisters in order to be able to carry out their beautiful purpose in seeking unto its realization. And even there they found it difficult ; for the Brotherhood and Sisterhood Communities early became inoculated with the views of the Pagan and Jewish barbarism which passed for the true consecrated life. They ate the flesh of the sentient creatures and drank fermented wines to the glory of God. They followed in the wake of the Churches, looked upon the taking of the lives of the creatures as necessary and just, and thus defiled the temple of the body which they professed to have surrendered as a meet sanctuary for the indwelling of the Holy One.

Now and again voices were heard proclaiming against the terrible degradation of the whole concept of the Jesus-life. But the Soul-blinding and desolating customs prevailed. Tertullian ;[1] the Author of the Clementine Homilies ;[2] Marcion ;[3] Clement of Alexandria ;[4] Chrysostom of Constantinople ;[5] and the best of the Gnostics, ancient and modern, have appealed in vain. And this is the more surprising when it is known that, so far as history can be trusted, the inner group of the disciples neither ate flesh nor drank wine. References to this are found in the writings of Clement of Alexandria,[6] and in those of the historian Hegesippus, as quoted by Eusebius.[7] These show that the disciples of the inner group lived lives of true asceticism, and that they understood and interpreted the Jesus-life.

How is it, we may ask with much reason, that the leaders and teachers of the people have passed over this aspect of life so obviously indicated in these early writings ? How came it that those consecrated to what ought to be the very purest and holiest of ministries, have never awakened to the terrible wrong done to the Master by the extremely mixed and, in many respects, contradictory narratives ? Why have they been so long blind to the monstrous thing that was done to His sublime Christhood when the custom of eating flesh and drinking fermented wine was foisted upon the new religious movement in the name of the Master ? Is it because they too have been blinded through following the traditions of the elders ? Do they not worship at the shrine of literalism when they accept these Gospel Records as true statements of fact concerning the Life and Teachings of the Master ?

Perhaps the greatest contributory factor to this lamentable

[1] *Vide* DE JEJUNIIS : ADVERSUS PSYCHIOS, Chapters vi , xv., xvi., xvii.
[2] CLEMT. HOMILIES, viii., chap. 15 to 19. xii., ch. 6.
[3] ANTITHESES, in which Marcion upholds the doctrine of abstinence from flesh-foods on Humane, Moral and Spiritual grounds.
[4] PÆDAGOGUS, II., ch. 1. STROMATA, Bk. vii., ch. 6.
[5] HOMILIES, xiii., chapters 3 and 4 ; xix., chap. 3. LXIX., ch. 4. LXXIX., ch. 3.
[6] PÆDAGOGUS, II., ch. 1. STROMATA, Bk. vii.
[7] HIST. BOOK II., chap. 23.

condition of things is to be found in the Epistolary Letters
sent out in the name of Paul. For in some strange and un-
accountable way, these Epistles have exercised more influence
than the Gospel stories upon the kingdom which grew up in
the name of the Master. The Redemption taught in them is
objective to the Soul ; and so mysterious that it is impossible
to understand it. Concerning our grounds for this statement,
it is only necessary to remind our readers that they are supplied
by the manifold views held by various sections of the Churches
as to the real nature and extent of the Redemption. This is a
striking commentary. The Pauline Epistles did not treat of the
Life of the Master, though they dealt with some of the Logia
which He spake ; but without understanding the meaning of
these. How evident this is may be gathered from the confused
utterances in these letters concerning the doctrine of the
Redemption. It was lifted out of the spheres of a true empiricism.
It was made historical rather than experimental, objective
instead of subjective, judicial in place of profound inward
realizations.

It is indeed remarkable how large the place is that is given to
the Pauline Letters in the history of Christian doctrine. The
personality of Paul dominates it. He is the brilliant first magnitude star of the new religious movement ; the disciples of
the inner group who knew the Master and heard the Teachings, are but stars of the sixth or even tenth magnitude. In the
teachings of all the Reformed Churches, he even eclipses the
Master. *Yet Paul did not know the Master.* His first knowledge
of Him was gathered from the oral tradition. He knew nothing
of those profound Teachings given to the inner group. He had
not come under the influence of the Life of the Master, and had
no vision of its glorious purity and sweetness. Had he done so,
he could never have said what he did concerning the eating of
flesh and taking of wine ; nor would the personal element have
found expression as it does in these letters.

The Epistolary Letters did not contribute to the realization of the Jesus-life in the lives of those drawn into the movement. These latter joined the Churches as members of that movement ; but most of them were allowed to carry with them many of their Jewish and Pagan habits. And so in the very heart of a movement which should have led to the full realization, by attainment, of the Redeemed Life, there existed that which made that attainment utterly impossible ; which violated the fundamental laws of all true Being ; which repudiated the sacred doctrine taught by the Master of *the oneness of all true life :* which rejected the Laws of the Divine Love—laws of mercy, compassion and pity ; which associated with the Life and Teachings of the Master, the violation of those sublime Laws ; which attributed to the Divine Father the fashioning of the creatures for the purpose of sacrificing them to the barbaric habits and customs of His fallen children ; and which so blinded the Soul that the Light of the Eternal Spirit could not be received.

It is impossible to express in any adequate terms the awful disaster which befell the whole of the Human Race when the writers of the various New Testament Records so grievously misrepresented the Life and Teachings of the Master, and founded in His name a kingdom whose members were not illumined regarding the true meaning of the Jesus-life. For those who would have entered the Kingdom it was an unspeakable tragedy, because the true meaning of the Jesus-life was quite obscured. With the vision clearly before us of what the Master meant by the Jesus-life, and of the manner in which He beautifully interpreted it in His own way of living, the history of the Churches is truly appalling. To have seen (as it has been vouchsafed to us to see) how transcendently pure and beautiful He was in *all* His ways—eating, drinking, desiring, feeling, purposing, serving,—and then to witness the thing that has professed to be the interpretation of that Life, is to pass from the vision of the full radiance of the Sun beheld on the heights to enter some deep valley where the darkness prevails. It is as if we turned away from the vision glorious beheld upon the delectable mountains, and descended to enter the valley of the shadow of death ; for on the one there abides the Light of the Life of Love, whilst in the other there dwells the darkness of spiritual death.

Yet the full resultant of that tragedy included much more than the obscuration and misrepresentation of the Teachings of the Master concerning the nature of the Jesus-life, and His transcendent interpretation of that Life, as we shall now see.

D

THE CHRIST-CONSCIOUSNESS

IN the Mission of the Master, the Jesus-life was not the end or fullness of discipleship. It was all important, but it was only preparatory to something more transcendent. The training of the Twelve began with the Jesus-life, the life of self-denial issuing in the life of Self-sacrifice ; but *the finale* to which this was *the prelude* was something greater, an attainment yet higher, an experience far more profound. The narrow door and the straitened way led into the realization of the Jesus-life ; but the Jesus realization was the initiation into the way which led unto the attainment of " the crown of Life "—the Christhood consciousness. The Life of beautiful purity, goodness and compassion was an attainment to be desired for its own sake ; but when realized, it became also the prophecy and harbinger of a yet deeper consciousness of *Life*. It led on to experiences as much more glorious in nature in their realizations of the Divine Light, Life and Love, as the radiance of brilliant noonday exceeds the early dawn.

As a natural sequence, the following of Jesus led to the finding of Christ. It is after the Baptism in the river Jordan that the disciple is invited to the dwelling-place of the Christ. Indeed it is only after that full Baptism that the disciple enquires—" *Master, where dwellest Thou?*" For the Baptism of John in the river Jordan was the baptism unto purification in the river of spiritual truth, so that all righteousness might be fulfilled in the ways of life. The event was not outward but inward, though in the outward life the effects were made manifest. It was the baptism into the Jesus-life. It was the initiation of those who desired to know Jesus :—that is, desired to enter upon the path which led into the realization of the Jesus-consciousness. To follow Jesus was to follow that path ; but the crown of Life would be the finding of Christ. To enquire for the dwelling-place of the Christ and to enter in to abide with Him, was to enter upon the path of experience that issued in the full Christhood consciousness. For the term denoting Christ was not a personal name, but, like the term Jesus, represented a beautiful Soul experience. And it expressed the second part of the Master's mission, and the sublime Manifestation given through Him. As Jesus represented the *purified* Life, so the Christ spake of the *illumined* or divinely anointed Life. The one had to be made manifest unto all Souls ; the other could only be revealed unto the Jesus Initiates—those who had entered into the sacred meaning of that Life, and purified themselves.

WHAT IS A CHRISTHOOD?

The misapprehension of the meaning of Christhood is remarkable. It has had given to it, and it still has given to it, such a *personal* ring, that the real significance of it is lost. The personal Master has been so greatly confounded with the Divine Christ who overshadowed Him, that the true meaning of His Christhood cannot be seen. He was the Christ because He was the Illumined One, but in His Christhood *He knew nothing from Himself :* the Father within Him was the One who made manifest. This obvious truth religious teachers within and outside the Churches must needs learn, *that Christhood is always impersonal.* It is an attainment of the Soul. It is the *fruit* of the Jesus-life. It is a condition of Life within the Kingdom of the Heavens. It may be described as a state of inward glorious illumination in which the Divine Wisdom has become the heritage of the Soul. As the full realization of the Jesus-life is the perfect realization of the Divine Love, so the fulness of Christhood is the realization of the Divine Wisdom. It is therefore a consciousness of the Divine indwelling, the resultant of the perfect unfoldment of the Divine within the Soul.

But, like the attainment of all other states of consciousness, it follows its own law of growth. There is first the blade, then the ear, to be followed by the full corn in the ear. And its spheres of action are entirely spiritual ; for it is *the life* of the Kingdom of the Heavens in glorious fulness, the fruition of all the divine potencies of the Soul. We may write of it that it is the coming to perfection of the Divine Image within man— the Redemption through the baptism into the Jesus-state, followed by the full realization of the Jesus life ; then the Life Transcendent which rises from glory to glory as ever increasing illumination breaks upon the Soul from the Divine Radiance, until those sublime heights are attained upon that exalted spiritual state known as " the mount of the Lord," where Life is so rarefied that the Beatific Vision is beheld with open countenance, and the consciousness of the individual Soul becomes *one with the Divine.*

To Whom made Manifest

Such is Christhood, that holy state unto which the Jesus-life led, and unto the attainment of which the Master called those disciples who were able to tread its path. The training of the Twelve was unto this glorious end. Unto them did He reveal the Kingdom of the Christhood. He could not make that holy estate manifest unto all, for all could not have understood it. *" How is it that Thou dost make this manifest unto us, but not unto the world ? "* Because it was of the innermost, and could only be apprehended as Christhood by those in whom the love-principle triumphed, and the intuition was awakened and purified. Hence the reason for the Teachings given to the inner group of the disciples. Only they were able to hear them. The Teachings contained the Divine Wisdom which had been hidden for untold ages, and only initiated Souls could receive them. And these Teachings were the evidence of the Master's own sublime state of Divine Realization. So profound were they that even the inner group of disciples could only receive them gradually.

If these Teachings, notwithstanding the mutilated form in which they are found in the Gospel Records and Pauline Epistles, now appear to be wonderful to spiritual men and women, what must they have been to those who were privileged to hear them in their purity ? It is indeed difficult for any one to understand how wonderful these Teachings were to those who heard them as they fell from His gracious lips, spoken as they were with all the deep feeling of His being. They revealed the glory of the Divine Love, the radiance of the Divine Wisdom, and the sublimity of the Divine Purpose towards all Souls. The holiest of Mysteries, no one could understand them except through following on to know the Christhood. Unto such alone was it given to know " the Mysteries of the Kingdom." All could understand the Teachings concerning the Jesus-life ; but only " the elect," " the chosen ones," the Souls who had passed up into the higher states of realization, were able to receive with the understanding the profound Teachings of the Christhood. These were they who, in the purpose and vision of life, were born, " not of bloods, nor of the flesh, nor of the will of man, but of God," and unto whom it was given to have " the power to become Sons of God," or Christs.

For such an attainment was to be the end of the training of the Twelve. They were to triumph over the local, social, and racial distinction of " bloods "—the birth-mark ; the personal material desires and dominion of the senses—the ways of the natural and animal mind ; the ambitions which mark the way of the unredeemed mind and will ; and find their full life in God alone. Born into *the consciousness of Sonship*, they were to gather power to reach the consummation and be crowned with Christhood.

How it is Misunderstood

No one could have imagined that these sublime Teachings would be overtaken with such a disaster as befell them at the hands of the writers of the Records. None of the privileged Souls who heard them dreamt that they would all be materialized and that, at times, almost beyond recognition. Yet that which befell the Jesus-life as interpreted and revealed by the Master, likewise became the lot of the Christhood. For the holy estate was made personal, local and national. That which was a state of Soul exaltation attained through the realization of inherent divine potencies, in which there was a profound consciousness of the Divine Overshadowing, was made purely personal. It was related to the outward personal life. The birth of the Christ-consciousness within the Soul became only the birth of a human child. And the birth of the Christ in the Soul who had realized the Jesus-state was made local, in that He had to be born in Bethlehem of Judæa—a small town in Jewry ; whereas the meaning was entirely spiritual, and was related to the Jesus-life, Bethlehem signifying the little House of the Lord, or Jesus-life. And then the Christ was made a national hero ; for Jewry claimed to be the national and religious stream upon which the Messiah would come. The priests and scribes interpreted the prophetic allusions to the Christhood in such a way as to make the Messiah the head of their own local, national and religious life ; so the Christ is represented by the Jewish writers of the Gospels as in the direct line of the Kings of Israel and the House of Levi, representing the nation's regal and sacrificial systems.

The person of the Master was thus confounded with the sublime Manifestation given through Him. The writers of the Records did not understand the beautiful impersonal Soul-significance of the term, and took it to have reference to the personal life, and to be a mere name of the Master. And by thus changing the relationship of the term from the Divine experience which it represented, they destroyed its meaning, obscured almost to obliteration the Christhood vision which had been made manifest for the guidance of those Souls who were ready to seek unto its realization, and gave a wholly wrong direction to the religious thought of the entire West.

THE MASTER'S TEACHINGS WERE CHANGED

And what these writers did with the term expressing the Christhood estate, they also did with all the precious Teachings in which the reality of the exalted nature of the Christhood of the Master was revealed. Not apprehending their deep spiritual import, they took them to be outward events. As we shall presently show, they all lost their intrinsic value for the Soul, and had given to them a fictitious value which in the case of many of them has, all through the ages, led to polemics of the most unenlightening and unedifying nature. Not only in the four Gospel Records were these Teachings obscured and changed in their meanings, but they passed through the like process in the Epistolary Letters. For many of the sayings concerning the Christhood and the Sin-offering which were spoken through the Master in the hearing of the inner group of disciples, were found by Paul when he visited the Brethren at Jerusalem, and were made use of by him in building up his doctrine of the Sin-offering. This much we have thought it well to say here, because of the undue importance given by many scholars, even in these days, to Paul's teaching concerning the Christhood. Later we will have to speak more fully about this astounding thing which has had such far-reaching effect upon the whole of the development of historical Christianity. Many of the most remarkable of the " Sayings " Paul applied to himself, Logia which spake of the burden of the Sin-offering borne by the Christ-Soul. The " hard sayings " were of these very precious Logia. These had their inner meanings destroyed. Others were embodied in some of the Theses of these Letters with their meanings still apparent. These are they which refer to *the Christ within*. They still reveal the real inwardness, the beautiful spirituality and the absolute impersonal nature of the Christhood. In their original form they showed *how* the Christ was formed within the life, *how* it grew unto fulness, and *what* that fulness was. In due course these precious Logia will be given in the form in which they were spoken by the Master, and in their true relationship to the indwelling Christ, the Christhood of the Soul, the Divine Purpose hidden for ages, and the Sin-offering.

E

THE MASTER'S TEACHINGS

IN such public ministry as the Master took part, He generally spake in parables. In this way He illustrated the nature of the Kingdom of the Heavens, the Life of that Kingdom, and the true and only way to the attainment of it. But the parables were understandable by those who spiritually discerned. Those who had the unstopped ear to hear, the open vision to see, and the sincere heart to conceive beautiful things, could discover their meaning. The parables were *not* made use of, as reported in the Synoptic Records, to obscure His meaning. Such an act on His part would not only have violated the whole spirit of the Jesus-life, which is that of true love, compassion and pity made manifest unto all Souls, whatever their state ; but it would likewise have been the very way to court defeat in the sublime mission He had undertaken. The purpose of the Manifestation was too vast in its importance for anything of that nature to be done. Indeed, its very sublimity and divine character made any such conduct on the part of the Master impossible. There are many great truths that can only be apprehended by means of parable in the case of those not initiated into the higher Soul-experiences. And they were great truths which the Master illustrated. They were all of the Soul—its nature, its value, its inherent powers, its possibilities, the nature of the Life which it was fashioned to live, and how it should perform its service of life. These were the Teachings which the Kingdom of the Heavens had to communicate ; and the parabolic Teachings of the Master beautifully illustrated them, as we observed in writing of the Kingdom.

THE OUTER AND INNER MISSION

Whilst the parabolic Teachings were associated with the first part of the mission of the Master, and in this respect were more directly connected with the manifestation of the Jesus-life, the Teachings concerning the Christhood were of a more profound order and could not be given except to the few, as we have seen. This will be obvious when we remember how few disciples there were in the inner group. For many of the followers who belonged to the outer group of disciples, went back from Him. The Teachings, and the Life to which these called, were too much for them. Is it not recorded that some of them were hurt and offended, *even some of His brethren ?* The conditions of discipleship, such as were imposed upon the inner group, were more than they could respond to. Indeed they do not appear to have truly responded to the conditions of the Jesus-life.

They were those who followed " afar off " in their lives. They were impressed ; but they found the conditions irksome.

But very different conditions existed in the hearts of the disciples of the inner group. They gladly responded to His call to follow the Redeemed or Jesus-life, and they had all arrived at the Jesus-state. They had " left all " to follow the way of life whose path was pure, and strewn with the grace of love, compassion and pity. They were those Souls who were ready for the Manifestation, children and heirs of the prophetic spirit, a remnant of the long lost Israel, members of the once ancient order of Christhood. To them no hard conditions became an obstacle to the full surrender of themselves. They were initiates of a high spiritual order ; graduates in the Great White Lodge of Christhood, who were pressing forward to the full realization of the glorious Life found in that exalted spiritual state. It was no mere Masonic Lodge with a meaningless ritual and dead symbolism of which they were members. Theirs was a sacred group—not because they were a secret body, but because they all loved to be of its membership for the blessed fellowship, and the sublime Life to be found through it. The themes spoken of, and the purpose for which they were spoken, lifted the fellowship out of the Earth into the Heavens. " The fellowship " was in a sense a Hierarchy, but it was purely heavenly ; it was a Priesthood, but it was of the Soul ; it was a true Church, but only as a " communion of saints " : for the fellowship was with the Angelic World, and, finally, with the Divine World.

The Teachings given to the inner group transcended those given concerning the Jesus-life. As the manifestation of the outer part of the mission was embraced in the Jesus-life, so the manifestation of the inner part of the mission was embraced in the divine vision. But the divine vision could only be entered into by means of the realization of the Christhood consciousness. *The Teachings were concerned with that holy estate as revealed in the Master. They were of the constitution of the Soul ; the remarkable history of the Soul ; the nature of Christhood ; the Divine Pleroma ; the sublime purpose of the Father in the manifestation of both the Jesus-life and the Christhood ; the reason for the Sin-offering ; the nature of the burden to be borne ; the duration of it ; the outcome of it for the Soul ; and the Parousia.*

Many of these Teachings were set forth by the Master in allegories. To this order belonged the Birth-stories ; some of the events chronicled as miraculous, like " the stilling of the storm," " walking upon the Sea of Galilee," " the great draught of fishes," " the feeding of the multitudes with two small fishes and five barley loaves," " the turning of water into wine in Cana of Galilee," and " the sleep and awakening of Lazarus "; some of the reported incidents and conversations, such as the story of " the Woman of Samaria," " the anointing in the House of Simon," " the anointing in the House of Mary," " the Temptations in the Wilderness," " the story of the Good Shepherd," and " the Washing of the feet of the Disciples."

But the profoundest of all the Christhood Teachings were those given in the Logia of the Upper Room, which comprised those sayings setting forth the divine nature of the Christhood of the Master, and the estate into the inheritance of which all Souls were by their very inherent nature called ; those Logia which revealed the divine nature of the work to be accomplished by means of the tragic Sin-offering ; those Logia wherein the depth of the sufferings of the Soul who bore the Sin-offering were revealed ; those Logia which in themselves made manifest the nature of the Sin-offering, the terrible burden of it, and its duration ; and those Logia in which was explained the nature of the Parousia.

a
THE BIRTH-STORIES

The Teachings contained in the Birth-stories were at once

both beautiful and profound. The legend or myth assumption is childish. It is lacking in virility. It contains no satisfactory solution of the mystery of the existence of these stories ; and it is a sad commentary upon the enlightened condition of that mind which rejects sublime truths which it is unable to understand. The literal interpretation is impossible to men and women who are set free from the superstitious worship of the letter, and who are truly seeking for a rational explanation of them. But the legendary assumption, and the interpretation accepted by the worshippers of the letter, fade into insignificance like artificial lights fading with the coming of the glorious dawn, when the true spiritual meanings of these stories is made manifest. They were allegories, in part concerning the Christhood of the Master and the Divine Manifestation through Him ; in part concerning the Sin-offering ; and in part concerning the history of those Souls who formed the inner group of disciples, and others of the same order, as well as the manner in which the Christ-state was born within every one who sought it.

The stories were records of facts ; but the facts were of Soul-histories and events. They were allegories of realities ; the realities, however, were not in the objective world. They belonged to the realm of *true* history ; but the history was empirical. They were wonderful cryptographs. Here we can give only an indication of their meaning, and we must refer the reader to the Unfoldments of these Mysteries given in the several chapters for a more adequate interpretation.

The Annunciation was a beautiful Soul experience, and had naught to do with the Motherhood of the body of the Master. It concerned the birth of Christhood within the Soul. For the Christ-life is " the holy thing begotten within " Maria the Soul, from the Holy Breath. And it is that holy state which bringeth with it Light for all Souls. Unto every one in whom such an event is taking place, the Angel of the Lord appears and affirms the nature of the event.

The appearing of the Angel of the Lord unto Mary and Joseph was a blessed fact. But Mary and Joseph were not the personal names of the earthly parents of the Master. They represented spiritual and divine states. Though in a very special sense these terms spake of the Master's inner experiences, yet they represented the experiences through which all Souls pass on their way to the realization of the perfect Divine Life, the two representing, as their names imply, the feminine and masculine modes of the Soul. In relation to the Master they revealed the high estate of realization to which He had reached in having become *Maria Ioseph*—a Soul with Divine consciousness, and one overshadowed by the Adonai. The Virgin Mary was the Divine Soul (virgin meaning a pure Soul) in and through whom the Christhood was to be made manifest.

The going up into Bethlehem and the birth there, had an exceedingly beautiful meaning. For the term Bethlehem, as we have already indicated, meant the outer or little House of the Lord. It was known to the ancient Hebrews as containing that meaning, and was made use of by them to express the Jesus-life. It was " a little city," " the least of all " the glorious Soul-states associated with the Christhood, yet it was that one out of which the Christ should appear. For without the Jesus-life, Christhood could not be born and realized. And in order to make manifest the fulness of the glorious Divine Christhood, the Master had to know, by beautiful experience, the life of the Bethlehem.

The Angel of the Lord appearing unto the Shepherds upon the plains (planes) of Bethlehem, and the Song of the Heavenly Hosts heard by the Shepherds, contained profound experiences relating to the Christ-Soul and the Christhood Order. On the one hand it was the embodiment of experiences which are actually passed through by every Soul on the way to Christhood, and during its dwelling on the planes of Bethlehem or spheres of the Jesus-life ; whilst, on the other hand, it was an echo of what took place within the ancient Order of the Christhood long ages prior to the Advent, when that sublime Manifestation was foretold.

The Magians, and His Star appearing unto them to inform and lead them to the place of the Christ, was an allegory of beautiful spiritual import, and signified the state arrived at by the Soul, and the degree of the Christhood to which it had attained. For the Star was the sign of Divine Christhood ; and the three Magians represented the three Divine Principles within the Soul bowing in reverent worship before the Divine, and the consecration of their special gifts unto the Christhood service.

The Flight into Egypt is perhaps the most remarkable of the Birth-stories, for it represents in succinct form the wonderful history of the Sin-offering. The Christ going down riding upon an Ass signified the Soul functioning through a lower mind that would bear it into Egypt, or the land of Soul-bondage, oppression and darkness. And the story revealed the part played in it by the Divine Love. All the details are significant— the Angel of the Lord appearing unto Ioseph, the taking of Mary and the Christ down to Egypt, and the return.

The Slaughter of the Children of Bethlehem by Herod was a monogram of a sad and tragic history. For the children of Bethlehem were those who had been in the Jesus-life ages prior to the Manifestation, but who had been overwhelmed by the emissaries or powers of the astral or elemental kingdom. For Herod signified such power. And the weeping Rachel and the crying in Ramah, spoke of the sorrow of the very Heavens over the event. This story was a monogram of one of the ancient knowledges associated with the long past history of the Planet. But in a remarkable way it likewise anticipated just what happened as the result of the betrayal and crucifixion of the Christhood ; for all the children of Bethlehem, or those who were ready to enter into the realization of the Jesus-life, were spiritually slain. Through the evil influences of Herod and the semi-religious world power, the Jesus-life was made of non-effect.

The Presentation of the Christ in the Temple by Mary and Joseph, and the meeting with Simeon and Anna, was an allegory embodying the consecration of the Life to the service of the Divine Love, though it had very special reference to the con-secration of the Christ-Soul for the work which He had to accomplish. The very details are full of beautiful teaching which may be still discerned, notwithstanding the Jewish set-ting given to the whole incident. Even the offering of " the doves " in sacrifice as an act befitting what in the story is called " the purification," is a symbolic presentation of deep Soul experiences.

b

ALLEGORIES CONCERNING THE SOUL'S UNFOLDMENT

Amongst the supposed historic events in the Life of the Master were a number of beautiful allegories of the Soul which were told by Him to the inner group of disciples. Of these the most important were the following, whose full interpretation will be found in the Unfoldments.

The Marriage in Cana of Galilee was a story of sublime spiritual beauty, and contained within itself a Soul-history rich and glorious in realizations. The conversion of it into a physical and social event of a Jewish order, with an atmosphere of the miraculous, totally destroyed its profound meanings. To gaze upon the historical picture and interpret it as relating to the outward life, is to miss the picture of the Soul event as drawn by the Master. For this latter was a portraiture of one entering into that spiritual state expressed in the terms " married to the Lord." It betokened the attainment of the Christhood estate by that one, and the first great work that would be wrought by the Soul in such an exalted spiritual state, namely, the turning of the water in the waterpots used for purification, into wine. When the Soul arrives at the state known as the Christ-hood-consciousness, it is married or united to the Lord who then may be said to overshadow it. And when such a union takes place, the Truth (water) which at first is only for cleansing (leading to the Jesus-life), becomes the very wine of the Divine Love. The apparently insignificant details will be found to contain precious meanings.

Of a like nature is " *The Christ walking on the Sea of Galilee,*" " *The Stilling of the Storm on the Sea of Galilee,*" " *The miraculous draught of Fishes on the Sea of Galilee,*" " *The Feeding of the Multitudes on five barley loaves and two small fishes.*" All these, even in many of the details, are fraught with a wealth of blessing for every one who is able to rise to the meaning of them ; for in them they will find echoes of their own history in past ages, luminous pictures of their innermost experiences, testimonies to the divinity within them and the need for its perfect realization. They will find in these allegories something of infinitely more value than mere outward histories, light for the mind and nourishment for the heart, visions of the transcendent Christhood of the Master, and the glorious nature and powers of their own Soul.

The Christ walking on the Sea of Galilee, The Stilling of the Storm on the Sea of Galilee, and the miraculous draught of Fishes on the Sea of Galilee, were wonderful embodiments of the marvellous power which comes to the Soul when it has entered into the experience of Christhood. For the Sea of Galilee was *not* the Sea of Tiberias or Genesaret, but the Higher Mind. The term was symbolical. It is within the Higher Mind that all the conditions suggested in the narratives are to be found. It is within the Higher Mind where are discovered all those forms of thought which give rise to Soul perplexity. It is within that sea of thought that the waters of divine truth flow for recognition and Soul uses. It is the sea which at times is storm-swept ; for its waters are disturbed by the elemental spirits, the astral conditions which set up conflicts within the spiritual system of the Soul. It is the sea upon which the Understanding (Peter) finds itself unable to walk, even though it fain would, and must needs cry out lest it be over-whelmed. It is the sea wherein the little ship of the Soul is tossed to and fro until all its attributes cry out for the awakening of the Divine, until the Christ-consciousness is born within, and comes forth into manifestation, commanding the storm-winds (elemental spirits) to cease their astral revelry, and the tempestuous waters of thought to be still, until at last the life becomes filled with a great divine calm. For, when the Christ within is fully awakened, the fearful tempest of the earthly conditions is not only quelled and the divine peace realized, but *the Soul becomes able to walk upon the waters of the deep Mysteries*, having henceforth power over them through knowing their nature and understanding the meaning of all things. And in such a state, the Divine Christ within is able to bring forth from that deep the great draught of fishes, and that even in a miraculous way. For the " Fish " was the ancient term and sign for a profound truth, a hidden message ; and to bring out of the Sea of Galilee a great draught of fishes, was to bring out of the waters of knowledge the Mysteries of God and the Soul. And thus the narratives concerning the Sea of Galilee will be found rich in the lore of the most Ancient Wisdom.

The Feeding of the Multitudes on two occasions was likewise allegorical. The stories illustrated *how* and upon *what* the people had to be spiritually nourished. Every detail is of value, and contains spiritual significance, sometimes of the most beautiful character, at times of the most profound order. They reveal the comprehensiveness of the Divine Love in His dealings with the Soul. The Desert-place, the lack of Bread, the anxiety of the Disciples because of the lack, the five barley Loaves and two small Fishes, the breaking up of these and the distribution, the gathering up of the Seven Baskets full, and the

Twelve Baskets—these are treasures indeed in their revelatory character.

ALLEGORIES CONCERNING THE SIN-OFFERING

The Teachings concerning the Sin-offering were far more numerous than any of the interpreters of that supreme subject seem to have imagined. These are not isolated texts, but whole allegories which have been applied to objective things and historical events. Looked upon by the readers of the Gospel Records as literal stories containing accounts of events and experiences passed through by the Master during the days of the Manifestation, and as miraculous acts performed by Him, it is no wonder they have remained hidden in their inner meanings. Placed in other than their natural and true relationships, they were materialized beyond recognition as great spiritual pictures illustrating the most momentous work a Soul, even though divine in its attainments, could have undertaken. Thus there were lost to the whole world of religious thought the most precious and invaluable assets contained in the Gospel Records (such as these are) to the reality of that stupendous work. When it is known that these events were all connected with the Sin-offering, and are descriptive of various aspects of it, they become luminous even to being transformed.

Of these allegories those which describe *the Two Anointings* are most suggestive, the one preceding and the other following the accomplishment of the Sin-offering. For the anointing by Mary of Bethany was said to be done with a view to " the burial " of the Christ ; whilst the anointing in the House of Simon by the woman who was said to be a sinner, was not only the expression of most wonderful grief and exquisite devotion on the part of the woman, but her action was also a beautiful service rendered to the Christ *whose feet were travail-stained*—a service neglected by Simon. The first was the dedication of the

Soul through whom the Christhood was made manifest, to the sublime sacrifice implied in the Sin-offering; the second was the rediscovery by that Soul of the vision of the Christhood. It was the awful anguish which filled the Soul, consequent upon that discovery, owing to the consciousness of the Sin-offering tragic experiences; the discovery of what had happened unto the Life through a recovery of the past; the recovery of the consciousness of the glorious Christhood as it was realized during the days of the Manifestation, that the sublime vision given in that Manifestation had been betrayed and even the Jesus-life obscured, and that it had been done in the House of Simon to whose threshold the Divine Christhood had been invited. In both stories the names, the situations, the actions and the Sayings of the Master are burdened with Soul-meanings of profound nature.

Two more of these wonderful Sin-offering pictures are to be found in *The Flight into Egypt* and *the Temptations in the Wilderness*. We have indicated in a paragraph on the Birth-stories, what the Flight into Egypt meant, that it is the story of the going down of the Christ-Soul into the state represented by Egypt, to there bear the heavy burdens which all Souls have had to bear, so that the astral kingdom might be changed, and the way back to the Jesus-life and the Christhood realizations be found for all.

The Temptations in the Wilderness illustrate the nature of the trials that beset the Soul amid the wilderness life into which it went down, and the momentous experiences which had to be endured. Again the details are significant—" the tempter," " the turning of stones into bread," " the pinnacle of the Temple," " the exceeding high mountain," and the terms made use of. The wealth of sacred but sorrowful story buried in the historic narrative, is immense. From first to last the story is of *the Soul and its burden.*

Next in order of importance are the two supposed historical

incidents of " *The Woman of Samaria* " and " *The Christ washing the Disciples' Feet,*" followed by two more equally profound and illuminating, namely, " *The sleep and awakening of Lazarus* " and " *Mary Magdalene in the Garden after the Resurrection.*"

It is impossible in a few words to give even the faintest idea of the invaluable spiritual lore buried beneath the outwardness of these histories. Yet it is there for all who are able to bear the burden of the truths which they illustrate. The key to the meaning of the story of " The Woman of Samaria " is contained in the expression, " *And He must needs pass through Samaria.*" For to pass through Samaria was to go through some of the saddest and most painful experiences. The esoteric meaning of the terms must be understood, and not their mere outward historical application. The experiences were of the Soul—those experiences which the human children on this Planet had gone through, and many are passing through even now ; but very specially had they reference to that beloved Soul whom we know as the Master, during the Sin-offering, by which He was made like unto His Brethren. For the Woman of Samaria was an embodiment of the state represented by the term ; and in bearing the burden of the Sin-offering He had to enter into that state.

" *The Washing of the Disciples' Feet,*" though differing in some respects from the above, also illustrates the same great Mystery. It is perhaps the most wonderful of all the Sin-offering allegories. The transcendent Love revealed, the depth of the Humiliation entered into, the infinite Sacrifice made, the insight given into the process by which the Great Work was to be accomplished, the mysterious Logia spoken by the Master, and the profound meaning of them—these are beyond any adequate exposition. They have to be realized to be fully understood.

Three distinct Acts are, however, revealed.

1st. The laying aside of the Christhood Estate implied in the laying aside of " His Garments."

2nd. The Humiliation in passing down from the High Estate of a Divine Christhood to be as a Soul divested of all such beautiful raiment, and to then gird the loins with a towel, *i.e.*, to enter into the experiences signified.

3rd. The pouring of the water into the basin, followed by the work of cleansing.

These three Acts reveal the stupendous nature of the Sacrifice, the depth of the Humiliation, and the process by which was accomplished the tragic Sin-offering.

" *The sickness and death of Lazarus* " and the miraculous event of his resuscitation, embodies yet another aspect of that same profound Mystery. It was sickness that was not unto ultimate death, " *but for the Glory of God*." All the terms made use of and the Logia said to have been spoken by the Master, are pregnant with great meaning. The absence of the Divine Christhood from the House of Mary and Martha ; the sickening of Lazarus with the " fever " that had come upon him ; the going down into death ; the burial ; the fourth-day events through the approach of the Divine Christhood ; the sorrow and sayings of Mary and Martha ; the Divine sorrow and inward grief ; the awakening and calling forth of Lazarus ; the unloosening of " the grave clothes " ;—all these have inward meanings which the historical setting and exoteric interpretation have obscured. When these material environments fall away from before the vision, the allegory becomes luminant, And its light reveals still more fully to the wonderment of the discerning Soul, the depth of the Divine Love and the sublimity of the Divine Wisdom.

Then there is the wonderful story of *Mary Magdalene in the Garden* upon which Renan said the history of Christianity was built up. What a misfortune it was when such an allegory of the Soul was changed into an outward history ! Literally, the story was impossible. Spiritually, the very details of the allegory are full of significance. To the question, *Who was Mary Magdalene ?* we have an answer in the very terms themselves understood in the light of their esoteric significance. And to that yet further question, *How was it she sorrowed so terribly, and was so long in recognizing the Divine Lord who appeared unto her ?* we have the answer in *the aftermath* of the Sin-offering upon the Soul who bore the burden. For Mary Magdalene represented a spiritual state of that Soul ; just as " Mary of Bethany " and " Mary the Mother of the Lord," represented spiritual realizations. For Mary the Mother of the Lord represented the divine consciousness within the Virgin Soul ; and Mary of Bethany represented spiritual Christhood—that state in which the Soul loves to sit at the feet of her Lord ; whilst Mary Magdalene represented a state of intense spiritual darkness and abandonment to the sense-life. Mary was still the Soul, but as the Magdalene she was divested of even the attributes of spiritual Christhood.

Hence the intense anguish manifest in the House of Simon on the rediscovery of the Christhood vision and life ; and also her unspeakable grief in the garden of sorrow, when she could not find her long-lost Lord. For it was *that very profound sorrow* which prevented the Soul from arriving at the clear vision of the Divine Lord *within*.

And the allegory has found its complete fulfilment only in these latter days, a fact that will be better understood when the resurrection story is apprehended in its true light ; *for the Soul who bore the burden of the Sin-offering, after having been the vehicle of the glorious Divine Manifestation, has passed through these very experiences in these days in which we live.* For the resurrection days are with us now. The risen Lord (not the Master, but the Adonai) has appeared unto many (in Soul vision). And He who was known as the Master has accomplished *the great work* given Him to do by means of the Sin-offering. He has awakened once more to find the Christhood in the House of Simon with unwashen feet and unanointed ; and He has sorrowed with a sorrow none but the Divine Love could comfort. He is that Maria who has washed those feet with her tears and wiped them with the covering of her head, and anointed them with the precious ointment of her love ; who has grieved more than other Souls over the loss unto her of the vision of her Lord—the loss of the divine consciousness consequent upon bearing the awful burden of the divine work, and has sought unto it again with yearnings too great to find utterance, until at last the Soul has found her Lord once more in the dawn of that consciousness.

d

THE LOGIA OF THE UPPER ROOM

But beyond all these marvellous Teachings on the Sin-offering there are others equally important. There are other Logia of the Upper Room—the *Logia of the Lord's Supper and the Passover ; the Logia of the Gethsemane ; and the Logia of the Cross.* For the events with which these are associated were not such as the New Testament Records would seem to imply. *The Lord's Supper* was other than an evening meal in fellowship with the twelve. It was composed of higher elements than earthly bread and wine. It was a most solemn event between the Soul of the blessed Master and the Divine Lord. The Supper was the Lord's. It was the last exalted realization of the Divine Presence by the Master prior to His passing-over (The Passover) to take up the work of the Sin-offering. In that hour He ate of such bread and drank of such fruit of the vine as had been His meat and drink—the Divine Wisdom and the Divine Love, but which were to be no more known to Him in such blessed fulness until the Sin-offering was accomplished.

And *The Passover* was the last act, the passing away to take up that stupendous work, the divestment of all the attributes of Divine Christhood so as to take upon Himself the weakness, infirmities and afflictions common to all Souls upon the Planet, in performing the work of the Sin-offering.

The Gethsemane which is placed in the Gospel Records immediately after the Lord's Supper, was a most tragic affair. Even in the account given in the Gospel stories it would appear to sympathetic Souls as appalling. The profound anguish of it ; the mysterious agony so very manifest ; the dire sorrow ; the bitterness of the thing to be done ; the implied burden to be borne ; the awful nature of it which made the Master agonize and shrink from undertaking it ; the prayer for deliverance from it were it possible in harmony with the divine purpose—all these impress the Soul profoundly. Yet the picture drawn of it in the Gospels is indeed small compared to the reality. It is only a miniature, and imperfect as that. For *the real Gethsemane was a process of revelation to the Master*. It was the revelation to Him in a series of awful visions of the various spiritual states He would have to enter, and the things He would have to do as He travailed and trod the wine-press alone. In the Unfoldments it will be found what these visions were. And the knowledge of their nature will show the true reason for His awful anguish, and His prayer to be delivered from such an experience. It overwhelmed the Soul. Not a brief hour, but many days, did the Gethsemane cover. It was a time of the most profound mystery to all but Himself. Those who were nearest Him were overawed in presence of such inexplicable sorrow, such outbursts of anguish, such awful agony. *If all the Churches realized the meaning of the Gethsemane, they would become interpreters indeed of the Christhood, and make manifest the Jesus-life unto all Souls.*

It is in connection with the Gethsemane that *The Logia of the Cross* must be interpreted. In the light of the experiences

passed through in that momentous Soul-episode can their
meanings alone be understood. That they were not uttered on
the Roman Cross will be shown in the chapter which treats of
them. And that the meaning of these Logia went beyond
anything attributed to them in the interpretations put upon them
by scholars, will be most evident unto all who are prepared to
find the esoteric and Soul significance of things. For they had
relation to the Gethsemane vision and the taking up of the
dread burden of the Sin-offering. They covered all the scenes
in the Gethsemane, and the last hours of the Master's dwelling
upon these outer spheres as the vehicle of the Divine Manifestation. They were uttered in the hours of His intense anguish
as He saw all that was coming to Him, and where few heard them
or beheld the agony. What wealth of revelation they contain
concerning the nature of the Master's Christhood and the death
He was to experience ! *What assets to the reality of the Sin-
offering they are when understood in their esoteric sense !* The
Churches have not known, and none of their teachers appear
to have understood, the meaning of these profound Sayings.
Had they done so they would surely also have discovered that
the sufferings testified to were not borne upon the Cross on
which the Master was crucified by the order of the Roman
Judge at the instigation of the Jews, but upon that Cross borne
by the Christ-Soul as He performed the work of the Sin-offering;
and they would likewise have discovered that these Sayings
were not only a testimony to the reality of the sufferings, *but
also in themselves revealed the cause and the nature of the Sufferings*.

But herein also the whole Western World has been in the dark,
though doubtless it has had light of a sort. Concerning the real
significance of the Jesus-life, the true nature of a Christhood,
the profound purpose of the tragic Sin-offering and the nature
and work of it, not to speak of the true nature of the Resurrection,
Ascension, and the Parousia, the light within the Churches

has not been illuminating, and in a very real and painful sense it has even been as the darkness. Had the light of the Holy One, the Divine Breath—the only Illuminer and Inspirer of the Soul —dwelt within the Churches, then would the Jesus-life have been made manifest in no uncertain fashion. The various Christian Communities would have been venues for the revelation to the whole world of the Redeemed Life, the true and only Redemption for all Souls. Within all these Communities there would have been those who not only found the Jesus state, but who followed on to know the Christhood estate ; for the teachers within these Communities would have understood the nature and realizations of Christhood, and would therefore have been able to encourage and strengthen all those who in their spiritual state had become Initiates.

Nor would the tragic *Sin-offering* have been so grievously misunderstood and misinterpreted. It would never have become the cause of such fierce polemics as have been waged in its name ; for its nature and work would have been apprehended by all the teachers and leaders of the Communities. It then would not have been the instrument by which the glory of God was obscured, and a false vision of His sublime Love given to the Soul, but the great accomplishment upon the astral kingdom by means of which the purification of that kingdom was effected. The meaning of " the graven images " which were upon the " middle wall or partition," and which had to be broken down and blotted out because they were inimical to the Soul's spiritual growth, would have been known ; and such profound teachings would never have been related to anything connected with the ceremonial of Jewry.

The Redemption would have been a blessed realization through all the members of the Communities living the Jesus-life ; for them no such meaning would have been given to it as that which the Churches have held all through the ages. Never would it have been received as something objective to the Soul and accomplished apart from it ; for the meaning would have been obvious unto all, that it was an attainment through purity in all the ways of life.

The most sacred doctrine of *the Atonement* would likewise have been apprehended in its true inward significance, and understood through beautiful experience, as the profoundest of the Soul's realizations, and transcendent in its blessedness— *the oneness of the Soul with the Divine Life, Light and Love.* Under these conditions of high and beautiful spiritual experience, the astounding ecclesiasticism which grew until, like an upas tree, it spread its deadly influence everywhere in the West, overshadowing all spiritual purpose and service, and retarding every good movement which had for its aim the upliftment of the Soul to its own true realm, could never have found any place. For *Priesthood* would have been a beautiful Soul reality ; not the official thing it is to-day, whose insignia are purely ecclesiastical, and whose dominion is over the conscience and spiritual outlook of the Soul. And *Prophetism* would have been a living force within all the communities, an essential part of the divine ministry to the Soul ; for it is of the very nature of a full spiritual Priesthood. Nor would the high office of *Seership* have been relegated to the past, and viewed as only possible during that past ; but it would have been regarded as a most essential part of the divine ministry to the Soul. Its visions would not have been judged of according to the present Christianized methods of Jewry ; for the Traditions of the elders would have been founded upon knowledge received at first hand from the Divine World, and not the mere mental equipment gained in the schools comprising the knowledge of languages and outward history. And so the Church would have been a *living organism*, a glorious spiritual community, a blessed fellowship, an enlightened congregation, a mighty People, a royal Priesthood—the true embodiment of the Kingdom of the Heavens upon the Earth, universal in love, wholly spiritual in purpose, truly heavenly in vision, and as the Divine in all its work. And by means of it the entire Western World would have been uplifted to the purest and noblest ways of life, and to the most enlightened outlook. It would have been raised to the purity, goodness and nobility of the Jesus-life; and there would have been given unto it the Light of Christhood through the outshining of that Divine Light in the illumination of all those who had risen into that holy estate. For in these would the Holy Breath have dwelt whose sacred Flame is the Radiance of the Divine Love.

When the Master in His Life and Work is beheld by the West as He was, blessed indeed will be the vision unto the mind; and when His Teachings are understood by all who ought to know them, then will it indeed be a time of Soul enlightenment, issuing in a very real Christhood manifestation.

John the Baptist

*Being an embodiment of the first part of
the Master's Mission, and showing
the way of Initiation into the
Jesus-life, with expositions
concerning the Baptism
of Christ and the
doctrine of the
H o l y
Spirit.*

A

IS THE STORY BIOGRAPHICAL?

" *THE Baptism of John, was it of men, or was it from the Heavens?* " The question is said to have been asked by the Master when the Pharisees sought to dispute the authority which He claimed for the Teachings He gave. And in the Records it is so presented as to make it appear as if the Master sought to confound the Pharisees and the Scribes—men who were the religious leaders and writers of their times—because, whilst they had given a hearing to the message of John through the fear which they had of the multitudes who were moved and influenced by his message, they nevertheless opposed the Teachings of the Master concerning the mission of the Christ.

It is sad to reflect that the story of John the Baptist has likewise been reduced to mere outward literal history, and changed into the biography of a man. As an historical narrative it seems so natural at first sight; and yet when examined seriously it is all so strange. The story of John's mission appears to be very real as the story of a man who suddenly issues from the desert to begin a work of purification as the preparation for the coming of the Christ; and yet there is much that lacks the true elements of reality, much that is unreal as regards any mere biographical portrayal of a man. Mystery surrounds him from his birth to the tragedy that closed his mission. Though he is said to have had a large following, and that his special mission was to prepare the lives of his followers to recognize and follow the Christ, yet few could have been so prepared, or the blessed Master would have had many true and noble followers, men and women ready to receive His more profound message, and His beautiful vision of life and service for the Soul. If it is a true story of the mission of a man named John the Baptist who came to prepare the way of the Lord in order that the Christ who was coming might be received, and the life to which He would call all Souls be entered upon and realized, then it was a mission that failed in its object. He is said in the Records to have been a Messenger of the Divine, one sent upon a mission at once wonderful in its meaning and glorious in its issues, one sent to recall the people to ways of true repentance expressed in purification of life and goodness of heart ; yet the Messenger and his message are represented as having lamentably failed in their original purpose, so few really brought forth those fruits which were the meet of true repentance, so very few, if any, were prepared to follow the Christ when He made His appearance. Indeed so few followed the Messenger who was sent out to prepare the way, that the Christ, when He came, had to find and call His own disciples.

That the story contains sacred history is not only unquestionable, but it is most obvious. The history, however, is not that of a man preaching a new way of life unto multitudes, but the history of the Soul on its way to the Kingdom of the Divine. John the Baptist must precede the Christ ; the baptism in the waters of the Jordan is essential to following the divine path ; the voice of the Baptist must be understood ere the voice of the Christ can be heard ; the way of John is the path by which all must walk towards the Holy City where the Christ is made manifest.

How full of profound meaning the story is will be recognized as we unfold its spiritual significance.

B

WHO WAS JOHN THE BAPTIST ?

IN ,the Records the forerunner of the Christ is spoken of as the cousin of the Master. The Birth-stories find a place for him and show how intimate was the relation between his birth and that of the Master. In birth he is made to precede the Master, and likewise to know even before he is born that the Christ is about to come ; for he is said to have leapt for very joy in the womb of his mother when the news was broken to her that the Virgin should bear the Christ. His coming also is foretold by the prophets and heralded by Angels ; for the prophets spake of the coming of the Messenger of the Lord to prepare the way, and the Angel of the Lord, Gabriel, appeared unto his father Zacharias within the Temple to announce his birth. Though in a less degree, yet in as true a sense, it is an event as miraculous as the Advent of the Christ ; for it is the outcome of divine interposition, and is attended by angelic ministry. It is an event which is not only spoken of as the shadowing forth of the coming of the Christ, but one that was absolutely essential to that coming, a prelude to the full drama of Christhood. Not only does he precede the Christ in His manifestation through being first born, but he also precedes Him in the order of ministry. He is a voice proclaiming the Christ's Advent, a purifier making the Advent possible. His voice is heard on the borders of the wilderness, and his message is one burdened with judgment. He proclaims the way of the Lord, and calls all who hear him to purify themselves that they may follow it. His life seems stern and rudely simple, as one whose ways are of the desert ; but it is pure. His diet is not such as men and women nourish themselves upon, being only the food of the desert dwellers ; but, though rude fare, it is the diet of " one sent " from the Lord. His message reverberates with the strident tones of the prophets, even as if spoken through an angelic trumpet, the horn of salvation which sounds forth the Word of the Lord. He baptizes with the Waters of the Jordan, and in that river, all who come unto him that they may begin the new life ; and then he points out to them the Christ who alone taketh away the Sin of the World. Even of him is the Christ baptized in order that all righteousness may be fulfilled. And concerning the Christ and His mission he proclaims that He will increase ; whilst of himself and his work he affirms that he will decrease, as the new and higher baptism which the Christ gives, is received. He acknowledges himself to be less than the Christ, and that he is not even worthy to unloose the Christ's shoes ; and the Records state that the Master afterwards spake of him as less than the least within the Kingdom of the Heavens, though he was the greatest amongst men.

What John Represented

Perhaps our readers have already discerned something of the marvellous truth connected with the mission of the Baptist. If so, they will have discovered that he was not a man, but a state of life ; that he was not a mere physical personality moving out of the desert, but the life of the Soul leaving the desert wherein no spiritual realizations are found, that desert which has the fiery trials within itself, the arid sands and impoverished wilds of a mere material existence. For the mission of John the Baptist was a part of the Christ-mission within the Soul. It was that part of the mission which made possible for the Soul the coming of the Christ, or Christhood. It was the purifying Breath of Divine Love blowing upon the life to separate the chaff from the wheat, the dross from the pure gold, the things that were wholly material from those things which were entirely spiritual. It was the voice proclaiming the approach of the Kingdom of God ; the voice of the Divine Word crying amid the wilderness of Judea (the wilderness conditions of life upon the Planet) ; the voice whose message was that all the things of the flesh were as grass, and all the goodliness of the sense-life as the flower of the grass ; the voice whose call was unto righteousness of conduct, purity in the ways of life, self-denial in the world, and the Baptism of Truth, the cleansing waters of the Jordan (the Spirit).[1]

---

[1] The river Jordan was the river of the Divine Spirit flowing through the interior of Man's spiritual system. It was applied by the Jews to the river which flowed from North to South of their country. The purifying Waters of the Jordan were and are the purifying spiritual truths with which the Soul comes to be baptized.

John the Baptist, therefore, represented the initial stages of the new life unto which the Soul was called in the Teachings of the Master ; just as the Christhood represented the Pleroma or fullness of that life. His message is that one which must always precede the message of the Christ. There can be no Christhood without the realization of the Baptism of John. Purification of life must go before heavenly vision and inward spiritual realizations. The fruits of the first love must be brought forth ere the Vine within the Soul (the Divine Love) can bear precious grapes, or the Fig-tree blossom and give forth tender figs (the Divine Wisdom unfolding within the Soul). The Redemption of the life must be accomplished ere the Crown of Life (Christhood) can be won.

C

THE BAPTISM WITH WATER

THE whole story of the work of the Baptist seems to be in keeping with the elaborate ceremonial religion for which Jewry stood. Though the message of the Messenger was full of fire with which to search and purify, by means of separation, the lives of all who heard it, yet was it set in the cumbersome ceremonial of baptizing with water, as if any mere outward rite could contain or impart the divine virtue or power which was necessary for the purification of life. The ceremonial was not unlike the priestly acts with which the Jews were acquainted, and it lent a seeming value to the outward rite which it did not and could not contain, and which was in direct opposition to the whole of the Teachings of the sublime Master. Whilst the message is in harmony with those stirring appeals made by the true prophets, in which the people were urged to change their ways and purify their affections ; yet is it beset with those formulæ which the true prophets always denounced as hindrances to the pure life and service of the Divine. It is the message of the prophet with the prescriptions of the priest.

It is a call to spiritual life, the beginnings of true life for the Soul ; but the initiation into this life is made by means of outward ceremonial. The Soul is to seek for the realization of the prophet's message ; but it is to seek it through the means provided by the priest. It is to find a new and blessed experience but it is to find it through rites and ceremonies.

What the Baptism meant

" *The Baptism of John, was it of men ? or was it from the Heavens ?* " If the story were literal, truly it would be of men. It would be a combination of prophetic message for the Soul with those priestly limitations which are entanglements. And as it stands and is read and interpreted by the Churches, it was and is such a combination as we might expect from men such as those were who wrote the received Records of the ministry of the Christ. In this respect it is in keeping with nearly all the other stories in the Records ; for they are mostly changed into material histories, and the sublime and profound meanings are hidden almost beyond finding.

The Baptism of John was not of men, but from the Heavens. It knew nothing of outward ceremonial, for it was of an inward and spiritual order. It was a sacred rite ; but it took place within the mind where the eye of man could not penetrate, though its effects were made manifest in the outward life. It was from the Heavens in the sense that it was heavenly in its character and results, and that it was given from the Divine Lord through the Messenger whose work it was to purify the Heavens of the Soul. It was from the Heavens because it was of the life of the Soul, appertaining to the Kingdom of the Soul, having for its beautiful purpose the purification of the conditions of the life so that the Soul might be sphered with all the elements essential to the true unfoldment of spiritual being. It was from the Heavens in that it was a baptism begotten of a new and blessed purpose in life, the birth of a new spirit, the outcome of a new vision ; for it followed the new endeavour after purity in the ways of life, the nobler feelings awakened within the mind, the higher call heard and responded to by the Soul. It was from the Heavens because all its influences were heavenly. Its results were beautiful in the life of the one baptized, and beneficent in their power over others. So heavenly in character was it that it pointed to a yet higher state than the life John the Baptist represented ; for it clearly foreshadowed the coming of Christhood, pointed out the path to that blessed state, and counselled the Soul to follow the Christ. It spake of the Christ-hood baptism that would follow, the baptism of the Holy Spirit and Holy Fire. It pointed to the Christhood as something greater, whose increase would be assured even when the more outward life which it represented grew less and less to the vision of the Soul.

" *Except ye be born of water and the Spirit ye cannot enter into the Kingdom of the Heavens.*" These words are attributed to Jesus in His conversation with Nicodemus. The truth im-plied in them is profound. And the first stage of the experience spoken of is expressed by the Baptism of John. It is the Baptism of water. And it is a baptism with the waters of the Jordan.

Water is the symbol of Truth. Cleansing with water is the symbol of the purifying power of Truth. To be baptized with water is to pass through the baptism of the cleansing influence of Divine Truth revealed unto the Soul. To enter the waters of the Jordan for the baptism, is to enter into the realization of the Spirit of Truth in the purpose of life. For the Jordan represents the land of the Spirit within a man, whose waters flow through it as consciousness upon the various planes of Being, through which consciousness the Soul apprehends upon these planes the Truth as it comes unto it from the Divine. The river Jordan is the river that divides the true Human Kingdom from the elementary Human Kingdom, that separates the true Man from the animal rudimentary Man, that divides the desert from the land flowing with the milk of spiritual nourishment and the honey of heavenly sweetness.

To be baptized in the Waters of Jordan by the Messenger, was and is to arrive at the consciousness of the redemptive powers of Truth, and to pursue it unto the full realization.

The materialization of the sacred inner meanings of the Baptism of John has led to disastrous results. It not only hid the Truth from the seeker for the true path, but it sent the Soul along a wrong path. It withdrew the seeker's attention from the inwardness of the message and the life to which it called, and set forth the experience and the initiatory rite as entirely external. It changed the prophetic and spiritual character of the proclamation, and made of it an external ceremony and priestly function. It gave to the mission of the Messenger an entirely exoteric meaning, and thus completely veiled the esoteric significance of the initiatory experience for the Soul. It was not simply an endeavour to visualize the inward experience so as to impress the mind with the truth implied ; it was the bringing down of the whole of the spiritual meanings signified, to have relation to outward things only, and to find their interpretation in them.

The writers changed the beautiful recovered Redeemed Life represented by the Messenger, into a man performing an outward ceremony by which men and women were made disciples of a new life. They made of the man a fore-runner of the coming Christ, and of the baptism a preliminary or initiatory step to following Him. They presented the man as one coming out of the desert, and as having almost the wildness of the desert-life in his ways ; yet they presented even the Christ as one of the subjects for the Messenger's baptism, as if the Messenger were greater than the One to whom he pointed and concerning whose coming his message spake. And thus they associated the blessed Master with outward rites from the beginning of His beautiful and altogether spiritual ministry, and so gave to the Soul a vision of Him which was the very antithesis of the way He took when He came to make manifest the Christhood and interpret for the Soul the way unto its realization.

THE EFFECT OF MATERIALIZING TRUTH

The disastrous results of such a calamitous materialization of deep spiritual teachings, may be found in the history of ecclesiastical Christianity. Almost from the foundation of the Church as an outward and visible Kingdom, the doctrine of baptism as an initiatory rite was held as vital to the Soul. So great was the delusion resulting from the materialization of the spiritual truth implied, that the scholars of the various schools of thought which arose as the outcome of different views of the nature of Christ and the purpose of His mission entered into conflict with one another. And so bitter at times did that conflict become, that men and women persecuted each other both secretly and openly. What pain and sorrow the error brought upon many who desired to find the true path ! What anguish of Soul and agony of mind many had to endure as the result of the mistaken way which the scholars took ! What a religious history was written by the various religious schools whilst these conflicts were waged ! Considering the supposed foundations of the Churches, the wonderful claims which they have always made as to their divine origin and purpose, the high and blessed life which they professed to represent and call all the world to realize, the history which they have written is dark indeed, and amongst the saddest the world has known.

Nor in these days of a greater spiritual enlightenment when the whole world seems moving upward unto a life of spiritual realization beyond anything that has been experienced for untold ages, do the Churches seem to have awakened from the stupor which overtook them as the result of the delusion.

Indeed the delusion is still upon most of them, even the most enlightened. The rite of baptism is one of their sacraments. The outward ceremony is valued as an important part of the spiritual life. In most cases it is viewed as essential to the salvation of the individual. Nay, many of them teach just what the Records appear to teach concerning its inherent value, namely, that it is the gateway into the Kingdom of the Heavens, the initiation of the Soul by which it is made a child of God, the act whereby the individual life is made sure of an entrance into the Kingdom of God.

A Question of Great Moment

Was there ever a greater delusion foisted upon the children of the Divine Father ? Was there ever a greater travesty of a sublime spiritual experience ? Was there ever a more tragic thing done in the name of the Divine Love ? How great must the darkness within the Soul have been when such a delusion found acceptance ! How intense that darkness now appears unto us when we know that even those who were desirous of finding the true path of life, entered into conflicts with one another, and that these too frequently ended in dire persecution ! How appalling is the blindness of the schools represented by the various Churches whose leaders must be familiar with the sad history of these conflicts and the present state of the Western World, and who must witness the utter impotence of any such outward rite and ceremony of baptism, howsoe'er and whensoe'er administered, to effect the redemption of the life, and to initiate the Soul into the life of the Kingdom of the Heavens ! When will the Churches, every one of them, awaken from the deep sleep that for ages has characterized them in their ways, worship and interpretations, to behold the inner significance of these divine things, and so purify themselves from their gross materialism ? When will they indeed hear even the voice calling amid the wilderness of life, and enter into the experience represented by the baptism with

water ? When will they awaken to recognize the Divine
Messenger as no mere man, but the redemptive and purifying
power born within the Soul, that divine power by means of
which the life puts away every evil thing in order that it may
be able to follow the Christ ? When will they hear the voice
of the Messenger whom the Divine Father has sent to prepare
the way for the coming of the Christ, calling them unto the
life of outward as well as inward purification ? When will they
awaken to the fact that the pure life is one full of tender pity
for all creatures ; that the true life glows with a beautiful
merciful kindness ; that a life truly noble would scorn to make
any creature suffer for any purpose whatever, whether for
food, clothing or health ? When will they come to understand
the true meaning of redemption, and see that there is no
redemption that does not make the life pure in its ways, the
mind noble in its thoughts and purposes, and the heart over-
flowing with pure affections and boundless compassion ? When
will they arrive at the blessed experience implied in the baptism
with water, see the truth with the eyes of the Soul as it is lit
up from the Divine, and take their place as true centres of
redeeming activity in the world, communities founded upon
love for ministry unto all Souls, pilgrims on the way to the
only Holy City worth finding—the realization of all that is
implied in the Christhood Estate ?

AN APPEAL TO THE CHURCHES

*O Church of the Living God, begotten in the Divine Thought
as a Community of Souls pure and spotless ; chosen from the
foundation of the world as a spiritual system before the present
cosmos or order of things arose ; chosen to be the venue of the
Divine Manifestation unto the little children growing up within
the Heavenly Father's Household ; appointed unto the most
sacred office of spiritual priesthood to minister before Him in the
interpretation of His Love and Holy Wisdom ; when will ye arise
out of the darkness and come into His glorious Light ? When will*

ye break the bands of your captivity and shake off the dust of your humiliation, and clothe yourself in the garments of your ancient priesthood, garments of purity and truth and light, garments whose phylacteries are goodness and compassion, whose stole is the sign of the Divine Cross-bearing, and whose mitre is the Crown of the Divine Life ? When will ye throw off the yoke of materialism by which ye have been directed and even ruled through so many long ages, and step forth into the glorious spiritual liberty of the children of God, putting for ever behind you the sensuous and ceremonial that ye may again know the inwardness of things, and arrive once more at the knowledge, through experience, of the divine ways of entering the kingdom ? A voice upon the midnight air of your life is calling you to awaken and arise and come forth into the Life, Light and Love of the Divine and ever-Blessed One. The voice is that of the Messenger of the Lord. Ye are called to leave the desert wherein all your spiritual forces have been impoverished, and the Divine Image within you has been miraged, and come to the waters of the Jordan which flow from the divine uplands, the waters of truth whose cleansing power makes clean the life, and purifies all the elements of Being until all things are renewed and have become wholly spiritual and divine. Ye are called unto the baptism of the Messenger, the forerunner of the Christ ; to pass from the desert-life into the life of The Redemption, the life whose every way is pure, compassionate and pitiful. Ye are called to forsake the life of mere outward ceremonial for the inward realization of the truths of which your ceremonials should have spoken unto you ; to cease the vain oblations which ye have offered unto the Divine Love, and make your altars pure ; to destroy and sacrifice no more the beautiful creature-lives for food, adornment and purposes of science, but rather to eliminate from your life everything that would hurt or destroy any living creature and the Divine Life of the Soul. For nothing that hurts or destroys, nor those who hurt or destroy, can approach unto the Holy Mountain of the Lord, the Mount of the Assembly of the First-born—the Christs of God.

Behold how without your camp many are hearing and responding to the voice of the Messenger, and are being baptized with his baptism! The new redemptive movements are all outside your borders ; tarry ye not lest ye be left behind.

D

THE BAPTISM OF THE CHRIST

IN the Records it is set forth that the blessed Master was baptized by the Messenger, and that He submitted to that Baptism in order " to fulfil all righteousness." In this way is it made to appear a righteous thing to submit to the outward ceremony, and as if the Master had given His sanction to such a view, and lent His authority to the priestly function. It thus represents the Master as believing in these outward rites and ceremonies as things essential to the redemption of the Soul, as viewing them as gateways into the higher and more blessed life, indeed to be the actual initiatory acts by which the individual passes upward into more spiritual experiences, and the life is prepared for the coming into the Soul of those profound realizations implied in the Christhood.

But any one who truly understands what Christhood means, will also know that any such action on the part of the blessed Master was impossible. He was no priestly occultist emphasizing outward things, and transferring the true significance from the innermost spheres to the physical planes. He was no follower of the schools of the priests, scribes and pharisees, whose righteousness consisted so much in the rites and ceremonies of Jewry. Even the Gospel Records, notwithstanding the blurred image they present, in other parts of their narratives make that obvious to the reader. The righteousness of a Christhood is born from within. It is Divine Righteousness. It is a mode of manifestation of the Divine Life. The rites associated with it, both in the attainment and the manifestation of it, are all inward. It has no relation to anything outward other than its own manifestation. It could not look upon outward symbolic rites and ceremonies as anything more than the most temporary aid to Souls who were still in their spiritual childhood, and who required some objective sign of the inward meaning to help the mind in a manner not unlike the aid rendered to the child-mind by the kindergarten method of imparting knowledge. And a Christ would require no such helps ; for a Soul who is in a state of Christhood such as the Master knew, knows all things from within himself or herself. The righteousness which such a Soul fulfils is the righteousness of the Divine Love made manifest in a life of most beautiful purity, goodness and compassion. And, knowing this, we may thus see what a travesty of the truth the writers of the story presented for the West, and how that world has been deceived and deluded by it.

The Baptism an inward Reality

Was there then no such baptism of the Christ as is implied in the story ? Was there no baptism of Him by the Messenger with the waters of the Jordan ? Is the story in this respect a fabrication in order to attach the name of the Master to the outward ceremonial ? The story was true as originally told, and the baptism of the Christ was a reality. But it was not an outward rite, nor performed as an outward priestly ceremonial. The Baptism of John was from the Heavens ; it was not of men. It was an inward realization with an outward manifestation. It was the baptism of truth received from the Divine Spirit, and revealed in the true life. With Him it was not a baptism unto repentance, but one unto manifestation of the meaning of the life unto which all Souls were being called. For Him it was not a Baptism into a new life, but one through which He showed forth the nature and purpose of that new life for humanity. It was a baptism through which He fulfilled all righteousness, fulfilled the Law of the Lord in walking in the ways of purity upon every sphere of experience. He knew no wrong in His ways. He ate no flesh of any kind, nor did aught to bring hurt to any creature. He kept His body pure as well as His mind and Soul. The Baptism of the Messenger was unto purification for the world; for Him it was unto the manifestation of the true and pure life, that the world might know the meaning of the purified life through beholding it in Him. It was a Baptism of Truth, the vision of the true life, the descent of the Life of the Heavens unto the planes of the Earth. And, had those who wrote the accepted Gospel Records understood these things and truly presented them, the history of Christianity would have been one full of the most wonderful spiritual changes and achievements that would have shown forth the Christhood gloriously, and brought the whole world into the Redeemed Life, subduing all evil, conquering all wrong, establishing everywhere the righteousness of the Divine Love, bringing in the reign of the Christhood with its blessed Life and Light, making the Golden Age a reality, Paradise restored, and the whole world the Home of the Gods through the recovery of the blessed consciousness of the Divine Presence within the Soul.

The Master fulfilled all righteousness. All who would follow Him must do likewise. They must go in the way of the baptism with the waters of the Jordan. The life must be pure. Every way of life must know the cleansing which the Messenger brings. There is not one way for the Master and another way for the disciple. The seeker who would know the Lord has to follow on to know Him by means of the path which leads to the vision and realization within the Soul. Righteousness has to be fulfilled; that is, it has to be lived. To fulfil righteousness is to live the righteous life. The truly righteous life is pure; it is compassionate; it is pitiful. Its one aim is to have all its ways pure, so that there is nothing done, or purposed to be done, that would militate against that beautiful intention. Unto this end the body will be kept pure. It will be nourished only on the purest food. It will be kept apart from the contaminating evils in the world. It will never be the instrument of inflicting directly or indirectly, pain and anguish upon others, even if these others be only the creatures. Rather it will be the medium through which goodness and compassion are interpreted, the vehicle for the noble expression of tender pity, the consecrated instrument through which even the creatures are sheltered from those who would oppress them and take from them their lives for purposes of pleasure, food, clothing, or in the pursuit of knowledge for any purpose whatsoever.

When once a man is baptized with the baptism of the Divine Messenger, who is always in every life the forerunner of the coming Christ, his righteousness will be no longer that of the scribes and pharisees, but that of goodness, purity, compassion and pity. And he will bless in the service of his life, all Souls, Human and Creature.

E
THE OPENING OF THE HEAVENS

WHEN the Christ was baptized with the waters of the Jordan there was vouchsafed unto him who bare record, a vision from the Heavens. The Heavens were opened, and from the glory there came forth the form of a Dove. And the Dove descended from the glory until it rested upon the head of the Christ, whilst from out of the glory there was the voice of One who spake, saying, " *This is my Beloved Son; hear ye Him.*"

Even the writers of the Gospel narratives have told us that the vision beheld was the baptism of the Divine Spirit descending upon the Christ. And when the symbolism is fully understood, profound depths of meaning may be discovered in it. For the opening of the Heavens implies so much, the appearance and descent of the Dove adding to the depth of meaning ; the glory and the voice from out its midst only increasing the blessed mystery.

In its inner meaning the story is sublime. It is dramatic ; but its drama is of the Soul, It is wonderful in its spectacular ; but the phenomena are all heavenly. As the baptism of the Messenger is from the Heavens and not of men, so the baptism of the Spirit is *within* and not without. *The phenomena are all inward, and are of the Soul.* The Heavens which are opened are not stellar ; they are those of the Soul whose life is crowned with the state of inward Divine Realization represented by the term Christhood. They are the Heavens of the Divine Presence within the Soul, Heavens which cannot be opened until the life is purified upon all its spheres, through the baptism with the waters of the Jordan—the baptism which the Messenger gives unto all who truly seek the Divine. The opening of the Heavens indicates the unfoldment of the inner life, the discovery by the Soul of the Divine Presence within its sanctuary, the beholding of the exceeding glory of that Presence, the realization of the inheritance of the Spirit, the power to hear the voice of the Presence and to understand the message which is spoken from the Divine Kingdom. And what a blessed experience that is when the Heavens are opened and the Divine Presence is henceforth known as a *realization !* How profound is the realization when the glory of the Lord overshadows the Soul ! What beautiful heavenly awe is present, that reverence which none may understand but those who have passed that way !

THE MEANING OF THE DOVE

With the opening of the Heavens the glory of the Lord is beheld streaming forth upon the Christ : it is the glory or light of the Divine Love to be expressed in the Christhood Life. The glory of the Lord rests upon Christhood : it is the testimony of the divine realization. The Soul in the Christhood estate is the venue through whom the glory of the Lord is made manifest unto the world, the medium through whom its blessed light is to break and be distributed upon the life of men and women. It is the glory of perfect Being ; of life pure and spiritual in all ways ; of knowledge born from the Divine—that heavenly Wisdom which the world-mind cannot receive, neither understand, Wisdom which is not of men but of God ; of love which is the interpretation of the Divine Love, that knows no measure in its giving nor limitations in its ministry, whose service is one of boundless compassion unto all Souls and illimitable pity unto all creatures.

With the streaming forth of the Divine Glory, there also descended the Holy Spirit in the form of a Dove until it rested upon the Christ. The descent bespeaks the descent of the Adonai or Logos to make Himself manifest in and through the Christhood of the Soul. The Dove is the symbol of gentleness upon the spiritual planes. When it is white it is the symbol of purity. But, upon the innermost planes of vision, it speaks of the Divine Nature, of the attainment and realization by the Soul of that Nature, of the unfoldment of a divine consciousness within the Soul in which the Soul knows itself one with the Divine. It is the At-one-ment, the entering into the perfect realization of the One Life. The baptism of the Spirit thus symbolized is not simply the baptism in that measure which brings upon the soul its first heavenly influences ; but that baptism which is without measure, and imparts unto the Soul the consciousness of the Divine Overshadowing.

The Voice from out the Glory

When the Holy Spirit descends from the Glory to rest upon the Christ, there is heard the Voice from out the Glory saying, " *This is my Beloved Son ; hear ye Him.*" Truly it is " the crowning act to the imperial theme ; " for it is the blessed testimony to the nature of the life unto which the Soul has attained, the Soul hearing the divine language concerning the Christhood Estate with the vision of the Divine Glory. It is indeed an unspeakable mystery which must be realized to be understood. The sound of that Voice is *not* outward. It is heard within the Sanctuary. The message of the Voice is one which no man knoweth until he has prepared himself unto the understanding of the innermost. But it is translated for the Soul into terms which it may come to understand. It is a message profound in its meanings for the Soul, and encouraging to the earnest seeker. Unto the blessed Master it spake of the Beloved One who was with Him, the Divine Christ, the Eternal Son, the Adonai, the Manifest One of the Unmanifest One, the embodied glory of the Invisible. *Him the Master was to hear always within Himself.* He was the One from whom the Master lived, worked and taught. The words which the Master spake were the transcription of the divine language spoken within Him from the Adonai.

For the Soul the message is again transcribed. That which the beloved Master made manifest was true sonship to the Divine, the Christhood as the state of " the beloved ones." It is the realization unto which Souls are called, the fulness of life towards which all Souls are to travel. From out the Glory within the innermost sanctuary of the Soul's spiritual system, the Divine Voice calls to every one to hear the words of the Christ.

F

JOHN'S DESCRIPTION OF THE CHRIST

" BEHOLD *the Lamb of God who beareth away the Sin of the World !* " These are the terms in which the Christ is described by the Messenger. That they are profound in their meaning will be understood by all who know what the office of the Cross meant for the Christ. That the deep significance of them has been misapprehended and misinterpreted may be gathered from the whole history of the doctrine of the Redemption as promulgated by the Churches. The sufferings of the Christ through the sinful conditions of humanity is a subject which has engaged the thought of all who have felt the power of evil, and who have been taught in the doctrines of the Christian Religion as expounded in all the Churches. That there is a profound mystery in it, all readily acknowledge ; but the endeavours to expound that mystery have not only been manifold in their diversity, but often disastrous in the results.

The Sin-bearer was said to be the Christ. Of Him it was affirmed that He would carry away all the sin of the world. Was the Christ, then, in the manifestation of His Christhood, a Sin-bearer ? Did He, in that State, carry away the sin of the world ? If so, where did He carry it to, and how did He bear the awful burden ? Has the world had no sin since then ? Has the history of Christianity witnessed a real redemption from sin ? Have not men and women their sin still ? Have not the sins of men and women brought dire trouble upon themselves, their posterity, and the whole world since the days of the Christhood ? Does not the entire world still groan under the burden of it ? Is not society to-day in its constitution, with all those evil elements whose ramifications are to be found and seen everywhere, the direct outcome of the sin of men and women ?

It must be obvious to any one who thinks seriously, that the sin of the world has not been taken away, and, therefore, that the Christ during the blessed Manifestation, nor even by the Roman crucifixion, could not have borne it away. For were all the sin in the world taken away, then indeed would Eden be regained, the Earth become a Paradise, and all the spheres of human experience would be Elysium. Love would be regnant, Righteousness triumphant, Goodness universal, and Peace, even the Peace of God, abiding. The worldly mind would find no place ; the oppressive spirit would be unable to exist ;

the self-seeking life would pass, even as the darkness passes with the dawn. Strife between man and man, between nation and nation, between race and race ; militarism in every form ; conquest in every degree of the things of this world, whether in commerce or national life—all would pass with the coming of that new Life whose glory is manifest in love, compassion and pity ; tenderness, gentleness and merciful-kindness ; righteousness, goodness and peace.

WHO HEARD THE ANNOUNCEMENT ?

What then could have been the meaning of the saying ? Who were they who were to behold the Lamb of God ? What was it they were to behold ? Where were they to behold it ? Those who were counselled to behold the new phenomenon were those who had been baptized in the waters of the Jordan and cleansed from their evil ways. Unto them was a new and very blessed truth made known, namely, that the Christ was amongst them making manifest the meaning of the new life unto which they had been called ; that He was the interpreter of the Divine Mystery, and the carrier of the sinful burden of the world. The appeal was unto Souls who were on the threshold of the Kingdom, Souls who had taken the first step of the cross by which the Kingdom is won, men and women who had arisen from the dust and humiliation of the sense-life bondage into the liberty of Souls whose faces were henceforth Zionward (that is, towards the higher spiritual realizations, as the term originally meant ; for the state known as Zion was that of spiritual Christhood. The Soul born in Zion was blessed). It was not to the multitude, nor to the traditionalist, nor yet to the mere scholar, that the Christ was pointed out ; but to those only who had received the baptism, and were ready to hear the things pertaining to the inner life and the Kingdom. They were the disciples of John, the beloved one, men and women who had indeed heard the voice of the Messenger, and who had responded to it.

Unto such Souls were the words spoken, " *Behold the Lamb of God, who taketh away the sin of the World.*" How the sin was to be carried away, they could not then know ; it was only the fact that was announced to them. But, like all deep things of the Soul and the Kingdom, by and by as they were able to apprehend the inner significance of the saying, the truth of it would unfold unto their vision. Spiritual things can only be interpreted unto spiritual men and women ; and that only in the proportion that they are able to receive them. Only that which the Soul has known of old can be thus given unto it again ; according to the sphere of life experienced by the Soul has the truth to be broken. Unless the inner eye be open to perceive, and the ear to understand, the Soul cannot see and understand spiritual and divine things. There are things purely Human, things purely Spiritual, things entirely Celestial, and things altogether Divine. The Soul must pass through the lower spheres first, and then rise ever upward to reach the highest. It must apprehend and understand the things on the levels ere it can hope to apprehend those on the distant uplands and heights. To reach the highest it must climb up from the levels ; and as it does so, its path will narrow even as the mountain narrows from its base upwards. But the horizon will become more and more extended ; the air grow more and more rarefied ; the vision become ever greater, clearer and more intense ; and the resultant life be an ever-increasing blessedness, free and still more free from every influence of the magnetism along the lower reaches, until it attains that inward realization when the divine consciousness awakens and passes into fulness in which the Divine Glory stands unveiled to the Soul.

G

THE DIVINE MYSTERY [1]

THE Lamb of God who bore away the sin of the world
was the Divine Love. It was affirmed of no man, though
it applied to the Christ. It was of the Divine Lord in Him of
whom it spake, and not of the outward personal life through
whom the Christhood was made manifest. It was of the Divine
Love in a sacrificial capacity and in the Office of the Cross.
And it was of that Love in its sacrificial capacity revealed in
the Office of the Cross, that it spake when this was affirmed
concerning the Christ ; for He was the manifestation of the
Divine Love in His Christhood, and after His Christhood
He was taking up the burden of the Office of the Cross that He
might bear away the effects of the sins of the children of this
world which they wrote long ages ago upon the then magnetic
plane of the planet, but known now as the astral kingdom. It
therefore pointed to the work of the Divine Love by means of
which the work of the Christhood manifestation was to have
effect given unto it.

The profound mystery is not easily understood. It is most
difficult to conceive how the Christ-Soul laid aside His
beautiful Christhood in order to become the bearer of the sin-
burden of the world. Only unto those Souls who are able to
receive it, can it be understood in its inner significance. How
very difficult it is to fully understand may be gathered from
the history which has been written by the Churches in their
endeavours to expound it and convert the world to their view.
The theories of its nature and results are many, ranging from
the recrudescence of the most commercial doctrine of commutation and the Jewish vision of the manifestation of the
Divine Judgment upon the frailties of all His children, to the

---

[1] The full treatment of this profound Mystery can only be given when
we are able to write fully of the Nature and Work of the Sin-offering.

doctrine of a mere meaningless exemplary sacrifice by the Christ of His outward life, to show man how to die, if need be, for his work's sake—that is, meaningless in the sense of the death being a Sin-offering, or an act of sacrifice which took away sin and its effects. Yet, though the Churches contain within themselves the various schools whose interpretations of the mysterious doctrine are so manifold, no unifying interpretation has ever been given by any of them. Either the Sin-offering becomes to the expounder and interpreter the basis of a manifestation of what they call the Divine Justice and Righteousness, but which is the most awful exhibition of injustice and unrighteousness when viewed in the light of the most beautiful expression of human love and compassion ; or it becomes a meaningless term having no great mysterious divine significance, but only an exemplary manifestation of moral courage amid difficult situations, and in the face of cruel persecution. Even in these days of a new awakening amongst Souls as the outcome of that most marvellous work performed by the Christ-Soul as He bore the Sin-burden of the past history of this Planet in His Office of the Cross, the different schools of thought represented by the various Churches, are only able to *guess* at the meaning of the Sin-offering, and so remain in the dark concerning the true inward significance of the very real foundation-truth of their doctrine of the Redemption.

Yet when the full significance is understood of the expression " *The Lamb of God who taketh away the sin of the world,*" the Sin-offering is seen to have been most real, the sin-burden of the past to have been too awful even to imagine fully or describe by means of any terms, the Office of the Cross to have been such a ministry performed by the Christ-Soul, as no one has dreamt of. And all the work by which it was accomplished may be seen to be the exhibition of the Divine Love, the redemptive process by which that Love sought to make possible the perfect redemption of all Souls upon the Planet, a work full of the most beautiful righteous purpose wherein no element of injustice may be found nor such a thing as anger expressed, but only love beyond compare, tenderness irreproachable, pity unfathomable in its depths to which the Christ-Soul descended, and sacrifice immeasurable since it was even unto the uttermost.

A Vision of the Church

O Church of the Christhood, the professed interpreter of the blessed Master's mission, and manifestor of the Divine Life which He revealed and taught ; ostensibly founded to rear the Temple of the Christhood in all souls upon the planes of this world, through making manifest the true nature of the Redeemed Life in thy ways, and the true meaning of the Divine Love in thy ministry : what a loss thine is that thou dost not even yet know the meaning of the Redemption, the nature of the Redeemed Life, the glory implied in Christhood, and the work accomplished by the Christ-Soul ! Alas that those who laid thy foundations should themselves have been in the darkness ! Tragic in the extreme has been thy history throughout the ages, how tragic none may know even from the outward phenomena through which thy history has revealed itself, unless they can behold it from the Kingdom of the Soul ! What is that history which thou hast written as to the interpretation of the Divine Love, Light and Life ? Where in that history of thine has the Divine Love truly triumphed over the evils in the world which, alas ! have so often found their adumbration and exposition in thine own ways to the detriment and even the degradation of the Soul ? Where in that history has the Divine Love revealed itself as boundless compassion unto all Souls, even the most faltering, and measureless pity unto all the creatures ? Where in thy history do we find that triumphant Love which maketh always for purity, goodness, harmony and peace ? That Love which divideth not but uniteth, which smiteth not but healeth, which curseth not but blesseth, which condemneth not but ever trieth to restore ? That Love which thinketh not evilly of others ; that beareth all things on its cross ; that hopeth beautiful things of all Souls ; that

wearieth not in its burden-bearing ; that faileth not in its tender-
ness and forgiveness or healing power ? Where in thy history may
be found, in glorious brightness, the Light of God by which Souls
are guided into the true path and vision, that Light so pure and
unerring, the which when a Soul has, he knoweth the Divine Wis-
dom ? When in thy history hast thou given a gracious welcome to
that Light when it has come to thee through the illumined Souls
who have shone amid the darkness as stars in thy firmament ?
When in that history didst thou hear with gladness the messages
of those who were as thy watchmen in the night, and receive them
as the inspired servants of God ? How strange that in every chapter
of thy history thou hast not only refused to hear their messages,
but hast sought to silence their voices through driving them out
from thee by oppression and cruel persecution ? Where in thy his-
tory may we look for the manifestation of the Divine Life, that
Life so full of everything beautiful and glorious, that Life which
is the perfect expression of the Divine Nature—pure, gentle,
righteous, glorious in its power to bless ? For the vision of the
Christhood unto which the blessed Master called the very Souls
who laid thy foundations, we seek in thy history in vain. That
vision thou hast never known in thy history or it would have been a
history written with the spirit of Eternal Love, and not with
the very life-stream of those who sought the true Vision with its
ever-blessed Life, Light and Love.

Behold ! the axe is laid at the root of the tree thou didst plant,
to cut it down that it may no longer cumber the ground. The voice
of the Messenger cries unto thee to repent and bring forth fruits
worthy of thy great and high profession ; to forsake the ways of
oppression and follow those of blessing ; to no longer know the ways
of cruelty towards the helpless creatures by oppressing them to
gain knowledge, and taking their lives in order to provide the body
with food and raiment ; to put away the priestly spirit from thy
midst and replace it with the prophetic priesthood of the Soul ;
to make of thy communities centres of true fellowship and venues

of true worship ; to live the life of the Redeemed and fit thyself to understand the Christ-life ; to make all thine altars pure and thy sacrifices spiritual ; to know nothing of the world-mind which appraises everything from its commercial value, but to seek only the mind of the Christ which sees the spiritual and eternal to be the only abiding things, the value of which no man can appraise ; to seek that increase which is of God whose riches are abiding, rather than the increase which is of men whose riches often not only enslave thy powers, but do, alas ! too frequently act as demagnetizers of the Soul and corrupters of the life.

If thou doest these things, then thy work may yet become glorious, and thy share in the Travail of the Redemption be a Reality.

H

PART II.

The Birth Stories

The Angelic Vision and Song

*Being a beautiful Soul-history of most ancient
times, an event which took place upon
the lower spiritual planes ; as well as
the prophecy of blessed spiritual
experiences into which
many are now
entering.*

A

WHAT THE VISION WAS

THE Angelic Vision associated with the birth of Jesus into this world, is an exquisite gem of spiritual history. It is a Soul-poem, for its language is of the inner life. But it was not anything outward, no objective picture like some heavenly landscape presenting itself to the eye ; rather was it a beautiful inward spiritual experience, a reality to the Soul far greater in its issues than any outward and visible pheno-menon. It was a vision seen by the soul ; the result of the opening of the Heavens unto it ; the recognition by it of the Angelic ministry sent from the Father, the ever Blessed One. And it was a vision which proclaimed the birth of the Christ-child *within*, the attainment by the Soul of such a measure of spiritual consciousness as enabled it to enter upon the Christ-hood path, and pass up into the Christhood experience. And the Angelic Song was the heavenly harmonies heard within when the Soul arrived at that stage of its spiritual unfoldment, harmonies none the less real because they were inward ; indeed far more real through being altogether spiritual.

When the Soul approaches that state in which Christhood is born within it, it is not only able to have the vision of the Angelic World within its sanctuary, but to hear the harmonies of that world. And the message which it hears proclaimed is, " *Glory to God in the Highest, and on Earth peace and the good pleasure of His will.*" For it is the message which Christ-hood brings with it unto the Soul, and through it, unto the world. The glory of the Lord rests upon the sanctuary, and upon the earthly house abides His peace and the gladness or pleasure of His will. For the " Highest " is within the Soul. There are the Heavens reflected. There is the glory of the Lord seen when the Soul is in the silence and seeks to ascend unto " the Hill of the Lord," the blessed spiritual altitudes where the atmosphere

107

is pure and rarefied, and the vision glorious. And the
" Earth " is the lower or outward spheres of life, those spheres
within which the noises of life and the world's altitudes find
their echo and reflection ; and these are to be filled with the
heavenly peace, and the pleasure of doing the Divine Will.
They are to know the peace shed by the Christ-spirit within,
the peace of God which passeth all understanding ; because that
peace is born from the beautiful inward life of spiritual
realizations, realizations of the Divine Presence within.

The Angelic Vision, Song and Message are, therefore, for
all Souls who can behold, and hear, and receive them. They
were not local experiences on the physical plains of the little
city of Bethlehem in Judæa, but universal in that they were
wholly spiritual, and experiences which every one should enter
into. They were those experiences which Souls had passed
through in their attainment of the Christ-spirit and Christ-life,
and who were called by the blessed Master to seek to enter
upon them once more. It was unto that sublime end that the
experiences were portrayed by the Master, that the setting
of them forth might aid these Souls to awaken unto the consciousness of that life, and bring unto them its beautiful
realizations.

IT IS A RECOVERED TREASURE

How that wonderfully beautiful and blessed vision has been
misunderstood throughout the ages of the Christian era ! It
has lain buried amid the materialized history of the Christ,
like lost treasure buried amid the ruins of some ancient city
overthrown by tremendous seismic conditions. Difficult indeed
is it to impress Christian men and women with the truth of
its storied wealth for the Soul, and bring them into that blessed
state when they themselves shall know it as the portion of their
own experience, the sublime realization within their own
spiritual system of the Divine Love, Life and Light. To restore

that long-lost Soul-vision to its true place is not an easy work to accomplish ; nor to lift it out of the débris amid which it has been buried, to let its beautiful image become once more pure and clean, so that all who have the true willinghood to understand its meaning and realize its blessing may again behold it unto full realization. So long has it been lost as a history experienced within the Soul ; so long has it been regarded as history upon the physical planes ; so long has it been related to pastoral shepherds watching on the fields outside a town in Judæa ; so long has it thus been made local rather than universal, outward instead of inward, material history in place of spiritual realization, that now it is most difficult to impress upon men and women that it is the blessed embodiment of the experience of a Soul who has accomplished its Redemption from the dominion of the sense-life, interpreted that Redemption through the Redeemed Life which it lives in the world, and has arrived at that beautiful experience when the Christ-consciousness within the Soul has been born. It is almost impossible to impress those who ought to know the truth, that it is *a most real experience within the Soul*, that the vision of the Angelic Life and ministry is actually beheld within the Soul's sanctuary, that the Angelic Song is there most assuredly heard, that the things seen and heard are not imaginative, but most tangible.

O blessed Vision of the Soul, how beautiful thou art !

O Song of the Angels sung by the Heavenly Hosts, what glorious harmony may be brought into the life when thou art heard !

O Message of the Father through His Angels, have we not felt the heavenly influence of thy meaning, the blessed power which comes upon the life in whose " Highest " there is " Glory to God," and upon whose earthly parts there is the breath of a Divine Peace !

B

THE BLESSING GIVEN UNTO ABRAHAM'S SEED

THE Angelic Vision which was said to have been seen by the tenders of flocks on the plains of Bethlehem in Judæa on the night when the Master was born into this world, and which has throughout the whole of the Christian era been regarded as a true history in the experience of these shepherds, and as a sure testimony to the heavenly nature of the Master, is now being repeated in the experience of many Souls. Many are coming from the East and the West, the North and the South "to sit down within the kingdom of our Father Abraham"; to behold the glory of the land given unto him for a possession, and to his seed for ever; to know the joy of His salvation who hath caused the Star of the Day-spring to arise upon us. For many are the Souls awakening all over the world to the realization of the Redeemed Life and the beautiful visions of the Christhood. The North and the South, the East and the West, represent the manifold states in which Souls are found—those who seek the inward spiritual or eastern life, and those who seek the outward material or western life; those who find life in the cold northern or intellectual conditions, and those who seek them in the volatile southern atmosphere of the emotions. And they are all coming into the kingdom given unto our father Abraham and to his seed for ever, the goodly land of Christhood on which the glory of the Lord never sets, and which is full of the riches of His Love and Wisdom; for Abraham was and is the divine estate of this Planet, the state in which it was when the whole world was young, that golden age ere "the Gods slept" (the planetary systems of Sol), the state the Planet was in prior to that unfortunate experience which is now known as "The Fall," a state in which all was pure and true and beautiful upon every plane and within every sphere, and unto which the Planet is once more being redeemed with all her children.

THE COMING OF THE REDEMPTION

The coming of the Son of Man upon the clouds of the Heavens through the restoration within the Soul of the vision of the Christhood Life, is showing itself everywhere; for there is an awakening of the Souls of all peoples who once knew that vision and lived that life, to seek again unto its realization. The descent of the Angelic Heavens to encompass the Earth, is now a glorious reality; for the Divine Love has purified the intermediate kingdom (the astral spheres) so that the angelic ministry is not only possible now, but is realized by every Soul who has unfolded its life through purifying its ways. The days of the Redemption are upon us; days full of great changes in and for humanity; days full of the separating fires of righteousness wherein evil is consumed and the gold of good is purified; days full of travail for the Soul as the breath of the Spirit passes over its life, winnowing the chaff from the true grain of good; days prophetic of the victory of truth over error, purity over evil, and love over lovelessness and hate. For the coming of the Son of Man is as the rebirth of the Christhood, the day of " glad tidings unto all peoples," the heralding from the Heavens of the coming of the Deliverer in the form of the Christ-child Jesus to be born within the Soul, the sure Redeemer of the life from all evil, and the manifestor of the glory of the heavenly Father. For the true Redeemer of the Soul is the Divine Love who, by His approach unto it through the Angelic Heavens, has not only heralded the coming again of the Son of Man, the Adonai, the Logos, upon the clouds of the Heavens (or true spiritual conditions which give true spiritual phenomena within the Soul), but has enabled all who were in a spiritual state to behold the vision, to once more look into those heavens of angelic ministry and hear the harmonies which fill them. And the true redemption of the Soul is the purification of all its ways, from the centre to the circumference of its experience, every sphere made to respond to the life and service of the Divine Love.

111

SIGNS THAT THE VISION HAS BROKEN

The coming again of the Angelic Vision unto the Soul is the surest testimony we could have, or desire, of the second advent or coming of the Son of Man. It is a testimony transcending anything of an outward or personal nature such as is looked for by those who still expect the return of the Master in the form in which He lived the Christhood, more glorious in its results for the Soul, and further-reaching in its redeeming and regenerating effects upon the whole world. For if men and women do not recognize the vision of Christhood when it is shown them, but refuse the interpretation of the Redemption as that path to Christhood which must be taken by all who would truly follow the Master, we may be quite sure that they would fail to understand or even be attracted to the Master were He to again appear to live the Christhood ; nor would they follow out the Teachings He would have to give, nor carry out the demands which He would make upon them as preliminary steps to their finding the Redemption which leadeth unto the path of Christhood. If they hear not the prophets concerning purity in living, neither would they hear Him. If they refuse the ways of repentance proclaimed by the John the Baptists of our own age, they would not be likely to accede to the high demands of the Master. But if men and women have awakened to the sublime reality of the life of the Soul, and have brought forth fruits meet for repentance by changing their habits of living, putting away every evil and impure thing, feeling purely toward one another, acting compassionately unto all Souls and pitifully towards all the Creatures, scorning to wound any living thing or cause it hurt or suffering in any way, making the body pure through pure food, and the mind through pure thoughts and feelings, seeking only the truest, best and highest, then such Souls will go on to know the Redemption as the blessed state in which the life is redeemed from evil until all its impulses, desires and purposes are to seek after and fulfil the Divine Will. They will live on the fruits of the Earth. They will have no creatures destroyed to find nourishment or adornment. They will be the protectors of the creatures from cruelty wherever practised. They will oppose the ways of vivisection and vivisectors. They will require no creature to suffer to provide drugs or serums for their bodies. They will oppose all the unclean and degrading methods pursued ostensibly on behalf of the Medical Faculty, not requiring such impure protective aids themselves, nor believing them necessary for others. They will thus live the Redeemed Life, and influence others to go along with them. They will follow the Jesus-life until they also arrive at the vision of the Christ. And they will at last come into that blessed experience when the Angelic Heavens shall open unto them, and they will behold again what the shepherds are said to have beheld upon the planes of Bethlehem. They will hear once more the glorious harmonies of the heavenly Hosts in their praise of the Ever Blessed One, and realize within themselves the beautiful and profound meaning of all that the angels sang. And then they will know and understand the meaning of Christhood.

C

A STORY TOLD BY THE MASTER

HOW profound in their meaning were the words of the song which the angels were said to have sung ! Who now pauses to inquire concerning their significance, what is the true poetry of them, and what their full splendour ? They are embodied in Litanies of Praise, and set by some of the great Masters of Harmony to music born in them of the overshadowing of the Heavens. They are sung in many sanctuaries, thrilling those who feel their sublime meanings (though as yet they see not these), moving Souls to nobler impulses and more beautiful experiences. Yet they remain in their innermost meanings like a sealed casket whose outward form is beheld as rich and beautiful, but whose treasures are hidden from the gaze of all who cannot open the casket. For though the language is much thought of, yet the real significance of them for the Soul remains unseen. And why ? Because men and women have been taught to regard them as words spoken only concerning the birth of the Master ; whereas they are the language of the Heavens unto the Soul itself when the Christ-spirit is born within it.

The story of the Angels' Song was not preserved unto us by the Shepherds who were said to have heard it ; it was told by the Master unto the inner group of His disciples as an exposition of the experiences through which the Soul passes as it approaches the beautiful realizations implied in the term *spiritual Christhood*, when the Soul has found the Redeemed Life and attained unto it, and is following on to know the Divine. This birth-story was one told by Himself ; but not concerning His own birth into this world, not His own Christhood, but rather concerning the experience of every one who rose from sphere to sphere until the Angelic World found its correspondence within them, so that its Life could be imaged within the Soul's Heavens, and the echoes of the heavenly song be heard there.

How rich and beautiful the blessed Master's Teachings were, how profound in their far-reaching meanings and comprehensive in their scope, has yet to be made known. And this Angelic Vision was one of them. It was told by the Master not only to inform the Soul of those experiences which come to it when it has accomplished its Redemption, and is in the path to the blessed realization of Christhood ; but it was told primarily to awaken within those who heard it (the disciples of the inner group) memories of long ago, memories of a past whose history contained that very experience. For the Shepherds of Bethlehem were those spiritual teachers who were as the messengers of the Father unto the children of this world

114

in the days prior to " the fall " or descent of the whole system from pure spiritual conditions to conditions largely and, in some instances, wholly material. The flocks upon the planes were the little human children who were being tended by these devoted Souls ; and Bethlehem itself was a condition of life, a consciousness of spiritual experience upon the planes of the Planet where these little children dwelt. For Bethlehem originally meant the little House of the Lord, the state of such simple, yet beautifully spiritual, life, that to live was to praise and to serve was to pray. The flocks upon the planes of Bethlehem were those children who had risen up in their true evolution from the simple elementary life of the creature kingdom to the complex life of the Human Kingdom, many of whom were almost ready to rise yet another stage higher, even unto the realization of the angelic life. And the Souls who were spoken of as the Shepherds were those who had long ago been crowned with the angelic life, Souls who had once been like those within the little House of the Lord, or Bethlehem, upon another planet, but who had evolved and unfolded until they had attained the high estate of sonship to God, and who were known as " the Sons of God " or " His Christs " upon the system of Sol. And some of these were members of the innermost circle of the disciples of the Master.

CONTAINED ANCIENT HISTORY

The story was not only the embodiment of the experience which comes to every Soul who is on the path to Christhood, but it was one which these Souls had passed through when they were the spiritual helpers of the children of Bethlehem. They had arrived at the experience of the angelic vision and song of the heavenly hosts, individually ; but they had likewise had an experience of it collectively during the dark times which overtook " the Bethlehem," when the elements of the planes of the Planet were changed in their nature, and the evolution of the children was interrupted and at last suspended.

Darkness fell upon the Earth, and the Night of the Soul came.
The magnetic conditions of the Planet had become so changed
that even those who ministered as Christs found the Bethlehem
to be other than the little House of the Lord. They kept watch
over the flocks, *but it was night with them.* The Heavens seemed
far away—the Heavens of the Lord reflected within the Soul,
with all their hallowed images and sacred signs ; *for it was
night around and within them.*

It was at that time that the heavenly vision was sent. They
were all, as it were, lifted up on to the angelic heavens where
they beheld the angelic vision and heard the angelic song.
And the purpose of it was to inform them of the coming of
a Saviour and Deliverer who would redeem them from the
bondage imposed by the darkness, and deliver all who were
made captive by the enemy, namely, the changed elements ;
and that their Lord would be that coming One, made manifest
in Christhood, and born within the Soul as Jesus, the Redeemer
from all evil.

PROPHETIC : PATHETIC : PROFOUND

The Vision was prophetic : it foretold the necessity for a
Redeemer, and that He would be forthcoming. It was pathetic ;
for it was the outcome of the endeavours of the Angelic
Kingdom to communicate with this world amid the most
difficult conditions, after it had been for long ages struggling
on amid the darkness which had overtaken it as the outcome
of its descent from a pure spiritual state to one in which the
magnetic conditions were all changed. And its meaning was
profound ; for it informed the Shepherds or Christ-souls, that
it would be necessary for the Divine Love and Wisdom to
descend from the Heavens in a sacrificial capacity to effect the
necessary redemption and deliverance.

It was also prophetic in that it anticipated for the Shepherds
the coming of that Life within them, which once they knew ;

those most blessed experiences which were their constant heritage, the angelic visions, communions and fellowships which they once had as their perpetual portion ; that inward knowledge of the divine life and consciousness of the Eternal Presence associated now with Christhood. It spake to them of the restoration of these through the work of a redeemer. It was in this way likewise pathetic ; for its very prophecy of the restored conditions within them implied so much as to their own past, showing what they once had been before the Night overtook them upon the planes, and all that they had lost amid the darkness arising from the changed conditions. And in this respect was the meaning of the heavenly vision profound ; for it not only spake of all that they once had been, what they had lost through the changed conditions, but also how alone the restoration could take place, both for them and the whole of the Bethlehem.

The Angelic Vision was therefore, prophetic, pathetic and profound in its meanings for all Souls, and even for the Divine Love. It was glorious in its anticipations, pointing, as it did, to the time when Christhood should again crown the lives of all who once knew that blessed state ; and when the planes of the Bethlehem or little (that is, in experience of Soul-consciousness) House of the Lord should all be redeemed back to their original state, when life for all the children would be pure and beautiful, when there would be " Glory to God in the highest " states of experience through the Soul reflecting His glory in the life and ministry of Christhood, and " peace on Earth," or in the lower states of experience, through the restoration of all unto the purity they once knew and the wonderful harmony and concord born of that purity in them and the conditions around them. For " Glory to God in the Highest " was not simply meant as a poetic expression of the glory rendered unto the Eternal and Ever-Blessed One upon the Heavens. It was the testimony of the Soul's true nature, function and service, and an injunction to render within the Soul wherein " The Highest " has His abiding-place, the glory of life and service : for *the Soul is the highest place*, and wherever the Soul is, here on these outer planes, or on those higher, or upon any other spiritual system, it is always within itself that it must first give the glory of the divine Life in beautiful service. And through the giving forth of that real and blessed glory in " the highest," will the earth-spheres, the lower planes of experience, be filled with the divine peace ; for only through the restoration within the Soul of " the glory of the Lord " as a realization, can the Redemption be truly and fully accomplished.

The Christhood must be sought unto its blessed realization ; and unto this end must the Christ-child or Christ-spirit be born again within the Soul.

D

TESTIMONIES THAT THE VISION IS SEEN

BEHOLD in these latter days the awakening of many men and women to seek unto the Christhood life and service, and the realization of the Divine Love made manifest in all the redeeming powers which are in operation upon the Earth ! Witness the outpouring of the Spirit of the Lord in the awakening of many unto a new consciousness of their own nature and heritage, and their endeavour to find the meaning of these things ! Recognize the signs of the coming of the Redemption in all the excellent endeavours put forth to reclaim those who have gone far afield in their experiences, and to restore all men and women unto the true ways of living once more ! See and understand how it is that many of the most beautiful Souls amongst us are called to pass through experiences of the strangest nature, alone and misunderstood, full of pain and often anguish, as if their lives were afflicted by some divine judgment which had overtaken them, and see in these things the sure signs of the days of the Regeneration !

In all the true reform movements—Vegetarian, Anti-Vaccination, Anti-Vivisection, Social Purity, true compassion, pity and love manifesting themselves in the redress of great evils which have for ages been imposed upon the defenceless children, human and sub-human—we may behold the fruits of that awakening of the Soul to a higher consciousness of *the true meaning of Life*.

These are all testimonies to the coming realization of the meaning of the angelic vision and song. They are like the shooting forth of the new life at the dawn of springtime, and as such are the prophecies of great good. They are the testimonies to the passing away of the long winter of spiritual coldness and impoverishment during which the real life of the Soul has been almost quiescent, and the harbingers of the reawakening of the very Gods themselves (the Planets of the System of Sol), who have long slept because of the changed conditions which overtook the Earth. They are the evidences of the reawakening of all Souls from that spiritual sleep in which the Heavens were shut so that " no open vision " was vouchsafed, to the consciousness of the reality of those Heavens and to desire and seek after the heavenly vision. They are the first fruits of the coming forth of all who went down into the graves of matter symbolized in the going down of Israel into Egypt, and there finding sorrow and oppression ; the rising up into the light of a new and great hope of the whole " House of Israel " under the leadership of Moses—the sacred name by which the Divine Love was known unto the most ancient Hebrews. They are the immediate results of the first resurrection consequent upon the coming again of " the Son of Man " upon " the clouds of the Heavens," and the entrance into the " Resurrection Life " of all who are able to ascend to the heights of its most blessed realization.

Such are the portents of the age in which we live, planetary and human, spiritual and social, racial and national. The Heavens are telling of the dawn of the New Age in which all things shall be made new. The angelic visions are coming unto many to testify of the birth of the Christhood realizations which are to be. The planetary influences are once more in favour of the true upwardness of the Earth, and all her children, notwithstanding the devastating magnetic storms which in these latter days have been filling many with fear and dismay, and leading the students of the Heavens to all sorts of conjectures as to the cause of them.

E

THE CELEBRATION OF THE CHRIST-MAS

THE return of the Christmas season is also the return of the time when the angelic vision, song and message are recited in the Churches of the West. For Christmas is the great time of joy in home and sanctuary ; a time of great gladness shared more or less by all ; a season of devotion when gifts are bestowed and the needy ones are specially thought of. The home is the scene of very special festivity, and the sanctuary a centre of praise. And all these things are supposed to have their origin in the " glad tidings " heralded by the angels concerning the coming of the Redeemer, the advent of the Christ.

Very beautiful is the celebration of Christmas in so far as there is good in its Joy and Praise, Devotion and Gifts : these are beautiful when true and pure. They are full of true poetry. They are the expressions of the noblest feelings of the Soul, and should be prophetic of wonderful fulness of spiritual realizations such as point to the attainment of the Redeemed Life crowned with Christhood. There is something sensuously delightful in hearing the recital of the angelic vision, song and message when set to inspiring music; and there is real good in the arresting of the mind busily engaged with material things so as to present to it the story of the Advent of the Redeemer, and to impress it with the reality of His having come in the life and ministry of the blessed Master.

But that is not all the meaning of the Christ-mas. If it be, then no wonder the season has failed to lift humanity up out of the depths of the evils associated with its celebration, as illustrated in the fearful tragedies of the abattoirs and shambles; the unspeakable suffering thrust upon the defenceless creatures; the indescribable shame presented in the streets where their mangled forms are exposed for purchase, and in the homes of the people, even of many who profess that they are the friends of the creatures, where the mangled remains are served up as fitting diet and nourishment for those who would enter into the meaning of the angelic vision, song and message. Throughout the centuries of the Christian Era the celebration of Christmas has not been prophetic of the coming of the Redeemer and the Christ; but rather of the awful carnival which it has become in these later ages. It has not been the harbinger of a coming redemption for the race; instead of anything so blessedly hopeful, it has been the perpetuation of the most revolting cruelty to the creatures, and degradation to humanity. It has not foreshadowed the birth of the Christ-life and spirit, but rather an order of things which are the abrogation of any such experience.

When a Redeemer brings redemption to a people, the chains of their captivity are broken, and the means of their bondage are overthrown; but the celebration of the Christ-mas has only served to bind the western world more firmly in the bondage of the flesh-pots. It has not brought deliverance but increased the captivity. It has filled the creature kingdom with anguish unspeakable, and blinded the Soul to any true heavenly vision. So intense has the darkness been that those who truly desired to live the true and pure life have not been able to see the way. The would-be humane and truly pitiful Souls, who in their innermost Being love the creatures, have been so grievously misled that they have too often partaken of the terrible feast in the western world's terrible way.

Such have been the effects of the celebration of Christmas.

THE STAR OF BETHLEHEM HAS ARISEN

But the hour has struck when the new Redeemer was to make His appearance. The star within the eastern Heavens has arisen to herald his coming and proclaim the birth of the Christ. The Magi have beheld it and have sought out the Christ in Bethlehem. The Shepherds of the planes have been awakened in the dead of the western world's night through the approach of the angelic world unto them ; and they have beheld the vision of the heavenly hosts and heard the angelic song. For the Souls who once were the true teachers upon this Planet have both seen and heard those angelic things which mortal eye hath not seen nor ear heard ; to them " the heavenly hosts " have once more made themselves manifest, and the song sung has been re-interpreted. The magian Souls who have always sought to understand the movements of the spiritual heavens, who have sought their highest wisdom in the heavenly know- ledges gained through communion with those heavens, who have longed for the realization of their beautiful aspirations and profound yearnings in the crown of Christhood—these have beheld the arising in the Orient of the sign of the birth of the Christ-child ; for the Orient signifies the Divine within the Soul. And the star is the sign of Christhood within the Soul, " the bright and the morning star " given unto all who overcome. The Redeemer has been born. The Redemption has been entered into. The deliverance of many who sat in bondage has been accomplished. The cruel chains which bound many in slavery have been broken. For the Redeemer is the

Divine Love within the Soul finding expression in a redeemed life, the life purified upon and within every sphere ; the Redemption is the attainment of victory over all the sense-feelings, desires and affections, the mastery over the outwardness of life, so that all the senses are under control from the innermost and are only its servants to do the Lord's service and not their own ; the Deliverance is the liberation of the whole being from the bondage in which it has been held by the earthly conditions, the snapping of the bonds or fetters which hold it down, the setting free of the whole spiritual man for the true worship, service and life of the Divine Love.

The hour has struck that heralds His coming : the star has arisen that proclaims the birth within the Soul of Christhood ; behold how the Redemption proceedeth through the purifying and uplifting movements, and how the Christhood is once more coming upon the Earth ! For the true *Christ-Mas* is being restored to the Soul.

F

AMAZING CONTRADICTIONS OF BELIEFS

IT is sad to reflect that where the Angelic Vision and Song should have been most expected, they are almost unknown as an experience, and their meaning is misunderstood. The channels of the Divine communication to the world have, as a rule, been found outside the recognized traditional venues. These latter have valued, stereotyped and guarded the letter of such Revelation as they have had handed down to them ; but the spirit of the things signified has most frequently had to find a dwelling-place elsewhere. From their own confession and claims, the Churches should have been the vehicles through which the Angelic Heavens communicated their messages from the Divine, and the interpreters of those messages for all Souls ; yet do they repudiate the very thought that it is even possible for a Soul to commune with those Heavens and receive messages from them. They jealously watch and guard the literal sense of the Records wherein accounts of heavenly visions are given ; yet they deny that such visions may now be the heritage of the Soul. To them the days of open vision are no more. The visions of the Adonai seen by the ancient Seers are accepted by the Churches (though they seem not to understand either the nature of the visions or how they were vouchsafed unto the Seer) ; yet do they deny the possibility of such visions coming unto the Soul *now*, or they reject the vision when it is presented to them. They believe in the reality of these things in the past, and proclaim the glorious times which are to come ; but for the present they see not, neither do they believe in, these beautiful realizations. *Their faith is still intellectual rather than spiritual, and looks along the planes of outward history rather than within the vail of the spiritual world.* They profess spiritually without realizing ; they confess belief in a spiritual world which they do not know. They believe that angels once visited this world and communed with men and women ; but they do not accept the fact that angels even now are communing with Souls upon the Earth, that " the heavenly vision " is being seen and the angelic song heard. They believe (according to the things which they confess) that the angels are " ministering spirits " sent forth from the Divine to minister unto all who are heirs of salvation ; but who the angels are, what their nature is, and how they minister, are to them things unknown.

A WORD TO THE CHURCHES

Ye Churches founded upon the name of the blessed Master as the means of communicating to the whole world the vision of his most beautiful Life, the Redemption which He is said to have brought to men and women, and as the interpreters of the profound spiritual Mysteries of the Soul and the Divine Love and Wisdom —how great is the darkness which is still within your courts ! How sad that ye know not the vision which ye were ostensibly founded to set forth to all men ! How grievous that ye understand not the redemption ye proclaim! How pitiful that the interpretations of the Divine Love and Wisdom made known by the blessed Master should yet be unknown to you!

What is it that hath overtaken those who should have been, and who yet profess to be, the repositories and interpreters and manifestors of the Divine Love and Wisdom? Whence hath it arisen that the altars upon which the Light of the Divine should now be brightly shining, have only those lights which are kindled by men and women? Why is it that the redeemed Life which the blessed Master so beautifully interpreted, has always been unknown unto those who were its supposed interpreters and manifestors?

TO THE CHURCH CATHOLIC

Church of the Living God, glorious in thy garments, and radiant with the light and beauty begotten from the Divine; truly Catholic because Universal in the divineness of the spirit of which ye are born; Spiritual and not Ecclesiastical, because ye are of the Soul; wherein no evil thing finds shelter, nor cruel practices are condoned; through whose sympathy the Creatures are defended, and the Shambles, Abattoirs and Physiological Laboratories are to be abolished; Church of the living Christhood, whose Light is from the Divine, whose Life is the Divine in manifestation, and whose Love is the Divine Love interpreted unto all men; in whom there is no schism, no sectarian strife, no impurity, but whose garments have been washed in the Blood of the Lamb (the Life-stream of the Divine flowing through the whole life of the Soul), when will ye be raised up upon the earth once more to shed abroad the Glory of the Lord?

The Star of Bethlehem

*Being an allegory of supreme beauty and interest
wherein is set forth the Soul's attitude towards
the Highest Things, her recognition
of Divine Events, and her setting
out on the journey of life
that takes her to
Bethlehem and
Christhood.*

A

THE STORY OF ITS APPEARING

THE story of the Magians is a beautiful one. It is beautiful even as it is found in the present Gospel Record, notwithstanding its materialization. It is beautiful even as an outward history when applied (as it now is generally) to the event of the birth into this world of the Master. But if it be beautiful as a story of such outward events, what must it be when its real meanings are beheld by the Soul and realized as an experience ? If its charm as an outward history associated with the birth of the beloved Master into these outward spheres, be so great, what shall we say of its spiritual charm and its transcendent glory when it is understood in its true inward meaning ? If as a literal story its wonderfulness is beyond the understanding of many, is there any wonder that its inner meaning should appear beyond the apprehension of all who have never gazed into the spiritual heavens, never beheld the angelic objects of those heavens, never seen a star upon those heavens, and know not the meaning of such an appearance ?

Yet the story may be understood by all who have functioned upon the angelic spheres and beheld the heavenly visions there. For the Star which it is said the Magians beheld in the Orient, has once more been seen. The Magians who then beheld it and went to Bethlehem to find the newborn Christ, have beheld its arising once more and have gone forth to seek out the one born in Bethlehem who is to be Redeemer and Christ. For it is the age in which that Star was again to make its appearance ; and those who have scanned the Heavens, as anxious observers seeking to discover some new object on the celestial spheres, have beheld it rising above the eastern horizon, the place of divine manifestation. They have interpreted its heavenly meaning and have now set their faces towards Bethlehem, led by the Star, carrying with them treasures of Gold,

Frankincense and Myrrh, to lay at the feet of the new-born Christ.

The star which the Magians beheld in the Orient was that of the Christhood. The star denotes Christhood. " *He who leadeth many unto righteousness, shall shine as the Stars in the Firmament* "—shall be as a Christ, full of the Light of the Divine. " *Unto him who overcometh will I give the bright and morning Star* "—the Christhood estate whose Light is of the nature of the Everlasting Day. " *And I beheld a wonderful sign in the Heavens ; behold there appeared a woman clothed with the Sun, her feet resting upon the Moon, and upon her head a crown of twelve Stars* "—a wonderful picture of the attainment by the Soul of an exalted Christhood, when the glory of her life is the Divine Love ; her Understanding (or as it is named there, the feet) resting upon the Moon or Mind whose office it is to reflect into the Understanding the light which is broken upon it from the Sun or Divine Love ; and her head or Life crowned with the twelve-fold attainments of spiritual realization, when all those graces known as the Christian or Christ graces become an absolute inheritance.

The star arising was therefore the Christhood arising before the vision of the Magians. It was the Christhood of the blessed Master which they beheld arising in the Orient of the Heavens, that is, in the Divine ; for the East denotes the Divine. It was His Christhood to which they were attracted, the outshining of the divine light which was in him, the sacred star whose light had been kindled from the Divine. He was the star of Bethlehem which shone so brightly in the heavens, the star of the Redeemed Life whose purity was beautiful to behold, the star which attracted Souls to Bethlehem (the Redeemed Life) when the Christ-child was born within the Soul.

THE STAR OF THE CHRISTHOOD ORDER

The reappearing of that star in these days is the certain sign that the Christhood is rising up above the conditions of the world which are spiritually dark, to shine with the light of the Eternal One within the Soul, testifying to the beautiful truths that the inner life has become as the little city of Bethlehem, the city of the Redeemed Life, the purified way amid which the Christ-consciousness is born. The new arising of that star is the herald of the return of the Eternal Christ to the Soul ; the awakening of all God's Christs ; the harbinger of the glorious day of the Lord ; the ushering in of the year of His Jubilee for His children, when they shall all return into their own possessions and know the blessings of Zion (Christhood) once more.

The interpretation is a glorious one. It vibrates with the pulsations generated from the heavenly hierarchy. It is illumined with a glory whose radiance is the reflex of the radiance of the Divine Love, and guides with all the inerrancy of the Divine Presence. It brings a new vision to the mind, blessed, luminous and beautiful ; and it constrains the Soul to a new, a higher, and a more glorious life. It reveals the real meaning of the Master's Christhood for the world, and shows how true the prophecy was that the Christ should be born in the City of David, in Bethlehem the city of the ancient kings, the state of the Redeemed Life. To all who have given unto it a physical meaning, it shows that the true science is spiritual, having its foundation and interpretations in the Divine, and that there is a very real and very profound significance attaching to the symbolism of a star. It restores the story to its true place as a *spiritual history of fact*, a history always repeated when a Soul is beholding the approach of that blessed state we speak of as Christhood. It annuls the myth theory of which so much has been said both in relation to this story, and the whole of the so-called birth legends ; whilst, on the other hand, it changes the literalism of its setting into spiritual imagery of deep and blessed value. It thus makes manifest the precious gem within the casket, and carries the admiration, wonder and value from the casket to the sublime treasure which it contains.

B
WHO WERE THE MAGI?

WHO were those Magians who beheld the star and followed its course even unto Bethlehem, and the manger outside the Inn wherein the Christ-child was born? They have been thought of, spoken of and written of as the three Kings of the East; representatives of the ancient cult of Astrology; students of the stars in the stellar heavens; watchers for new phenomena amid the stupendous systems of the skies, and who read the history of Souls from what they there beheld. Just as the star is supposed to have been (by those who accept the literal presentation as the true meaning) some physical phenomenon, so the Magi are looked upon as ancient Astrologers.

But, as with the Star, so with the Magi. Here likewise we have to pass from the outward spheres, to the inward; from the phenomena upon the physical planes, to those of the spiritual; from the region of mere astrological study and speculation, to that of the Soul; from the action of three earthly ancient potentates, to that of the three beautiful Soul-powers represented by the three disciples who were said to have been the most intimate of all the Master's followers—John, Peter and James, disciples who beheld the Christ transfigured, who witnessed the Master's Gethsemane, and who are said to have shared the Cup of which He drank and the Baptism with which He was baptized. For the three Magi, most ancient watchers of the spiritual heavens, readers of the history of the Soul and the Planet, and indeed the whole of the system of Sol, as that history was found written upon the spiritual heavens of the Planet and the Soul; the three Kings of the East, potentates of a divine order who gave up their lives to the pursuit of celestial things, who beheld the star in the Orient, who followed it unto Bethlehem and the manger, were none other than *the three divine principles within the Soul*, the representative *trinity* within the perfect human microcosm—the Love principle, the Intuition or spiritual perception, and the Spirit of beautiful fidelity to the Divine, " the faithful one " within. These are they who truly watch for the arising of the star, who scan the spiritual heavens of their own system for the arising of the light of Christhood within them, who know His star and follow it whithersoever it leadeth, who always find their way to the little city of Bethlehem where Christhood is born, the city of a life purified within every sphere. For it is the Love-principle directed upward and inward to the Divine, that seeks unto finding the highest realization ; it is the Intuition purified through seeking only the purest and most beautiful ways in life, that always recognises, through its spiritual power to discern, the meaning of Christhood ; and it is the Spirit within the Soul itself, ever faithful to the way of life unto which the Divine calls it, which enables it to set out and follow the path by which the Christ-child can be born within, then found or realized in fulness of Christ-consciousness.

Such is the inner meaning of the Magian story, the reality of the picture which has been presented as an objective history, having its full meaning upon the physical planes. The *innermost* meaning we have indicated elsewhere.[1]

STILL NO ROOM IN THE INNS

But there is yet another application of the profound truth embodied in the story, which has to be presented for all who cannot yet behold the innermost and inner meanings, those relating to the Christhood of the Master and the attainment of the birth into Christhood by the Soul ; for the story of the Magi in its objective significance was meant to awaken Souls to the importance of watching for the approach of the spiritual world with its angelic and glorious phenomena. It has its

[1] *Vide* " The Transfiguration Unfoldment."

message for all who require objective pictures of truth, in that it invites the Soul to become a watcher for the arising of the star of Bethlehem, the star of the Christ-child within the Soul, the star which leads the Soul to the Redeemed Life—the life filled with goodness, purity and love upon every sphere. It may speak to them of the approach of the New Age in which we are now living ; of the arising of the star of the Redeemed Life in the great redemptive movements springing up on every hand ; of the coming to the birth of the new great hope for humanity, through the purified life brought to the threshold of men and women by those in whom the Christ-child has been born. It has its message for the age, for the West, and for the Churches. They are the true Magians to-day who are watching for the star of hope, the light of Christhood, the birth of the Christ-child within the Soul, the arising of the ancient Christhood in the West to bring unto all men and women the sure *redemption of life*, the purified path for the Soul, the narrow way which leadeth unto Life Eternal. The Elect Souls, those who once knew these things, need to be fully awakened to the reality now breaking upon the life of many, the shining forth of the star once more to point the way to Bethlehem—to the life of purity upon the physical planes as well as upon the planes of the spiritual life.

O that the members of all the Churches were like the Magians ; that they were Souls who watched for the sign of His appearing, and who knew His star when it arose in the Orient ; that they were true and pure seekers after the Christ, students of the spiritual heavens looking out for the manifestations of the divine approach, Seers and Prophets of the new dispensation, witnesses and interpreters of its life and glory, manifestors in their own ways of life of the path along which the star of Bethlehem moves, leaders and guides to the blessed conditions amid which the Christ-child is born again within the Soul !

O that they all knew the meaning of the wonderful story,

and realized within themselves and upon their altars all its profound spiritual significance !

How strange it is that there is no room in the Inn for the birth of the Christ-child ! There was not in the days of the Master. And the ecclesiastical Inns have not yet found any room. To those outside of Jewry, the star appeared ; so has it been in the new awakening and rebirth of the Christ-child. Outside of Jewry was the Master born and reared ; to-day, beyond the traditional religious centres is the Christ-child again born.

But the hour is coming when all those within the darkness caused by the vails of Idolatry, Blood and Materialism shall also behold the star and set out to find the Christ-child.

C
THE MANGER AND ITS MEANING

THE Magians found the Christ-child in a manger outside the Inn in the little city of Bethlehem. It was truly a lowly place in which to be born and cradled. But the Master was not born and cradled there in any mere literal sense. Yet there is a meaning in it of deep import for all who are seeking to find the Christ. He is not born out of and amidst conditions whose use is to minister unto the sense-life. He is not born where luxury and sense-gratification are sought, but in the pure and lowly life. He is not born where earthly ambitions prevail, but in the meek mind and gentle heart. He is not born where the proud oppressive spirit rules, nor where the life of the helpless creatures is hurt and taken from them. He is born rather where mercy and truth meet each other, and righteousness imparts the kiss of Divine Peace.

The life of that one in whom the Christ-child is born must be a friend of the creatures. It could not be otherwise. The ox in the stall, the ass in the stable, the sheep in the byre, the dove in its cote, and all creatures in their several degrees of unfoldment, are related to such a life by indissoluble ties, even that of *the Oneness of all true life*, and by the fact that the gentle creatures have been the venues through which the Soul has passed upwards in its true evolution before the Divine Love. To be born in the stable or byre, and cradled in a manger, therefore, means very much more than to be born amid lowly conditions. For the Soul truly was cradled amongst the creatures. And when the Christ-child is about to be born within the Soul, the life awakens to the consciousness of its relationship to all the creatures, its duty unto them, and the service it must perform in making manifest the Divine Love then awakening within the Soul.

Of course all this implies the Redeemed Life for the individual. It pre-supposes a very genuine sympathy with all the creatures, a sympathy so rich and full in manifestation that it could not hurt the creatures for its own pleasure, nor cause them to be wounded, afflicted and killed on any pretext whatsoever. It shows how the Soul will look upon the creatures when once the Christ-child is born within ; how it will spread over them the mantle of true pity, and protect them ; how it will recognize them to be, not only the venues by means of which souls came up on to the Human Kingdom, but members of the Father's Household. It teaches us how impossible it will be for those who are born into the Jesus-Life to have the creatures killed for food, clothing, purposes of pleasure or healing. It reveals that beautiful state of love which could not consent to the creatures suffering so unjustly. Unto such men and women the Abbatoirs will be as hells in all their conditions. The cruel sport indulged in with such zest by so many men and women whose power and joy of life are manifested in the destruction of vast numbers of the beautiful creatures whose place in the economy of the world so few seem to understand or even think of, will be to such Souls the most ignoble of pastimes, the most heartless of pursuits, the work of all who unconsciously are the emissaries of evil. The Physiological Laboratories where those creatures which have had the misfortune to fall into the hands of the Scientists who there pursue their nefarious traffic in the lives of the helpless ones, and make them to pass through the very " fires of gehenna "—scientific inquisitors who are bereft of pity as they try to wring from the fearfully afflicted lives the secrets of their being—they will be led, through their consciousness of *the Oneness of all Life*, to see in the light of the Christ-spirit, the Christ-love, the Christ-compassion, to be the very apotheosis of ignorance and wickedness.

What a profound meaning is to be found in the picture of the birth of the Christ-child within the refuge for the creatures, and His cradling in the Manger ! Great is the depth of meaning that may be found in this story which makes the birth of the Master and His cradling to have taken place amongst them ! When we know its inner spiritual significance, the literal story is changed into a veritable treasure-house full of invaluable riches. In the Advent the creatures were concerned as well as the Human Races. In the birth of the Christ-child and the full Manifestation of Christhood lay the hope of the groaning Creation. Unto this end was the story told ; unto this end is it now interpreted.

D

THE TREASURES OF THE MAGI

WE have seen who the Magians were who beheld the Star of Bethlehem and sought out the Christ-child ; what the star was whose light illumined the Orient ; the place where the Christ-child was born outside the Inn ; why He was born amid the conditions which spake of an indissoluble relationship to the Creatures ; and now we would ask of these Magians who sought and found the Christ-child, what it was which they brought as gifts unto Him. For it is said in the story found in the first Gospel that they brought of their treasures and laid them at His feet—*gold, frankincense, myrrh, and their worship.*

Of what intrinsic value were these gifts to a new-born child ? How could any child make use of them as aids to its enrichment ? Could any mere child understand the presentation of such gifts, and receive the worship of the donors ? Were these in their literal sense such gifts as the magian Souls would be likely to present to the Christ-child ? Were not they themselves kings of the East, princes of the Divine Love and Life, seekers after the Divine Light, searchers for the manifestations of the Divine Presence, watchers for the Christ Advent that they might hail it and pour out their treasures upon the new-born life ? Was not even the star which they beheld, *spiritual ?* Was not the star beheld by them also a sign upon the spiritual heavens, and not an objective sign upon the stellar heavens where celestial bodies are seen ?

The Gold of Ophir

And so were their beautiful gifts of the like order. They were purely spiritual. They were those beautiful precious treasures of the Divine Spirit within the Soul symbolized by gold, frankincense and myrrh. For what does gold stand as a symbol ? It is the Divine Love. It is " the Gold of Ophir " inwoven in the garments of " the Queen " described in the forty-fifth Psalm. It is the gold out of which the most sacred vessels of the Temple were fashioned. It is the " gold tried in the fire " which the Seer counselled the Laodiceans to buy. It is the gold out of which is built up " the Crown of Life " which the Saints shall wear. It is the Love Divine within the Soul, ever blessed in its ways, ever pure in its desires and purposes, ever beautiful in all its services, yearning always for the highest realization, craving always for its noblest fulfilment, ever giving of itself to the Christ-life, happiest when giving most. It is that Love which finds no adequate expression anywhere upon the outer spheres, that experiences no satisfaction in the ways of the sense-life, that must seek until it finds the Christ, that manifests itself always in reverent spirit, that bows before the Christ of God worshipfully—the Eternal Christ—and pours out its treasure of love.

It is the most precious treasure that the Soul can give unto the Divine ; for to give love unto the Christ-child is to give that which will enable him to grow in stature, and in the knowledge and grace of the Divine Love and Wisdom. For the growth of the Christ-child is not any mere physical unfoldment implied in the growth of the powers and functions of the vehicle through which our Soul makes itself manifest upon these outer spheres. It is the unfoldment of the Life of the Soul ; the manifestation of the Christ-spirit which is always child-like ; the ever-increasing realization of the Divine Love by means of the in-flowing to the Soul's sanctuary, and thence through all its spheres, of the Divine Life-stream ; the growing consciousness of the Divine Presence, a consciousness which increases and deepens until it issues in that yet higher consciousness of the Divine Overshadowing, when the Soul knows the Divine Presence as its continual Light, Life and Love.

Priestly Frankincense

Love was the first gift brought by the magians and laid at the shrine of the Christ-child. It was a love, beautiful and glorious, vibrating with the divine energy within it, radiant with the inherent divine potencies of which Divine Love is built up. And that gift was followed by another treasure from their treasure-stores. They laid at His feet *frankincense*.

How beautiful also was this gift, and how suitable for the Christ-child ! It was like the magians to bring it for His service. For what is *frankincense* if it be not the innermost aspirations and desires of the Soul ? As the incense of the temple-service is none other than the prayers of the saints ascending to the Divine Love, so the frankincense offered to the Christ-child by the magians is none other than the aspirations and desires of the innermost life of the Soul (which is Divine Life) for the welfare, the nurture, the beautiful unfoldment, the perfect manhood of the Christ-life : that is, *Life of a Christhood order*.

How significant is the thought herein presented ; how rich is the storied urn of this long buried treasure ; how full of profound things for us all ! What more beautiful service can we render unto the Christ-child born within us than to give the gold of our purest and noblest love, and the *frankincense* of our deepest and noblest aspirations and desires ? For these are of the very elements from which all spiritual strength flows into the sanctuary of the Soul. They are of the nature of the Divine Love, and in their service they are Divine. Without them the Christ-child within us could not be enriched and strengthened, nor sphered in the necessary atmosphere and environment of a divine temple ministry. The frankincense surrounds our life so that it is encompassed by an atmosphere whose magnetic conditions are generated by pure and beautiful prayer.

THE CROWNING ACT OF DEVOTION

But to the " gold " and " frankincense " there was added the gift of " myrrh." It was likewise a gift full of significance ; for it was the crowning act of beautiful devotion. Love makes itself manifest in the spirit of worshipfulness and tender ministry. Pure desire and aspiration reveal themselves in generating an atmosphere of beautiful spiritual feeling. But where these qualities are found manifesting themselves, there is also found the spiritual power symbolized by " *myrrh*." " *All thy garments smell of fragrant myrrh* " had a meaning more profound than most readers of the ancient Scriptures suppose.

They take it often as referring to the Christ, but without discerning its deep significance. For it implies the beautiful purity of the garments of the Soul in a state of Christhood, and the purifying influences which they send forth. It is something divine ; no outward aromatic, but a blessed spiritual quality. " *All thy garments drop myrrh* " is true of the Christhood, that full stature of the manhood of the Soul in whom the Christ-child has been born.

This was the gift of the magi to the Christ-child, the acknowledgement by them of the beautiful estate which it represented, the crowning act of their worshipful spirit, the natural accompaniment of the gifts of pure and beautiful love and devotion, the exquisite grace of all their endeavour, the realization of these graces and powers in the attainment of the Christhood estate when the garments become fragrant with the heavenly aroma emanating from such purity, goodness and love as only that one can know who has come to realize the Divine Light, Life and Love within himself. It was the very fulness of life poured forth in sacred oblation to the service of Christhood.

How blessed and how glorious is the vision now presented to us in that wonderful story of the star of Bethlehem and its appearing unto the magi ! How full of profound meaning for us in these days whilst we serve upon these outer spheres, and when the star has once more arisen to tell the wonderful story unto all who are able to receive its hidden meaning, that the Christhood is again born in Bethlehem, the city of David and of the ancient Kings ! How wonderful is the hidden wealth contained in the ore of the literal story, wealth of Divine Light, Life and Love !

E

THE WORSHIP OF THE CHRIST

THE magi are said to have worshipped the Christ. Had the literal sense of the story been the true one, then the little man-child would have received, not only the love, aspiration and devotion of the magi, but also that adoration which must ever be given only unto the most Blessed One. It would have been the worship of the person of the child ; and that would have been just another form of the idolatrous worship practised by so many in the eastern countries.

That the objective picture is beautiful and very fascinating, need not be questioned. Like a miracle-play, it would furnish a remarkable and striking spectacle, which could be made most impressive. As a religious drama on these outer spheres, it would not be lacking in dramatic power and scenic effect. But as such it would be only that kind of spectacle which an unfolding child-life would require, not such as the more advanced Soul initiated into spiritual things would desire. The outward presentation might appeal to the senses, but it might also change the entire meaning and purpose of the wonderful story. Indeed that very thing has happened ; for the story is taken, literally, and all its significant Soul-teachings are lost. There are those who seem still to require that kind of kindergarten spectacle, the objective pictures to impress the mind (as in the Roman and Greek Churches) ; but the spectacular story should not be confounded with the profound spiritual truths for which it stands. The objective is but the shadow of the reality ; the subjective is ever the substance of things. All outward forms and ceremonies, all symbols and literal records of precious truths, were meant only as aids to the mind of those who still required a visualization outwardly of the things signified. It was never intended that the forms and symbols should be accepted as the things themselves, rather than the embodiment of the ideas.

It was not Personal Worship

From this it will be understood that the worship of the personal Master was never intended ; that the story should be understood spiritually even in this. We have seen that the star was spiritual, and that the vision was beheld within the Soul. We have also seen who the magi were, both as divine qualities within the Soul itself, and as seekers after the realization of Christhood. Likewise we have seen that the gifts of the magi were entirely spiritual, the gold, frankincense and myrrh denoting spiritual and divine qualities and conditions. And having seen these things from the spiritual standpoint, and recognized their inner and innermost meanings, we need have no difficulty in arriving at the true understanding of the worship of the Christ. *We shall see that it could not have been the worship of the person of the blessed Master.* For, as the gold was the Divine Love within the Soul pouring itself forth in glad service upon the Christhood Life, the frankincense the Soul's most beautiful aspirations and desires towards the fulness of the Christhood realization, and the myrrh the very Life of the Divine within the Soul which made the garments or raiment of one in Christhood to give forth heavenly fragrance, so the worship of the Christ was the adoration of the Divine Love and Wisdom of which the realization of Christhood ever speaks —the realization of the glory of the Divine Life within the sanctuary of the Soul.

It is the Divine One alone that the Soul ever seeks to worship. It is the Divine Father-Mother only that the true Soul seeks. It is the Divine Vision for which the Soul supremely longs. It is for the realization of the Divine Presence that it yearns with inexpressible desire. Outward forms, symbols, ceremonies and literal presentations of truth may aid the mind and bring to it degrees of comfort ; but nothing short of the realization of the Divine Love, the Divine Presence, the Divine Vision, can ever bring healing and satisfaction to the Soul. Whatever fails to aid it in the realization of these things, is lacking in spiritual purpose.

GOD ALONE TO BE WORSHIPPED

The worship given by the magi to the Christ-child is therefore burdened with the profoundest meanings for us. It carries us away from an atmosphere of merely personal worship of the Master, into one of beautiful impersonal spiritual and divine conditions. It lifts the vision above the elements of the personal life and enables us to behold the innermost significance of things, to understand who the Christ was whom the magi worshipped. It raises the Christhood out of the elements of the earth to the kingdom of the Divine, from which it should never have been brought down by the writers of the New Testament, nor kept there by the misled teachers in the Church. It changes the whole character of the worship by transferring the object from the outward spheres to the innermost of the Soul, from the objective world to the world within us, from the spheres amid the stellar universe to those within the kingdom of the heavens. And the deeper the experiences within us, and the higher these rise above the influences of the Earth, the more fully will the individual enter into the realization of this most sublime truth. It is the worship of the divine within ourselves, the Soul bowing in adoration before the ever Blessed One by whom it is overshadowed. *For the consciousness of such an overshadowing comes to it in Christhood.* It is the entering into the inheritance of the Spirit of Divine Awe, and the making manifest of its sublime power. It is Life crowned with the Elohim.

When we know these blessed truths as parts of our experience, we cannot fail to wonder at the materialized form in which the Churches hold them to-day. We cannot but be struck by the apparent idolatry in the service of them all (we say apparent idolatry, for though it is very real yet it is not intended by most). We cannot close our eyes to the fact that rarely is the Divine Father-Mother as such, worshipped ; whilst the personal vision of the Master is mostly what is adored. It is Jesus who is sung of, prayed to, and worshipped, instead of the ever Blessed One whose beautiful Love the Master interpreted and made manifest.[1] It is not the Divine Love who is adored for His bountiful and gracious manifestations, but the vehicle through whom the Christhood was interpreted and made manifest. It is not the Infinite One whose compassion is unfailing and whose pity knows no limits, who is entreated to show forth His sublime Presence in the true healing of all the worshippers, but rather the vehicle through whom compassion and pity from the Divine One were most fully and wonderfully broken upon the world. It is the personal Master whose image looms so largely in all the Churches, with rare exceptions, from the Roman Catholic to the lowest orthodox evangelical, rather than the Divine Vision within the Soul's sanctuary. The altars have all been reared to the personal Master[2] instead of to the Divine Love whom He so beautifully interpreted in His life and ministry.

Its Effects upon the World

It has been an unspeakable calamity for the whole world that such a view of the purpose of the life and teachings of the sublime Master ever found soil in which to grow. And it has been equally calamitous for the Soul and for the Master. It has led the seeker away from the true vision of Christhood which the Master revealed, to attach it to a personal life, and

---

[1] If any testimony to this statement is required by the reader, let him or her study the Hymnology of the Church. The great majority of the hymns of Praise and Prayer are made to gather around the name of the Master, to the exclusion of the Eternal One.

[2] How true this is will readily be recognized by earnest truth-seekers. The altars within the Church of Rome are all of the personal human order ; and the worship given within the various sections of the Reformed Church is almost exclusively personal, and related to the Master.

think of the person of the Master as the Divine Christ. It has wrought a grievous and disastrous work in obscuring and falsifying the beautiful divine purpose of the Master's coming, through bringing down to the personal and physical spheres that which was altogether spiritual in its nature and divine in its manifestation. And it has made, to a large extent, the manifestation of the Christhood to be of non-effect, because of the materialization of its beautiful divine meaning.

Is it any wonder that the whole of the western world has lain for ages in gross spiritual darkness ? Is it any wonder that men and women should worship outward things rather than inward, and set value upon the material things rather than the spiritual ? Need we be surprised that the hero-worship of the West is so personal, that the qualities most appreciated are chiefly physical, that the attainments upon which the highest value is set are merely of a social, commercial and intellectual nature ? Need we express our surprise at the ignorance of men and women (many of whom profess to be enlightened in other ways), concerning truly spiritual things ? That the West does not understand Christhood is only too evident from the attitude of the leaders of religious thought towards all that the estate implies. It worships the personal Master, but ignores the Christhood Life He so beautifully made manifest. It bows the knee at the name of Jesus, but does not understand the spiritual and interior meaning of its own objective act. It confesses His name as high above every other name ; but it sets high above the life unto which He called all Souls, every material thing—wealth, ambition, social power, dominion, pleasure, and all manner of sense-gratifications. It professes allegiance to Him, but fails to behold whither He calls all to follow. It proclaims Him the world-saviour, yet refuses the way of salvation which He makes manifest. It sings of Him as the redeemer, and prays to Him to deliver and save ; but it will have none of His redemption, because its path is " the narrow way." The passing season of the Christ-Festival, known as Christmas, will reveal *how little* the West understands the blessed Master and the Christhood He made manifest.

It is all a momentous tragedy !

G

THE FEAR OF KING HEROD

IN the story of the magi it is recorded that when Herod learnt of the appearing of the star in the Orient, he was deeply troubled, and great fear came upon him. The magi had informed him of the appearing of the star and their setting out to find the Christ-child ; and he professed to be eager to learn of the new-born King, where he had been born and how he fared. He requested the magi to return unto his court after they had found the Christ-child that he might learn these things from them, and also go and render homage unto Him. But the magi are said to have been warned in a dream not to return to Herod.

Here a new factor is introduced, and it is one that is somewhat difficult to explain to readers who have not come into touch with a true esotericism, or even with occultism. For the term will have to be understood in a symbolical sense.

Why should king Herod have been so full of fear at the birth amid lowly conditions of any child who could have no claim whatever or title to the rule which he enjoyed ? Why should he have feared for the stability of such a throne as he sat upon, and the power he was able to exercise ? Was not his sceptre the gift of Rome, the delegated power of the Cæsars ? Why should he fear for such a sceptre with Rome behind him ? What had he to dread in the birth of the Christ-child, even supposing the great endeavours of those who wrote the two chronological tables found in the first and third evangelists had been based upon facts, and that the Master was in descent

(in His personal life) of the lineage of the kings of the Jews ?
The new-born king, supposing Him to have been of such
kingly descent, could not have come to the throne for many
years, and then only by the consent of Rome.

This part of the story is like the rest of it ; it is impossible
as a history upon the outer and historical spheres.

Who was King Herod ?

Where then may we look for the meaning of the part of
the story which relates to Herod ? And how may we find
its interpretation ? Simply by viewing it as another part of the
story upon the spiritual spheres. For it is in that way only
that the nature and conduct assigned to Herod can be understood. Just as the star signified the birth of Christhood ; as
the magi symbolized the three spiritual and divine qualities
of the Life within the Soul seeking for the vision of Christhood ;
as the birth in Bethlehem signified the awakening of the Soul
within that little city of the eastern kings which represents
the redeemed or purified life ; as the hostel of the creatures
and the manger implied the beautiful lowliness of the mind,
the Soul's kinship with all creatures, and the cradling of the
Soul amid the creature kingdom ; so king Herod, his rule,
nature and conduct, find their meaning in their spiritual interpretation. They relate to very real experiences through which
the Soul has passed and still passes. They are not such as men
have supposed from the narrative, but experiences imposed
upon the Soul from the astral kingdom. For king Herod was
and is that kingdom. He holds sway within that part of the
circulus of the present magnetic plane (what we understand
by the spiritual heavens of the Planet) whose constituents
were originally all pure, beautiful and spiritual, and were aids
to the Soul seeking Christhood, and not a hindrance.

How Herod Treats the Christhood

The astral kingdom has for ages and ages been the oppressor

of the Soul. It has sought to rule all its desires and prevent any Christhood from being born within the life. It feared the arising of the star in the Orient when the blessed Master was born into the world. It followed His path and pursued Him with its destructive work. It made His wonderful Christhood manifestation of non-effect through the influence it brought to bear upon the minds of those who compiled the present Gospels ; for they knew not the meaning of the Master's Christhood, and so could not write of it truly. They understood not the nature of such an exalted spiritual state, and so could not truly represent it. They were not even in sympathy with the beautiful life which He lived, the life of wonderful purity in every sphere of experience. They ignored in their writings the first essentials of Christhood, and presented the Master as one who ate flesh and drank wine like other men and women, and countenanced and encouraged the taking of the life of the creatures for food, and sacrifices such as men and women offer unto their gods. They betrayed His Christhood by misrepresenting it, crucified it by obliterating its Divine Vision, and buried it in the grave of their materializations of His sublime Sayings. Such was the result of the influence of Herod upon them.

And what Herod did to the Christhood of the blessed Master, he has tried to do unto all who have sought the Christ. He has persecuted them with his materializing powers. He has always tried to blind the vision of the Soul, to prevent it from beholding the Christ-vision lest he should be dethroned and lose his power. He has always professed to be deeply interested in the Christhood of the Master and of the Soul ; but he has also always tried to destroy the vision lest the Soul should attain to divine power and become a king anointed from the Divine Love. For the astral kingdom is a living kingdom, a kingdom whose elements are full of conscious power, but which, being in a state of impurity and so out of spiritual equilibrium, operate for evil more than for good, influencing all who are functioning upon it, inverting all heavenly images, miraging the angelic truths which are sent down to Souls for their sustenance and guidance, and materializing every beautiful symbol and sign of spiritual and divine things, changing heavenly histories into earthly ones, making of the Christhood a personal and even a physical inheritance.

AN APOCALYPTIC STORY

When we speak of the astral kingdom in apocalyptic language, and personify it, it is because it is the combination of elements and forces whose magnetism is still at variance with the magnetic attraction of the Divine Kingdom—influences and forces whose nature is well expressed by the term Herod. The term is symbolical of the misuse of powers through the perversion of the elements. It was this Herod—the astral kingdom —who slew the Innocents of Bethlehem; who was outwitted by the magi ; who was said to have had John the Baptist beheaded in prison ; of whom it is reported that he sent for the Master and asked him to perform some notable work, and then insulted and heaped indignity upon Him, clothing Him in mock regal robes, and giving Him a dummy sceptre to hold in His hand whilst he smote Him. These supposed outward events, and many others, were spiritual experiences of the Soul, and of the Christ Himself before and during the Sin-offering lives,[1] brought upon them through the action of the astral kingdom. For Herod has always feared the Christ and all relating to Him. Ever since he founded his kingdom has he feared the arising of the star in the Orient—that is, the Christhood within the Soul. He has always feared the Christ, because the life of Christhood lived by all men and women in this world

---

[1] What this implies will be explained later. The Sin-offering was something accomplished after the passing away of the Christhood of the Master, and all through the Ages of the Christian Era, and has only quite recently been finished.

would mean the end of his kingdom as at present constituted. It would mean the cessation of the order of life which is now lived by all who function upon the astral kingdom, that is, those who make the outward sense-life everything, and set little value upon the inward spiritual and divine realizations ; who love the flesh-pots of Egypt more than the manna of heaven in the wilderness ; who long for the fulfilments of the flesh more than the sublime experiences born of the Divine Presence ; whose deepest yearnings are for earthly attainments rather than for the angelic life ; and whose greatest ambition is to have power in this world, rule over its elements, and be crowned a king by world-seeking men and women, rather than possess a kingdom from the heavens, and be crowned Son of God.

The birth of the Christhood may well bring fear to Herod who loves not the life unto which that blessed estate calls all Souls. He feared the coming of the Christ to restore the Soul to Christhood, and so he set to work to defeat His sublime mission. He tried to make that beautiful mission impossible, and only too well succeeded through those who compiled the present Records, and those who in the name of the Master laid the foundations of the great ecclesiastical systems which have ruled in the West since then. He succeeded in preventing the Master's Christhood from having the effect of awakening all those Souls who once were the Seers, Prophets and Teachers upon this system, and whom he overwhelmed untold ages before. By miraging the true vision of the Christ and the meaning of Christhood, he succeeded in presenting a false vision to the Soul, led the seeker into a form of Hero-worship which was idolatrous, prevented him from beholding truly the vision of the wonderful life and realizations unto which the divine manifestation called him, inverted the glorious image of the Divine Love which the Master made manifest, and drew a veil over the teachings concerning the indwelling presence of the ever Blessed One.

A Great Change is Impending

For great cycles of ages the kingdom of Herod has been firmly established in this Planet's spiritual system. It came into existence when the whole planetary system went down into non-spiritual conditions. Through the great change wrought in the elemental kingdoms, the astral kingdom which was originally the magnetic plane of the Planet, was fashioned. And when the children of the Planet were all drawn down into spiritual states in what is known as " the fall," through the changes within the elemental kingdoms, the astral kingdom became their home for untold ages. And then it drew down those Souls who had been ministering to the children of the Planet upon the outer spheres of the lower heavens known as the Bethlehem, and in doing so slew their Christhood. For this latter was the primary meaning of " The Slaughter of the Innocents." Herod overwhelmed them. The astral kingdom, a changed magnetic plane, drew them down. And since that time he has never ceased to strive for the over-throw of the Christ within the Soul, lest the Christ-child should attain unto the stature of full manhood or Christhood.

But the rule of Herod is coming to an end. His kingdom is being divided through the purification of the spheres embraced by the astral world. The effect upon it of the tragic Sin-offering is now making itself manifest. The days of his oppressive government are passing, and those of the redemption of all the children are coming. The elements are being changed, melting with the fervent heat of the Divine Love, and giving place to new and nobler conditions. The day is hastening when all its spheres will be so purified that once more it will be restored to its original condition and become a very true and very real aid to the spiritual evolution of the Soul, instead of the hindrance it has been for unspeakable ages. For the Divine Love has prevailed. The Christhood has once more been restored. And the awakening of all the Souls who once knew that blessed spiritual experience is progressing, as the true vision of the Divine Love and Wisdom breaks upon them. And in and through all such lives will the Eternal Christ be triumphant.

H

THE DREAM OF THE MAGI

IN the story it is said that the magi were warned from God in a dream not to return to Herod, and because they did not, Herod was filled with wrath.

From all that we have said in the previous paragraphs it will be readily apprehended what the warning meant. It will be understood why the magi should not return unto one who loved not the Christhood, but had ever been its enemy. It will be understood how the Soul with all its powers, must avoid that kingdom whose elements are opposed to its true progress, whose magnetic conditions are yet out of harmony with the Divine Love. For the astral kingdom is the Soul's greatest enemy. It is the kingdom personified in the Apocalypse as " the kingdom of Satan." It is the kingdom which the Christ was to overthrow, the kingdom wherein the saints have been persecuted since the beginning of the world as it is—that is, as a fallen spiritual system or cosmos. It is that kingdom which has heaped upon them sufferings untold and unnameable, as they have fought their way through it to find the kingdom of God within them. It is the kingdom wherein the beast is said to reign for a period—for the beast represents the awful prostitution of the powers of the Soul to the worship of matter, the degradation of the spiritual functions of the innermost being to find their fulfilment in the sense-life. It is the kingdom wherein the fearful dragon had sway for a time, and persecuted the saints—the dragon of spiritual negation, the materialization of everything that was originally spiritual and divine. It is also

153

" the great city " which is said to have been built upon " seven hills," within which every kind of abomination was wrought, with which all the Kings and Princes of the Earth have commerced, which not only drew within its gates all the people, but set upon their forehead " the mark of the Beast."

WHAT HEROD HAS DONE

For the astral kingdom as it is, has been the great hindrance to the Soul's Redemption. It has materialized everything that was purely and beautifully spiritual and divine. It has made the work of the redemption of all the Souls whom it overwhelmed by its impure elements, much more difficult. It has made the wonderful mission of the Master so long in bearing its true fruit, that even the Heavens have wept because of the pain, sorrow and anguish which became His portion as He performed the Office of the Cross in His astounding Sin-offering—that sublime but sad offering by means of which He changed many of the elements of the astral kingdom, absorbed in His Sin-offering lives the terrible fluidic and magnetic images which filled that kingdom and tortured Souls who were in the way of the Cross, and thus enabled those Souls who had been of the Christhood Order upon the Earth to once more rise up through the astral kingdom and function upon the angelic spheres. It changed the beautiful Teachings which the Master gave, into material histories ; drew off the earnest spiritual ones from the worship of the Divine Love, and led them to worship the person of the Master ; turned the inward kingdom of God which he taught, into an outward kingdom ; changed the entire meaning of the Church as a true spiritual fellowship between the Soul and the spiritual heavens, to mean such ecclesiastical communities as have prevailed throughout the so-called Christian Era ; made the holy priesthood of the Soul itself into a religious hierarchy through whose members alone the divine blessing could be bestowed ; transformed the Divine Hierarchies through whom angelic ministry is performed, into the great materialized systems represented by the Roman and Greek Churches, and, in less degree, by the Protestant Episcopal Churches.

Such has been the history wrought by the astral kingdom, a history full of tragic experiences for all men and women, all the more tragic because the Soul was always deceived into believing that it was the right way to go towards finding the Divine Life, and the right thing to do in order to fulfil the Divine Will.

THE INNER MEANING OF THE DREAM

Perhaps our readers will now behold the real meaning and purpose of the dream of the Magi, and the warning from the divine kingdom not to return to Herod. They will see the great need for the warning because of the nature of the astral kingdom. It is a warning which has always been given unto the Soul in the day of its deliverance from the dominating power of that kingdom. " *Let him who is on the house-top, not go down again.*" " *Let those who have fled unto the hills, not return unto the City.*" The Soul is counselled even in the night-season to flee from " the city of destruction " where all the powers make desolation within the life.

The Magi dreamt. After they had found the Christ-child they experienced " visions in the night." The Divine One communed with them. The spiritual heavens were open unto them, and from these they were able to receive. " *God giveth unto His Beloved Ones in sleep.*" The dreams of the Soul are waking visions—real, tangible, glorious. How comparatively few believe in such exalted things ? How few of those who should know the meaning of Christhood believe in the possibility of such heavenly experiences ? The worldly mind laughs at the bare idea of such realities, and the average professed followers of the Master repudiate the thought.

Yet is the inner life thus aided and educated. In the quiet which night bringeth, and the silence which is found when all the out-works of life and the world have for the time ceased their activities, the Soul is approached from the angelic world to be ministered unto. Many of the beautiful thoughts, images and impulses which visit the mind in the midst of the duties of the day, are born within us through the angelic visions given during the night.

What a wealth of meaning is here for all who would know the truth concerning these sacred stories of profound inward spiritual experience ! What a wonderful message it is to break upon us with the roseate hues of the dawning of another day ! How blessed is the Life unto which it calls ! and how gracious is that Love who calls unto such a Life ! May Bethlehem's Star appear unto all who read this true story. And may the Star become their guide until they too find the Christ-child born within themselves !

The Flight into Egypt

*Being a Cryptograph of the true nature of the Christ,
the manner of the Sin-offering, and how He
entered into the states of life wherein the
burden of it was borne ; and the reason
why He had to descend from His
Christhood that He might
remain in Egypt until
King Herod was
dead.*

A
A MONOGRAPH OF PROFOUND MEANING

THE story of The Flight into Egypt is one of the most beautiful and remarkable in the whole field of sacred literature. It embraces more than one spiritual history of the Soul, having at once a planetary, an individual, and, in a special sense, a Christ-Soul significance. It embodied an historical incident which occurred upon the planes of the Spiritual World untold ages ago when Maria Ioseph was the vehicle of the Divine Manifestation unto all those Souls who were known in ancient times as " the Sons of God," and, in the language of the western Scriptures, as " the Israel of God." Therein it was the history of how one Soul who had risen from sphere to sphere, from plane to plane, and from kingdom to kingdom upon an unfallen system, descended to minister unto the Souls referred to who were then dwelling upon the spiritual planes, in order that He might help them to rise also into the same glorious estate. Concerning that ancient spiritual history we may not write further here, and have only named it to indicate one of the meanings contained in this wonderful story.

Then in addition to that ancient planetary history, it has reference to the experience of every one when the Soul enters the spiritual conditions which are described in the allegory. It is purely spiritual history, as the unfoldment will make obvious. All Souls in the path of their evolution go down into Egypt ; though the experiences of the process now are very different from those which the Soul entered into prior to the descent of the entire household of the Planet into conditions which issued in evil, spoken of as " The Fall." Originally, the going down into Egypt had no *evil* results, though it brought into the life many new and remarkable experiences which enriched it. But ever since the descent of the planetary household in what is understood as " The Fall," the going down has meant great trial, much sorrow, and, not infrequently, profound anguish for the Soul.

But in addition to these histories of the Soul, the story embodies another. It is a history having intimate relation to that profound mystery named The Sin-offering, and is a picture of the going down of the Soul who was the vehicle of its accomplishment, into the necessary conditions. Indeed, it is only a monogram whose signs embody the history of the most profound work ever undertaken by a Soul. It is cryptic; because its mystery had to be hidden from all who were not initiated or born again into the consciousness of the Christ-state. Nor has the monogram been deciphered since the days of the Brotherhood who gathered around the Master to hear from Him the Divine Wisdom, and learn more fully concerning the Divine Purpose, until in these days when its secret may be revealed. For its secret has been kept throughout the ages through the destruction of the spiritual meaning of the story and its conversion into a mere outward event in the life of the Master when as yet He was a little child. The Mystery shadowed forth in its signs was sealed up and lost to the vision of the Soul, when it was materialized. Yet the story contains evidence of the profound Mystery such as should convince any pure and earnest seeker for the Divine Wisdom, that the Sin-offering was a most tragic reality.

B

THREE CRYPTIC TERMS

The chief terms made use of in the allegory were cryptic. On the historical plane their meanings seem apparent to the general reader, for they are associated with places and persons; but their real significance is not obvious to any but the initiated, and even unto the inner group of disciples the innermost meanings had to be explained. The Master knew the derivation and original signification of the various terms; and such use did

He make of them. As these are unfolded, the beautiful story will be recognized as one containing teachings most profound. The truths couched in the language and imagery of persons, places and things will become manifest. The foliage of the dry plant will be transformed into bloom the most wonderful, exquisite in the glory of the love revealed, sublimely beautiful in the transcendent life poured forth in sacrificial service for the purification of the entire Heavens of the Planet, and the healing and redemption of all peoples. The outward history will grow into something far, far more wonderful than any such cruel story as that implied in the gospel narrative ; for it will be transfigured into history the most remarkable and glorious, and transmuted into things purely spiritual, and a service to humanity which is wholly divine.

In the story of the Flight into Egypt, the terms we meet with which have purely a cryptic meaning are, Egypt, Maria, Joseph, Herod, Nazareth and the Ass. These terms did not represent persons, places and a creature ; they rather denoted spiritual qualities, states and experiences. They were terms which had been in vogue in the pure schools in which the Mysteries had been taught, and were well understood by the Master. And, as we shall see, His use of them was entirely spiritual. For the Flight into Egypt is a story that was told by Himself to the inner group of disciples, and it followed the story of the Angelic Vision ; and it was told by the Master only a brief time prior to the passing away of the Christhood Manifestation.

In order to make the following unfoldment of the Mystery embodied in the story intelligible, we shall have to briefly explain the meaning of the terms.

THE LAND OF EGYPT

Egypt originally meant *the body*. In the schools where the sacred Mysteries were studied, it was so understood. In this sense it was the land of oppression, for the magnetic fires of the unredeemed body-powers were oppressors of the aspiring Soul. Pharaoh and all his hosts who were overthrown in the Red Sea, were these dominating influences overthrown by the Soul's divine power when she rose up out of her terrible bondage to the sense-life (the flesh pots of Egypt) in response to the command of the Divine Lord. For the history of Israel in Egypt was the history of the Soul, a purely spiritual experience and not such as Jewish history would seem to imply. And it is in this light alone that so many of the ancient Scriptures can be understood which refer to Egypt, and, with it, Assyria ; for, as the former symbolized the body, so the latter symbolized the mind. " *In that day shall the five Cities of Egypt speak the language of the land of Canaan* " ; for these cities or centres of activity were the five senses which, in a state of Soul-bondage, were opposed to the life of the Soul, and hence in opposition to the laws of the Divine Love ; but which came to speak the language, or live in harmony with the life, of the land of Canaan—the Soul in a purified state.

The City of Nazareth

Nazareth was a term expressing *a condition of spiritual life*. The term lost its full significance during the ages when all the Hebrew Mysteries were changed by the Occult Schools which grew out of the earlier schools of the Prophets. It was applied to men who lived in certain ways, whether or not they were in the spiritual condition which its inner meaning signified. In a way these men were like the eastern Yogoi. They meant well, and followed what they conceived to be the prophetic path. But, as a rule, the inner meaning of the thing they sought after eluded their grasp, for the materialization of the term deprived them of the vision to which it originally drew on the Soul. And it came to be associated with certain formulæ, and with rites of initiation into the outward state. For there grew up within the Occult Schools a communion known as the Nazarenes. And it was in this way that the village which was the centre of their fellowship, came to bear the name of Nazareth.

From the scriptures we learn that the condition of life which the term represented, was despised by many. Men and women did not like the impoverished life which it brought with it. They did not like its hardships, its loneliness, its self-denying rules, its self-sacrifice. Originally it was despised because of its purely spiritual nature. Men and women shrank from the spiritual things it implied. It was opposed to their material ways in life. What good could come out of it ? It bore no earthly fruit. Its riches were intangible, and therefore not such as to enrich this life. Its ways were those of hardships, earthly loss, pain, loneliness and even sorrow ; wherein lay its advantages ? Who would be the wealthier for following its ways ? What natural ambitions could it ever gratify ? What earthly powers could it ever acquire ? Could *any* good thing come out of Nazareth ? Yet it was the place or spiritual state in which the Master dwelt in the days of the Manifestation ; and it was the place or state in which He dwelt after the Sin-offering had been accomplished, and He had returned from Egypt.

THE ASS AS A HIEROGLYPH

The Ass upon which Mary and the Christ rode, had a profound meaning. In ancient symbology the horse stood for the Higher Intellect, and the Ass for *the lower mind*. If the remarkable apocalyptic visions found in the scriptures in which these creatures figure, are read in the light of such interpretation, new meaning will be found in them. The black, red, pale and white Horses of the Apocalypse, spoke of states of the Higher Mind : they symbolized spiritual death, spiritual conflict, spiritual famine or impoverishment, and spiritual power within the Higher Mind. And wherever these Horses were ridden, they carried with them the like conditions. And the conquest of all things, the overthrow of all evil, the victory of all good, the triumph of the Christ-Life, was accomplished when

" the Word of God " was written upon the vesture of the Soul, and the White Horse was ridden—the purified mind with a purified vision—by the Logos or Adonai overshadowing and filling the Soul of the one who was so mounted and equipped.

And in like manner the Ass was made use of as the symbol of the lower mind. Some have thought that it symbolized the Intuition, but this is surely a mistake and one arising out of some references in the ancient Scriptures, especially the story of Balaam's Ass. For Balaam knew by means of his intuition that he ought not to do the thing he purposed, yet opposed himself to his own best visions through his avarice and pride. And it was only *the fear* which overtook his mind on the way that prevented him from carrying out his purpose. He was astride the Ass of his own lower mind, trying to drive it to accomplish his end. In his way the Angel of the Lord stood whose presence even the lower mind became conscious of, and, full of dread, turned back.

The symbolism will likewise be found in the ancient prophecy concerning the manner of the manifestation of Christhood, though in later years it came to be associated with the appearing of the Jewish Messiah, and then with the Master in one of the incidents of His life.

" *Rejoice greatly, O daughter of Zion ; shout, O daughter of Jerusalem : behold thy King cometh unto thee. He is just, and having Salvation : lowly, and riding upon an Ass, and upon a Colt, the foal of an Ass.*"

Of the Master it is said that He rode into the city of Jerusalem upon an Ass, and a Colt the foal of an Ass. But the story has a most profound spiritual significance, and not a merely outward historical meaning. This we will interpret fully when we write of The Sin-offering. But here we would point out that the symbolism is perfect, for the Ass symbolizes the lower mind, and the Colt the foal of an Ass, is the body which is the vehicle of the lower mind. And upon these two, garments were spread, and then the Christ was set thereon. And on His way He passed from Bethany to Bethphage, and thence into the City—Bethany and Bethpage also symbolizing spiritual states.

It is with this meaning that the term has to be read in the story of the Flight into Egypt.

C

WHO WAS IOSEPH?

IOSEPH was no man. The term was a most sacred name associated with *a most sacred state*. It was originally a Divine Name. Traces of this may be found in the Hebrew Mysteries and in the Psalter. But the term came to be associated with a man, as instanced in the story of Joseph who was sold to the Egyptians, and who arose in their midst into great power, manifesting great wisdom, and becoming the preserver of those of His Father's house who went down into Egypt. But that story was not outward history, nor the experience of one man and one family; it was spiritual history, and was of a planetary nature. The story belonged to the Mysteries, like those of the bondage in Egypt and the deliverance from it, together with the wearisome wanderings through the wilderness; and the history which it recorded was of the Soul amid the changed conditions which overtook the Planet when its elemental kingdoms were turned into the centres of opposing forces. And Ioseph came down into Egypt as the preserver of the children of Israel amid the spiritual famine which prevailed for many great cycles of ages. He was the manifestation of the Divine Love and Wisdom upon the plane of the mind to the House of Israel —those Souls who had overcome the elemental powers and had prevailed in their spiritual aspirations, and who had become princes or rulers for God, and teachers of the people. These were known as " the ancients " or " Christs," and in later years as " the Sons of God." The term was a cryptogram

M   165

which will be seen to contain the most wonderful teaching when we unfold its meaning.

Through its relation to the Divine Nature, and as a manifestation of the Divine Love and Wisdom upon the plane of the mind, it also came to be related to a spiritual state in the experience of the mind. It was applied to one who had reached that state and made manifest the service in life which it represented. And it is in this sense that we are to understand its use in the Birth-stories, and not in relation to any one man. For Ioseph was not the father of the personal Master, as we have already indicated, but the spiritual condition of the mind to whom it refers. In its primary sense it spoke of the Divine Love and Wisdom performing a very special ministry ; in its secondary sense it signified the ministry unto which the mind was called who was in such a spiritual state.

D

THE VIRGIN MARY

MARIA was no earthly woman. There was a much higher meaning attached to the term, and to the thought of " the Mother of our Lord." In various ways this will be revealed in the Unfoldments ; but for our present purpose it must be shown that the name was not a personal one. Like Ioseph, it related to a spiritual condition of the Soul. In its inner meaning the term is most significant, embodying as it does so much that is most beautiful in character and profound in experience. It was also related to the Mysteries of the Soul. Amongst the Hebrew Mysteries it may be found as Miriam, for the Song of Miriam was that of the triumph of the Soul over all the elemental forces implied in Pharaoh and his hosts. It was a song of the Soul whose references were spiritual, though the Jewish historians understood it to be otherwise. In the purer days of the Schools of the Prophets, the term was understood ; and it became the cryptogram for a Soul who had reached up to the exalted spiritual state implied in Christhood. It therefore spoke of the profoundest of realizations such as are indicated in the triumphant Song of Miriam, the Annunciation unto Mary, and the Transfiguration of the Master. And in the Unfoldments it will also be shown how the beautiful term came to be applied to the Soul in other states, such as those represented in Mary the Mother of Jesus, Mary of Bethany, and Mary Magdalene.

In its innermost meaning the term meant a state of Soul unfoldment in which the Christhood had not only been entered upon, but one in which the consciousness of the Divine Overshadowing and Indwelling Presence had been realized. It was more, in its meaning, than what is understood as the cosmic consciousness in a planetary sense ; for it was the Divine Consciousness. And it had a very special relationship to the Soul of Him who is spoken of as The Master, as we shall now show.

E

THE HIDDEN MEANING DISCOVERED

In the light of these explanations of the terms made use of, the cryptograph unravels itself and reveals its profound Mystery. The Flight into Egypt assumes a new rôle as a revelation of divine history. It ceases to be any longer the outward event men and women have believed it to be, and becomes dissociated from a supposed historical tragedy of the most overwhelming and devilish nature, concerning the truth of which there is not even the remotest vestige of historical data. It changes the venue of the whole incident as experimental history when it is known that the experiences were inward and not outward, spiritual rather than physical, profound Soul history written in the fulness of conscious life, and not in the state of a helpless child. Even the *modus operandi* is all changed ; and *the purpose* for which the so-called flight from the destructive powers of Herod was taken, is turned into a sublime one, even to endure that tyrant's yoke for a season in order to deliver all the children of the Bethlehem whom he had slain through his emissaries, and raise them up from the dead. The Flight into Egypt will be revealed as one in which the Christ is not preserved from persecution, but through it becomes a Soul full of sorrow ; that by means of it He did not escape from sharing the tragedy that overtook all the children of Bethlehem, but shared it in a way that made His sufferings and anguish more poignant and terrible than theirs. *For it was a cryptograph of the way and the accomplishment of the Sin-offering.*

F

THE DIVINE COMMAND

The Angel of the Lord is said to have appeared unto Ioseph, commanding him to take Mary and the child down into Egypt. Who was the Angel of the Lord ? Surely the Angel of *His* Presence who is within the sanctuary of every Soul, and is consciously realized by all who reach Christhood. It was the voice within the glory or cloud of the innermost of the Soul advising the line of action to be taken, the method by which the Divine Purpose was to be accomplished.

And we must remember that the Christhood of the Master was of a very high order. We may speak of it as Divine. In His spiritual nature He had attained the exalted state of realization of Being designated by the terms Ioseph Maria. *In mind He was one with the Divine Father : in Soul He was one with the Divine Mother*. He took unto himself the nature of the Divine and Ever-Blessed One, as He rose from kingdom to kingdom, thinking it not wrong or presumptuous to be of the very nature of God. He had assigned to Him the sublime office of Ioseph for the work of the Redemption on this Planet, even as He had given unto Him the beautiful office of Maria in giving birth to the Christ-child in the Jesus-life, and bringing into fulness of manifestation the glorious vision of a Divine Christhood. For the office of Ioseph was that of the Cross, the office of burden-bearing, the work of the Redeemer ; just as the office of Maria was to conceive, bring forth and nourish the Christ-Life, the Divine Life in interpretation. And when the days of the Manifestation had been fully accomplished, the Lord commanded that He should go down into Egypt. For it was there that the Office of the Cross had to be performed. So Ioseph took Maria and the Christ and went down into Egypt.

And they went down riding upon an Ass. Ioseph did not so ride ; only Maria and the Christ. But he accompanied them as their protector. And what was this mode of travelling into Egypt but that of the lower mind, since the Ass is the symbol of that mind. It was *by the path of incarnation* that Egypt was reached ; but it was incarnation through a mind and a body whose desires and impulses belonged to the land of magnetic fires. For, as the Ass was the symbol of the lower mind, Egypt was that of the limitations of the body. But they specially symbolized a mind and a body whose elements were un-redeemed, a mind and a body whose powers were responsive to the powers and magnetic forces of the astral world. In the life of the Christhood Manifestation, the Master had a lower mind and a body ; but these were not of the nature of the land of Egypt. They were in a purified state. Their desires and impulses were all beautiful. They did not hinder and mar the manifestation of the Jesus-life and the Christhood ; they fully responded to the innermost desires of the Soul. But the vehicles of the Sin-offering work were different. They had to be different. It was necessary that they should be conditioned for the special work which had to be accomplished by means of them. They had to be so magnetic upon the astral plane that they could attract certain magnetic forms which were there, and absorb them. For the work of the Sin-offering was of this nature.

This then was the meaning of The Flight into Egypt. It was " the flight " of the one through whom the Divine Manifestation had been made, from the state of Divine Christhood into the land of the magnetic fires spoken of as Egypt—magnetic fires which found response to their influences within the minds and bodies of men and women in greater or less degree. It was the descent from the state of the Bethlehem or Jesus-life wherein also the Christ-child was born and made manifest, to that state of experience which the magnetic fires represented. It was " the passing over " from a state of Christhood into that state of spiritual experience in which He became even as one of the least of His Brethren, bearing upon His own body and within His own mind, the weaknesses, frailties, and iniquities or spiritual diseases, by which they were afflicted. And it was in this sense that He was like a little child in His life of spiritual experience, still the Son of Maria, still attended and protected by Ioseph, but in realization of divine things in the outward life, always as the little child. His life in the many incarnations necessary for the accomplishment of the Sin-offering, was crowded with mysterious experiences which He, as the spiritual child, could not fathom ; for it was needful for the work to put Him under such great limitations. But Ioseph and Maria understood these—the Overshadowing One and the Soul. Amid the magnetic fires He endured untold agony ; for they filled His being with anguish as they afflicted Him. He was in Egypt in all the lives He lived to accomplish the Sin-offering, and these covered the ages from the passing of the Christhood until these days in which we ourselves now live. For the Sin-offering, has only recently been fully accomplished. It is only in these latter days that " The return from Egypt " has fully taken place. And in the return, the little despised City of Nazareth was chosen once more as the state of dwelling for Him ; and He returned there with Maria and Ioseph. For Herod had been overthrown ; his power was dead. The magnetic images whose presence upon the astral kingdom wrought such havoc with Souls, were destroyed by Him during the sojourn in Egypt ; and now all Souls may seek without fear, the Christhood born in Bethlehem, even as the Magi did, and lay their gifts of love, devotion and consecrated preserving service at the feet of the Christhood born within the Soul from the indwelling of the Divine Love.

Concerning all the experiences passed through in the land of Egypt ; the many lives lived during the Sin-offering ; the return in every life to the Jesus-state, and, in the last return, to the Christhood consciousness ; the meaning of the return to the little City of Nazareth in every life covered with the obloquy and scorn of those who would have none of that narrow way of life, and who looked upon Nazareth as evil, and Nazarenes as men and women to be avoided ; and the meaning of the last return as one travailing in unspeakable sorrow, pain, and anguish, returning from Edom or the land of forgetfulness, to Bozrah or the land of the consciousness and memories associated with Christhood, burdened with some dire load and throbbing under some envenomed fang, uttering the most mysterious prayers and watering them with tears, seeking the vision of the ever Blessed One amid the garden of sorrow as only one could who had known the blessedness of it in the past—of these things we may not here write further ; some of them will be shown by and by.

The Presentation in the Temple

Being an allegory of great beauty illustrating the true consecration of the Life to the service of the Lord ; but having very special reference to the consecration of the Master to the work to be accomplished through Him, and the Purification and Consecration after the Return from Egypt.

The Presentation in the Temple

A

THE STORY

THE Presentation of the Christ-child in the Temple, is yet another of the sacred Mysteries associated with the Christhood. It is at once full of power and spiritual beauty, though, in the presentation given in the third Gospel Record, these are not seen. Indeed, in the monograph, the true meaning is quite obscure to the general reader. For in the narrative the Soul mystery is changed into a literal history. In the story it is presented as the history of a Jewish mother observing the usual Jewish custom of going up to the Temple in Jerusalem to dedicate her male child unto the service of the Lord—such as the Jews thought that service to be. And the usual Jewish sacrifice is said to have been made in the form of two Turtle-Doves.

Truly it is sad to reflect that the beautiful life and mission of the blessed Master could have ever been associated from childhood with the Jewish custom of taking the lives of any of the creatures for oblations of sacrifice, as well as food and raiment. But that is just wherein the writers failed. They entirely misrepresented His life, and the blessed purpose of His redemptive mission. They changed into material histories all the wonderful and sublime Mysteries concerning the Soul which He taught to the inner group of the disciples, and which were originally embodied in the Logia of St. John. They understood not the profoundest significance of such interior histories relating to the kingdom of the Soul, but took them to mean outward things, purely material experiences, and presented them in their Records as such. As our readers will have seen from the previous studies, these Birth-stories are amongst the most wonderful of the Mysteries, and are rich in the history of the Soul. They will have beheld in them the narration of the Soul's experience in various stages, as well as spiritual histories relating to the Christhood of the blessed Master. And in this monograph of the Presentation of the Christ child in the Temple there will be found yet another of the beautiful histories which speak of the growth of the Soul until it attains to the estate of the Divine Man. It will be seen to have no mere material application, but an entirely spiritual one ; to be a truly subjective, not an objective one ; to have relation only to the Soul's conscious experience, and not to any unconscious act done by others on its behalf ; to actually be a beautiful service rendered unto the Divine One by the Soul itself after it has arrived at the consciousness of Christhood— that is, when the Christ-child is born within the Soul, the Christ-spirit leading the whole being to the act of consecration to the Christ-life, which experience again leads to the full realization of all that is implied by the term Christhood.

B

THE MATERIALIZATION OF THE STORY

THE ceremony of dedication which seems to have been the fulfilment of some law relating to the ceremonial of Jewry, was a materialization of the spiritual meaning. The outward rite was substituted for the beautiful truth out of which it had grown when the inner meaning became lost. The ceremonial was one of great interest and importance to the Jew, though it had no other than an outward meaning for him. What future blessing might come upon his child as the result of the ceremony to him, depended upon the rite being properly performed according to the traditional laws of the priesthood. It was like all other rites associated with ecclesiastical religion past and present ; it might have been a blessing to those who took part, but missed its real purpose through the beautiful inner meaning having been lost, and only an outward signification having been made to take its place.

So much for the effect of stereotyped forms, rites and cere-monies, for the materializing influences and powers of ecclesi-astical systems and priestly hierarchies. They have done despite to the truth in all ages, ever since they arose out of the great occult epochs which prevailed during the post-Hebrew times. They have always turned the truth into rites and ceremonies of an outward character, giving the people the shadow for the substance, the outward shell for the inward kernel, the symbol for the inner spiritual meaning. They have always succeeded in blinding the Soul to the beautiful significance of the truths implied ; and thus they have bereft it of its spiritual light by which it would have been enabled to pursue its way along the path leading unto Bethlehem to there find the Christ-child, and then make the Presentation in the Temple, and at last find the entrance into the full blessing of Christhood.

The terrible history of the Jewish nation is the fruit of the work of a non-spiritual occultism. The sad darkness which overtook the land of the Pharaohs, where wisdom is said once to have dwelt, and where it did indeed once find a dwelling in glorious fulness, as the great work of the Pyramid of Gizeh bears testimony, shows the Soul-blinding power of ecclesias-ticism.[1] The pathetic story of the once most marvellous people of India with their sublime religious vision, reveals, too palpably to be denied what materialization of spiritual things can do to impoverish the Soul. The Ancient Babylonia with its astonishing monuments of human power and genius and its still more remarkable religious effigies and inscriptions, testifies to the degrading and destroying powers of priestly hierarchies. The unnameable history wrought out by the Greeks (not-withstanding that at one time they knew the Mysteries and their

---

[1] The Great Pyramid of Gizeh, which has been written of so fully by Marsham Adams and Piazzi Smyth, and has been taken to contain a re-markable testimony to the Christian Era and the coming again of the Christ, was originally an embodiment of the path of the Soul in its spiritual evolution, and the way it had to follow in order to arrive at the Divine Life and Vision.

inner meanings, and in philosophic culture rose to a height which not even this age approaches) was the outcome of the loss of the inner spiritual sense through the establishing of priestly schools and hierarchies, and the introduction of rites and ceremonies as the true means by which the Soul could gain the goal of Christhood.

And what overtook these once great peoples, also overtook the whole western world after the days of the Master, and in the like manner. For almost as soon as the Master passed from His Christhood manifestation, the work of materializing all His beautiful Teachings began. Very quickly arose a new priestly system out of the ashes of the overthrown temple ministry of Jewry, and the effete paganism of Rome and Greece. Rites and ceremonies were established as the venues through which alone the virtues of the Christ could reach unto the earnest seeker after the divine life, and the priestly hierarchies grew stronger and stronger in their claims until, at last, the priest stood between the Soul and the Divine One. Within the hierarchy the Mysteries were regarded either as outward histories, or mere child-pictures necessary for the mind of the people ; only the very few regarded them as allegories of great spiritual facts. These mysteries may be found now within the Greek and Roman Churches, but they are like precious treasures lost amid the rubbish within these religious communities, for they are concealed from view through their gross materialization, hidden in gaudy caskets which attract the outer senses, and which are presented as the precious treasures themselves.

Nor is it much better in those Churches where the priestly power and claims have been rejected. For though as regards rites and ceremonies they make less claim, yet do they regard the stories in which the Mysteries are embodied as outward history ; and they will not brook any interpretation that shows the monograms and monographs containing the Mysteries to have always had a purely spiritual and divine meaning, having relation to the Soul, its origin, evolution and realization of such a measure of the divine life as to attain unto the realization of Christhood. They have, as Churches, professed more freedom in their outlook, more true spirituality in their application of truth ; yet have they been bound hand and foot in the bonds with which tradition maketh the Soul captive, until even those Churches which arose out of the Reformed Religion (the present Episcopal Churches) ; those which arose out of the earnest longing of the Soul to worship the Divine One free from all rites and ceremonies during the sixteenth and seventeenth centuries (as the Congregationalists, Baptists, etc.), and those which arose as the result of the great spiritual awakening in the times of the Wesleys (the various Methodist Churches) ; have all become so subject to tradition, and to the interpretations of the scholastic elders, that they have lost their power to discern spiritually, to penetrate the outward history and find the inner meaning. Nay, even that Church which grew out of the remarkable unfoldment, in part, of the doctrine of " Correspondences " as set forth by Emanuel Swedenborg, and which took to itself the name of the New Jerusalem Church, has likewise missed its way because of the rites which have been made to take the place of the inner meanings, the sad limitations with which its elders have bound it, *its far too personal view of the nature of the Lord*, its mistaken interpretation of the outward histories associated with the Master, and its misunderstanding and, as a result, its misinterpretation of the remarkable Sin-offering. With all its advance on the other Churches in its apprehension of spiritual things, it has nevertheless failed to understand the nature and history of the Soul, *the true nature* of the Master, the meaning of a Christhood, and the vision of the Divine Lord within the sanctuary of the Soul.

Such, in brief, has been the history of the Church since the days of the Master, one of the most astounding histories ever written in the name of the Divine Love, a history over which it would scarcely be too much to write the word *Ichabod* : for the Lord has been absent from it, and its glory has been very largely the garish show of the world, or the cruel triumph of the ecclesiastical, traditional and scholastic inquisition.

It would have been remarkable, indeed, if the Presentation of the Christ-child in the Temple had escaped materialization amid such conditions. But for even such a form of the allegory in which the Mystery is embodied as may be found in the third Record, we are grateful ; because something of the truth may yet be beheld when carefully considered and spiritually discerned. The very details which are given are full of profound significance. Mary, Joseph, and the Christ-child in the Temple offering a pair of Turtle-Doves ; with Anna the aged prophetess, and Simeon the aged sire, looking on with gladness of heart, blessing the child and praising the Lord—all have meanings so beautiful that they excel any possible outward history or material signification.

C

THE HOLY FAMILY

THE picture of the Holy Family is ever an engrossing one. It has attracted to its service the genius of some of the greatest artists who have endeavoured to embody their ideas in most beautiful works of art. There has always been a great charm about the subject. Alas ! that so few have discerned what it all meant. Mary, Joseph and the Christ-child have always been regarded as persons, rather than as individual parts of the system of the Soul itself representing distinctive states of spiritual experience. That there was a very real " Holy Family," into which the blessed Master was born, is quite true ; but it was not that holy family that is intended in the birth-stories. For all that is meant by the holy family is potentially in every man, and shall ultimately become so in realization.

The holy family is a Soul subject, and not simply something personal. It is an inward beautiful Soul realization, and not merely an objective experience in several lives related to each other in the flesh. It is a purely subjective history, and is not something found upon the material spheres. Let this be clearly understood ; for to get the true inner meaning, everything personal and material must needs be laid aside.

Mary the Mother of the Lord

Who then were the actors in this remarkable event ? The very terms are full of significance. Mary, the mother of the Christ-child, is the Soul as to her innermost divine nature. *She is ever Virgin.* What is conceived within the womb of the Soul is always of the Holy Spirit (unless the Soul loses her divine nature). It is Mary who hears the message of the angel announcing the coming to birth of the Christ-child. It is Mary who is astonished when the angel informs her that she is to bear the Christ-child. It is Mary who marvels that she should be counted worthy to receive so great honour as the birth of Christhood would confer. It is Mary who sings the song of the Soul in the beautiful Magnificat. It is Mary who bears the Christ-child and nourishes him through the goodness of the Divine Love.

The function of Mary is most important ; she bears the Lord *in* Life. She brings unto the fulness of spiritual unfoldment the divine powers latent within her ; and in her experiences she reaches the holy estate of Christhood, which is the manifestation of the Lord *in* Life. *She is, therefore, the Mother of the Lord in Manifestation*. And the thought is most beautiful, one full of blessing and hope.

Could there be anything more wonderful, more truly glorious for the Soul, more truly blessed for humanity than this vision of the nature and function of the Soul, and her attainment through inward realization of the estate of Christhood, the manifested Life of the Lord whose Presence is within her ? Could there be anything more beautifully spiritual, more transcendent in conception concerning the purpose of the Soul and the realization of the approach of the Divine and ever Blessed One unto her to enable her to rise into the blessed Life implied in Christhood, and even to that higher and still more sublime consummation when the Christhood is clothed with divine attributes, even as was the inner Life of the blessed Master ? Could there possibly be a nobler vision presented to the Soul than this in which her own divine nature is manifested, and the wonderful and holy purpose of her creation set forth ? Does it not transcend any mere material history, even though such might have been associated with the outward life of the Master, and show the birth incidents to have a value for the Soul surpassing anything that any outward history could have ?

The very term Mary, as we have pointed out in a previous chapter when writing about these Birth-stories, contains within itself a wealth of meaning. It is like a precious jewel, a true gem within whose elements its ancient inherent light is still visible, and ready to pour itself forth unto him who looks. As we follow the Master in the profound Teachings which He gave unto those who were able to receive them, we shall find yet deeper experiences associated with the term, larger meanings growing out of it, and a vision breaking upon the mind that the term had a very special application to the blessed Master Himself in His Christhood, and the experiences which came to Him as He made that Christhood manifest, and performed the Office of the Cross in the tragic Sin-offering.

Joseph the Father of the Lord

The reader will now be prepared to learn that Joseph was not a mere man any more than Mary was a mere woman ; that the one who is presented as the foster-father of the Master was the *Mind*, that mind whose function it is to reflect purely the spiritual and divine things which were given unto it, and whose office is that of reflector of the light of the Soul who is illumined from the Divine Lord. The *Mind* is the masculine aspect of the inner life, as the Soul is the feminine aspect. Joseph is said to have been well on in years, whilst Mary is represented as being young ; because, whilst the Soul is ever young, the Mind grows aged with heavenly wisdom. But the aged Mind is not to be understood as implying what is meant by aged when applied to the body of man ; for there is no loss of power, no lack of strength, no diminution of vital energy. Indeed when the Mind is in the state represented by Joseph, its strength is divine, its vital force is divine, its power is divine ; it is great with years whose ripeness is found in the heavenly wisdom learnt as the Divine Love, Light and Life have come to be realized ever more and more. It is no misfortune to the life to be aged in a heavenly sense, but a great and glorious blessing. For in such a condition there is no impoverishment, but an ever-increasing wealth ; there is no decrease of vigour, but a power growing more and more spiritually mighty as the life approaches the realizations implied in Divine Soul-consciousness.

The state of life represented by Joseph is therefore beautiful, and one to be eagerly sought for. It is the state of a purified Mind, because all the life is set Zionwards—that is, to the realization of the Divine Presence within ; a state which has to be attained as the Soul travels along the path of its true evolution unto its perfect fulfilment.

Such then was the aged Joseph who is said to have been the foster-father of the Master. He was the aged companion of the ever young Soul, the Mind stored with heavenly wisdom, the husband of Mary, the masculine mode of the ever feminine Soul. And herein we may behold a most wonderful mystery, one which shows how fully the Soul originally was constituted divine in her nature ; how she was always dual, male and female, with positive and negative forces, and so like the Divine Macro-cosmic Soul. And the thought is truly a beautiful one, one not only full of mystery but also of blessed inspiration for all Souls who would behold how the Divine Love originally fashioned them, and what wonderful and blessed realizations He always purposed should be their heritage. They will behold how, with the unfoldment, the mystery of their own being assumes a still more wonderful meaning, deeper, higher, greater, more sublime. And they will understand the depth of feeling in the language of old time when one said, " *O how wonderful are Thy works, Lord God of Hosts ! Who is like unto Thee ?* "

And beyond all this there is a meaning which had very special significance when applied to the Christhood of the Master, just as Mary had. In another place we have indicated the innermost meanings of the terms, MARIA and IOSEPH, showing their relation to the Divine One Himself ; for they represent, in their most interior sense, the feminine and masculine principles in the Divine Nature—the Divine Love and the Divine Wisdom. They represent the two modes of Deity—the Eternal and Ever Blessed One—the un-manifest and the mani-fest, the negative and the positive divine powers out from which all true life and manifestations have proceeded. The Maria who bore the Christhood of the blessed Master, and who ever brings to birth Christhood in humanity, *is the Divine Life within the Soul*. There could be no Christhood otherwise. And the Ioseph who espouses the Maria, and companions her, is none other than the Divine Love, the ever faithful guardian of the Soul who cares for the Divine Life within, and cherishes the Christ-child ; for without that beautiful Love no Christhood would be possible, and so there could have been no Master. It is of the Divine Life within the Soul that the Christhood is born ; and it is of the overshadowing Divine Love that the Christ-child is preserved.

Thus we may know the wonderful mystery of " the holy family " which the genius of many has endeavoured to embody —the mystery of the ever blessed Fatherhood-Motherhood of the Divine, and the Mystery of the birth of the Christ-child within the Soul.

" *Behold, what manner of Love the ever Blessed One hath bestowed upon us, that we should be named the Sons of God !* "

D

THE PURIFICATION

WHEN the days of the *purification* had been accomplished, it is said that Joseph and Mary took the Christ-child and went up to the temple. How beautifully natural it all seems, judged of from a human standpoint. The Jewish ceremonial law is apparently observed by Mary and Joseph, and then the way is clear for the visit to the temple and the dedication of the Christ-child. But what a false atmosphere surrounds the picture ! What a mistaken application is given to the wonderful truth that is implied in the act of purification ! How sad that it should ever have been diverted into a mere physical channel in which its meaning has become lost ! How subtly the truth has been concealed under the guise of the ceremonial bodily purification of Mary ! The evil view of motherhood held by the Jews has been wrought into the picture, and Mary is made to pass through the process of ceremonial cleansing. The writers did the Soul a great and grievous wrong when they gave such a presentation of the purification.

Its Meaning for the Soul

What then was this process which is spoken of ? What was the nature of the purification that had to be accomplished ? Let us change the picture in its nature and we shall behold how the truth will shine forth. See Joseph as the Mind and Mary as the Soul, and these together as the life approaching Christhood, and the light will break. It was their purification ; the elimination from them of everything that was of the sense-life ; the accomplishing of their redemption from mere earthly things. It was a purely spiritual process, an inward accomplishment, a divine cleansing of the whole being. The law that was fulfilled was not the Jewish ceremonial, but the Law of the Divine Love. For there can be no absolute and perfect dedication within the temple of the innermost Being until that experience has been accomplished.

The accomplishment of the purification is the attainment by the Soul of redemption in all her spheres. It is the elimination from those spheres of everything astral, whatever in any degree darkens the vision of the Soul and prevents her approach to the divine realization. It is the gradual uprising of the Soul out of the conditions known as the elementals, which are at present so impure on the Planet that they militate against the upwardness of the Soul. It is the overcoming of the world, the flesh and the devil :—that is, it is the conquest of the worldly spirit which dominates the mind when the life of the world is sought for as a source of satisfaction of desire, and as an end in itself ; the overcoming of the sense-feelings as venues of mere gratification, and the changing of them into venues of beautiful devotion to and service in the highest realms ; the repudiation of every way of life that leads to the negation of gentleness, goodness, pity, compassion, righteousness and love—such ways as are followed where pity is refused to the creatures, compassion to the poor and burdened ones, love to all Souls in whatsoever condition, and righteousness in all thoughts and actions towards others. To overcome the devil (who is the negation of all that is truly humane) is to purify oneself of the evil of flesh-eating and its accompanying horrors ; to repudiate vivisection and all that it stands for of heartless conduct and monstrous delusions ; to be no party to imposing most grievous burdens upon the poor and afflicted ; to refuse to have any lot or part in any system of evil by which Souls are hurt, lives impoverished, and misery generated ; to know no way in life whose foundations are not in righteousness and whose walls are not built of love, but rather to seek to heal and restore the life of the individual, the community and the nation, and indeed all nations, since we are all one great family ; to seek and make goodness the chief factor in all action towards others—that is the overcoming of the devil, the evil spirit that negatives and destroys all true Life.

To overcome the flesh is to rise above the dominating power of all desire born of the body and the lower mind, to make the senses pure in all their feelings, to make desire in any form only the venue for expressing the most beautiful affection and service in life, to chasten the taste so that only the purest things are sought for the upbuilding of the body, to purify the thoughts of the mind so that its images will always be beautiful and such as will be helpful in life. For the flesh means the fallen state of the body and mind, the merely sensuous ways so greatly sought after, the ministry to desire which is not soullic but animal, the craving for the fulfilment of desire through the lower nature. And the conquest means the setting right of all these things, the restoration to a pure and true state of all the powers of body and mind.

The overcoming of the world is the attainment of perfect mastery over all the ways of life in the world, the purification of the heart from all false ambition, from all aspiration after things which are not in harmony with the Divine Life, from all love that is without true spiritual foundation, from all purpose which does not lead to the realization of the most beautiful powers within the Soul, and from all service which has not its beginning and ending in the fulfilment of the Soul's highest quest.

The purification was, therefore, the redemption of Mary the

Soul and Joseph the Mind, from these things. And it did not *follow* the birth of the Christ-child, but preceded it. The redemption must always precede the birth of Christhood. *John the Baptist is first born, and then the Christ. The mission of John the Baptist must ever forerun that of Christhood. The life of purification must be experienced ere the Christhood can be born.* But when the purification is accomplished, then may the Christhood be entered upon, and the presentation made in the temple.

But the purification had also a profound meaning for the Master, as we shall presently show.

E

THE TWO TURTLE-DOVES

AFTER the purification there followed the presentation and dedication. The first act consisted in the offering unto the Lord of two doves. This was a most beautiful act, one betokening much more than a superficial interpretation could ever imply. It was an act of the most wonderful consecration of life in its two modes, the active and passive, the positive and negative, the masculine and feminine principles. The turtle-dove was the symbol of purity ; and the offering of such unto the Lord by Mary and Joseph, was the Soul and Mind in a purified state making an oblation unto the Divine Love. This was the original thought and meaning associated with the sacrifice of two doves ; and when the inner spiritual meaning of the symbol became lost the idea was transferred to the creatures. They were made the victims of Jewish darkness.

THE DEGRADATION OF THE SYMBOL

Behold what a fall was there, when the Jews, who knew not the meaning of the symbol, gave to it a material signification and changed the whole nature of the offering ! Think of the

Soul-blindness that took such a remarkable symbol of pure Being dedicated unto the service of the Lord, to mean that the lives of two harmless, timid, beautiful creatures were demanded by the Divine Love to be sacrificed unto Him ! Think of the degrading influences of a system that could not discern with what abhorrence the Divine Love must regard all such cruel wrong inflicted upon His creatures offered unto Him in sacrifice ! Need we marvel that the Jews remained in darkness all through their history, notwithstanding the fact that prophets and seers came unto them from the spiritual heavens and proclaimed the true way of the Lord and the only sacrifices in which He delighted ? Their degradation of the meaning of the beautiful symbol from a spiritual to a material thing, had not only disastrous results for themselves, but has had for the whole western world ; for the Jews who wrote the Gospels, gave the exquisite picture of the Soul's beautiful dedicatory act such a meaning as to utterly obscure the wonderful spiritual experience of which the presentation speaks. They gave to all the Birth-stories an outward significance ; and they made the most sacred act of consecration revealed in these stories, one in which life was taken from two gentle creatures, because in their ceremonial religion the Lord was said to have demanded them. And thus they not only degraded the Soul in its most sacred act, but also the very nature of the Divine Love. Is it any wonder that the western world is the theatre of such fearful animal cruelty found in the habits of flesh-eating and sport, and the vivisecting of the creatures in the name of science, when the religious scholars of that world teach that the Jewish Religion was divinely ordered, and that the holocaust of creatures laid on the Jewish altars as sacrifices, were demanded by the Divine Love ? Is it to be marvelled at that the same darkness which lay like a heavy pall over the whole Jewish history, should have been repeated in the history of the whole western world where the creatures have been and are still sacrificed in their millions on the corrupted altars of human desire ?

Why have not the Churches beheld the true and inner meanings of the wonderful Birth-stories, from the birth of the Christ-child in the hostel of the creatures to the dedication ? Why have they not had the power to discern wherein the truth lay, and to bring the precious jewels out of the casket ? May not the answer be found in the conditions within themselves ? Though they build no blood-altars such as were the leading features of Jewry, yet they have made of every life within their borders, an altar where the remains of the sacrificed helpless ones have been continually offered to the god of *Desire*, for one or all of these things—food, raiment, pleasure, adornment and healing.

WHEN WILL THE CHURCHES AWAKE ?

It is a sad picture, the more sad because it is impossible to fully paint it and embody all that it means. To see it as it is, one must rise on to the spiritual heavens. *It is a great and unspeakable tragedy.* Would that our voice could reach all the Churches to awaken every Soul within them to the terrible reality. Oh that we could impress upon all the various religious communities, what it means both for the creatures and themselves ! Oh that we might open the eyes of all who lead and teach within the Churches, to see the worse than battle-field scenes which the habit of flesh-eating has fashioned, and the hell-tortures imposed by the vivisectors ! Oh that we could impress all those Souls within the Churches who truly desire to " *do justly, love mercy, and to walk in humbleness of heart before God.*" and cause them to prayerfully examine the question of the *redemption* in the light of a truly redeemed life whose every way is pure, and is born of love for all Souls as well as for the Divine ! Then would there be a purification of life which would presage a temple presentation such as there has not been upon the planes of this Planet for untold ages.

F

THE DEDICATION

IT will not be difficult now for the reader to understand
how the Christ-child was presented unto the Lord in the
Temple. The presentation in the form of an oblation of the
two turtle-doves, or purified Soul and Mind, was the act of
one who had arrived at the beautiful spiritual experience
indicated by the birth of the Christ-child. The presentation
unto the Lord is a spiritual act, *one that takes place within our
own temple, one that denotes true surrender of the life unto the
divine service*. It speaks of a consecration unto the Lord of all
the powers of our being—Soul, Heart, Mind and Strength
(Body). In its meaning for the blessed Master it was indeed
profound, far, far more so than any human Soul has ever
dreamt.

But its meaning for all Souls is likewise profound. When the
Soul reaches the experience of which it speaks, the consecration
has to be complete. When the Soul and the Mind go up to
Bethlehem, or enter into the life of the redemption, and the
Christ-child is born there, then follows the presentation of the
Christ unto the Lord. The Soul will desire it. The service of
the Divine Love will alone be sought. And the consecration
will be so complete that the life will take up the burden of the
Christhood service, bearing *the cross of self-denial* crowned with
the cross of self-sacrifice, even unto *perfect self-abondonment* to
the divine will.

Could there be anything more beautiful than this picture,
one reaching the state of the redeemed life wherein the Christhood is born within—the Christ-love, the Christ-spirit, the
Christ-purpose leading on to the full Christ-Life ? Is not
the glory of it as the glory of the Lord covering the life, and
making it all beautiful and radiant ? What outward ceremonial

191

could compare with it for spiritual realization ? The gold of such love is a gold purified, and woven into the very garments of life. It is the gold of Ophir which is said to have been woven into the garments of the Queen of Solomon—the consecrated Soul at last attaining unto the Divine Christhood.

Here then is a story rich in lore. It is no eastern fable, as has been affirmed by many. Nor is it of the nature of a myth except in a true spiritual sense, for all myths have had a spiritual fact to build upon. Nor is it outward history except in the blessed revelation of the life. Yet it is very real, and full of the most beautiful truth concerning the experience of the Soul as it moves ever upward towards the fulness of the Divine Life. If any one who reads this unfoldment of its wonderful meaning should doubt its reality, let such an one follow the path of the Christhood as the Master made it manifest in the beautiful life which He lived, then that one will arrive at Bethlehem where the Christ-child will be born within, and he will afterwards seek the temple where the Holy Presence abides (the innermost of the Soul's own spiritual system) to make such an offering unto the Lord as it is said was made by Mary and Joseph.

THE TESTIMONY OF SPIRITUAL THINGS IS IN THEIR REALIZATION.

G

ANNA THE PROPHETESS

IN connection with the presentation of the Christ in the temple it is recorded that a prophetess named Anna blessed the Christ-child, and said that His arising was for the restoration of Israel. It may appear to many as if it were of no value whatever, as a part of the story of the presentation, but only an incidental notice of an unimportant action. But even in it there is also a beautiful significance ; for the prophetess, whose name was Anna, was the discoverer of the nature of the Christ-child and the purpose for which He had been born. It was " the year of the Lord," the manifestation of the Divine Life within the Soul, discovered by the prophetess or the Soul's own Intuition. The Prophet is always the illumined Intuition. When the Divine One has spoken through His prophets, it has been through Souls whose Intuition was open to be illumined from Him. It is the vision of the Soul, the seeing and discerning power within. And it is through that power, when the Soul has attained it, that the Divine One speaks. When the Soul has that power in a large degree, she is a prophet whose light is kindled from the Lord. And the prophetess Anna was the discerning Soul in " the year of the Lord." She knew by inward knowledge the nature of a Christhood. She saw in the Christ-child the birth of the divine consciousness within the Soul which would lead unto the arising of Israel, or all those who once knew the Christhood from experience. The intuition illumined from the Divine Presence is able to see those things which men and women do not see, and to hear those things which they cannot yet hear.

Thus new interest is added to the remarkable story. There are present Maria the mother of the Christ-child ; Ioseph the foster-father ; and then in the temple they are joined by Anna the prophetess. The Soul, the spiritual Mind, and the Intuition. The Soul, *ever Virgin*, bears the Christ who is begotten of the Holy One within her ; the Mind, the reflector of the divine glory unto the Soul, shields her and her new-born one. Then in the sacred temple where the Divine Presence abides, the illumined Intuition, the ever true prophet of the Lord, discerns that it is " the year (Anna) of the Lord," the birth of Christhood in the full stature of which redemption will be found for Israel, and through Israel (or all those who once knew Christhood) for the whole world.

What a presentation it was that took place when the blessed

Master awoke to the consciousness of the Christhood ! What depths of meaning may we not find in the story even as it stands in the third Record ! Who may fathom the " great deep " to the shores of which it leads us when it speaks of the accomplishment of the purification ? For, whilst the story in its more general application speaks of the Soul's experience when it approaches the state of Christhood, the incident was likewise a picture of the awakening of that Soul who gave Himself to be an offering for Sin—that is, to take up the burden implied in the Sin-offering—when the Sin-offering was accomplished, and the purification of Himself from the effects of that offering, and then the presentation of Himself within the temple as " the Son of the Highest." Who may be able to gauge the extent of the work implied in the presentation, all that is meant by " the purification " of Himself, what marvellous changes were wrought by Him in the lives which followed His Christhood, and which made up the Sin-offering process or burden-bearing ? Who can enter into the temple with Him when He presents Himself once more unto the Most High with the sacrifice of the " two turtle-doves " of a purified Mind and Life—that is, purified from all the effects of the burden of the Sin-offering ?

The presentation in the temple which has for so long been associated with the childhood of the Master, had nought to do with Him in his childhood, though it was a picture, not only of the Soul reaching the Christhood act of beautiful consecration to the service of the Divine Love, but also of the return of the Master from Edom where He went to purify the astral kingdom. And instead of it having preceded " the Flight into Egypt " recorded in the first Gospel, it should have followed it. For when He was taken down into Egypt, He was taken into the land of the flesh-pots, the land of oppression, the land of darkness for the Soul, the conditions amid which His sad Sin-offering was borne. And His return from Egypt and Edom, was His return from the conditions represented by these terms, " with garments dyed red " as one who had trodden out the wine, unto the state represented by Nazareth —the despised state, unpopular, accounted as of no good thing, and out of which no good thing could come. And it is in Nazareth that the purification is accomplished, the Soul restored unto the ancient estate when the divine one illumined her ; the Mind restored to its glorious heritage of being able to reflect once more the Light of the Divine Glory ; the Christhood born once more within the Life, and the Intuition once more awakened to behold all the past.

Anna the prophetess is said to have discovered the Christ and the meaning of His birth : once again has the Intuition discerned the true inner meaning of the Christhood of the Soul, and the significance of the Christhood of the Master. Again has the Intuition been able to discern what Christhood implies as to life and service, and the nature of the service rendered by the Christ-Soul when He performed the Sin-offering.

H

THE AGED SIMEON

FOR many years the " Nunc Dimittis " has formed a part of the religious worship of the West. It is beautiful in its archaic expressions, full of that pathos always associated with the sayings of the very aged ones, peaceful in the spirit which it breathes, and sweet with the cadences of a great hope. It is taken to be the inspired utterances of an old man concerning the Christhood, and his quiet confidence in the truth of the things which he uttered.

But the " Nunc Dimittis " has something far more beautiful and profound in its meanings than the Churches have yet recognized. Like the beautiful " Benedictus" and " Magnificat," it contains within itself much of life's history written by the

Soul; and, for the blessed Christ-Soul, it embodies the prophetic vision that the presentation within the temple has been for the salvation of all Souls. It contains within itself something far, far more precious than the outward blessing of an old man upon the Christ-child. It is rich in divine meaning for all who are seeking Christhood, and the whole world of Souls. The eyes which had come to see the " salvation of God " were not of the body only, but the eyes of both the body and the lower mind. For Simeon or Simon meant the lower mind. The mind through which the Mind of the Soul vehicles, was the aged one, one grown old amid the strange ways of the world, one full of that age which comes with the burdens of life, one bowed down with the great weight of experience, such as comes unto the Soul in its passage through the various conditions which beset it upon these outer planes. It was the lower mind and body with all their desires, feelings, ambitions and purposes at last beholding the meaning of *the redemption* and entering into it, seeing the Christhood and blessing it for its saving power, willing at last to take its own part in the glorious redemptive work on behalf of the world. For just as the prophetess was the Intuition discerning " the Year of the Lord," so Simeon was the lower mind discerning the meaning of the Christhood, and rejoicing in the redeemed life which the Christ brought. Simeon was not anxious to depart, as has been wrongly indicated in the story; he was changed, and in his redeemed life was filled with a great and blessed hope. It was the hope of salvation for the whole human race; just as the prophetess was filled with a great hope for the arising of the Christhood Order, or the true Israel.

ITS APPLICATION TO THE MASTER

Such is the meaning of this wonderful incident for all who are seeking unto the attainment of the redeemed life and the realization of the Christhood. But for the beloved one whom we know as the Master, there is even a deeper and further reaching meaning. For Him there is a significance in it more profound than any human Soul may yet enter into, the depth of which none may fathom except those who became like Him in that they shared His burden in the tragic Sin-offering. Indeed no one now may understand the significance of it unless it be given such an one to realize from above. The Soul has borne her burden nobly, that burden the nature of which the world-child is as yet unable to apprehend ; nor even those who are the leaders of religious thought, though these latter guess at its meaning. Within that Soul has the prophetess spoken again, discerning " the Year of the Lord " ; for the Intuition has awakened to perceive the innermost meaning of things. For that beloved one has Simeon at last come to see " the salvation of God " in the arising of the Christhood Order through whom the whole world is to be taught the way of the Lord, even the salvation of the life from every form of evil. It is the age of His return from Egypt to Nazareth, and from Edom to Bozrah—that is, from the land of the sense-life where He has borne His Sin-offering, to the land or state of the redeemed life ; and from the state of spiritual forgetfulness or loss of the divine conscious-ness, unto the realization of Christhood in which that conscious-ness is restored. For in His Regeneration or return from Egypt and Edom, He was to dwell in Nazareth—the despised life which it represents—until the presentation in the temple, when all the beautiful and blessed things implied in the presentation would be realized once more, when both Soul and Mind (as Maria and Ioseph) would attain the estate from which they descended when the sublime Christhood was laid aside, and present themselves unto the Lord in a purified state as two turtle-doves, the symbols of the twofold (feminine and masculine) Divine Nature in the possession of the Divine Love and Divine Wisdom ; and when the Intuition would again awake from its long sleep to perceive " the heavenly secrets " and discern their innermost meanings, knowing what Christ-hood meant, and how it was reached by the Soul ; and when

o

the lower Mind should so purify itself from the evil in the world and enter into the joy of the Christhood life and service before the Divine Love, that it also would come to possess the divine peace.

THE BURIED LORE RECOVERED

Who would have thought that so simple a story associated through all the Christian Era with the outward life of the blessed Master, contained such wealth of meaning both for the Soul in its approach to the divine realization, and for the beloved Master as the Soul who was the bearer of the burden of the Sin-offering ? Who would have dreamt that such an ordinary Jewish narrative (for such is the manner of its presentation) would have possessed within itself one of the most profound incidents in the spiritual unfoldment of our being, and one of the most wonderful incidents in the history of the tragic Sin-offering ? What gems of divine truth the Gospels contain, buried amid the historic stories with which the writers built up an outward picture of the life of the blessed Master ! What precious treasures may be found hidden in the field of the literal story ! What pearls of great price may be discovered by the earnest seeker, in those depths where the shallows of the literal stream are lost through them giving place to the clear, deep, pellucid waters of the Divine Truth where *great fish* (or Mysteries) are to be found, and where *the fishers* (Seekers) find precious pearls ! What a rich increase of the profoundest spiritual truths may be possessed by the Soul from this brief story, when the literal gives way before the discerning vision of *a quickened faith*—faith being the very eye of the Soul, the discerning Intuition !

WHY CANNOT THE CHURCHES SEE ?

We wonder ever more and more what the teachers within

the Churches have been doing all through the Christian Era with this wonderful story, and indeed with all the Birth-stories, not to have discerned something of the inner meanings, not to speak of the innermost significance. We cannot but marvel at the terrible darkness with which all of them have been smitten, and that they should not have discerned the darkness and sought for the light. But we are constrained to marvel most of all at the attitude of the Churches toward the true inward meanings of these stories when they have been presented unto them, the insistence with which they claim for themselves the true knowledge of the meaning of the Birth-stories, though indeed they are full of divisions concerning the exact interpretation to be put upon them. For we know that they are not even open-minded concerning any inner or innermost meanings which these stories contain, and view any suggestion of such inner meanings with suspicion and distrust.

What a sad and sorrowful spectacle it is to behold all the Churches founded in the name of the blessed Master, ostensibly to interpret His glorious Christhood and tragic Sin-offering, grovelling to-day where they have been for the whole of the Christian Era. They remind one of the vision shown in the House of the Interpreter in Bunyan's " Pilgrim's Progress," of the Man with the Rake gathering unto himself all the straws he could find as if they were precious and greatly to be desired, whilst overhead the Crown of Life is held by an Angelic hand which he sees not, so intent is his gaze away from the Heavens. For the teachers in the Churches do gather all the straws of an historical and a literal evidence concerning the Gospel Records as if these were of immortal value, and are always gazing outwards and downwards for more, whilst the Angel of His Presence is unseen by them standing overhead with that crown of gold, the possession of which would enable the seeker and teacher to discern spiritual and divine things, and find the real value of this wonderful story, and all those related to the Master, in the inner and innermost meanings which they contain. When will the spectacle change, and those who ought to know these things cease to look downwards instead of upwards, and outwards rather than inwards ? When will the charm of the literal records grow less in its power to enslave the Soul and blind the Intuition, and the Soul come to behold the grace and power of the sublime spiritual and divine meanings which they contain ?

Brethren, we speak not with words of enticement fashioned by men, nor born of the wisdom of this world, but in words born within us from the Spirit who understandeth and knoweth all things, even the deep things of God.

For the widsom of this world is unto God as the language of the child who must needs learn through objective images the meanings of things not beheld—all which wisdom is foolishness when the outward image is mistaken for the inward signification.

But the wisdom of God, which appeareth as foolishness unto those who account themselves wise in this world, maketh the Soul ever rich when it is discerned by the Spirit of the Lord who is within.

Only unto spiritual men and women can spiritual things be interpreted.

O Love Divine ! Ever glorious and abiding in Thy ways towards all Thy children, ever steadfast and sure in Thy holy purposes, how shall we bless Thee for Thy great goodness ? Through Thee and Thee alone have we been found again and brought back to the land of the Soul, that land so full of angelic light, life and love. It was of Thy seeking that we were found ; it is of Thy goodness

200

that the darkness has passed and the light been broken. It is of Thy gentleness that we have found healing, and through Thy grace we have gained strength. It is because of Thy approach unto us that the inward vision has been restored, and the wonderful mystery of Thy Love and Wisdom has been made to unfold itself unto us. We pray that our life may be a Living Psalm for Thee in the blessed service of our ministry.

Amen and Amen.

PART III.

Allegories of the Soul

In Cana of Galilee

*Being no physical miracle performed at an earthly
Marriage Festival, but an allegory of the Soul's
Marriage to her Divine Lord when she enters
into Christhood and attains to such union
with the Divine that she has the
power within her to change the
waters or truths which
were for purification,
into the Wine
of Christ-
hood.*

A

THE MYSTERIES UNVEILED

" THE Lord maketh all things new : He taketh away the
letter to establish the Spirit."

The first miracle said to have been performed by the Master
was the turning of water into wine at the marriage feast in
Cana of Galilee. The story is well known to every reader of
the fourth Gospel. It is classed amongst the remarkable works
of the Master, and has often been made use of to prove His
divine power. How strange it seems to one who knows wherein
that divine power lay, that spiritual men and women should
require any such evidence of the divinity within the Master,
that they should for a moment imagine that the outward powers
of any one were testimonies to commensurate powers within !

Many of the greatest wonder-workers in the world have
been far removed from the attainment of divine love and life.
Where world-power has most triumphantly manifested itself,
spiritual power has been most conspicuously absent. To seek
for great outward signs and wonders in the Master's life as the
testimony of His divine nature, is to reveal the sad truth that
the seekers do not understand the nature of Christhood. If
they knew what a beautiful spiritual state it implies, they would
not be seekers after outward signs. Nor would they be filled
with alarm when the outward works, supposed to have been
wrought by the blessed Master, were attacked by rationalism
in its varied forms ; but they would look deeper than the outward
phenomena to see if there were not some hidden meanings
to be found in the narrative. They would know that a Christhood meant the interpretation of the Divine Wisdom as well
as the manifestation of the Divine Love ; and that that Wisdom
had to be embodied in such a fashion as would prevent those
who were not in a state to receive its holy meanings, from
understanding it before they were prepared, lest they should

make a wrong use of it. Is not this the reason why it is said the Master spake unto the people in parables, and that without a parable spake He not unto them? And what was true of any general public ministry which He gave, was equally true of the Teachings which He gave to the inner group of disciples. How frequently it is reported that they wondered what He could mean. There is an impression abroad in the Churches, and indeed outside of them, that the profound Mysteries of the Kingdom of Heaven unfolded by the Master, were such as anyone, without preparation, could understand. But the teachings given by Him which anyone could easily understand, were those concerning the purification of life, the path of the redeemed life, the realization of the redemption by all who followed that path. And it was only after a disciple followed that path that he could fit himself to receive the meanings of the profound Mysteries of the Divine Love and Wisdom.

To Whom the Mysteries were made Known

Somehow these palpable truths seem to be entirely overlooked where naturally we should most have expected them to be understood. So many are there who not only profess to earnestly seek after the Divine Wisdom, but who are on the path now which leads unto the light of that Wisdom, who yet speak and write concerning the Teachings of the Master as if they had all been gladly received by the people generally, and readily understood by them. Unto the inner group of the disciples was it given *to know the Mysteries of the Kingdom ;* but not unto the multitude, nor the Scribes, nor the literalists of those times. In the natural fitness of things there had to be preparation through purification of all the ways of the outward life, and the intuitive perception of spiritual and divine things. Men and women had eyes to see and ears to hear, yet heard and saw not, *because the conditions about them and within them made it impossible.* Even to the inner group of the disciples some of the most profound teachings were spoken in the form of allegory.

The story of the marriage feast at which the water was turned into wine is of that order. It was not an outward incident in the experience of the blessed Master, but an inward glorious realization for Him in the Manifestation of the Christhood: that in the first place. And, in the second place, it was a beautiful illustration of the spiritual power acquired by the disciple who was approaching Christhood, namely, the power to turn the water of truth into the wine of God. It was the first work which the Master is said to have wrought after the baptism of the Spirit; and it is the first work wrought by the disciple after he has been baptized with the Divine Spirit. The miracle concerns the Divine Love within the disciple. It is accomplished through the Christ; and it is the manifestation of the power of Christhood.

How beautifully it illustrates that power will be seen as we unfold the meaning of the allegory. We shall find ourselves carried far from the literalism that blinds the intuition and buries the precious treasure out of the Soul's sight, into a region where the air is rarefied, and the vision is clear and wonderful. Angels walk whither we are led by the story. The winds of the spiritual heavens are wafted to us. " The Holy Breath " is felt, with all its harmonizing and peace-giving influence. For the marriage in Cana of Galilee is a beautiful function of the inner life of the disciple, in the performance of which the Christhood will be made manifest.

B

THE MARRIAGE FESTIVAL

" WITHIN thee, O man, is the Universe; the thrones of all the Gods are in thy temple."

What could this festival be but the marriage of the Soul?

For after the baptism with the Divine Spirit the Soul becomes, as it were, married to the Divine. That is, the Soul in all its beautiful aspirations, desires and purposes, becomes divine. It is no longer only potentially divine in its nature, it has unfolded and become divine. It has attained its At-one-ment. Henceforth it is one with the Divine. It will henceforth live only for the Highest. It will think divinely, feel divinely, love divinely, serve divinely. Its joy will be the Joy of God ; its gladness will be the gladness of one who knows the Lord ; its love will be as the Love of God ; and its sorrow will be even as the divine sorrow over those of His children who have gone far afield like the lost sheep in the wilderness.

The marriage of the Soul is one of the most wonderful events in its history, far more wonderful than any one or any language can adequately describe. There are depths of meaning in it which are unutterable, so blessed are they. There are ecstasies born of the sublime realizations which cannot be expressed by any terms.

But there are likewise griefs unspeakable to be borne as the Soul enters into the realizations of the past history of humanity and the Planet, and indeed of the entire system of Sol. For, when the Soul is married unto the Divine One, it knows divinely. It sees from the divine kingdom all things in their true relationships. The vision is a true one, for it is begotten of the divine consciousness unto which the Soul has attained. There is no wrong perspective. The meaning of things is clear. The light of the Divine Wisdom shines within the sanctuary. It is even as one who has set out to climb a lofty mountain, rising up out of the valley and gradually reaching the various stages in the ascent, passing upward, still upward, with an ever-extending horizon, beholding the vision to be had in the valley, but also the greater vision of the ever-widening outlook, until having reached the summit the climber beholds all that may be seen from that height as he stands amid the rarefied conditions and the glory of a cloudless sky ; for the Soul who has climbed to that blessed estate when it is said to be married unto the Lord, has reached that lofty summit where the atmosphere is that of the angelic world, and the light is the glory of the Divine.

The vision then is of the very highest. It is of the most extended nature. It is most glorious in that it takes in the Angelic World, and even still greater things. It truly reveals the divine purpose. It makes manifest the works of the Father in their true nature. It shows to such a Soul the beautiful creative processes, and the wonderful issues. And the vision reveals the true past of the Planet. It shows to the Soul how that past was also glorious, as all the works of the Divine One are. The vision takes the Soul back to the time when the Gods walked upon the earth, and slept not ; when the footsteps of angels were often heard, and their beautiful ministry unto the children upon the Planet was well known and felt ; when the life upon all the planes of the world was unsullied, and all experience was pure and beautiful ; when the whole earth rang with the laughter of unalloyed joy, and the Soul was full of music and gladness.

AN ALLEGORY OF THE SOUL

But, alas ! the vision has also its dark side ; for it makes to pass before the Soul in dioramic pictures, not only the past glory, but likewise the passing away of that glory and the coming of the awful darkness, sorrow and woe into the life of the Planet and all her children. All things are made clear in that blessed altitude. The meaning of the terrible history written upon the various kingdoms and planes of the Planet is understood. The true interpretation is at hand to the Soul. It knows from the Divine Presence within. And it knows how the redemption of the Planet and all her children can alone be accomplished.

Such is the vision that breaks upon the Soul of the disciple who has entered fully into the blessed relationship implied in this story. And so we have presented in the allegory of the marriage in Cana of Galilee a profound Soul-mystery that cannot be understood in its sublime meaning except by those who have entered into the realization.

The story is fraught with great blessing of good. For the festival is no mere earthly experience. It is the Soul as the Bride receiving the Divine Bridegroom. It is the festival within the sanctuary or innermost of the Soul, " the guest chamber " of the Lord, the Upper Room where even the Pascal Lamb is partaken of. The company are all heavenly, as we shall see. The rejoicing is angelic. The wine drunk is the wine of divine joy, the new vintage within the Soul. The wonderful work wrought by the Christ is another wine, said to be the best, and partaken of only after the other has been well drunk of.

How beautiful it all is ! How wonderful the actors are as they stand out before the vision ! O the transcendent meaning of the allegory ! How everything literal pales before its glory ! How the earthly setting of it forth seems so poor, so inadequate, when the sublime experience is realized ! What words were ever found sufficient to express a great and beautiful love ? Has language yet been found adequate to perfectly interpret the yearnings of a Soul ? What symbolism was ever invented that could fully illustrate the profound realizations within as the disciple of Christhood approaches the height implied in the divine marriage ? All are inadequate—pen and brush and tongue. All are insufficient—story, symbol and picture. To know it is to have entered into the realization of it.

C

THE REQUEST OF MARY

" GIVE me to drink of the wine of thy Cup, that I may live for evermore."

In the story it is represented that Mary the mother of the

Master approached Him with the information that there was no wine ; and, though it is not stated, yet is it implied, that she suggested to Him to perform a miracle and provide wine for them. And it is represented that the Master rebuked her, saying, " *Woman, what have I to do with thee ? Mine hour is not yet come.*"

If this had been literally true, what a very different aspect it would have given to the meaning of Christhood. Indeed it would have destroyed the Christhood of the Master. It would have been such a manifestation of power as would not only have been other than consonant with His Christhood, but would have been diametrically opposed to it. For Christhood powers are of a divine order, and therefore could not be exercised in such a way nor under the conditions implied, had the story been literal. For the guests had all drunk the wine provided ; and no divine work could ever be accomplished under the excitation arising from the imbibing of wine. The very conditions would all be non-spiritual. The atmosphere would militate against the Soul, its divine vision, and all its powers.

Many do not seem to apprehend this most elementary truth that, for the unfoldment of true Soul-life, there must be true and pure conditions, and that these conditions are generated from true spiritual aspiration, desire and purpose, and that these alone make for the realization of the consciousness of the Divine Presence. They have an idea that a Christhood can work miracles with the elements by changing them at will for any such purpose as is here implied in the literal story, just like an occultist who uses his Soul-powers to work wonders for personal ends, or a magician who sets out to entertain the public with wonderful works of illusion. To them Christhood powers seem to be like the outward powers of those who have great dominancy in the elemental kingdoms, rather than beautiful spiritual and divine attributes whose influence over the elements is only unto purification and rectification of equilibrium. The powers of a Christ could not destroy the nature of the elements ; nor could one in the state of Christhood make use of any of them to create what would undoubtedly be injurious to body, mind and life. Water when pure is a most valuable element ; but its value is lessened as its original properties are changed. And as regards wine, the purity and uses of the water are destroyed through the other dominating destructive element. It is, therefore, quite certain that the Christ could not have provided such an element as wine ; that He could never have made use of His sublime powers to create anything destructive of the very life of the Soul ; that He could not have countenanced in any way the creation of wine, nor its uses. Nor could the Mother of Christhood have suggested any such step.

The beloved Master has indeed been greatly and grievously misrepresented ; and His earthly mother knew Him too well, and loved Him too devotedly, to have ever suggested to Him a way of action which would have been a betrayal of the beautiful Christhood which He had to make manifest.

THE VIRGIN SOUL

Yet is there a great truth contained in the story to be discovered and unfolded. It is a truth whose very preciousness makes it somewhat difficult to write of. It is of the *innermost*. Who is Mary ? Have we not already spoken of the wonderful meanings contained in the term Marias ? Have we not also pointed out the profound yet sublime significance of the saying that she was Virgin when she bore the Christ ? The blessed Virgin Mary is no mean term, though its wonderful significance has long been lost. Its sublime meaning was bemeaned through being materialized and made personal. For Mary is the Soul who has borne the Christ (the Soul who has attained to Christhood). She is " the Mother of the Lord " within the sanctuary ; for it is only through her (the Soul) that the blessed consciousness of the Divine Love and Wisdom can be realized, and the divine vision beheld. She has to be virgin to bring about such an exalted realization : that is, *her elements must all be virgin or pure.* And she must desire to be the channel for the manifestation of the divine life. It is her service in life to first bring forth the Christ-child, to nourish it and guard it, to see that the new life grows up into the full stature of the manhood of Christhood ; and then it is her province to follow the Christ whithersoever He goeth, that is, whithersoever the state of Christhood may take the Soul in the service of the Highest.

O the wealth of divine meaning underlying this story of The Marriage in Cana of Galilee ! The wonderful history of the disciple which is silently implied in the allegory, who would have imagined it ? How full and rich in blessing is the picture for all who see its remarkable inward beauty and seek unto the realization of that ? How blessed to be able to gaze upon the picture and see nothing of its outward historical setting, but only that drama of our inner life, whose blessed realizations it represents ?

THE MEANING OF MARY'S REQUEST

Let us now look at the counsel given by Mary to the Christ. And as we do so, surely for you, reader, the Light of Heaven will now shine upon the saying ! Surely for you the outer curtain will move aside to reveal the inner glory !

The feast has been held ; the marriage has been accomplished ; the wine of the divine joy has been drunk. This would have seemed sufficient under any other circumstances. But not so with the Soul, from whom Christhood is born and by whom it is nourished. She knows the Christhood is not yet made manifest, and she would fain behold it in manifestation. The Soul longs to be in the state of manifested Christhood ; not simply to have attained the marriage, and have drunk deeply of the wine of divine joy which it brings, but also to be in a position such as the Christhood implies of divine manifestation, in order that she may show forth the power and glory of the estate. Her very love for the Christhood is the cause of her extreme anxiety to know that He is manifesting Himself. And such is the meaning of the request which it is said Mary the mother made to her son, the Christ. She desired Him to provide new wine, to do the works of Christhood. But He said unto her, " Woman, what have I to do with thee ? Mine hour is not yet come." The reply is just as significant as the request. It likewise is full of deep meaning. It is no rebuke, as it might at first sight seem ; it is rather a question of inquiry, and an explanation when the works desired were not wrought at once. What is to be done with the Soul that so longs after the manifestation, that it is disturbed and restless because the wine of the divine joy has been drunk, and there is no more wine to take ? What is to be done with the Soul who, having drunk deeply of that wine of joy, is now impatient to have the full manifestation of the power and glory of Christhood ? She feels within herself as if she could not wait in patience for the manifestation to come. Yet must she wait in patience until the hour of the manifestation has come when the Lord (the Divine One) shall reveal Himself, and turn the water-pots into vessels full of the most precious wine of the Wisdom of God.

O wondrous truth for the disciple whose desires are all aflame with the energy of divine passion, whose holy yearnings find no fulness of satiety, whose one purpose is to live only for the Divine Love ! First, fulness of inward realization of the Divine Presence ; then the nuptials which make the Soul and the Divine within, One ; then the divine joy begotten of the realization of the Love and Wisdom of the Father, the deep draughts of the Wine of God ; and then the manifestation of the Lord in the power and glory of Christhood ! The water will now be turned into wine that all may drink of the wine of Christhood, and rejoice that it has been kept until the last.

D

TURNING THE WATER INTO WINE

" **B**UT that Scripture is the more excellent which is exceeding fruitful and brings forth abundant signification."

Then the Christ, when His hour was come, commanded that they should fill all the water-pots to the brim. And when they drew it forth to serve, behold it was wine. For the hour was come when the Christ should be made manifest, the hour in which He should accomplish His first great work. It was, therefore, *the hour of Divine Manifestation through the Soul*. The hour was come when the yearnings of the Soul could be satisfied ; when the blessed and holy cravings for realization in service could be acceded to ; when the almost impatient longings after an outward Christhood ministry might find fulfilment ; when the power and the glory of Christhood should be revealed and interpreted.

Such is the experience of the Soul who attains to the divine state represented by the Marriage. The story in the fourth Gospel is an allegory of the history of the Soul as it enters upon the blessed estate of Christhood when there is real conscious union with the Father-Mother Life. It illustrates that union, and the power and glory begotten of it. It is, therefore, a picture of our own history ; of the way our life passes in its upwardness and inwardness of experience ; of the consummation which comes through treading the path to Christhood, and the realization of the divine within the Soul's sanctuary. It is a picture of the sublime life unto which *all Souls* are called ; a grouping together, for the purpose of embodiment, of the most wonderful experiences which can come into a man's life, experiences which are all quite separate and distinct, though so closely related to one another. In words it is like one of the finest embodiments in art wrought by one of the great spiritual artists, in which he groups together for some historic purpose, several events all quite separate in their order, but all dependent one upon another.

This truth becomes more and more salient as we unfold its inner significances. How obvious are the meanings of even the details as, in true perspective, the history of the marriage of the Soul to the Divine appears before the vision. The mother of the Christhood may direct all the servants to obey the Christ when He giveth instruction, and the request is fulfilled. For who are those servants within the house where the marriage feast is prepared ? Who are they who wait upon the Lord of the festival to perform His will ? Who are they, if they be not the powers of the body, mind and life ? the powers of the Soul itself upon the various spheres of its system ? For are not these the servants of the Lord in any one seeking to attain to the blessed union implied in the marriage of the Soul ? *Are not all the powers of the life—those of the body, those of the intellectual mind, those of the spiritual or intuitional mind, and those of the love-principle of the Soul itself—consecrated unto divine uses as the disciple enters into true divine union ?* These are the servants who ever wait upon their Lord to do His will. For that purpose are they within the spiritual household of the Soul.

O joy, joy divine, to behold even this meaning of life within the allegory ! For it speaks in a language so very different to the language of men and women concerning the purpose of all the functions of the body, mind, heart and Soul. It reveals what their office in the Soul's ministry should be ; and it implies their beautiful obedience to the divine way. They know no will but His. They hear no voice to obey it, but His. Mary as the Soul in the state of union with the Divine Life, is the expression of His image and the interpreter of His purposes. And the Christhood is the fulfilment of the Soul's life, the crown of its evolution, the consciousness of such heavenly union when henceforth it is the Father who speaks *within and through* the Soul. It is the Father Himself who does the wonderful works of spiritual interpretation of the Mysteries, causing His Light, Life and Love to break upon the world with their healing, redeeming and perfecting power.

THE SIX WATERPOTS

Surely herein does the mystery of the Soul deepen and the divine wealth within her multiply ! For the marvellous nature of the Soul is seen more and more as the powers within are unfolded, the realizations of life are entered into, and their meaning is interpreted. And the mystery is only made the more profound, and the nature of the Soul seen to be yet more wonderful, when the command of the Christ within is issued to fill all the water-pots unto the brim, that He may work the works of God by turning the water into the wine of Christhood. For, to fill the water-pots with water until they are full to the brim, is to fill the whole system of the Soul with the waters of truth, the waters which are for purification first, and then, at the marriage feast, for the wine of Christhood.

There were six water-pots. And these speak of the various spheres of the Soul which lie toward the outward life which must needs be purified ere an entrance is effected into the guest chamber ; meaning by that, that the divine realizations implied in the marriage of the Soul, cannot be entered into until the life upon every sphere is purified by means of the waters of truth, the cleansing power of the Divine One within. *The outer spheres must be purified ere the inner life can come into the blessedness of divine union.* And when that is done, and the marriage is accomplished, the hour of manifestation arrives when the whole being upon all spheres is filled with the beautiful waters of divine truth, now to be used for the sacred purpose of meeting the new needs of the Soul. For the waters of truth are not only expressive of the cleansing of the life through the operative power of the Divine Spirit, but they are likewise expressive of the life-giving power of love. Hence the expressions met with in sacred literature concerning " the river of life " flowing from beneath the divine altar, or from the heavenly throne, or from the east gate of the temple.

To turn the water into wine, even the wine of Christhood, is to be able to show that the waters or truths with which the mind is furnished and enriched, are in very deed the wine of God, the light of His holy wisdom, the interpreter of His holy purpose, the meaning of His holy will for and concerning the Soul, the Planet, and the whole spiritual system of Sol. It is to make the Divine Love towards all Souls a reality, by revealing what is meant by that Love in the ways and service of life, It is to know and interpret the " mysteries of the kingdom"; to bring out of the barren rocks of the letter the living waters for refreshment ; to reveal the glory of the Divine Love through unfolding the beautiful divine purpose ; to illumine the history of the Soul and the Planet with the light which breaks from Him, that these may be beheld in their true light, and be understood even where they appear to be most contradictory ; to work the works of God in changing the intellectual apprehension of the truth into a Soul knowledge of things divine. To be able to change the water into wine means that the Soul has arrived at that experience in which it not only sees divinely, and knows divinely, but is able to interpret divinely " the hidden wisdom of God," and so to provide the wine of life, the wine of Christhood, the wine of the Divine Power, the wine of the Divine Love, the holiest, the most exhilarating, the most inspiring cup of blessing for the refreshment, the inspiration, and the illumination of all who would themselves partake of that marriage feast of the union of the Soul with the Divine Life.

O Life most blessed ! O work most gracious ! O transcendent experience ! To know the joy of God in a blessed Soul-union ; to drink deeply of the wine of that joy ; to long for the fulfilment

of the Christhood of which it speaks and is the precursor ;
to have that fulfilment at last in the blessed work of changing
the water of truth into the very elements of the vine, the Divine
Love—that is indeed Life ! And it is unto such a Life the
allegory of the marriage in Cana of Galilee calls us.

E

THE CHRISTHOOD MANIFESTED

" NOW the Kingdom of God is with us ; that is, it is interior,
invisible, mystic, spiritual."

The Christhood has again been manifested in Cana of Galilee ;
and it has been manifested in turning the water into wine.
It has been manifested in the little city of the Soul, *the
spiritual mind ;* for the Intuition has once more recovered its
power to perceive the inner meaning of things, to behold the
true nature of a Christhood, to discern wherein the Christ-
power lies, and to understand what that power is. For the
spiritual mind is Galilee itself whose calm clear waters ever
reflect the Heavens above them, and whose uplands are the
homes of angels, " the hills " and " the mountains of God."

And the little city of Cana in Galilee where *the spiritual
vision* is found, is that spiritual state in which there comes
to the Soul the power to perceive heavenly secrets, to enter
into their meaning, and to thus bring into the consciousness
the treasures of the Divine Wisdom.

The manifestation of the Christhood is, therefore, *in Cana
of Galilee ;* because it is through the intuitive perception of
the Soul that the manifestation of Christhood is recognised.
And it is in Cana of Galilee that the marriage festival takes
place ; for it is through the Soul's perception of the nature
of the divine life within herself, and the Christhood fulness
unto which she is to attain, that enables her to rise ever higher
and higher into heavenly conditions, until the day arrives

when she is able to enter into the blessed state expressed in her marriage to the Divine Lord.

And the Christhood is manifested in the first great work of turning water into wine. For the work of God is wrought in changing what were only waters for purification, into the wine of God. The truth within the life has accomplished its first mission, that of the purification of the whole life unto its perfect redemption from all the dominating influences of the world spirit and the sense-life ; and the Soul enters upon its sublime experiences of Christhood, and progresses in that state until it is fully united unto the Divine Life : is, indeed, one with the Divine Lord. Then comes the manifestation ; for the truth that cleansed is changed into the truth that inspires. The water that refreshed the travel-stained life becomes the wine of Life. The water which was for the healing of the life, is changed into the wine of God whose cup is precious, sparkling as it does like the very vintage of the Gods. It is the very life-stream of the divine within the Soul by which all her pulses are quickened in their heavenward motion, and she at last comes to be filled with the powers of the Divine. It is the wine that fills the cup of the Immortals, whose fragrance is sweet as the Breath of the Eternal and Ever-Blessed One, with whose Love and Wisdom it enriches the Soul.

O Love Divine, ever blessed and glorious, what hidden depths of meaning are to be found in Thee ! What fulness of Life for all Thy children ! What intensity of Life for all who are able to receive of Thy fulness ! What awe-inspiring heights and splendour of vision and realization, are possible unto those who drink deeply of the Wine of Thy Love ! How vast is the vision which breaks upon all who climb these heights ! How immeasurable is the outlook that opens unto the disciple who has attained to these transcendent spiritual altitudes ! How wonderful are all Thy ways towards Thy children ! How great is the sum of Thy thoughts unto them !

" *What is Man ? Thou art so mindful of him !* " *Through the Son of Man (the Christhood) in whom Thou visitest him, Thou crownest him with honour and glory. Thou dost give unto him a knowledge which is divine. Thou revealest unto him the wonderful works of Thy hands. Thou makest known the secrets of Thy Counsel concerning the Life unto which Thou hast called him. Before his vision Thou unveilest the past so that he may behold it in " the light of Thy Wisdom." The earth and the fulness thereof as these once were, Thou showest unto him, and makest known what Thy perfect works were, and how wonderful and beautiful Thy holy purpose was. In the blessedness of " her former glory " Thou unveilest the Holy City of Jerusalem (The Planet) unto his vision, that glory which she had ere the stranger (the evil conditions) laid low all her beautiful terraces (planes) and palaces (the dwelling places of all the Human Race). And Thou revealest it unto him how that glory is to be again restored when the redemption of all her children is accomplished. Thou dost graciously unveil to him the mystery of the Soul so that he knoweth henceforth the meaning of her going away, and the way Thou hast taken to restore her once more to her ancient heritage.*

How exalted, holy and blessed are Thy ways ! O that all Thy children could know Thee as Thou art, and behold how beautiful Thy purposes always are ; that all of them could even now drink of the Wine of Thy Love and know the power which it imparts ; that all men and women could now understand the holy and blessed mystery of the Soul's nature, and the end for which Thou didst fashion it ; that they were able to enter into the realization of Thy Love as found in the redeemed life; that all who have reached the redeemed life could now enter into Cana of Galilee for the marriage there, to drink of the Joy of God, to understand the yearnings of the Soul, Mary, for the manifestation of the Christhood power, and then to realize the unspeakable blessedness when the disciple in Christhood is able to change the waters of truth into the wine, and drink the cup of the Immortals !

And what shall we wish for the Churches whose citizens should have known these things ; whose mission it should have been to realize them with an ever-increasing fulness, and then to have made the glory of them manifest in the ways and service of life ? How shall we show to these all the things they should have known, and the blessedness and glory they have missed ? For them we would pray that *the threefold veil* which now darkens their vision may be drawn aside :—namely,

The Veil of Blood, even the blood of the creatures which they still have shed upon the altars of their desires, their tastes, and that they may put from them this abomination of slaying the creatures, and partaking of their flesh :

The Veil of Idolatry, the veil generated as the outcome of worshipping material things in any form, the earthward things ; the literalism that destroys the spirit, the form that obscures the substance, the outward in place of the inward :

The Veil of Materialism, that which has arisen to blind the Intuition and deprive the Soul of her vision ; that has made faith a thing of belief and forms, instead of the power to understand the substance of all things ; that has changed the very nature of life for the Soul, placed her in gross darkness, and caused her to walk along wrong paths ; that has made it impossible for the Divine One within to make Himself manifest, or the light upon the altar of the innermost to throw out its rays through the spheres of life.

These three veils still shut out the Churches from the realizations of Cana in Galilee and the Christhood vision. Nor can the blessed realizations come to them until these veils are put away.

F

THE WINE OF CHRISTHOOD

" I have said unto men, ye are Gods ; ye are all in the Image of the most High."

When the servants of the household wherein the marriage was celebrated, drew the new wine which had been created out of the water, and gave it unto the Governor or Lord of the marriage festival, he is said to have proclaimed it the best, though, contrary to usage, it had come last. But is it not ever so with the Divine Love ? His blessings increase as the Soul rises in the scale of life. The realizations are more and more profound as the Mount of God is climbed. The glory and blessedness intensify the nearer the disciple approaches the Divine Kingdom. The powers of God within become ever greater as the Soul in its ascent takes height after height. The Wine of God which fills life's cup is stronger as the Life takes unto herself " the crown of the Immortals." It is " life abundant " for the one who is able to drink abundantly. It is life that grows from glory to glory the more abundantly it is realized.

Who is the Governor of the Feast who recognizes the difference in the Wine ? Is He not the Lord Himself whose dwelling is within the sanctuary, the Lord of the marriage festival, the Divine Presence within the Soul when fully unfolded ? Who but He could recognize the change from the wine of the marriage festival when first it was celebrated, to the wine of the Christ-hood manifestation ? Could any one but He distinguish between the wine of the joy of God drunk at the union of the Soul with the Divine Life, and the wine of the power of God drunk at the manifestation of the Christhood in accomplishing His first work ?

And so we may perceive the meaning of the best wine being

kept until the last, the end of the feast. For the wine of the divine power created by the Christhood in manifestation, is far, far stronger and better than the wine of the marriage festival, the joy of God. Joy, divine joy, wells up within the household of the Soul when the marriage with the Divine Life is accomplished ; and unto the Soul it would seem as if there could be no wine to equal it, not to think of any wine that could surpass it. Yet in the history of the Soul's growth Godward, the wine of Christhood which comes last is far more transcendent in its power ; for it is not only the realization of the Divine Life but the attainment of that life with full power. That is the best wine which cometh last after the other has been well drunk. The Christhood manifestation is the highest. It can only appear within the Soul as the result of the marriage with the Divine.

Nor is the manifestation to be confounded with the birth of the Christ-child within ; for that is a much earlier event. The manifestation in Cana of Galilee is *the attaining to manhood*. There are yet greater works to be wrought, other manifestations of the divine power to be given when the hour for them has come ; for Christhood has likewise many stages between early manhood and that sublime realization of divine fulness of being unto which the blessed Master called all Souls. There is in the Christhood unfoldment a vast difference between the manifestation in Cana of Galilee, and that in the Upper Room where He washes the feet of the disciples and wipes them with the towel with which He is girt. For in the work of changing the water into wine, He becomes the Interpreter of the Divine Love and Wisdom ; but, in washing the feet of the disciples, He becomes the Redeemer. In the first work He reveals the divine power within Him ; in the last He reveals that power as the very Divine Love itself. In the former He changes the truths for the life into truths for the Soul ; in the other He changes the life within the Soul into life for redemptive purposes. In the first work, the waters provided for purification are changed into Soul-inspiration ; in the last work, the blessed life attained in the fulness of divine power is given to accomplish the Redemption of the human race. And if the mystery in the first work be great, how much greater is the mystery of the last ?

Thus much do we write that there may be no misunderstanding of the profound meaning implied in Christhood for the Soul, and very specially in the Christhood of the beloved Master. *The Christ-child must not be mistaken for the Christ-man ; nor must early Christ-manhood be interpreted in its works as the same Christhood when crowned with " fulness of days."* " The fulness of days " implies a wealth of wisdom and service far outreaching the wisdom and service of early manhood. It signifies that that Soul is even as one of the ancients seen around the throne of the Ever Blessed One, patriarchs indeed, disciples whose vision and service transcend even those upon the angelic kingdom. For thus do the Christs who are appointed to accomplish the work of Redeemers, behold with a vision and serve with a service transcending the vision and service of Souls who have only celebrated the marriage feast and accomplished their first work of turning the waters of purification into the wine of divine power.

Thus it will be seen that the degrees in the realization of Christhood are as great as the degrees in the service of life.

G

MANIFESTING HIS GLORY

" THE Manifestations are inward ; and the spirits which speak unto thee are of thine own kingdom."

We have seen what is meant by the divine marriage within the Soul, and the manifestation of the divine power of Christhood in changing the waters of purification into the wine of God. Now we have to behold the glory of the manifestation. The wine of the feast was crowned with the wine of Christhood, and the manifested divine power was crowned with the manifested divine glory. The divine power was shown forth in the Christhood when the new wine was created for the Soul to drink—the new wine of a pure spiritual interpretation of its own history, nature and life ; and the divine glory is now revealing itself in the interpretation being given of the divine purpose in the Soul's history and redemption, and *the true* meaning and vision of the Christhood unto which it is called. The divine glory has been obscured for untold ages, indeed ever since the passing away of the Christhood made manifest through the beloved Master. It was early eclipsed by the false view of the manifestation which was presented to those groups who formed themselves into Churches, to all who were influenced in their thought by the Pauline letters, and finally by the equally erroneous view that was sent forth by the writers of the four Gospels.

But that glory is once more making itself manifest in the Teachings concerning the Divine Love and Divine Wisdom which are now being restored. The divine power of the Christhood was witnessed in the changing of those waters or truths which had been given by the Master as the baptism of John— the baptism unto purification of life ; and the divine glory of the Christhood was made manifest in the unfoldment of the divine mysteries known as " the Greater Mysteries "—the Mysteries connected with the divine purpose, the nature and operation of the Divine Love, the history of the Soul, the past of the Planet, the history of the Redemption, and the coming of the Regeneration and Restoration. The baptism of John, the purification of life through the waters of truth, was for all Souls ; the changing of the waters into the new best wine was only revealed unto those who were within the household where the marriage took place and the festival was held ; but only unto those who were of the innermost circle of the disciples, was the glory of the Christhood made manifest.

" *How is it Thou dost manifest Thyself unto us, and not unto the world ?* " What a wealth of meaning there is couched in the question as seen in the light of our unfoldment ? And the like truth breaks upon the Soul to-day. The purification through the baptism of John is for all. Unto it must all would-be disciples of the Christhood come. Through its experience must all pass. Without it there can be no realization of any degree of Christhood, and, consequently, no attainment of the marriage of the Soul unto the Divine Life. The wine of the divine joy is for all who are able to enter upon the experience of the marriage of the Soul with the Divine Life. The wine of Christhood—the wine of the divine power—is only for those who have passed through the realizations of " the marriage feast," and who have prepared themselves for the more profound realizations. And unto them only is the divine glory made manifest in the Christhood.

DEGREES OF THE CHRISTHOOD

We have said that the Christhood was as varied in the degrees of its realization, as the experience of life is of manifold degrees. Perhaps this will enable all who are looking out for the return of the Christhood to recognise the many degrees of spiritual unfoldment in these days as the various expressions of the degree of Christhood. For *the return* is with us, and the Christhood is being restored. The Divine One, the Adonai, the everlasting and overshadowing Christ, is making Himself manifest in every state of spiritual experience, according as the Soul is able to receive Him. Through the baptism of John unto purification of life He is preparing the multitude for the larger life. The various purification movements all testify of His coming again. In the baptism of the Holy Spirit unto illumination of the Soul with the inward divine light, He is returning in the Christhood of Souls. The new light breaking everywhere testifies to His approach. As the wonder-working Christ is He coming again unto all who are able to receive Him. The divine power of the Christhood, revealed in the spiritual interpretations of the purpose of all life and all service, bear rich testimony to this truth. And He is also coming in His glory unto those who are in the spiritual state to receive the divine vision. Of this the unfoldments concerning the inner history of the Soul and the Planet ; concerning the very nature of the Soul and the Planet ; concerning the original condition of them both, and the beautiful purpose of the Divine Love towards them at all times ; concerning the presence of evil in the world and the Redemption from it through the operation of the Divine Love ; concerning the Regeneration when all Souls should enter into their own ancient inheritance, and the Restitution of all things when this complete planetary system of Sol will be restored to its pristine glory—these all speak of the re-manifestation of His glory, the glory of the ever-Blessed One made once more manifest *in the New Interpretation of the Wisdom of God which has been hidden for ages.*

Marvellous are Thy ways, O Lord of the Heavenly Hosts ! Blessed and glorious art Thou. Who is like unto Thee ?

H

THE WORKS OF CHRISTHOOD

" FOR the Interpretation of hidden things is at hand ; and man shall eat of the precious fruits of God."

The first works of the Christ have again been wrought. He has come for whom all Souls long. Into Himself has He gathered up all the messages of all the Messengers sent forth from the Divine Kingdom. The work of purification has revealed His presence. The voice of one crying in the wilderness unto Souls to prepare for His coming, has been the testimony of His approach. The awakening of Souls is made manifest in the numbers who have sought for the baptism of John with the waters of the Jordan—a baptism unto repentance from evil and purification of the ways of life, and one which speaks of the awakening within the breasts of many of that true humane feeling which makes the Soul to see the awful systems of eating the flesh of the creatures and afflicting them in the name of God, to be an inhuman, unspiritual and wicked thing, and something to be put away from them. For the new Humane Movement manifest in all in whom it is the outcome of a truer, purer and nobler vision of life, is the living palpitating testimony that the first part of the Christhood return is being accomplished, that the way into the larger kingdom of life is being proclaimed, that the first path in the way of the Christhood is affording many the joy of the redeemed state. In this way may it be truly said that the Buddha has come to the West also ; for the Christhood contained Buddha in the days of the Master, was indeed first of all a repetition of the work of Gautama—a work of purification.

And such is it to-day. In the return of the Christhood in the work of purification of the life as the path to be trod, Buddha has come to claim his own (all who are able to follow that part of the way unto Christhood). For the work of Buddha was a work of purification, a work of redemption for body and mind, a work of upliftment by which the Soul was raised out of the gross conditions into which it had gone down as the result of the materialization of all the sacred Mysteries contained in the religion of Brahmanism, a *work that was meant to prepare the way for the coming of the Christ.*

Where Christhood Dwells

But this most essential first part of the Christhood mission is also being followed by the next in the order of sequence. After the baptism of John there were those who approached the Christ to enquire of Him where He dwelt. " *Master,*" said they, " *where dwellest Thou ?* " To whom He replied," *Come and see."* And they followed Him, and became His disciples. *" For it was about the tenth hour,"* a most significant thing.

And here a most profound truth is presented, to understand which we must get away from the personal. We must remember that though the Christhood was gloriously manifested through the beloved Master, yet is it always *impersonal*. So let us understand this essential truth, that following the Christhood was not, and is not, simply following the man through whom the Christhood is manifested. The two things must never be confounded. In the past it has always had disastrous results both for the Soul and the truth taught. To follow the Christ was, and is, to follow the path unto Christhood, even unto the full realization and divine vision which it brings. To follow the Christ to the place where He dwells is no easy task ; for it is to follow Him up to the blessed spiritual experiences of Christhood. It is to follow Him along the threefold path of *Self-denial, Self-sacrifice* and *Self-abandonment* to the divine service. It is to have realized the purification, then the redemption, and then the regeneration. It is to manifest pity unto all creatures, to show compassion unto all Souls, and to have love, even the Divine Love, in fulness of manifestation. It is to know purity in all life's ways, devotion always to the highest in all life's action, and to make of life a perfect service unto the Divine Lord.

The Christ dwells where the atmosphere of the Soul is pure, where the air is spiritually rarefied and life's vision sublime. He dwells on the heights far above the murky conditions which accompany the low-lying ways of human experience, where no evil obscures the Soul's noblest vision, and where the light of the divine glory never sets. The feeling where He dwells is angelic ; the purpose of life is angelic ; the service of life is also angelic. His house is the threshold where angels tread ; the altar where the Seraphim worship ; the most sacred sanctuary where the Divine Presence is known, and the divine vision is beheld. And so, when we are asked to come and see where He dwells, we verily are asked to much more, infinitely more, than we ever dreamed of in connection with following the Christ.

Yet, blessed to relate, there are those in these days who have not only asked the question and received the answer, but who are entering into the dwelling-place. With them also it is " *about the tenth hour.*" They have sought not only the purification in the waters of the Jordan, but the baptism of the Holy Spirit—the Holy Breath, the inflowing Spirit of the Divine Love—that they may follow on to know Christhood. They are not only seekers unto the full realization of the redeemed life, but they also desire to give themselves in beautiful devotion to the ways of the heavenly service. With them " *the tenth hour* " is come, for they have passed into that condition of profound spiritual longing after the divine realizations which only the attainment of the Christhood can ever satisfy. And so they seek to follow the Christ to the place or spiritual state in which He dwells. Hence the wonderful uprising of so many Souls to seek out the inner meaning of Christhood that they may enter into that Blessed Life.

THE GREATER WORKS BEING DONE

Thus, that other work of the Christ is being accomplished in which Souls who are ready are being called unto discipleship for the Christhood. The Divine Spirit is finding the Simons and Andrews, the Philips and Nathanaels, the Jameses and Johns—Souls who are ready and willing to follow on to know " the crown of life " as a blessed spiritual inheritance.

And so the works of the Christhood will now proceed apace, for the disciples are being called ; and some there are who have already realized much implied in the sublime estate. Indeed there are those who are passing into those realizations expressed by the term " *the eleventh hour,*" and even " *the twelfth hour.*"

There are those following the Christhood now who will soon enter into such realizations of the Divine Love and Wisdom as will enable them to perform the works of God even as the Christhood through the blessed Master performed them— works of Divine Light and Love ; of interpretation and enlightenment ; of unfoldment of the Mysteries concerning the Soul and the Planet ; and all the systems in the household of the Sun ; of the whole past of them all, and the glorious future unto which they are all to be restored. For in the realization of divine Christhood the Soul cometh to know all these things ; and there are those now upon the earth who are entering into that exalted state. Nay, there are upon these outer planes those who formed the inner group of Souls who followed the beloved Master during the manifestation of the Christhood, unto whom alone He unfolded the awful nature of the Sin-offering and its necessity for the accomplishment of the redemption of the human race, and who were in some measure sharers of the unspeakable burden. And these will be able to remember the Blessed Manifestation, and to write of it as it was.

O the depth both of the Wisdom and Love of the Father ! How unsearchable have been all His ways, and how profound His thoughts ! His path is upon the Heavens, and His ways are on the Great Deep.

If the first works of the Christhood which are now beginning to be made manifest, be so blessed, how much greater must be the blessedness of the greater works yet to be accomplished ? If turning the waters of purification into the wine of Christhood be a great work, what shall we say of those works in which the wine of the Christhood, the wine of the vine, is changed into Divine Being ?

Yet that is what will take place. In all who follow the Christhood unto fulness shall there be realized this exalted state. As those who drink well of the wine of the marriage festival

234

in Cana of Galilee are also given to drink, when the hour has come, of the wine of Christhood ; so all who drink deeply of the cup of Christhood, at last are given to drink of the cup of the divine fulness. They are made members of the innermost group, those unto whom even the Mystery of the nature of the Divine Life is unfolded. They sit at the table of the Lord ; they eat the Bread of the Divine Body ; and they drink the wine of the Divine Spirit ; and thus are they nourished.

Deeper, ever deeper, grows the mystery of our Being as we rise into the altitudes of spiritual realization. Greater, ever greater, grows the vision of life as the Soul enters into the divine experiences unto which Christhood calls. Ever more and more wonderful does it all appear, the further we go along the divine path, the higher we climb the divine heights. The glory is ever increasing ; the wonderment is without end.

" *Great and marvellous are Thy works, Lord God of Hosts* " ; *for Thou makest us to be Thy sons with the image of Thee within us, and the power of Thee realized by us.*

On the Sea of Galilee

*Being the Record under the form of an Allegory of
most Ancient History relating to the Soul, whose
miraculous elements were spiritual and not
physical ; and also a remarkable embodiment of the elemental influences
that play upon the life of all
Souls now, and the trying
experiences which
have become the
portion of
all.*

A

THE STORY OF THE TEMPEST

THE true character of the Teachings given by the Master, and the depth of their inner significance, will become even more wonderful when the inner meaning of another incident is understood. It is an incident recorded in the synoptic Gospels. In these Records it is written of as if it had been an event upon the outer planes, an experience of a material kind. Its sublime and profound meanings are therefore lost to the Soul. In its present form it is only an outward history, having no direct bearing upon the innermost life. Yet it was an allegory of the Soul, the story of a profound spiritual event in the history of the Soul. We refer to the miracle of *The stilling of the Tempest*.

It was an allegory told by the blessed Master to the inner group, setting forth the experience of the Soul in its path across the Deep as it moved from the shores of the outward or sense-life, to those of the divine life. It embodied what has been, and what is now, the experience of every one who seeks to leave the outward life for the inward, the material for the spiritual, the sense realizations for those which are of the Soul. For ever since the elemental kingdoms of this world became changed in their nature, the Soul has found her path most trying and difficult. Since her fall into matter she has had such a history of trouble and sorrow as was never anticipated, and such as few could form any conception of. Her path has been one beset with hardships, full of contrariety in the influences to which she has been subject. Her difficulties have not been simply such as were necessary for the development and strengthening of life, but also such as might be expected to arise out of wrong conditions and contrary powers. Of these contrary conditions and powers we have already spoken, and we shall yet have further words to say concerning them. For, to thoroughly understand the conflicts into which the Soul has now to enter, it is absolutely necessary to understand the conditions through which the conflicts are brought about, and to witness the influence which they exercise over the whole of life.

The allegory of " *The stilling of the tempest* " was a picture of the powers of the elémental kingdom, and the fear which these powers awakened within the Soul as they played upon her frail life, and especially as she crossed the Deep from the shore of the world-life to that of the spiritual heavens. It pictured the setting out of the Soul ; the sleep of the divine consciousness within her ; the arising of the new and overwhelming conditions, and the great fear awakened within the Soul through them ; the arousing of the sleeping Lord, or the divine consciousness within her ; the Lord's command to the elements, and the stilling of the tempestuous winds and seas ; and, at last, the restoration of the vision of the Soul.

These profound experiences are embodied in the story, so that there is a wealth of history in it little imagined by the general reader, a history transcending in meaning that of any merely outward and physical events. And it, therefore, has a value exceeding in importance any experience with the elements such as the story found in the synoptic Gospels would imply, since it deals with *the inner history* of the life of man rather than the outward. For it is a spiritual history and not material. It is the embodiment of universal experience on this Planet rather than a mere personal narrative. And its value is enhanced greatly when the Soul can behold in it not only her own experience, but also, in part, that of the Master after the passing away of the Christhood. For the states He entered into during the days of the Sin-offering, are portrayed in it. He truly became like unto His brethren ; passed through the like experiences ; was tried as they have been and still are ; traversed the storm-swept waters of life in all the lives of the Sin-offering ; knew the meaning of the sleep of the Lord within the Soul, the overwhelming fear begotten of the powers of the elements, the sad consciousness of the loss of the awakened and realized Christhood, and what it meant to feel so utterly forsaken as to cry out in agony of Soul, " *Carest Thou not that we perish ?* "

WHAT THE ALLEGORY REVEALS

The allegory was one spoken by the Master to the inner group of disciples for the purpose of helping them to understand the meaning of the terrible conflicts which were and still are so obviously a part of the experience into which every earnest disciple enters. It was told by Him in order to deepen their trust in the Divine Love, to impress them with the ever-blessed truth that never fails to accomplish for the Soul absolute conquest over the elemental kingdoms. For the Master knew what lay ahead of them after the passing of the Christhood. He had beheld in the Gethsemane vision the fearful conditions which would arise as the result of the materialization of the Teachings. He foresaw the arising of the conditions which turned the whole spirit of Christianity into one that sought and delighted in mental and even physical conflict. He knew how the inner life would be overwhelmed by the tempests generated from such a spirit ; how the sea of experience, across which the little ship of the Soul must needs pass, would be turned into tumultuous waters ; how the storm-spirits, the elemental influences, would be let loose as the result of the intellectual conflicts and ecclesiastical claims and oppression, to hold revelry upon these waters ; how great would be the sufferings of the members of the inner group of disciples, as well as all earnest Souls. Hence the aim of the allegory.

And what a picture of the thoughtfulness of the Divine Love we have in this allegory told by the Master ! What tender care is revealed in this vision of coming events, wherein the Soul's difficulties are anticipated. How great is the love revealed in the forward look on their behalf, the endeavour to prepare them for the coming hardships, and to guard them against the influences of that evil day. With what sorrow did He foresee the changes that would take place in the conditions amid which they, and indeed all earnest truth-seekers, would find themselves ; and with what tender solicitude did He yearn over them and endeavour to prepare their minds to meet the turbulent conditions without allowing these to effect any permanent change in themselves. What pathos there was in the message as He gave it to them in the allegory of the storm-swept sea, and the trying experiences of the little ship and all aboard her. To understand the depth of feeling with which it was spoken by the Master, one must have been present to hear it.

Ah, there were meanings in the beloved Master's teachings which have never been discovered until this day of the Redemption and the Regeneration, depths which none could fathom unless it were given them to understand from the innermost and the highest. How deep the teachings were in their meanings may be perceived by those who read these unfoldments, and who may be able to receive them with the open understanding. For their intrinsic value is to be found in their inner meanings—those meanings which find the innermost life of a man or woman, which carry the vision away from the outward and physical to the inward and spiritual, from the lower reaches of experience to the higher, and even the highest.

How very different seems the vision presented when we get a true point of view. How wonderfully expansive and how beautifully soullic. The phenomenal world recedes, and the world of the Soul comes into vision. The miraculous element upon the outer planes gives place to *a world of divine power within the Soul*. The storm is within as well as without ; but the elements are changed from within. The miracle is of the Soul ; and it is wrought by the Divine Presence within her. The quelling of the elemental conditions whose tempestuous ways have almost overwhelmed the Soul, and filled her with distrust and fear, is from within. All these things are seen when the true point of view is reached. And there is more still to be discovered, much more for those who are able to receive it, of which we shall speak by and by.

Lord God of the heavenly hosts! Who could have found out these treasures unless in Thy goodness Thou hadst revealed them unto us? May the light within our Lamp be thine alone, for we would know only from Thee.

B

THE LITTLE SHIP OF THE SOUL

IN sacred symbology a little ship upon " the great deep " was the emblem of the Soul borne upon the bosom of the Eternal Spirit. Upon the waters of the great deep of the Divine Mystery, the Soul has to perform her evolution from the shores of the outer kingdoms where her life as a spiritual organism began, until she reaches that shore upon which life's fullness awaits her. She has to move upon the face of the waters through *the potential divine energy within her ;* and the Holy Breath, as that most sacred power, is sent forth from the Divine Love. From state to state of experience she moves, gathering store by the way, like a ship sailing through the ocean from Isle to Isle ; for the Isles amid " the great deep " are the various stages of her evolution, the temporary harbours for which she has to make on her great voyage. For her the Isles amid the divine sea wait with their treasures to enrich her. As she passes from shore to shore her freight becomes more and more precious, more and ever more valuable to herself, the world, and the Divine Love ; for her attributes grow in strength and unfoldment, and these are potentially of the nature of the Divine Life.

THE ATTRIBUTES OF THE SOUL

How precious those attributes are will be recognized when it is also understood that within herself the Soul has, in a latent form, the beautiful attributes of the Eternal One. In nature she is of *the One Life*, a child of the Infinite and Eternal Father-Mother whose beautiful Life pulses through her whole spiritual system, and composes her very Being. Within herself she has, in latent form, those powers which signify the Trinity within the Divine Nature. For she possesses the positive and negative forces of the divine nature, the masculine and feminine modes; thus having as an inheritance the twofold divine powers expressed by the terms Fatherhood and Motherhood, and the threefold divine powers expressed in Christhood—the Father, the Holy Spirit, and Childhood known as Christhood. She is of the Sacred Seven, the Elohim, in whose Image she is fashioned; and in this way she has given to her as her portion, when fully unfolded, the sevenfold life of the Gods. Thus she has potentially within her spiritual system " the Seven Spirits of God," " the seven Thunders " or Voices or Tones, the Holy Spectrum or Tinctures of the Divine, " the Sevenfold Amen " —*the perfectionment of spiritual being*.

The Soul's History

It will thus be seen what a sacred vessel the Soul is, how wonderfully she has been built up, and how great her possibilities are. And it will be understood what a terrible loss overtook her when she went away from her true path, and found herself overwhelmed by elements whose conditions made them inimical to her true progress. The inner meaning of the allegory will now be more easily apprehended; and the reason why it was spoken by the blessed Master to the inner group, will be seen. For He knew what was *in* man, not only in the sense in which that remarkable saying is so frequently interpreted, but in the most profound sense. He knew what the human Soul was in her nature and possibilities. He understood *the real Life* as well as the superficial. He knew and understood what the voyage of the Soul meant for her even under the best conditions, and was able to speak with authority of the difficulties of the way, and of the glorious issues. And He likewise had the vision before Him of what the conditions had become, and the dangers which now beset the Soul in her voyage to the shores of the divine realizations.

In the allegory we may, therefore, behold the setting out of the Soul on her great journey; the helpful conditions which prevailed when she first found herself upon " the great deep " ; the change which took place in these conditions through disaster to the elemental world, and the trying and anxious ages the Soul had whilst the Divine One within her sanctuary or inner-most parts, slept ; the awful fear which overtook her amid the tempestuous elemental contrary forces, and her feelings that the Divine One did not even seem to care whether or no she perished in the way ; the cry of the Soul for help upon the storm-swept seas, and the awakening of the Christ who had gone to sleep within her ; the manifestation of the power of the Christ within her rebuking the evil and hurtful conditions, quelling the stormy elements around her, and bringing forth out of the tempest the peace of a great divine calm.

And then in a more particular sense we may discern in it the anticipation of coming events, the taking of the Christ into the little ship " *just as He was* "—a saying full of profound significance ; the beautiful setting forth upon the placid waters ; the going to sleep of the Christ after the passing away of the Christhood Manifestation ; the arising, unexpectedly by the Soul of the fearful storm, and the wild winds lashing the waters into a perfect fury, until the little vessel seemed as if she would be completely overwhelmed amid the conflicts of the elements ; the loss to the Soul of her true vision in the decadence of Faith or spiritual vision within her, until her once beautiful trust in the divine goodness toward her and care for her, waned and died ; her agony and fear amid the tempestuous experiences when nothing but absolute disaster seemed to lie ahead ; the

R

discovery of the sleeping Christ, and the awakening once more to the realization of her ancient divine powers ; the overcoming of fear, and the subjugation of the elemental kingdoms to her will ; the coming of the great peace of the Divine Love into her life, and the restoration of the true vision of her Lord.

THE CAUSE OF THE CONFLICT

In all these experiences we may get a gleaning of the history of the Soul prior to the coming of the Christhood into her life ; the sad experiences through which those Souls passed who had arrived at the Christhood state, but who went down with the children of the Planet in their fall ; and what actually took place within these very Souls after the passing away of the glorious Christhood manifestation. Our readers need only reflect upon the history of dogmatic and ecclesiastical Christianity to have evidence of the truth portrayed in the allegory. And as to the truth of the former statement, the conflict of the Soul with the elemental kingdoms is now almost universally recognized, which not even the philosophy of Eastern Religions has been able to explain, further than to accept the fact and interpret it as part of the divine scheme in the Soul's evolution, that she should go down into the lowest depths of evil in order to know, by contrast, the blessing of the highest good—a belief that does violence to love, and so to the thought of the Divine Love as governor of this world.

The conflict is apparent, but not its cause. Every Soul has the conflict to engage in with the elemental kingdoms. Some feel it, mourn over it, and wonder why it is so. Only the very few have ever sought to solve the mystery. The fact has been accepted by many as something in the nature of the Soul's evolution, a provision made by the Eternal One whereby the Soul should work her way up through the elemental kingdoms in a state of conflict with them. The antagonism between the elementals and the Soul is thus accepted as a part of the divine scheme in the evolution of the Soul and the government of the world.

Under such conditions the bosom of " the great deep " can never have been in a state of calm for the Soul. The waters of life can never have been placid, but always in a state of trouble ; and the Soul can have known no restfulness and blessed peace since the day of her setting out as a conscious spiritual organism. In the light of that interpretation the little vessel must have been launched amid the tempest. That thought may be in harmony with the doctrine of material evolution, but it cannot be in harmony with a true spiritual philosophy. It may harmonize with the phenomena observable by physical science, but not with those phenomena of the Soul with which the earnest spiritual student has become acquainted. It may agree with a bald materialism which takes the world, and the whole celestial universe, as the manifestation of unconscious non-spiritual forces, but it does not and cannot accord with a true conception of the universe, including our own world, as the expression of potencies born of the Divine Love and Wisdom.

Indeed it is impossible to conceive of such a method of Soul evolution in the light of a radiant love ; for it is opposed to all human conceptions of the best conditions for the true and safe unfoldment of life upon the outer planes. No human love would ever thrust its beloved ones into such conditions, not even those who accept the elemental conditions as part of the divine scheme with all the evil and suffering born from them. For they also shield and guard their children. And we cannot conceive of the Divine Love being less than human love in its manifestation. Indeed, the whole of the religious experience of the race shows that the beginning must have been different. The Great Religions have all taught that the Soul had a period of beautiful childhood, a world to live in whose conditions were harmonious, ages of experience in which the earth was the scene of angelic ministry long ere the Gods went to sleep, a time when " Eden " was a reality and God dwelt within the Soul. And these religions have all attempted to explain the change which came over the world and the Soul, the cause of its coming and its disastrous results. And they have all anticipated a time when the Soul and the world would be restored to their pristine glory by means of The Redemption. Thus have they tried to set forth the very truths underlying this beautiful allegory, to show what was the past heritage of the Soul, the tempestuous conditions which overtook her, and the restoration through that beautiful divine power implied in the Christhood.

C

THE STORM-SWEPT SEA

IT was during the voyage of the Soul that the storm arose. All was right when the little ship set out upon her journey. She had travelled far from the outermost shores along the placid waters of life, sustained upon the bosom of the great deep, and wafted by the gentle Holy Breath of the Divine Love. The holy mystery of spiritual Being had been felt by her long ere the terrible change came over the elemental kingdoms. Then it was a joy to live. Her world was full of gladness. The winds which beat upon her and played within her, were full of the music of the heavens. There was true rhythm in her path, and harmony was born of all her movements. The great winds which came upon her, sounding forth the mighty tones of the Divine Life, had in them none of the elements which produce the tempest. They were exhilarating and inspiring, carrying her forward on her journey as she was able to spread out her attributes to receive them ; but even in their great strength and depth they were gentle with her, even as the gentleness of the zephyr winds, and never left hurt and dread behind. Her heavens were all clear. No storm-clouds swept across them blotting out her Sun. The elemental kingdoms were her friends. They had their part to play in the drama of the evolution of her wonderful life ; for they were the messengers of God sent forth to do His bidding. All of them were under the control of the Divine Kingdom of the Planet, obeyed the divine behests in performing the mission on which they were sent.

But as the Soul journeyed towards the shores of the innermost realizations, a great change took place in the elemental kingdoms. The elemental spirits which had ministered to her, gradually ceased to perform the offices for which they had been generated. They passed beyond the control of the Divine Kingdom of the Planet, and they lost their power of ministry unto the Soul. Their magnetic conditions underwent so great a change that they became, as it were, a law unto themselves, gradually refusing more and more to respond to the divine magnetic attraction. Not only did they cease to aid the Soul in her true evolution by their ministry, but they became obstacles in her path, and at last her enemies. Everything was changed in the outward kingdoms of the Planet, and then in the outward kingdoms of the Soul. More and still more was she drawn down in her life by the new, strange, and inimical conditions, until she found her whole life full of storm and stress. The waters of life for her were troubled from the depths, and the winds that played upon her were contrary. She found herself tossed to and fro upon the mighty deep of experience, helpless in herself, and knowing not whence to find succour. Her world was changed indeed. The gladness and joy of life went out of her. No longer were her kingdoms full of beautiful harmony ; they ceased to be resonant with the music of the heavens. Troubles hitherto unknown assailed her, and at last she found herself overwhelmed.

Such was the way in which the Soul came to know the great

changes that swept over her life, and drove her hither and thither upon the bosom of the great deep of experience upon this world. Such was the origin and nature of her first fall under the dominion of the elements. How tragic it was for her those Souls will understand who are now able to look back upon the terribly sad history, and perceive the true inner meaning of it. They will know once more the pure and glorious state in which the world then was when the Soul rightly performed her evolution ; how beautiful and harmonious life was upon every sphere ; how contributary to the growth and unfoldment of the Soul's attributes the elemental kingdoms were ; how very real the Soul's progress was toward the Divine ; how blessed, how peaceful, how joyous life was for her. What the storm-swept seas were they will understand. They will see the meaning of the awful devastations in the elemental kingdoms, and be able to interpret rightly the meaning of the fearful strife which has filled the planes of the Planet for untold ages. A new and true explanation will be theirs of the unspeakable conflicts in which the Soul has shared. The origin of these strange conditions will be understood ; and they will behold how the Soul has suffered in her path across the deep ever since that planetary change. The inner meanings of the Soul's struggles will be obvious unto them. They will now understand her anguish in the hour of trouble, her dread lest the Divine Love should fail towards her and cast her off. They will be able to rightly interpret her cry for succour, and her sore travail amid the tempestuous conditions of life. For in the light of the Divine Presence within will they behold her, so that the true meaning of her history will all be clear. For them will this allegory have new meaning. Its outward and physical aspects will give place to those which are wholly spiritual. The story will be transformed in its character, its beautiful purpose stand out in a new light. The personal element will melt away before its universal and soullic application. The small event upon the lake of Tiberius, with the manifestation of occult powers, will grow into a great history of the Soul as it is lifted out of its material environment and placed upon the true plane of spiritual experience. Yea, they will behold even the Christhood in a new light, the meaning of His going to sleep, and the awakening to still the tempest and bring unto all Souls the peace of God.

D

THE SOUL AMIDST THE TEMPEST

" *CAREST Thou not that we perish?* " It was a cry of despair in which we hear the agony of Souls overwhelmed by the conditions around them, and the consciousness of the utter hopelessness of their position. The cry is not that of one Soul, but of all Souls upon this Planet. It is the universal cry of men and women who have felt evil deeply, and have feared its power. How full of that cry of anguish is the sacred literature of all peoples, wherein the agonizing of the Soul may be both seen and heard. It reverberates through all ages of sacred story until it culminates in the awful cry of the Christ-Soul in His anguish and despair ! The Hebrew Psalms are mostly the expression of that anguish and fear, though the profound meaning is obscured through the localization and materialization of the song. The conflicts of the Soul with the elements may all be found there. The feeling that God has forsaken her may be heard expressed in varying degrees.

" *Deep calleth unto Deep at the noise of Thy Thunders ; all Thy waves and Thy billows are gone over me.*"

" *They go down into the deep and are lifted up again ; to and fro do they reel like drunken men.*"

" *My God, My God, why hast Thou forsaken me?*"

These are but illustrations of the Soul's crying with which the Psalms abound. And they reveal what depths of suffering the Soul has known. They are not the cries, the agonizing utterances, of mere animal men and women, of Souls in a low order of development. They are those of spiritual Beings of a high order who are full of great anguish, because overwhelmed by their conditions, and fearful lest amid them they should spiritually perish. The awful doubts, the unspeakable dread, the anguish born through the sense of loss—these are the fruits of the changed conditions which assailed her in those sad and terrible ages of which the allegory spoke. And when we find in any sacred literature these very states revealing themselves in expressions which show the uncertainty of the trust and hope of the Soul, her anguishing because the Divine Presence seems to have withdrawn from her, her agony in moments of deep feeling lest the Lord of Life should cast her off for ever, and show forth unto her His loving kindness no more, we may recognise in these things the results of the bondage and even slavery to the elemental kingdoms into which she was drawn down from her pure spiritual state and experience.

The Elemental World

Who could read the history of this Planet in its physical bearings, such as material science has shown to us, without feeling how awful that history must have been out of which the present mountains and valleys were formed, the mineral kingdom known to science came into existence, and the animal kingdom as it now is ? Does not science indicate, though it be with faltering words, the unspeakable forces that must have been at work for untold ages, and the frightful tragedies which must have been witnessed from the heavens during the ages in which all these conditions were brought into existence ?

What was the meaning of these great changes, and why were there such awful forces at play ? Physical science answers that the world was in the process of its evolution, and was being fitted as a dwelling place for the animal races, and then the human races. But the day is upon us when even that position taken up by science will be untenable. And physical scientists will have to learn at first hand that all the history written by these tremendous forces was *not antecedent* to the advent of man upon the Planet, but that it was done long ages after the human races had performed their evolution through the vegetable and creature kingdoms. They will also have to learn that the fearful devastations within the outer kingdoms of the Planet were witnessed by many Souls, and that these things filled them with unspeakable dread. In other writings we have given an explanation of much that then took place ;[1] and here we may not dwell upon it further than to show how profound was the inner meaning of the allegory. For the devastating forces resulting from the new magnetic conditions, the changed vegetable kingdom, the still more changed creature kingdom, all exercised a malevolent influence over the Soul and retarded her true life, turning her magnetic forces towards the elemental kingdoms, and changing the entire environment for her. These kingdoms were all out of harmony, and were therefore contrary forces playing upon her continually from the time of their arising. They often overwhelmed her life on the outer planes, and caused her great suffering. They tossed her to and fro upon the great deep of her experience ; for she was thrown down into the most fearful animal forms which had been generated by these tempestuous elements, and suffered such things as can never be told. Whilst she sought to rise up out of the awful states her agony was often such as to " rend the heavens." And the like experiences followed her through long ages. It is not therefore to be wondered at that she wrote such Psalms of sorrow and anguish, of doubt and despair, as may be found in sacred literature.

THE WISDOM OF THE MASTER

The Master understood the Soul as no other teacher who

[1] *The Herald of the Cross*, Vols. I. to VII.

had visited the earth had done. He knew what her past had been, and how history kept repeating itself in her experience. He knew how all Souls passed through the tempestuous conditions, and were at times like helpless vessels upon the raging waters. He was able to speak of it in terms which embodied the sad universal experience, to show wherein the Soul's great trials were found, the nature of her terrible conflict, the effect of that conflict upon her life, her anguish and agony, and the dire extremity in which she often found herself.

It was His sublime mission to recall the Soul to her true heritage ; to awaken and bring back those who once knew it and had it as a glorious possession ; to lead the thoughts of all true seekers for the higher life away from the outwardness of things to the true inwardness, from the material to the spiritual history of life, from the phenomenal experience upon the outer spheres to the real inward life born of the Divine Presence within the Soul.

It was part of His mission to show that the phenomenal conditions upon the outer spheres had spiritual causes ; that the mystery of life was to be found in the tree, the herb, and the flower ; that the unseen mysterious powers behind the outward were originally all spiritual ; that in all the strange contradictory manifestations in the elemental kingdoms were to be found many of those things which barred the Soul's progress ; that the very tempest upon the outer planes had a message, which could be understood through understanding how it was the elements were at war with each other, and often set up conditions which made life hard and trying, and how all these overwhelming experiences were to be overcome by the Soul.

It was part of His mission to interpret the inner meaning of the history of this world, of her children, and of all those who once were the spiritual Teachers upon the Planet ; of the Divine Love and Wisdom made manifest in all ages—that Love which has followed the children all through their long chequered history, and that Wisdom which has been hidden for unspeakable ages because of the state of the world. And nowhere is the Divine Love made more manifest, and the Divine Wisdom revealed more wonderfully, than in the teachings contained in this beautiful allegory, wherein the Soul's history is indicated as to what it was and what it became ; the manifestation of the Divine Love in the hour of the Soul's dire extremity ; and the beautiful revelation of the Divine Wisdom in making the path of the Soul one in which the tempestuous elements are all hushed, the whole of the conditions changed, and the waters of experience made beautifully peaceful as she moves towards the divine shore.

O Love most wonderful ! O Wisdom unsearchable ! How Thou hast led and succoured the children of Thy creation in all those dark ages when the tempestuous elements tossed them to and fro, and filled them with the awful dread of Thee, and madst them to cry out as if Thou wert of those who leave and forsake their own !

Thou wast beautiful in Thy ways in the hour of their dire extremity. Their cry Thou didst regard though they knew it not. Thou art our Father-Mother and our Redeemer : evermore blessed art Thou ! We are all Thine own : we would love and worship Thy Holy Name in the service of Thy Love.

E
THE CHRIST ASLEEP

BUT *the Christ was asleep in the hinder part of the little ship.* What depth of significance is to be found in this saying ? Taking the story as literal history there might not seem much in it, for there would be nothing unnatural in the Master having been overcome by sleep, and even sleeping through a storm after an exhausting ministry during the day.

Indeed there could have been nothing more natural, and certainly not anything to call forth the surprise of the disciples. But when we leave the material planes and find the story to be a spiritual history ; when we pass from the personal to the impersonal and universal meaning ; when we see in it the history of an event which took place within the spheres of the Soul, and not simply one on the physical planes ; when we understand that the action is not upon the phenomenal planes, but is wholly of an inward character, and that all the phenomena associated with the history are only manifestations of great spiritual forces, then we are constrained to recognise that the incident of the Christ falling asleep is not natural, though it was universal experience, and that it should not have taken place, and would not have taken place but for the conditions which arose to environ and then envelope the Soul.

For the sleeping Christ was not the personal Master, but the divine consciousness within the Soul. It was not the personal Master asleep in a fishing boat, but *the Christ within the Soul*—that consciousness of Life which, whether latent only or fully unfolded, is the Divine Life within us. It was that Life which had gone to sleep. In the case of those who had once known the Christhood realization, the Christ within them had fallen asleep. *They had lost the consciousness of Christhood. The divine powers within them were quiescent.* Though once they were the Illuminati Community and the Teachers of divine things, yet they had gradually but surely descended with the children of the Planet into a state of bondage to the elemental kingdoms as a result of the changed magnetic conditions, until all their once beautiful attributes and powers were suspended.

Thus the Soul slept. It was the mythical sleep of the Gods. It was then that Pan seemed dead. The elemental world was triumphant. The spirits of the elements passed to and fro as they would. None could hinder them. The upper as well as the lower firmament was changed. The human races became as thistledown before the breeze, children of circumstances, unable to resist the conditions upon them, helpless little vessels amid most tempestuous seas whose pilot had gone to sleep. For the elements held revel, and the Christhood was in deep slumber. The spiritual conditions became appalling ; the Soul was as one forsaken by the Lord. What could Souls do in such a state ? Only cry out in their helplessness. They grew conscious of their own impotence, conscious of the fact that unless some help were forthcoming they must be overwhelmed amid the tempestuous seas of experience.

The Care of the Divine Love

Hence the anguish-cry of the Soul in the allegory. " *Lord, carest Thou not that we perish ?* " It is just how the Soul has thought of the Divine Love. She has often thought that that beautiful Love was asleep when it was the divine life within herself which slumbered. She has not infrequently thought and felt as if the Divine Love had cast her off for ever, and that His tender mercies were no longer towards her. She has felt as those on the little vessel are said to have felt, that the tempests of life's experiences would overwhelm her, and that the Divine One slept peacefully and unconcernedly through it all. She has wondered why the Christ wakened not to still the raging waters and bring her to the desired haven.

Who could blame her if her trust became broken, her spiritual vision dimmed, her hope uncertain and even changed to despair? Has not her history been a most chequered one, full of sadness, pain and anguish ? Has she not suffered untold miseries during the long ages of her experience away from the spiritual kingdom where her true life alone is found ? Has she not lost much that she once possessed, and been like one crying in the night of her sore travail for some beloved one who did not come ? What have been all her wonderful yearnings for the Divine Presence, but the crying out for the recovery of what she had lost ? Even those sad anguish-cries, those words uttered in her agony in which she has seemed to reproach the Divine One, what were they and what are they but the sad outpourings of one who has been greatly spiritually afflicted, and is distraught with the sorrow and despair of it all ?

But the Soul must learn that the Divine Love has neither slumbered nor slept. That Love never forsook her amid the tempest of her experience. Though the Christ within her frail little ship went to sleep, God did not. Though on the outermost spheres the ages seem to testify of disaster to the planes of the Planet, the tumultuous raging of the elements, the waters of the most bitter experience surging around the Soul ; yet upon the innermost planes the Divine Love was operating to bring about the necessary change in the elemental kingdoms, and to awaken the Christ-consciousness who slumbered within the Soul. Had not the Divine Love been operative upon this Planet, she would long ages ago have been absolutely lost, and all her children with her. But the Divine Father in His Love and Wisdom has saved the Planet, and is now saving all her children. He has changed the elemental kingdoms so that the evil that was in them is gradually becoming less and less. He has purified the elements so much that they are now more responsive to the magnetic attraction of the innermost Kingdom, and more helpful to the true growth of life. He has wrought such a redeeming work upon the astral kingdom that now the Soul may pass through it without experiencing the awful tempestuous conditions which in the past Souls have known there. The work which He hath accomplished for this Planet, no words could describe ; indeed, few could possibly realize all He has done even could we tell it.

But all this has been wrought on behalf of the Soul. It has been accomplished out of love for her. The great purpose of it all was and is the Soul's deliverance ; the sublime end of it the awakening of the powers and attributes of the Christ within the Soul. *The sleeping Christ must be awakened; the tempest must be allayed; the little ship of the Soul must be saved; and the Divine Love alone could have accomplished so much for us.*

" *Beloved ones! Now are we the children of God. And it doth not yet appear what our becoming is to be; but we know that when He shall appear (i.e., in us), we shall be like Him.*"

F

THE AWAKENING OF THE CHRIST

OUR readers will now understand what is meant by the awakening of the Christ. They will recognize this beautiful truth that it is the awakening of the Soul to the consciousness of her divine life, the realization of the Divine Presence within her, and the manifestation of her divine powers. Unto that sublime end did all the Messengers of the Heavens appear, the Prophets proclaim their various messages, and the seers tell their heavenly visions. They were the agents of the Heavens unto the Soul to help her back to the knowledge of her beautiful inheritance, and the attainment of the life which once was her sacred possession. In that light must all the ancient teachings be understood, whether they be Hebrew or Egyptian, Greek or Indian. The theme is one, however set; and the end is always the same. The message is of the Soul; her conditions, her glorious and inglorious past, the life she should ever seek, and the blessed future which is yet to be hers. Whatever be the movement of the song, the purpose is never changed nor hidden. The music has always the one end in view, namely, the awakening of the Soul from her sleep, the arousing of her dormant energies, the calling forth of all her beautiful attributes. Her deliverance from bondage, her redemption from evil, her restoration to the state she once enjoyed, the crowning of her attributes with the divine life—these are the underlying thoughts of all the messages which have reached her from the Heavens through Messenger, Prophet and Seer.

But it was not an easy task to awaken the Soul to a divine consciousness. Through great cycles of ages she had slept ; and though she had been awakened to the consciousness of her bondage and need for help, yet for ages upon ages she had to remain there. The condition of the astral world prevented her from rising farther. Within her the power of the Christhood still slept. Nor could that power be fully awakened until the evil conditions were all changed.

And herein was the majesty of the Divine Love made manifest. The Heavens knew what these conditions were which so hindered the Soul. They knew the difficulties in the way of having the evil conditions changed. They saw how it alone could be accomplished. They foresaw the awful burden which it would lay upon the Divine Love. Yet that Love faltered not in taking up the burden and bearing it for all the children. *The terrible Sin-offering was the response to the cry of the Soul.* What the Messengers, Prophets and Seers could not accomplish the Divine Love purposed to accomplish by means of the Christhood Manifestation followed by the tragic Sin-offering. The Christhood manifestation was to recover for the Soul the vision of her true life, and the Divine Wisdom which was her ancient inheritance ; whilst the Sin-offering was to change the astral kingdom by the purification of its elements, so that *all* Souls might be able to return to the realization of the true life. By the Christhood manifestation was the Christ within to be awakened in those who had once known Christhood, those elect Souls who once were the Christs of God upon this Planet ; and by means of the Sin-offering was it to be made easier for all Souls to rise out of the bondage in which they found themselves, and become conscious of the divinity of their nature, and alive to the divine potencies playing upon them from the Heavens, and the God-given powers which they themselves latently possessed. The Christ within all the elect Souls of Israel (those who as Christs had served in the Office of the Cross) was to be awakened, that through the restoration of their ministry the outward spiritual conditions might be changed and purified ; whilst, on the other hand, the work of changing the elements of the astral kingdom was to be accomplished by the Christ-Soul, so that the angelic world might be able to approach the Soul to aid her in her efforts, to influence her directly towards the Divine Love, and thus to accomplish, at last, the awakening of all Souls to the consciousness of the Jesus-life, and then the Christ-life.

A Beautiful Purpose

Now this great and blessed work should have been proceeding all through the Christian Era. The true awakening of Souls should have been continuous ever since the days of the blessed manifestation. The passing of the Christhood manifestation, and the taking up by the Soul of the burden of the Sin-offering, should not have been followed by the disastrous conditions which arose immediately after. The history of Christianity in its initial stages (speaking historically) should have been of a very different order. It should have been a history of Christhood interpretation—the manifestation of the redeemed life and the meaning of the Christhood estate. The whole unfoldment of Christianity should have been one in which the *true meaning* of Jesushood was revealed through those who knew it *living the life*. Through that manifestation of the meaning of redemption, all Souls were to have had presented to them the true life to be lived. It was in this way that the Redemption was to have been accomplished ; and all the Souls who were so drawn into the path of the redeemed life, were to have become helpers of Him who was accomplishing the momentous work of changing the elements of the astral kingdom. They were to have been fellow-labourers with that Soul ; for the effect of their purifying lives was to have been such that His labours would be backed up by them, and the evil images on the astral kingdom the more easily and speedily changed, the burden of the Sin-offering greatly lightened, and the unspeakable anguish and agonizing sorrow accompanying it, very much lessened.

How it was Frustrated

But the unfoldment of Christianity took an entirely different form. At the very foundation of the Chruch, a wrong bent was given to the mind. False views of the meaning of the Redemption were set forth by Judaizing teachers who understood not the meaning of the Christhood and the Jesushood. The underlying doctrines of Jewry were substituted for those contained in the teachings of the Master. The Redemption became something accomplished entirely outside of the Soul ; some mysterious change in the divine attitude to all the children, in which man had no part except to believe that it had been accomplished for him, and without understanding what it was that had been done. Instead of a true Redemption of the life as the result of the serious endeavour of man to purify all his ways, it was turned into something which called for man's acceptance as a statement of fact, the fact being nothing more than an intellectual affirmation.

That this interpretation of what happened at the founding of the Church, is the correct one, the history of Christianity will testify. For in no age of this era has *the meaning of the redeemed life* been known ; and only now is it breaking upon the Soul : upon the Church it has not yet broken. The Redemption is now coming through all the beautiful purifying and uplifting movements around us ; but as a whole the Churches continue to believe in and proclaim the astounding affirmation of a Redemption accomplished eighteen and more centuries ago, which has proved to be no redemption at all, since it has left the western world without even the vision of what a redeemed life means. It is one of the most tragic things on record that a religion which professes to have Christhood for its foundations, should be so absolutely in the dark as to the twofold meaning of Christhood, namely, *a life of beautiful purity and inward illumination, a life so pure that it could not endure the thought of inflicting pain upon any living creature; and so enlightened from the Divine Love and Wisdom that it knows divinely, lives divinely, and serves divinely.*

Yet it is so with the Churches. Though here and there in individuals there seem to be faint glimmerings of the coming of the light ; yet are the Churches toiling and rowing in the night, just as they have done all through the dark night of this era, without catching any of the great and precious truths that are awaiting all earnest seekers. They are still like the little ship amid the tempest, tossed to and fro by the elements, having the Christ of their beliefs, but not knowing that the Christ lies sound asleep within themselves, and that the change in the outward conditions will only be effectually wrought when He is awakened to make manifest His power through the regaining of the consciousness of the Divine Presence.

COMMANDING THE ELEMENTS

It is only now that the effect of the most wonderful Christhood manifestation through the blessed Master is being felt. The Divine Christ, the Holy and Blessed One within the Soul, that should have been awakened through the manifestation, has slept on through the long ages of this era because of the materialization of the beautiful Mysteries, and the blotting out of the wonderful vision of Soul-life which He revealed. The tempest has raged throughout all these ages, filling men and women with great dread. The entire history of ecclesiastical Christianity has been one of conflict—the conflict of beliefs forms, powers and principalities. It has been ceaseless in its raging, because, in not one of the ages has the Church known true spiritual calm, nor her members the divine peace.

Sometimes the conflict has been upon the outermost spheres ; at other times upon the spheres of the mind. The Soul has known no rest in the western world for many long ages ; that which should have brought rest unto her became the means of only accentuating her distress. The West was made the battle-ground of the most malignant forces. Instead of the tempestuous seas of experience being stilled, they were lashed into unspeakable fury by the storm spirits let loose in the various conflicts. Christianity was taught by the various Schools of Thought which early arose, as made up of certain forms of belief rather than a life to be realized ; and the Church was regarded as an ecclesiastical system rather than a spiritual fellowship, informal and purely soullic. Who has read the awful history, ecclesiastical and intellectual, which Christianity has written, without being filled with sore amazement that it could ever have been done in the name of the Divine Love, and ostensibly upon the foundations of Christhood ? Who has read that history with a holy yearning for the truth only, without wondering how it could all have arisen out of the beautiful sayings of the beloved Master ?

One stands face to face with elements the most opposite in nature to those that should have been found where the Christhood was said to be understood, and the Divine Love practised. The most fearful religious conflicts the world has ever been the theatre of, have been begotten of the evil spirits let loose by the ecclesiastical authorities of the various Schools. Pagan Rome was truly bad, and gave the disciples of the new religious cult a terrible time ; but it was no worse than what Christianized Rome has given to her own religious citizens. Indeed, the works of the latter have surpassed in wickedness those of the Pagan world. Even the Reformed section of religious communities were caught in the meshes, and, in their turn have become oppressors and persecutors of all who sought another way than that along which they themselves went.

Truly the tempest has raged until this age. The Souls of
" the Faithful " have been anguishing all through the three
long nights since the Christhood passed—THE THREE NAROS
WHICH HAVE BUT ENDED, nights of veritable spiritual darkness.
They have been crying out in their distress for help from on
high. They have been amazed that no answer was forthcoming
in response to their prayers. *How long, O Lord, how long wilt
Thou tarry in Thy coming to deliver us from our sore distress and
dire extremity ?* The sleeping Christ, the Lord in the *within*
or Holy Place of the Soul, was appealed to at last. The glorious
truth once more broke upon the Soul that the tempest could
be subdued only by the awakening of the sleeping Christ
within. The true Mystic Souls are awakening all over the world,
and the Christ within them is coming forth once more into full
and blessed manifestation.

And this general awakening of the Christ within all who
once knew Christhood is the harbinger of better times for the
world. Already are the elements changing upon the outermost
spheres, and the tempestuous conditions are being subdued.
The tumult of the raging elements has grown less of late days,
and many of the most evil spirits amongst them have been
quelled. The stilling of the troubled waters is proceeding ;
divine calm is coming to the Soul. The awakened Christ is
speaking ; now are the new conditions coming upon the waters
of experience. The Naros in which the divine peace will become
realized within the Soul, has at last broken upon the world,
and men and women shall behold the works of an awakened
Christhood. The fruits of the awful Sin-offering will soon be
witnessed, and the Christ-Soul see of His sore travail ; for so
changed now, as a blessed result, is the astral world, that the
angelic heavens are able to approach the earth and give direct
ministry unto the Souls within the astral kingdom, as well as
to all earnest Souls upon the outer planes. So changed are they
that all who have the desire to rise up into those heavens to

receive direct teaching from the angels who minister there, may now do so.

The Christ arose and rebuked the winds so that they obeyed Him ; and there was a great calm. And thus it is now within many.

G
THE STRENGTHENING OF FAITH

" *WHY were ye so fearful ? Have ye no faith ?* " Such are the terms in which the Master is said to have addressed the disciples. Was it a rebuke to them for their lack of trust, or was it simply a question of inquiry ? Was it really personal in any sense ?

The question asked was addressed to the Soul. And it was asked of those who had once known Christhood. It was asked in a form which throws a somewhat different light upon its meaning to that suggested in the Gospels. It was a question of most tender solicitude whose purpose was to strengthen the Soul's faith, and restore her confidence in the goodness of the Divine Love. For the long tempestuous experiences had brought with them a great sense of loss, and filled the Soul with fear. Her struggle with the elemental spirits had been for many great cycles of ages, and these conflicts had given her a deep sense of dread. Whatever distrust had come into her experience had been caused by these fearful conflicts. She had battled with the raging elements ; she had been thrown down by them ofttimes ; she had felt herself utterly helpless amidst them and had cried out in her anguish for a help which never seemed to come, until her once beautiful trust was completely broken, and her wonderful faith dimmed.

There had been a time when her faith was great, and her trust in the divine goodness absolute. It was indeed a beautiful state in which she then was. Her spiritual vision (faith) was strong and clear. She saw and understood. The spiritual heavens were open unto her. She communed with angels as she trod the earth, and she even walked with God. Her buoyancy was divine. Her whole life was a song of hope.

But the changed conditions wrought great changes in her. The elemental spirits prevailed against her to such an extent that her spiritual vision became more and more obscured, until at last her heavens were shut, and the angelic communion was interrupted. And so terrible and so long were her sufferings amid the awful tempests in her experience, that her hope well nigh perished as her trust became utterly broken. She fought against her doubts and despair, but often had to yield to them.

THE DIVINE REPROACH

The saying attributed to the Master will, therefore, come home to the reader with a new and larger meaning. It will be understood as a beautiful exhortation. In it the Divine Love and Wisdom will be recognized addressing the Soul. The question is intended to encourage, and is not meant in any sense as a rebuke. It is exhortatory, and has as its purpose the recalling of the Soul to the consciousness of what she once was in spiritual estate, and what she should now be. " *O ye whose faith is not little, wherefore do ye doubt ?* " It is an appeal to the spiritual vision, to the inward life, to the power to discern divinely, to that faculty by which the Soul sees into the heavens even of the Divine Kingdom, and understands divine things.

So there is something most beautiful in the saying, something so full of tender regard, something that reveals the Soul's past greatness, and which should fill her with great hope for the future. It is of the nature of a divine reproach ; but not such a reproach as men and women are in the habit of using against one another. It is rather of the nature of that most tender love which in its solicitude for its beloved ones, seems to chide them because they have not the trust and confidence they should have, and fail to perceive the meaning of things which should be apparent to them. For the divine reproach is always of that nature. It is not rebuke, but tender regard for the Soul. It never discourages her in her upward path, but has for its beautiful purpose the uplifting and strengthening of her life. And to recall her wonderful past is to do this. To impress upon her how noble she once was is surely to chide to such effect as to restore her to her ancient estate. To say to her " *O ye whose faith (spiritual vision) is not little, wherefore do ye doubt ?* " is surely to encourage her to rest confidently in the goodness of the Divine Love, to try to discern His hidden and wonderful purpose, and to be assured that He will accomplish for her all things through the perfect realization of the Divine Life, Light and Love within her.

THE SURPRISE OF THE DISCIPLES

" *What manner of man is this that even the winds and the waves obey Him ?* " Such is the saying attributed in the Synoptic Records to the disciples. The stilling of the storm filled them with surprise. They marvelled at the power of the Christ. They had inquired whether He cared at all for them in their sore distress, and when He delivered them from the power of the elemental spirits by quelling the fury of these latter, they were filled with wonder. They could not understand it. What manner of man could He be whom the elemental furies obeyed ?

There is something profoundly significant in the picture, though its meaning is not to be found in the personal form in which it is presented in the Synoptics. There is a depth of real experience touched, but it is not simply that of the few disciples of the earthly teacher, but rather the universal experience of the Soul. The spiritual attributes represented by the disciples (their very names implying them) are often filled with amazement at the work of the Divine Chirst who is within, when Christhood consciousness is once awakened. They are sometimes even filled with fear as the result of the things accomplished. The Christhood consciousness is awakened amid the tempestuous conditions ; and when the Lord speaks through that consciousness to the elemental spirits, and commands them to cease their raging so that a great calm takes the place of the storm, the powers of the Soul are filled with wonder and the Soul herself is constrained to stand in awe. She wonders at the change, and questions the nature of the power within her through which it has been effected. For it is not immediately that she discerns her own *divinity*. That takes time to grow upon her. She cannot avoid the inquiry, " *What manner of man is this that even the winds and the waves obey Him ?* " She must question concerning the nature of the Christ within. And the whole tendency of the revelation which comes to her is to impress her profoundly with a sense of divine nearness, and the marvellous powers which become her heritage as her consciousness grows more and more intense, and she is led to fully realize the Divine Presence. She becomes filled with that Holy *Fear* which is said to be the beginning of Divine Wisdom ; for, through the awakening of the Christhood within her, the Light of the Divine Wisdom shines, her lamp is kindled from the Lord. The sense of the Divine Awe grows upon her— the effect of the work of the Seventh Spirit of Elohim, the highest colour in the divine spectrum, the divine voice at whose sound all the earth-powers are silent. *There can be no irreverence where the Christ is awake. Where His powers are made manifest a holy atmosphere pervades the Soul.* The Soul's amazement is not idle curiosity ; her questioning is not mere speculation. She is amazed at the marvellous nature of the powers called forth ; she inquires only to understand more fully the nature of Christhood. To her a new experience has come ; the old beautiful heavenly life is restored ; the elemental conditions are changed ; the storm-spirits are overcome ; the storm-tossed sea of experience is stilled ; so she is filled with wonder more and yet more at the new conditions wrought on her behalf, and is amazed at the blessedness of her experience. And so her wonderment grows with her growth in the new and blessed life.

The Innermost Meaning

But here we would present one more deep meaning for the Soul. The work of the Christ in the incident is what was accomplished by the Christ-Soul. The stilling of the Tempest is the embodiment of the changing of the elemental kingdoms by the Christ-Soul. The work or process was that of the tragic Sin-offering, the power by which it was done was that of the Divine Love. The Christ awoke in every one of His sad lives in which the work was performed, to realize how fearfully evil the conditions were, and how dreadfully the elemental spirits raged against the Soul ; and He became so filled with the terror which these conditions inspired within Him, that in every life He awoke to a consciousness of great dread lest He should utterly perish amid them and lose His own divine childhood. He awoke to the consciousness of His own loss of divine power as He was buffeted by the storm-spirits of the great deep, and cried out in agony to the Divine Love to save Him.

And so the allegory deepens in its meaning when we understand its inner significance, and the tragedy of it is intensified. But for that tragedy the wonderful and glorious awakening now taking place all over the world would never have been ; the tempestuous elemental spirits would have prevailed in their raging, and the Soul could not have risen into the spiritual heavens. The Christhood could not have been fully restored. The children of this world would have found it impossible to overcome the elemental kingdoms and rise up in the true evolution of their life into the heavenly conditions absolutely essential to Soul growth. But now the conditions have all become changed. *The elemental spirits are subject to the Christs.* The

Christ-Soul has accomplished His great work in changing the elemental kingdoms, blotting out the awful graven magnetic images which were against the Soul, and so purifying the astral world that those who were bound in its prison-houses are now able to rise out of them, and all who desire the angelic life may enter into its most blessed experience.

Such is the meaning of this new and more blessed age. The elemental spirits have been overcome ; the Christ within the Soul is awakening everywhere, and the works of Christhood are being done. The Souls of the ancient Christhood Order, the Cross-bearers of the World, are entering into their ancient heritage ; for the Christ has accomplished His Travail, and the days of the Son of Man have returned.

The Feeding of the Multitude

*Being an allegory of profound spiritual things, wherein
are illustrated the Divine Compassion and the
manner in which the Divine Love ministers
to the needs of the Soul ; and likewise
the showing forth of those events
which then were taking place,
as well as those events
which are now
breaking upon
the whole
world.*

A

THE NATURE OF THE MIRACLE

THE story of the Feeding of the Multitude is one which contains many beautiful spiritual truths. These truths, however, are hidden in the earthly and material setting which was given to the story by the writers of the Gospels. When the story underwent such a change that it was turned into a miracle upon the physical planes, its wonderful spiritual history was also changed, and its profound inner significances in the Soul were transferred to outward and material things. To the human imagination all true works of the divine are miraculous ; but men and women mostly think that the truly miraculous is always upon the physical planes ; and the *spiritual works* are not thought of as miraculous, though, indeed, if they were understood, they would be seen to transcend all outward phenomena both in their majesty and the results accruing from them. It has been through the teaching given for ages within the Churches that the truly miraculous is considered to be the phenomenal, until men and women cannot think even of any other kind of miraculous element in the life and teachings of the blessed Master. They do not understand the spiritual world and the wonderful works accomplished by it. They do not understand the nature of the Soul, nor the remarkable works accomplished within it. The laws of the heavens in their operations are enigmas unto them. They see and hear and feel upon the phenomenal world ; but that world behind the phenomenal they have never seen, and it only exists to their mind as an article of belief, or to their imagination as a vague dream. Its beauties, its glories, its marvellous powers its blessed ministries, its wonderful works, its angelic visions, they have never realized as Souls should whose true life is derived from that world.

275

It was an Allegory

Now, this story of the feeding of the multitude was not the story of a great work performed upon the physical plane by the Master, but an allegory illustrating the nature of His work, the purpose of it, and the extreme difficulty associated with it. It is unfortunate that it is so cast in the Gospel Records that its allegorical nature is hidden, whilst there is also given to it a relationship to the outer planes which it did not possess. The multitude is represented as having followed the Master into the desert without having made provision for their temporal requirements, and that, when the Master discovered it, He desired that provision should be made for them by the disciples ; but, as these latter could only find five barley loaves and two small fishes, He multiplied these loaves and fishes so that more than five thousand were fed, and twelve baskets of fragments left over.

Thus the allegorical significance of the story is lost through having been changed, and the miraculous element is transferred to the material spheres. The Master is made to perform a work of the most astounding character : for He is represented as changing the elements so greatly that what would have met only the needs of a few, is made to meet the needs of a multitude. He is thus endowed with occult powers over the elemental kingdoms, and to have changed them at will. The work is of the nature of transcendental physics : it is the work of the alchemist upon the physical planes. The Master becomes a magician whose magic word and touch change the laws that operate within the physical kingdoms, in order to make manifest His sympathy towards those who have followed Him into the desert. Beyond that there is no spiritual meaning in the story. There is no appeal to the Soul in it. It begins and ends with providing food for the body. The only spiritual element in it is the natural and obvious compassion of the beloved Master. This latter, of course, is beautiful ; and, the miraculous element taken away from it, is a testimony to His constant thoughtfulness towards all Souls, and such a lesson as we all require in our attitude towards others. But His compassion was divine in its nature. It was the compassion of a great Soul. It was more than philanthropic, as that beautiful term is now understood. It sought to do more, much more, than minister unto the physical necessities of men and women. It was born of the divine vision within the Master, and it was as comprehensive in its scope as the divine vision itself. It aimed at finding the *real* life within, in order to nourish it with spiritual food, to make manifest unto the Soul the divine power, to bring unto it the consciousness of the Divine Presence even amid the desert planes in the earth-life's experience. And in this wonderful allegory we have given unto us a picture of how the Divine Love has to nourish His children amid the spiritually desert-life which is the portion of the multitude, how they have to be ministered unto by those who know the Christ, and how they have to be helped towards higher things.

It is all most wonderful when the inner meaning is seen.

THE ALLEGORY CHANGED

The allegory was spoken by the Master unto all the disciples. It was told by Him to illustrate how desert the spiritual life of the world was, and the way in which the Souls upon its planes had to be nourished. In the true form of the allegory the story beautifully illustrated how men and women found their way into the desert-life with all its most sad and impoverishing conditions ; how difficult it was for them to maintain even a bare spiritual existence, not to speak of the fulness of the Soul's life ; how they had to be approached and ministered unto from the heavens ; how the Divine Love had to be revealed unto them as compassion ; how they had to be impressed with the Divine Wisdom in its simpler aspects and meanings ; and how the Soul had to be nourished.

The story of the miraculous feeding of the multitude is only part of the original allegory. The other part is found in another connection in the Gospel Records. The separation of the two parts, the changing of the expression from the Divine Love to the personal Jesus, and all the spiritual significations to material and phenomenal work upon the physical spheres, accomplished the transformation of the allegory concerning the divine compassion and the way in which the Divine Love sought to minister unto all Souls, into two distinct historical events wherein the compassion of the Master is the dominating thought, and the manifestation of alchemic power the preponderating action. The *personal* is made to obtrude itself and thus obscure the vision of the Divine, since it is *Jesus* who has compassion on the people and not the Divine Love ; and the magical power to change the elements at will is ascribed unto Him who always said that He not only knew nothing from Himself, but could do nothing from Himself, and that all the wisdom He spake and the divine work which He was able to accomplish, were the outcome of the presence of the heavenly Father within Him. He always disclaimed *personal* power, and insisted upon everything being related to the Father-Mother. And through thus breaking up the allegory and changing the form of the teaching, the beautiful and profound significance of it became lost.

It was just another act of the writers of the received Records materializing what they did not and could not understand. They made personal what was impersonal ; turned into material events what were spiritual facts. They gave an entirely physical meaning unto symbols relating to the human Soul and the Divine Lord. And thus they not only changed the allegory into the story of a most marvellous phenomenal work, but also misrepresented the whole nature of the ministry which the blessed Master had to give. He was presented by them as one who drew multitudes unto His ministry by means of the miracles which He wrought ; whereas His ministry was one of teaching the Divine Wisdom and manifesting the Divine Love. It was one of the most marvellous works of spiritual enlightenment for all who had the open ear to hear, and of the most wonderful interpretation of the Divine Love in His beautiful purposes for all who had the open eye to behold. It was such a ministry as men and women little dream of. There were works of blessing done by Him. He healed many of their infirmities and diseases ; but the healing was from *within*. The works were accomplished through the mind and Soul. HIS WORKS WERE ALL SPIRITUAL. Where the people were unprepared for the spiritual, He could do no mighty works. The works He wrought were done in accordance with the *faith* of the recipient ; and *faith is the perception of things spiritual*. Without that He accomplished no works of healing. There was no miscellaneous manifestation of power ; had it so been, there would not have been left in all Palestine one who was the victim of infirmity or disease. The blessed Master was a Physician ; but He was *not* merely a magnetic healer of physical ailments. He was such a physician as men and women then required, and whom they now require, one who could not only alleviate them by removing the outward manifestations of disease, but whose great work was to heal the *inward cause* of all disease, and make the life of the individual invulnerable to evil of any kind.

All His healing was Soullic. And therein lay the wonder of His works.

B

THE DESERT-PLACE

THERE is indeed a profound truth implied in the statement that the multitude followed the Christ into a desert place. The Master came into the world in a desert age. The ancient Religions had all lost their spiritual virility. They had been materialized until the spiritual meanings were lost in the outward forms. As a soul system, Judaism was spiritually dead. Its outward hierarchies had killed its inward life. Its priests were without spiritual vision. They had destroyed, during the process of ages of teaching within their occult schools, the inner sense of things, and they substituted for that inner sense a material meaning. They had brought down everything heavenly to the earthly planes, and related the things of the Soul to things of the phenomenal world. The Sanctuary they had turned into a house of death, even made of it an abattoir and public shambles. The Divine Ark had long been veiled, and the light of Shiloh had for many ages been extinguished.

Verily it was a dreary time for the Soul. Jewry had nothing to offer the hungry ones but its lifeless forms and ceremonies. Even to such inquiring ones as represented by Nicodemus, the consciousness of a higher birth than the earthly, was unknown. Souls were crying out amid the desert-life of Jewry for a divine shepherdhood ; but they understood not what it meant, so dimmed was the light within the lamp of the Soul through the effects of the awful system. And when Shiloh[1] came in the beautiful manifestation through the Master, they knew not that it was He ; for their spiritual eyes were sealed by means of the teachings they had received for ages. They understood not the meaning of Messiahship, nor what it was to be anointed by the Eternal Spirit. The sense of the spiritual world was almost lost altogether ; and indeed it was only awake in the few who sought most truly and earnestly for the realization of spiritual things. The most startling testimony to this statement may be found in the fact of so very few having been able to become complete disciples of the Christhood.

And what had happened to the things of the Soul through the priestly hierarchies of Jewry, had likewise happened elsewhere. Only a few elect ones could anywhere be found who

[1] Divine Christhood.

still appreciated divine things, and who sought the inner meanings amongst the outward forms and ceremonies. In Egypt the Ancient Wisdom had been lost for ages ; everything had been brought down, as in Jewry, from the spiritual spheres to the material. In Greece that same Wisdom had been changed from an inner spiritual history of the Soul and the Planet with the whole of the system of Sol, to one which grew into a mere intellectual philosophy on the one hand, and a Soulless mythology on the other. For the Ancient Wisdom which the Greeks knew in their purest days, became mere systems of intellectual thought and priestly superstition. The Orphic Mysteries were lost to them as effectually as the Mysteries of Hermes were lost to Egypt, and the wonderful Soul Mysteries known unto the ancient Hebrews were all lost to the Jewish people. To the East and the West, to the North and the South, the whole religious land was desert in the extreme. Here and there were a few centres founded, like the ancient Hebrew Schools of the Prophets, where the Mysteries were sought for by a few earnest Souls. But even in these centres the inner-most meanings were lost.

An Impoverished Humanity

It was in very deed a desert land into which the Master came as the vessel chosen by the Divine Lord through whom to make manifest the Christhood, re-interpret the Divine Wisdom, and show the true path by which alone the Soul could arrive at Christhood. And except to the very few Souls, like the inner group of disciples who were able to receive the more inward and profound teaching He came to give, His ministry had to be such as that set forth in the allegory. There was no other way of helping the people to a spiritual sense of the meaning of life. They were unable to understand more. Indeed, so far were they from a state of readiness to receive a fuller message, that even such teachings concerning the laws of life for the Soul as were given them, caused heart-burnings in many. And it is recorded in the Gospels that there were many who withdrew from following after Him ; and some even turned away in anger because of the things which He taught. The religious leaders and teachers were quite unable to appreciate His ministry, it was so far apart from the traditional schools of interpretation ; for these teachers were like barren fig-trees in relation to spiritual knowledge, and like wild vines in relation to spiritual life. They knew not the heavenly Wisdom ; they realized not the divine life within the Soul. They were as desert as the times and the land in which they lived. There was no heavenly spontaneity in them, and so the simpler truths set forth by the Master found no response.

ATTRACTED BUT NOT HELD

How desert the conditions of life were into which the Master came may be gathered from the history of the religious world written in the centuries which followed. The passing away of the Christhood was suceeded by the materialization of the precious truths which He had taught. Few accompanied Him in His Christhood, for they were unable to understand it, or to receive the deep things of the Wisdom and Love of the Father which it implied. The innermost group of the disciples alone were able to hear those things and respond to them. The " common people " as they have been called, heard Him gladly when He spake of the divine compassion, though they were unable to apprehend all that He meant by it, or to follow the path which would have led them to make manifest that compassion in their own lives. They were attracted through their great need for the loving sympathy He had to offer as the exposition of the Divine Love ; but they were astounded at and repelled by the demands which He made for purification of life as the first essential to the understanding of the Divine Wisdom and the realization of the Divine Love. And when He left, the outward manifestation of Christhood left with Him. For the inner group of disciples had soon to abandon their

" fellowship." They were no longer able to prevent the materialization of the beautiful Divine Wisdom which He had taught them. The betrayer had already done his work most effectively. The Mysteries concerning the Soul and the Divine Love which He had given to them had been changed in their meanings. From the inner group of followers had proceeded the original Gospel of St. Matthew and the Logia of St. John ; but these were misunderstood and misrepresented and thus destroyed by the writer who sent out the Gospel story from which the present four Records were afterwards built up. The story set forth in the Gospel by St. Matthew was that of the purpose of the Christhood manifestation and the path to be followed by the Soul in the seeking of Christhood ; and the Logia of St. John embodied the Divine Wisdom taught by the Master concerning the Soul, the Divine Love, and the Mystery of the Redemption. And the glorious vision of life in the one and the profound " Sayings " in the other, were taken and applied to persons, places, objects and experiences merely upon the outer physical spheres. The Christhood was made purely personal. It was related to the limited vehicle of the manifestation ; and its spiritual, impersonal, divine and universal nature was destroyed. And the profound Sayings concerning the Soul, the Divine Love and the redemption of the world, were built up into a philosophy of world redemption so contradictory, so confusing to the mind, so utterly at variance with the doctrine of true Love, that it made even more desert the whole western world where it was received.

HISTORICAL CHRISTIANITY

The history of Christianity in the West has not been one written in letters of the Divine Light, Love and Life ; but rather one written in spiritual darkness, loveless conflicts, and worldly conquests. The spiritual life of the people has languished amid the desert. They have cried for bread, and have had given to them stones. They have asked for the meanings of things, and have had presented to them interpretations which have only acted as scorpions. They have followed the name of the Christ, but have found the way desert. They have been attracted to Him, but not because they have understood the meaning of His beautiful life and profound teachings, for these they have not yet truly seen and heard because of the work of the enemy. They have been drawn to seek Him because of that *divine principle within them* which must of necessity seek for the realization and attainment of that Life of which He was the perfect exposition, though they have not understood the real meaning of the attraction. They have followed Him amid the desert of the spiritual conditions of the past centuries of this era, sustained on the fragmentary provision represented by the barley loaves and fishes. For though the Christhood dream has always been before some Souls during these ages, and the Christhood has been affirmed by the vast multitudes as the Saviour of the world; yet when they have sought the Christ, they have followed a name only, because they were taught that *the man* was the Christhood. They have sought the Saviour of the world to find healing, but have only followed a name without knowing its meaning. For they were taught that the Saviour was the Man of Nazareth who bore the name; that it was His name every tongue should confess; that it was before *Him* that every knee should worshipfully bow. For more than eighteen centuries have they bowed the knee unto the name, sadly ignorant of the fact that the one whom they thought they were worshipping was " *treading the winepress alone,*" and finding life upon the outer planes a sorrowful desert where even He Himself languished for " the bread of life " found in the Christhood realization. For during all the ages have they confessed His name before the world, without knowing the meaning of that name, all that it stood for of the Divine Love and Wisdom, and the life unto which it called all Souls.

The allegory was indeed full of deep meaning. It not only

illustrated what the Divine Love had to do in ministering unto His erring children ; but it likewise revealed what the conditions were which the Master found as He made manifest the Christhood, conditions which have reigned since then until this new and glorious age which has broken upon us as the outcome of the great work accomplished through the Office of the Cross as He bore the burden of the Sin-offering lives. It illustrated the way in which He had to minister unto the people who came to Him during the manifestation, except the few elect ones who were able to receive the deeper things ; and it foreshadowed the kind of provision that would be meted out to all who professed to follow the Christhood.

How true the allegory was will be recognized by all who are able to follow us as we interpret the remarkable story of how the beloved Master fed the Multitude.

C

THE DIVINE COMPASSION

WHEN the Master beheld the spiritual conditions of the people, He was moved with compassion for them. He beheld them to be like a flock of sheep without a shepherd. He saw how they were influenced by those who should have guided them, how far away from the true paths of life they were led by all who professed to shepherd them ; and it moved Him greatly. He loved like the Divine, for He was the exposition of that love in life. He felt as the Divine Father feels toward all Souls, and in His compassion He was the expression of the divine tenderness. Fain would He have shepherded all of them, and led them into the rich pastures of the Eternal Life ; but not only were the spiritual conditions amid which they passed their days, even as the desert, but desert indeed was the spiritual state of their Souls as the result.

Oh, it was beautiful beyond our telling, to witness the compassion of the Master for all Souls ; to behold how He was moved by the conditions of the people ; to magnetically feel the divine lifestream which flowed through Him, pulsing with wonderful life-giving powers, and longing to bestow these upon all who drew near to hear His word ! No one who was not of the inner group of disciples, and who therefore, did not behold Him in those hours, could conceive of the inexpressible yearning within Him to take all Souls along the path which led to the life and vision of the Divine Father. He was moved in a way and to a degree that men and women cannot imagine, not yet knowing the full meaning of divine compassion, nor understanding the nature and heart of a Christ. His was no passing pity awakened for the moment by the vision of the outward conditions of the people, and an endeavour to ameliorate their temporal experiences ; it was the divine pity awakened within Him through the vision of *the inner state of their life*. The compassion that flowed from Him was full-rounded in nature, taking into itself the *whole being*. Fain would He in His compassion have changed all the outward conditions which were so trying, mostly born of evil in various ways, and which militated against the upwardness of life ; and, with a view to the accomplishment of that, He longed to effect within the life of every one the changes which were absolutely essential. For He beheld that the conditions around them, both material and spiritual, were the outcome of the inward conditions, that the outward ways were the expression of the inward spiritual state. He saw the true relation of all things. He knew that the religious life of the people was as barren of deep spiritual realization as the social life of the leaders was lacking in genuine compassion and love towards all Souls. He knew that the religious life was the result of the materialization of the sacred teachings concerning the Soul and the Divine Love, the fruit of the false system of religious teaching and manifestation in worship which the occult priesthood of Jewry had established in the land, and He yearned with divine longing to save the multitudes from the awful system with its darkening and blighting effects.

HOW THE MASTER SAW THEM

The compassion of the Blessed Master had a depth of meaning that has not been yet fathomed. It had a depth of meaning which few have ever even faintly apprehended. When He was moved, the vision which moved Him was such as few have beheld. When He looked into the faces of the people, He beheld the spiritual state within them. He knew what was within a man. And what He beheld was not infrequently tragic. He saw the spiritual impoverishment of Dives, and the cankering sores of Lazarus. He beheld " the fires of Gehenna " at work in those who were passing through them ; and the wild beasts that prowled in the valley of Hinnom, where Souls were ravaged amid spiritual darkness. He beheld those in whom the fire of hate towards others burned ; and those who were anguishing amid the fires of passion and yearning for deliverance. As He looked upon the multitude, He beheld the awful desert state of them all, and it moved Him unspeakably. He sorrowed over the people. Their state filled Him with profound grief. If only we could impress our readers with the reality, they would understand all that we mean by our picture of the Master. And the hour has come for the picture to be restored which St. Matthew presented in his record of the Christ-Manifestation, and for the world to have revealed to it the kind of compassion which filled the Master, and what it led Him to do. It was indeed beautiful to witness *how* He loved all, and how His love moved them. *Those who were privileged to witness that love have come back to these outer planes to declare it anew, and re-interpret it.* They were indeed highly privileged then to look upon the Manifestation through Him ; they are now privileged to be able to recover that wonderful past, and tell of it unto all the world. They were sharers of that love manifested through the Master ;

they also became sharers of the burden by which the Redemption has been made possible through the Travail of the Divine Love. And now they have had it given unto them to behold all that that Love in *its travail* endured as it bore the burden, and what has been accomplished by it for the race.

Blessed be the Lord God of Israel for His abundant goodness unto all His children ! For He hath holpen us in our low estate, and raised us even unto the Throne of our father David. He hath revealed unto us the greatness of His Love towards all His children, and hath made us to be sharers in His kingdom and of its reign. He hath called us out of the darkness into His marvellous light and appointed us to minister before Him.

Ever Blessed be His Name !

D

HOW THE DIVINE FEEDS THE PEOPLE

HOW did the blessed Master feed the multitudes amid the desert place ? In the Gospel Records it is stated that it was by means of five barley loaves and two small fishes. These He is said to have multiplied to nourish fully five thousand, to have increased the loaves and the fishes in such a manner as to meet the demands of so great a number, that all were satisfied, and twelve baskets full of fragments remained over. According to the evangelists it was only a physical event. There is not the least suggestion that the event was a spiritual work. And in that light has it been received and understood through the eighteen centuries of this era in which the Churches have ministered unto the people. And in like manner has the other allegory recorded in the first two Records concerning the feeding of more than four thousand in the wilderness upon seven barley loaves and a few small fishes.

O it is sad beyond all words to think that these beautiful stories could ever have been so materialized as to have become mere physical acts in which divine power over the elemental kingdoms was made manifest, rather than the embodiments of profound spiritual truths. O the wrong that was done when these embodiments and teachings were destroyed by those who wrote the Records as we have them ; wrong wrought against the Divine Love and Wisdom and the Soul, when they so changed the spiritual meaning, that the truth could no longer be discerned.

In the allegory of the feeding of the five thousand upon five barley loaves and two small fishes, we should have had a manifestation of the divine compassion in stooping to meet the needs of the desert life of all Souls, so as to sustain them amid the impoverished conditions that they fainted not nor perished by the way ; and likewise in the feeding of the four thousand upon seven loaves and a few small fishes. For the two allegories revealed the divine compassion in a beautiful way. They showed how the Divine Love has never failed to find a means whereby the Soul might be reached and nourished even within the wilderness of this world and the desert conditions of its spiritual life. What could have been more beautiful than the revelation of the divine thoughtfulness in stooping to meet our requirements through the ministry represented by the barley loaves and two small fishes ? How wonderful is the divine tenderness revealed in the attitude of the Father toward His children in their fallen condition ? O how beautifully these allegories show forth His Love, that it knows no failure nor measure ; and how He would have all His children helped even unto fulness of Soul-life. For though the barley loaves were not " the Manna rained down from heaven," yet were they of the corn of that provision made for the Souls who were still in Egypt and Goshen, the corn provided amid the famine by the Divine Love and ministered unto the people through His servant Joseph. They were not " the shew-bread " which none can eat of until they have passed out of Egypt and Goshen, and even out of the wilderness life, into the land of true spiritual priesthood—the Christhood ; but they were of the bread provided by the Divine Love for all who went away into bondage and darkness, the bread that had to be broken, as it were, within the body, that had to be received through the senses of the body, that was so adapted unto the spiritual needs of all who were in bondage to the world-life and the inward darkness born of it, that the sacred things implied by the barley loaves might be apprehended. They were made up of those elements which were expressed by the parabolic teachings, the mystery embodiments and representations, the picture portrayals of events in the history of the Soul. They were the sacred things of the inner life brought down to the objective realm in order to impress the mind, through the vision of them, to reach the feelings through the visualization, and thus to move the whole spiritual nature to finer issues through awakening nobler impulses within the life.

It will therefore be seen how far from the true meaning of the story is the ordinary interpretation given to the feeding of the people upon barley loaves. For it was a great spiritual work to accomplish so much for the Soul in order that the truth implied might again be learnt, and its blessed effects felt.

THE PARABLES OF THE MASTER

The feeding of the multitudes by the Master had to be by parable. " *Without a parable spake He not unto them.*" They were parables which appealed to all the senses, the five avenues by means of which they could be fed. The eye, the ear, the taste, the feeling, and the touch, were all spoken to in these parables. Great spiritual truths were illustrated by them. They spoke of the true way of life, and the beautiful issues of following that way ; of the false ways of men and women, and the sad results which came to them. They set forth the value of the Soul in dealing with man as a spiritual unit, and how the Divine

Love sought unto the finding of every one willing to hear His word and receive its message. They made manifest the nature of the evil in the world which opposed the good, and the hardships it imposed upon all Souls ; and they revealed how that evil was to be overthrown, and the whole world of Soul-life redeemed. They illustrated many phases of the Soul's experience both sorrowful and joyful, and the profound love of the Father for all. They indicated something of its history in past ages, and implied the nature of the unspeakable loss which had come to it. They pointed out the way by which that loss could be recovered, and encouraged. The seeker to strive to regain what had been lost. The way of the redeemed life was clearly implied in them ; and there was made obvious the meaning of the blessed inheritance of the Christhood.

In this way did the Master teach and feed the people who drew near that He might address them. Many were " the barley loaves " which He brake and distributed amongst them as He sought to help them amid the desert conditions of their life. He appealed to their inner life by means of His parabolic teaching, seeking to reach them through the five avenues of their outward life, the outer senses. It was the only way in which they could be reached, so dulled was their spiritual power to receive. Their Intuition was veiled, and the inner consciousness of childhood to the Divine Love quite lost. They had eyes to see, yet saw not ; ears to hear, yet they heard not ; and hearts to perceive, yet they beheld not. Their spiritual vision had been destroyed through the terrible religious system of which they had been the victims for ages. They had no longer, as a people, the power to hear the divine speaking within the sanctuary of their innermost being, so dulled was the Soul with the terrible system which destroyed the divine vision within, and prevented its being restored. The darkest of veils had long been drawn across their spiritual mind so that the true sense of divine things was lost ; for no longer had they the power to discern spiritually. The sense-life had become everything to them : even their religion was nothing more than the craving to find divine favour, and to find it in the realization of those personal and national aspirations which were all outward, earthly and material.

How otherwise could the blessed Master approach such Souls than through the sense-life in its varied avenues ? How otherwise could He ever hope to spiritually nourish their desert-life than by means of parable which might appeal to their outward vision and feeling ? Nor are we to suppose for a moment that He only spake in parables in order that they might not understand Him, as seems to be implied in the Gospel Records ; for as we have shown in an earlier chapter, that could never have been possible in the case of the Master. Only too gladly would he have spoken more directly to the people had they been able to receive the teachings. It was *not* a question of counting them unworthy to hear the sacred things of which He had to speak, but entirely a question of their fitness to hear and understand. To have done what the Gospel Records seem to imply, and what many occultists affirm concerning the Mysteries and their communication to the Soul, would not have been in harmony with the ways of the Divine Love.

Herein then was the divine compassion shown forth by the Master. He beheld the low spiritual estate of the people, and went down to minister unto them. He loved them with the love of the Divine Father, and sought to awaken the love of the divine life within them. He pitied them with the pity of God, and spake unto them as they were able to receive. He yearned towards them with the longings of the Father to recall them to a consciousness of their divine childhood, and unto that end He spake His parables. And what joy filled Him when He beheld a Soul receive His meaning ! What gladness there was within the inner circle when one Soul awoke to the reality of its divine childhood ! How beautiful it was to witness the divine rejoicing when a Soul was known to have set out on the path of the redeemed life, determined to attain unto the Christhood realization ! It was indeed a blessed thing to be of that inner group to share the joy and gladness which broke upon it when Souls were influenced divinely.

E

THE UNFOLDING OF SOUL-MYSTERIES

IN addition to " the barley loaves " with which the Master fed the multitude, " two small fishes " were distributed amongst them. And our readers will now be prepared to learn that these were not two of the creatures whose home is in the waters. O how this wonderful work of the blessed Master has been made use of to maintain the habit of taking the creatures for food. How constant is the reference to the story in the Gospel Records as a plea that the blessed Master not only permitted flesh to be eaten, but actually gave it unto the disciples to distribute to the multitude. What terrible results have issued from the materialization of the truth taught by this allegory, and kindred teachings. What a sad and sorrowful thing was done when a spiritual allegory was changed into a work upon the physical plane by which two small creatures were sacrificed to feed a multitude, their flesh being multiplied indefinitely to meet the demand. What a dishonour was done to the Master when He was so misrepresented ; and what a betrayal of the divine compassion He so beautifully interpreted ! How little the writers understood the meaning of the divine pity and in what way it made itself manifest. Is not the picture a contradiction in itself as the writers of these Records drew it, when they presented the Master as one moved with compassion towards the multitude, *yet one who failed in that pity towards the little creatures, which is of the very nature of true compassion ?* How the misfortune has helped to change the whole vision

U

of the nature of a Christhood, none can know but those who arrive at the true vision, and see how the Christhood of the sublime Master was misrepresented. True, it is only one scene in the tragedy ; but it has exercised a most important influence upon the minds of many who would otherwise have been led away from the flesh pots of Egypt into the ways of the redeemed life. It has made many who had true compassion within them, and who felt it was wrong to take the life of any creature for purposes of food and clothing, wonder how it happened that the Master could have countenanced any such thing, let alone do it Himself. And to-day it is a stumbling block in the way of many entering upon the path of Christhood. Nor can the true path be clearly seen and understood until the terrible misrepresentation of the Master's Life and Teachings has been exposed, and the true vision made clear unto all who desire to truly follow His way.

WHAT FISH SIGNIFIED

The two small fish were not creatures. They were profound *Mysteries.* " The barley loaves " were many, " the fish " were few. It was not because there were few fish in the possession of the Master that only two small ones were made use of, for with Him there was an abundant supply ; it was rather because the people were only equal to assimilating as food those things implied in the two small fish, *viz.*, the two minor or lesser spiritual Mysteries. How little they were equal to may be gathered from the fact that so many baskets full of fragments were left over. They were spiritually satisfied with " barley loaves and the two small fishes." Was not the place " desert " ? As we have seen, their Souls were as desert as the place. So they could only take desert fare. Deep things, high things, strong things concerning life and destiny, God and the Soul, were as yet beyond their powers of perception, reception, and assimilation. Indeed so desert were the conditions then, and so desert did they continue after the passing away of the Christ-hood, that the Mysteries which He broke unto the people were never assimilated by them, nor by those who followed them, nor indeed by any during all the ages which have arisen and set since those times until the present age. Had even the " two small fishes " or Mysteries been understood by the teachers and the taught, the history written in the name of the Master during those centuries would have been very different ; and the western world would have been the theatre of very different activities to those which have dominated it. The present state of that world is the sure testimony that its inhabitants never have apprehended the meaning of the Master's mani-festation and teachings, not even the beautiful truths implied in the " two small fishes." But the hour is now come when they have to be re-interpreted for the Soul, and all the Mysteries unfolded unto those who are able to receive the profound truths they contain.

What then were the two small fishes which were broken and distributed unto the people ? They were *the nature of the Soul, and the character of the life unto which man was called :* the Soul as a spiritual organism and system whose value could not be outweighed by all the earth-life could lay at a man's feet, even unto the possession of *all* it could give ; and the life unto which man is called by the Divine Love, and for which he is counselled alone to labour. Let our readers turn to the parables spoken by the Master, and, notwithstanding that most of these are incorrectly presented in the Gospel Records, they will find that the value of the Soul of man as a spiritual system, and the nature of the Life unto which the Master called all, are there embodied. Let them read the parables in the light of what we have written, and even the most involved of them will become clear. The two small fishes were administered *with* the barley loaves ; for all the experiences of life portrayed in the par-ables gathered around these two beautiful and profound truths.

How remarkable it is that throughout all the long centuries since the days of the Master, the scholars should have missed the meaning of the term translated *fish* ? For the sign of the fish was used to denote deep things. Occultly it was the symbol of profound mystery. Even in the Zodiacal Signs we find the fish. Some of the early Christian Martyrs took it for their sign. It occurs many times in the Old Testament Scriptures with obvious symbolic meaning. In a like connection is the term *fishermen* used.

The word and sign mean *that which is hidden*. The fish was the sign of some hidden truth. It symbolized an unfoldment of such truth when the fish was said to be partaken of. To break up the " two small fishes " was to break up the hidden truths of the Soul's value as a spiritual system, and the high order of life unto which it is called, and distribute them with the barley loaves—the Parables ; for these were the two minor Mysteries of hidden things unfolded. The sign was originally taken to represent hidden spiritual and divine things, because the home of the fish was in the deep waters. And, as we have seen when treating of the baptism of John and the marriage in Cana of Galilee, the term *water* was the symbol of truth, and *deep waters* the symbol of deep truths ; so the fish became the sign of the deepest truths concerning the Soul and the Divine Wisdom. To partake of fish, in the language of symbolism, was to partake of *a divine mystery*. And to have given to eat fish broiled upon fire (as it is recorded the Lord gave unto the disciples), was to have *the divine mystery* offered in such a way that its acceptance by the Soul brought into its system the energy of the Holy One ; for that was symbolized by fire.[1]

WHEN THE CHURCHES UNDERSTAND

How profound were the Teachings of the blessed Master

[1] On this profound Mystery see the Chapter on the Lord and Simon Peter.

will be gathered from what we can only here indicate in passing ; and what a wealth of spiritual meaning lies awaiting those who once knew these things, and also for all who are able to follow the Christhood unto blessed realization ! How very different will be the Churches' ministry when all their teachers know these things, when the real Christhood is understood, and the profound Soul-teachings are rightly interpreted ? How beautiful will the life of the Churches then be with their various orders of ministry, comprising all Souls in their different degrees of spiritual experience, circles of communion according to the degree of their vision and realization, groups of disciples of Christhood from the first degree inward until the perfect degree is reached ? They will then not have to bid against each other for success such as official minds regard as the true measure of the value of the ministry ; they will not have to exist as denominations through depleting one another ; they will not be tempted to inveigh against each other because of doctrinal differences and ecclesiastical codes in order to attest their loyalty to the Christhood and the order to which they belong ; they will not vainly imagine that they alone possess the truth, and that those who step out from their circles and go beyond the bounds of their limitations, have stepped forth into the darkness of error ; for they will then see and understand the meaning of the various orders of communion, the various degrees of belief (not the erroneous beliefs many of them hold to-day, but truth in its manifold expression) held by these orders, and how they are all degrees of apprehension, reception and realization of spiritual life of the path to the attainment of the Christhood—an attainment unto which all Souls will then move forward.

In that day shall the Church universal be the Church of Christhood and so the Church of the Living God. It will be such a Church as the western world has not seen. It will be a Church in which the spirit of Christhood reigns, and where all

Souls within its borders are accounted the recipients of the Christ-life, from the Christ-child Soul in whom the heavenly consciousness has been but newly awakened, to the Souls in whom that life has been wonderfully realized. And it will be a Church whose labours towards the multitudes will not be carried out with a view to attracting them to come within the official recognition and communion ; it will rather be a beautiful ministry through its various orders and members by means of which the lot of the multitude will be changed, the desert conditions of life turned into such conditions as will enable them to grow spiritually ; it will be the Christhood life lived amongst them by all who know its beautiful purity, goodness and light, and divine childhood so revealed unto all the Father's children that they may come to understand what it means, be attracted by its graciousness, and leave the desert life to follow on to know it through blessed realization.

F

GATHERING UP THE FRAGMENTS

IN the narratives it is stated that after all the people had partaken of the barley loaves and the fishes, the disciples gathered up " *twelve baskets of fragments.*" There was to be nothing lost.

The statement is truly significant. At first sight it seems as if there was nothing of importance in it, beyond the fact that it showed how plentiful had been the supply provided by the Master. And, with the whole incident taken as a literal event, the abundance has often been used to illustrate the divine goodness in making provision for all His children—a beautiful truth which is always true of Him, but which alas ! is not always realized by His children because of the way of life pursued by so many. But it is true in a sense little thought of, that the divine provision is abundant. His provision is adequate for all His children upon *every sphere* of their experience. From the outermost spheres of life unto the innermost of the Soul, provision has been made to meet every requirement.

This may seem to be a contradiction of experience, so many are there who now lack. But they do not lack because there is no provision made by the Divine Love, but owing to the false and unjust conditions which prevail. If the conditions were right and true, the provision would be abundant, and more than abundant. Yet the needs of the outermost and the provision made for that life, pale before the marvellous abundance made for the inner and higher spheres.

NUMBERS HAVE SPIRITUAL VALUES

But the great truth revealed in the incidental mention of " the twelve baskets " full of fragments gathered up after the multitude was satisfied, is of a different nature, and testifies to the sad spiritual conditions of the people. It speaks of the utter failure of the presentation of the twofold mystery of the nature of the Soul and the life to which man was and is called by the Divine Love, to find response in the minds of the people. They had not partaken of the loaves and fishes in such a manner as to enable them to take even the first step in the path to the redeemed life and the Christhood realizations. The truth taught had not been assimilated ; and so the first spiritual experience of the Soul on the way to the realization of the redeemed life, had not been entered into. As far as the multitude was concerned, the ministry of the Master and the Manifestation of the Christhood through Him, were an utter failure in their appeal. So desert was the place, so utterly unspiritual were the conditions, so impoverished was the state of the Soul of the people, that, though the teachings were beautiful and adapted to their needs, they were quite unable (with rare exceptions) to receive and assimilate their meanings. It was, indeed, tragic. And the tragedy deepened when the Christhood passed away.

To what might those " twelve baskets " refer ? Had they any deep and hidden significance for the Soul ? The number *twelve* is a sacred sign. It is said that there were *twelve patriarchs*, that there were *twelve sons of Jacob*, and *twelve tribes of Israel*. There were *twelve apostles.* The New Jerusalem had *twelve foundations* and *twelve gates*. The woman clothed with the Sun had *twelve* stars. The Zodiac has *twelve signs*, and these divide the year of the earth into *twelve months* during which the earth passes through these signs. Like the earth, the Soul has to pass through all the spiritual experiences for which these signs stand. On its way to the attainment of the redeemed life it must needs enter into the experience of the spiritual qualities which the *twelve apostles* represent. For the name of each signifies a spiritual quality. It must needs pass through every gate into " the Holy City," the purified life, and possess *the twelve pearls* which crowned the gates. For the gates are " the labours " of the Soul in its overcoming of evil and its entrance into the inheritance of the powers which the twelve apostles represent.

And so the twelve baskets were significant. They revealed an amazing fact. Though the Master broke up and distributed the barley loaves with the two small fishes or " lesser Mysteries," yet so little did the people receive the inner meanings of the teaching that, when the Christhood was about to pass away, they had not accomplished even the first *labour of the Soul* nor entered upon the path by which all the labours would have been attained. Every labour or deep spiritual experience, contains its own nourishment for the Soul ; and the life learns as it passes through.

LETTING DOWN THE HEAVENLY TREASURES

The twelve baskets full were gathered. The beautiful truths

taught were not to be lost. They were there for use when the Soul was ready for them. *The twelve labours* to be accomplished ere the attainment of the redeemed life, were not yet entered upon by the people ; but the twelve baskets full of the truths of the Divine Love were gathered up to be preserved and kept awaiting them when their hour was come. Nothing of the truth has been lost ; the loss has been with the Soul, with all who have not sought to follow the Christhood through the ways of the redeemed life. The Mysteries were withdrawn from the earth, that is, from the knowledge of men and women ; because so desert were the conditions that the children were not able to receive these profound things with the understanding of the inner meaning, and they were withdrawn in order to preserve them that they might not be further misunderstood and so altogether destroyed. But they were to be restored again when the days of the Regeneration came and the true vision of the Christhood was restored. The Divine Love seems to have been slow in making Himself manifest to change this desert-world into a garden of spiritual fruitfulness. He seems to have tarried long ere making Himself known once more. The days of the Redemption have taken more than eighteen centuries to come and make plain the way for the divine manifestation once more to be made.

Yet has there been no tarrying with the Divine One ; for He is *never* slow to bless and redeem His children. He is never behind with His goodness and compassion. He fails not in what He promises to perform.

And thus it happens that we have the return with us now, the letting down from the Heavens of His dwelling of " the twelve baskets " full of the inner meaning of things ; the restoration unto all who are able to receive them, of the Mysteries learnt on the path of the Christhood ; the re-interpretation of the meaning of the Soul's nature and history as expressed in the Zodiacal signs ; the exposition of the twelve spiritual states represented by " the apostles " ; the profound significance of the meanings of the terms applied to the Soul under the guise of "the twelve tribes of Israel," and the even profounder meaning of the term " patriarch." These great and blessed truths have come as the expression of the divine goodness, the outcome of the *travail* of the Divine Love. They are with us to-day because they have been made possible through the great work accomplished after the passing of the Christhood. They are the fruits of the travail of the Sin-offering which He went away to perform. They are the blessed and glorious results of that burden-bearing by means of which the Divine Love through Him changed the whole astral kingdom, blotting out the magnetic images which were upon it, and which hindered the Soul in its upwardness—" the hand-writings which were against us " upon the walls of that kingdom. For by the process known as the Sin-offering that kingdom has undergone such great changes, has been made so much purer, that the way has been made clear for the Soul to once more perform its true evolution. The purification of the astral kingdom has led to the approach of the angelic world to the planes of the Earth with a ministry such as this world has not known for countless ages. True spiritual vision has not only become possible, but is a realization once more. The prophetic office is again restored. The eyes of the Seers are being opened, and the life of the heavens beheld. The angels of God are now beheld descending upon and ascending from the Son of Man. The Lord has again appeared in Galilee, on its waters and its mountains ; at Bethany ; and even on the Mount of Olivet. He has been seen in Jerusalem by those who have sought the silence and sanctity of " the upper-room." For the inner vision is restored ; the spiritual conditions have been changed ; and the Soul is now able to rise out of the desert state and find the angelic oasis within the wilderness, and even the garden of the Lord.

The Edenic Age Returning

How sad and yet blessed is the truth conveyed to us by the expression, " *Gather up the fragments so that nothing be lost ; and they gathered the twelve baskets full* "—sad because of the desert conditions of the people, blessed because the Divine Love has preserved the Mysteries for us and restored them unto us. Though the people's eyes were holden, and their ears dull, and their hearts heavy through the influences of the desert conditions upon them, that they could not receive the Teachings of the Master nor perceive the meaning of the Manifestation, who will gainsay the obvious truth that the Divine Love hath wrought great things for us in that He hath preserved for us the most precious spiritual things which we designate the Mysteries, until He had so purified the astral world that they could be given again unto His children, when they might be able to hear them gladly, to perceive the inner meanings of them, and to appropriate them in such a way as to enable them to follow on in that path whose way leads unto *the fulness* of the realization of the pure and blessed life, and so come into their true and full inheritance of the Divine Love, Light and Life, an inheritance incorruptible and undefiled and that passeth not away ?

Is it any wonder that there is breaking upon the world a great new joy ; a more beautiful and more illumined hope ; a truer and a diviner love ; a deeper and nobler consciousness of life ; a spiritual gladness that speaks of the return of the Soul to its divine childhood ; a greater longing for the realization of the edenic life when evil, want and wrong shall be no more, but peace and joy and fulness unto all ? None need wonder who know what it is to realize the Divine Love ; for it is the outcome of all that He has done for us. It is the fruit of His travail ; the blossoming and fructification of the Fig-Tree and the Vine whose fruits are the life of the Soul.

The Transfiguration

*Being the narrative of the sublimest of Soul-visions
beheld by those of the innermost group of disciples upon the Angelic World, and not such
a vision as is implied in the manifestations during a séance ; wherein the Divine
One was revealed as the Lord of Light,
Love and Life ; and also the nature
of the mysterious Sin-offering,
a history so momentous that
it was to be kept secret
until the present time,
and is herein
revealed and
interpreted.*

A

A TREASURE RARE AND BEAUTIFUL

IT is a wonderful story that is told by the writers of the Synoptic Records in which they describe the Transfiguration of the Christ. It is a picture most fascinating to " the faithful," and, indeed, to all who are attracted to the mystical side of things. Even in the form in which it is found in the Gospels with their varying sidelights, it is full of a strange suggestiveness. On the surface its meanings appear simple and obvious ; but to the true mystic they will reveal themselves as being most profound. If the picture seems to have no background rich in details whose meanings are not apparent, it is only because of the remarkably striking foreground, and the personal and local elements introduced ; for the whole framework of the story is local, and the treatment of it is personal. The world of the Soul is transferred from the subjection to the objective ; and the vision upon the heavens is brought down to the outer planes of the earth. The incident is presented as a transformation scene which took place upon the threshold of Palestine, and was accomplished upon the Master through the approach of the spiritual heavens. It even reads like a story of a Materialization, such as may be found in certain spiritualistic literature, wherein two great leaders and teachers of Souls are made to appear to the visual senses of three men.

Yet the story is one full of true beauty and power—beauty and power transcending anything of an outward and visual nature. It is a transfiguration of the most realistic order, though in nature it is altogether spiritual and not personal. The scene is of the most transcendent order whose glory is most real and translucent, though not such as may be produced at any materialization Séance on these outer spheres. For the story of the Transfiguration of the Christ is one of the most profound and remarkable of the many narratives found in the Gospels.

It is one which lifts us up and carries us away from the outer planes, from the threshold of earth to the threshold of the kingdom of the heavens ; from the objective world to the subjective realms of the Soul ; from the material spheres to those which are altogether spiritual, inward, and transcendently glorious. By the vision in it we are carried upward till we see face to face upon the spiritual heavens. So near is the divine kingdom brought to us, that we are permitted to look into it, to sense things which have been hidden from the Soul for long ages, to hear concerning those precious truths which belong to the most profound of the Mysteries, to witness the glory of a Divine Christhood, and to listen to the proclamation of the Divine One that such a Christhood is " the beloved son of the Highest " whose message the Soul is to hear.

In the Transfiguration of the Christ we have a gem of inestimable value whose chaste facets throw out the radiance of the glory of the Ineffable One in such fulness that it may be truly said that the whole wealth of that glory is reflected in them. It is a treasure of inexhaustible richness which has long been buried in the field of an impossible literalism ; and so there has been lost to the Soul a vision of the transcendent nature of Christhood.

THE MEANING HAS REMAINED SECRET

The Vision with its profound meanings was not to be told by those who beheld the wonderful drama until " the Son of Man " should be risen again from the dead. All through the centuries of this era since the present Gospel Records were written, has the drama remained unfolded, the marvellous vision untold, the remarkable spiritual history embodied in it, uninterpreted. The story as presented in the Synoptics has been known, and a limited interpretation given unto it ; but what it was, and what it meant in an esoteric sense, have remained hidden until these days of the arising from the dead of the Son of Man. In its spiritual and divine significance the Transfiguration of the Christ has remained a mystery. Those who beheld its glory had to keep the vision secret. It has been told to no man until these days.

What could that vision be that was to be kept so secret ? What could be the meaning of keeping it a secret until the Son of Man was risen again from the dead ? Nay, though it may seem a strange question to ask in the light of the history that is found in the Gospel Records, what is to be understood by the expression " *Until the Son of Man be risen again ?* " When did the Christ accomplish the decease referred to in the vision, and in what manner was His arising from the dead ? So accustomed are men and women to accept all the history given in the narratives as literal and personal, that it is with amazement they hear such questions, and imagine that the questioner is rejecting the truth because he rejects the literalism which they hold to be so vital, and seeks unto the finding of the inner meanings, *the real truths*, which are hidden from their view.

As we unfold the story these questions will receive their answer, and the hidden meanings will become clear. The inner significance of the vision will be understood. The reason why it could not be told until now will be obvious. In all things which are true and right there is divine purpose written upon them, and never more so than here. If the Mystery signified in the Transfiguration of the Christ, has been hidden all through the ages of the Christian Era, it has been so because of the conditions which followed the blessed manifestation. The localization and materialization of things universal and wholly spiritual, led to the most sad religious thoughts, systems and manifestations. Everything of a divine order was brought down to the level of the barbaric religious systems of the Jews and the Pagans, but especially the former. It was given unto the Master to forsee the coming of these things. He knew they would arise, as many of His Sayings testify. It was needful therefore that the inner meanings of the remarkable vision should not be told until the Son of Man had not only accomplished " *the decease* " spoken of, but should have again risen up from the dead ; for then the conditions would become changed, and Souls might be able to hear the message contained in the vision. And now that remarkable " decease " having been accomplished and the Son of Man having risen once more from the dead ; now that the awful conditions are changing so greatly and Souls are everywhere awakening and responding to the voice of the Eternal and ever Blessed One who calls to them ; now that the elect Souls who once knew the Mysteries in their innermost meanings, are seeking with pure and reverent desire to come again into the consciousness of the Divine Love and Wisdom, the vision may be told to all who are able to receive it. *For those who beheld the vision, are here also.* With the arising again of the Son of Man, they have also come, as was likewise foretold. They have come to bear their testimony to the Christhood, and to the interpretation of it which was given through the blessed Master. They have come to speak of the things which they both heard and saw when they sojourned with the Master in the days of the blessed manifestation.

B

THE MOUNT WHERE IT TOOK PLACE

THE Mount of Transfiguration has been located in Palestine, and it is generally thought to have been Mount Tabor. That is the result of the materialization of the story. In their spiritual darkness men and women have associated with a mountain upon the physical planes of the earth, what was a sublime inward state. With great zeal have archæologists endeavoured to discover the hill upon which this most marvellous vision took place, so wrapped up are they in the literalism which has been made to surround and clothe the event.

The uplands of the earth are doubtless more helpful to Souls who desire to rise on to the spiritual heavens, for the air is, as a rule, more rarefied than in the valleys ; and the breathing of exhilarating air is essential to the best conditions. It is also quite true that the blessed Master often sought the uplands for prayer. He knew the value of pure air, and how helpful it was to the highest realizations.

But the Mount of Transfiguration was not earthly in any sense. The uplands to which the Master and His three intimate friends went, were not physical merely. They sought the uplands of the hills only that the conditions might be more conducive to the blessed vision. *The real uplands were within them. They were spiritual. They led to the Mount of the Lord.* For only through the elevation of the spiritual within could the highest be reached. The kingdom of the divine is " an exceedingly high mountain," and the Soul who would ascend it must needs do so by prayer ; that is, by intense Soul-desire towards the Eternal Love. The disciple must live much in the uplands of spiritual feeling and thought. He will realize the absolute necessity for the pure and rarefied atmosphere where the breath of heaven may be freely breathed. The ecstatic vision comes in this way. Those who would behold it, must live in the heights. And these uplands have to be reached by the narrow way, the path into which the Christhood leads us, the steep ascent up which the Divine Love guides us.

AFTER SIX DAYS

It was after six days had passed that the Master is said to have taken the three intimate disciples up to the mountain. The simple detail, apparently without any relation to spiritual things, is full of significance. It contains a wonderful history in itself. For the six days were not days of twenty-four hours. Nor were they such days as are given us by the rotation of the Earth. They were days of the Soul, days full of great spiritual history for the three referred to, days in which they had grown towards the fulness of the divine life. They were days which represented the accession of such experiences as enabled them to reach that point in their history when they were in a state to ascend the Mount of Transfiguration. For following the sixth day comes the seventh ; and the seventh day is hallowed unto the Lord.

The seventh number is one that is most sacred. It is a perfect number. It signifies many precious things. It is of the Divine Nature. It speaks of the seven-fold Spirit. It implies many things for the Soul. One who has attained to that spiritual experience signified by the passing of the sixth day and the approach of the seventh, has entered upon a phase of inward history that must be experienced to be fully understood. The Elohim are seven ; and the Soul who attains to Christhood has the seven-fold Spirit. The spectrum colours are seven ; and the Soul who has reached the seventh day is taking unto herself the innermost colour, so that all may be blended in her nature. The seventh tone is necessary to the scale ; without it there could be no perfection of harmony. It is as the seventh voice of the divine within the Soul, a voice which fills the whole heavens of the Soul's spiritual system. When the Soul reaches that state she is lifted on to the innermost sphere of her own system—the Divine Kingdom—where she sees and hears unutterable things. *For it is the innermost plane of her being whence she beholds the divine vision.*

We have thus in this simple detail, the spiritual history of the three who were to be lifted up to that kingdom whence the vision of the transfigured Lord would be beheld. They had risen from plane to plane in their innermost life, until the seventh was reached. The other disciples did not accompany the Master to that sublime state. But these three were able to follow where some of the others could not ; and they could now ascend the mount whence the vision of the Transfiguration was seen : by and by they would also enter into " the Garden of

Gethsemane " where another and very different vision would be witnessed, even the vision of the Divine Anguish revealing itself through the agony of the Master.

C
THE VISION

THAT which the three disciples beheld was no man, but the Lord. The blessed Master was still with them ; they saw Him as Jesus only. But in the wonderful vision they beheld that One who was making manifest through the blessed Master —the Divine Christ. They then passed from the personal spheres to those which are impersonal ; from the more outward to the innermost ; from the lower spiritual to the highest. They went up into the mount with Jesus, and came down from it with Him ; but on the mount it was no man whom they saw, but the Lord of Glory. The outer world was lost to sense in the glorious vision. Everything earthly was forgotten.

In this sublime vision we have a picture of Soul-life in its perfection of being. It is a picture of the Glory of Adonai ; but the vision is within the heavens of the Soul. His face did shine as the sun in his fulness ; for the Divine Lord within the Soul is a sun unto her. " *The Lord is our sun ; He will give the glory of His grace.*" The sun in his fulness is the sun unveiled. No dense atmosphere obscures or dims his glory. He shines without interruption. His light streameth from afar, and reacheth the outermost bounds. There is nothing hidden from the glory thereof. And so is it in the Soul when her whole system is purified, and she is following the path of Jesus (the redeemed life), and seeking to be a true disciple of the Christ (to realize Christhood). The Lord is her sun ; for the light of His glory is the Soul's radiance. He shines within her beautiful system in sublime fulness : His countenance is glorious to behold within her sanctuary.

The perfected microcosm is even as the perfected macrocosm.

The divine is the centre of man's spiritual system ; and when the man rises in the scale of life and reaches the seventh tone, the seventh colour, and the seventh spirit of Elohim, he arrives at the divine vision to be beheld within the heavens of his own system. He ascends then the seventh plane, the innermost, the highest, where he finds the divine kingdom wherein the Adonai has His throne. There the " glory " breaks upon the Soul's vision. There all things are transfigured. In the valley it is the man who is seen : on the mount it is the Lord. On the lower reaches and planes of spiritual experience, it is the Jesus-life that is known : on the higher reaches and innermost spheres of life, it is the Lord who is seen in this Glory.

THE DIVINE RADIANCE WITHIN

The radiance of His countenance was so great, and His garments were so pure, that these glistened with the glory. His garments were whiter than any fuller's soap could make them, so pure were they to look upon. In their whiteness they reflected the glory which streamed from His countenance. And what might this vision mean to those who beheld it, and who may again behold it ? Surely this wonderful and most beautiful truth, that the garments with which the Lord clothes the Soul are always pure, so pure that they are white, and glistening with the radiance of the divine countenance. And what are the garments of the Soul with which her Lord clothes her in the days of her ascension to the mount of Transfiguration ? They are the white raiment of a purified life, a life whose ways have all been made white, a life whose ways have been purified until every one of them glistens with the radiance of His countenance and thus makes manifest His glory. For the way of Jesus is that of the purified life, the redeemed life ; and the path of the Christ is that of heavenly virtue or power born from the Divine Presence within the Soul, the path of heavenly Wisdom by which virtue or the inward power of the Divine Love is crowned. The wonderful garments are those of

Christhood ; for it is of the very nature of Christhood to reflect the glory of the Divine Life, Light and Love.

The meanings of such a vision are manifold ; and most of them will be obvious to those who are earnestly seeking the higher way, the higher thought, the higher realizations of life. They will see in the story the true vision of a Christhood, and understand how pure and beautiful the garments of the Master were. They will understand the glory that was in Him, and see how it was reflected in every one of His ways. Unto them will His garments show white, whiter than anything of an earthly order ; they will glisten all over with the golden radiance of the Divine Love and Wisdom. For such will there be no shadow upon them, shadow thrown through some obscuring weakness ; for they will all be beautiful with the radiance, and transparent in their glory. These will again behold the Christ as He was ; they will see the wonderful manifestation as it was given. They will know that His ways were all pure ; that His actions were great with the divine gentleness. They will behold the true meaning of love, and recognize its gloriousness as they witness it breaking in His compassion for Souls, and in His pity unto all creatures. To them will the Divine Love appear as He is, the lover of all, and the protector of every creature. The vision will speak to them of the kind of life the blessed Master lived as the interpreter of that Love, and the manifestor of the compassion and pity of the Lord. It will show to them that the horrors of the houses of cruel sacrifices, with their shambles and laboratories, could have had no countenance from Him ; and it will reveal to them that no blood-guiltiness in any form tarnished the whiteness of His raiment, that in His ways in life He had no part in anything which did not reflect the glory of the Lord. They will behold upon the mount the nature of His Christhood, and realize what it means to interpret the Divine Love and show forth the Divine Wisdom as He so fully and beautifully did.

D

THE APPEARING OF MOSES AND ELIJAH

HERE we have new factors introduced, whose presence on such an occasion is more than ordinarily significant. At first sight we might be inclined to doubt this part of the vision and think that the Jewish editor had introduced the two famous names for the purpose of connecting the Christ with the Mosaic economy as the Jews interpreted it, and associating Him with a prophet of their own religion. But the new part of the vision was very real also. It was so real that the vision remained with those who beheld it. They saw " *One like unto Moses, and one like unto Elijah*," talking with the Lord.

From the personal standpoint it looks more and more like a materialization of two notable characters such as have been associated with certain mediums and Séances. We can well understand Spiritualists taking the vision in that way. We can even imagine them falling back upon it as evidence that what are known as materializations were encouraged and sanctioned by the blessed Master. They do think and speak of Him as having been *the great medium ;* though He was not such a medium as they suppose. And it may be that many think that He was like a materializing medium.

But such a view of the subject would show how very little Spiritualists understand the nature of the Master, and the nature of the highest order of mediumship. He was a medium of the very highest order ; but His mediumship was always conscious. *He was not the vehicle of extraneous spirits, but always of the divine.* The Angel of the Lord was ever present to Him. The consciousness of the indwelling Divine Presence was at all times with Him. The voice that spake within Him was the voice of the ever Blessed One. The visions He beheld were upon the divine kingdom. *His mediumship was transcendent at all times.*

316

And we cannot think that He meant any word or act of His to be construed to mean such mediumship as one may find where the reality of the spiritual world is so much believed in, as it is by the Spiritualists, but where the heights of that world and its blessed realization are so little understood. The mediumship which He called the disciples to seek was that of the Soul. For the Soul has the power, when fully unfolded, to rise into the heavens to both see and hear and receive on the angelic heavens, and even upon the Divine Kingdom. It was to be like His own. For such mediumship were the disciples prepared by Him. They might by true spiritual culture, rise on to the spiritual heavens to see and hear heavenly things. They might, by preparing themselves through making their lives pure, reach the spheres of the angelic ministry. In time they might even arrive at an inward state when they would be able to rise on to the Divine Kingdom and see and hear even as He did ; for they were to seek to become as He was.

THE MEDIUMSHIP OF THE DISCIPLES

Thus their mediumship was always to be truly spiritual. It was to be a conscious office. It was to become purely angelic. And its supreme purpose must be always to serve the Divine Lord. For such mediumship is possible ; and it is blessed. It is the only mediumship worthy of our endeavour, for it not only comes to us as the natural result of our spiritual growth, but is the means of our approach to the fulness of spiritual manhood and womanhood. It is the venue of our highest education, the way of our illumination, the testimony to and the realization of the divine powers within us.

Such a mediumship is glorious. What the whole spiritualistic movement requires to lift it out of the false position in which it has come to be placed, is the recognition and cultivation of such mediumship. It needs such mediumship for true illumination, light to be thrown upon the path of life in which all who would reach those altitudes must walk, light for the understanding to reveal unto them from the Highest Source the meaning of purity in living. The movement requires such mediumship to exalt its ideals, to bear it up above the influences of the gross materialism which has overtaken it, to save it from spiritually perishing that it may fulfil some beautiful mission to the Church and the World.

It is also the kind of mediumship which all the Churches need, the mediumship in which they all profess to believe as regards prophets, seers and apostles, though they deny its continuity. They believe in the continuity of the priest but not of the prophet, of the mere ecclesiastic but not of the Seer. They lay great emphasis upon the outward form and transference of priestly powers, but understand not or ignore the glory of the inward state when the Soul is illumined from the Lord. They have yet no room in the Churches for true mediumship. They need greatly a belief in it as a possible and most blessed and beautiful realization for themselves, that they may be in the true line of the prophets, seers and apostles, and not mere worshippers of the past. They most require such mediumship for true illumination, that they may understand the things which they profess to believe, behold the vision of their Lord, and know the wonderful and glorious experience which is said to have come to the blessed Master with the three elect Souls on the mount.

Do the Churches Care for these Things?

How came it to pass that the line of the prophets, seers and apostles ceased within the Churches ? What has caused the whole movement of the latter days towards the higher spiritual realizations, to pass beyond their borders and find a home elsewhere ? How is it that within the Churches where all the teachings of the prophets, the Master, and the apostles are professed as things to be believed, the reality of Soul vision now is denied?

318

Would any of the Churches believe the story of a Soul who said that, like the prophet Isaiah, he had been carried by the Spirit on to the threshold of the Heavens where he beheld over again the wonderful vision that came to the prophet within the temple ? Would they find room amongst their teachers for a Soul who was lifted up out of the earth, like the prophet Ezekiel by the brook Chebar, and shown the most marvellous things described in the opening of the book ascribed to that prophet ? Would they give credence to any one who could tell them that the vision of the Adonai as seen by the seer who wrote the Apocalypse, had once more been beheld ? Would they extend the hand of true Fellowship to the one who was privileged to recover the vision of the Christhood and tell of that vision to the world ? What welcome would they extend to any one who could speak to them of experiences as profound as those which came to the three disciples on the Mount of the Transfiguration ?

Our readers will understand the pertinence and importance of these questions ; and they will no doubt recognize how the Churches have answered them.

MOSES A DIVINE MANIFESTATION

We have now to speak of the things seen by those on the Mount, to unfold the inner and real meaning of what was beheld by them. Let the reader remember that the vision was entirely subjective ; that it was of the Soul. What was beheld was reflected from the highest heavens into the heavens of the Soul. The vision was very real to the disciples who saw it, so real that the Soul could never forget it. But who was it that they saw ? *One like unto Moses, and one like unto Elijah.* Had they known Moses and Elijah ? Had they been dwellers upon the earth during the ages in which the two great teachers are supposed to have lived ? How suggestive such a thought would be, how full of significance for all who would fain believe

319

that Souls return to earth again and again for experience as well as service, for the full unfoldment of their attributes as well as to aid others by their ministry in life ?

" The Soul that rises with us, our life's star,
    Hath had elsewhere its setting, and cometh from afar,"

is a great truth, though the western world has been blind and could not see it. And in this we have a testimony that those who beheld the wonderful vision had known both Moses and Elijah. How else could they have recognized them ?

But we are here face to face with a profound mystery, which is also a remarkable history. In the story there are echoes of a long past. The three who saw the vision had seen Moses and Elijah. During the ages of the special mission of these Messengers, these three had played a part. The forms which appeared in the vision they knew, and the titles they were familiar with. They were able immediately to associate the distinctive titles with the distinctive forms. *The story is a testimony to the past of these three disciples.*

It is somewhat difficult to write further of this thing which happened, because it is all concerning the ever Blessed One in manifestation. For there never was such a man in Jewry as Moses,[1] any more than there ever was a man named Buddha in India, or Jesus Christ in Judea. These terms represented divine qualities, though they came to be applied to personalities. As we have observed elsewhere, the personal name of the Master was not Jesus Christ. The personal name of the one who came to be called the Buddha, was not that sublime title now associated with him. The family name of him after whom the Jews named their lawgiver, was not Moses. Like the terms

---

[1] Since the Illumination concerning the Transfiguration was received by the writer, the fact stated here has been also affirmed upon other grounds by Professor T. K. Cheyne in his recent work on *The Two Religions of Israel*. Dr. Cheyne does not think there is any real foundation for believing that Moses ever lived as a man.

Jesus, the Christ and the Buddha, the term Moses had only a spiritual and divine signification. *It was related to a special form of the manifestation of the Adonai.* And it was a manifestation that was unknown to the Jewish race, though it was known to the ancient Hebrews with whom the Jews associated themselves. It was known unto the Hebrews when they were dwellers in Upper Egypt long ages prior to the supposed exodus of the Jews. It was a divine name in that it was given unto the Messenger who communicated from the angelic heavens unto those Hebrews who were able to receive them, what are known as " the Hebrew Mysteries." The Mysteries revealed *the history of the Soul and the laws of life ;* hence the term Moses, the Lawgiver. The Mysteries contained the past history of the Soul prior to and after what is understood as the fall ; " the laws of life " by which the Soul performed truly her evolution when she was as yet unfallen ; the disaster which followed failure to observe these most beautiful laws of being ; the bondage into which she descended, now known as the bondage in Egypt ; the way of deliverance from that bondage through observing the true laws of spiritual being ; the exodus or passing of the Soul out of Egypt ; the hard and cruel conflicts of life amid the wilderness journeyings in the body ; the recovery of the vision of the Divine Love upon Mount Sinai, or the attainment of that spiritual state when the vision embodying " the laws of being " breaks upon the Soul ; the recovery of the vision upon Mount Horeb of the Lord as the Compassionate One, and the divine healer of the Soul ; and, at last, the entrance into " the land of promise," the land of the Christhood consciousness.

As Moses, the Adonai or Logos, gave these most wonderful teachings unto those who were prepared to receive them on behalf of the people. And these remarkable Soul-histories the Jewish priesthood found and wove them into an outward history of their own people. They knew not their true origin and understood not their meaning ; but they made such a use of them as destroyed all their relation to the Soul. They changed the laws of life which they found, into the Jewish decalogue ; and they made of the Messenger a man like themselves. In their ignorance they materialized every beautiful spiritual truth by changing all their sacred meanings, making of the sacrifices in life on the path of the Soul nothing but sacrifices of the creatures, thus violating the fundamental laws of living, ignoring the true law of sacrifice within the life, and degrading the Soul by making it write its history in the blood and sufferings of the creatures.

The vision of Moses on the Mount of Transfiguration was, therefore, not the vision of the image of any man : it was a divine form, the Adonai as Lawgiver. He was with the Christ : for He overshadows a Soul who is in Christhood. The Christhood of the Master was made manifest that the true laws of being might again be revealed and interpreted. The work done by Moses was gathered up and revealed anew in and through Him. And it was this vision which broke upon the little company. They beheld the Lord, the Adonai, clothed in the divine glory, radiant as the Sun. Such a vision they had seen in past ages. They were of those Souls who had received from Moses on the mount of the law (Sinai)—that spiritual state in which they were lifted up to behold the vision of the Lord, and receive from Him the laws of life. They had been of " the elders of Israel " in the true Hebrew days, who were called to ascend the mount. They knew the vision ; it had been engraven on their Soul. And when they once more beheld that vision in the ecstatic state into which they had been lifted up in their communion as the Master prayed, they remembered who it was whom they beheld.

Who was Elijah ?

But in addition to Moses, one like unto Elijah appeared.

They beheld him also in the glory. And here a very natural question arises in view of the fact that the history of the Soul is not of yesterday, but is the fruit of very great cycles of ages of the evolutionary process by which Being is unfolded, and led step by step to perfection. The question is this : Had they also been dwellers in the land when the prophet lived to whom that term was applied ? Were they of " the schools of the prophets " in those days, Initiates of the sublime Mysteries ? Were they of the company of Elisha who beheld Elijah ascend in " a chariot of fire ? " That they recognised the form is evident. They saw the Lord glorious as the sun, arrayed in the most translucent and transparent robes ; and they knew Him. They beheld the form they once knew as Moses ; and Him they recognised also. And when the form of Elijah appeared, they likewise recognised that form. Who was he ? And when did they come to know him ?

It is well for us to recall the fact that nearly all the remarkable terms used in Jewry were materialized in their meaning. They had been brought down to the physical and personal spheres. And this term was one of them. It had been applied to a man who had been sent on a mission.[1] But the name is full of significance, and would seem rather to apply to one who was revealing himself under a certain aspect. The term is compound, and means *The Lord is Jehovah*, the Eternal One, the God of Righteousness. Elijah's mission is said to have been that of the overthrow of the worship of Baal (and Baal was the embodiment of the materialization of spiritual qualities and things), and the setting up of the true worship of the Lord of Righteousness, the ever Blessed One. And that was doubtless the mission of the prophet. But the prophet was not Elijah ; rather his message was from Elijah. Things have been inverted. *The prophet saw and heard Elijah, the Lord Jehovah, revealed as the Lord of*

---

[1] Prof. Cheyne in the work referred to above expresses grave doubts as to the historicity of Elijah.

Righteousness. No wonder He is described, though unfortunately it is the man who is so described, as ascending in " a chariot of fire." That was the very symbol of the Divine manifestation to the world then, the consuming, purifying, restoring energy of the Eternal Love.

So it was the Lord whom the three saw, and not a man. It was the Elijah who purified the Soul like a refiner of gold. It was the Elijah who overthrew the altars of the Baal-worshippers by recalling the true Israel to the vision of righteousness. He whom the little group of high Initiates beheld was therefore none other than He whom they had known as the Lord in the days when he revealed Himself as Elijah whose " Chariot of fire " descended and ascended to purify the Souls of Israel.

Here then we have one of the most remarkable visions on record, transcendent in its nature in every respect. We have the Eternal One revealed under three distinct forms—The Adonai, glorious in His apparel, radiant with the Light of the Eternal and ever Blessed One, and overshadowing the Christhood ; Moses, the Divine Revealer of the true laws of being whose face had to be veiled before the people because of His gloriousness ; and Elijah, the purifier, the chariot of fire, the eternal energy of the Invisible One who restores within the Soul and the Planet—the Microcosm and the Macrocosm—the worship of Jehovah, the ever Blessed Father. And these three forms of the divine manifestation are gathered up into that manifestation of the Christhood which was given through the Master. The purifying Lord ; the life-giving Lord ; the radiant Lord ; *the Energy of Life, the Law of Life, the Light of Life*— were revealed and interpreted in His Christhood.

E

THE DECEASE AT JERUSALEM

FOR a moment we must look at the theme said to have been spoken of on the Mount, for it is of more than common interest. It is reported in the third Gospel Record that *they spake together of the decease to be accomplished at Jerusalem.* The words are few but pregnant with meaning. There is no hint given in them of the *nature* of the decease that was to be accomplished ; and the omission is significant. The nature of the Sin-offering could not then be told. That would be made known later. The innermost meaning of the vision had to be kept secret. The disciples of the innermost group alone were to be informed of " the Mystery." Only the three who beheld the vision heard what was said to the beloved Master ; for it was spoken unto Him. These were then initiated into the sublime Mystery that has been so terribly misunderstood by the whole western world, and which has been the cause of so many disastrous conflicts. Many things had the Master said unto them concerning the passing of the Christhood, the going away of the Son of Man, the betrayal and crucifixion ; here on the Mount the matter was freely talked of and anticipated. What He had said unto them was ratified in the vision.

Is it not remarkable that the Sin-offering, as something which had to be accomplished, the manner of its accomplishments and the results of it, the fearful burden which it entailed upon the Soul, the pain, sorrow and anguish born of the burden, should occupy so large a place in the stories found in the Records ?[1] What emphasis is laid upon it everywhere ; what importance attached to it ; what profound things are spoken concerning it. That it must have been something far, far greater than the passing of the Master from these outer spheres through the crucifixion of His body, might surely have been discovered

---

[1] For evidence of this see the chapters on Allegories of the Sin-offering.

long ago had not the intuition been blinded by the Maya of materialism, the delusive and deluding influences of everything literal and sensuous. The western world has worshipped the beloved Master as one equal with the Eternal One. It has thought of Him as absolutely pure even as the Father of All. Yet that same western world has thought of the beautiful life of the Master in no higher way than to believe that His pure and perfect body was capable of containing the elements of physical death, not knowing that in His pure state it was impossible, and that death could not touch Him. That He had to depart from the life of the manifestation is quite true ; but to do that He had to withdraw from the body in which the manifestation of Christhood was made. He did pass away from the outer spheres as the Christ ; but it was not in the manner supposed (a subject we have dealt with elsewhere). He did not die either on the Roman cross or afterwards in the sense in which death is generally understood. When the hour of His departure came which called Him to enter upon the work of the Sin-offering, *He had to withdraw from the body*. This the Churches should have known long ago. Indeed they would have known this most blessed truth had they understood the inherent life in a perfectly pure body. But that was hidden from them by the terrible delusion which came to the early Churches when they were taught that it did not matter what one ate or drank so long as it was done to the glory of God, *little dreaming that to eat and drink to the glory of God was to nourish the body upon pure things only, to build up all its cells so that each one should be pure and responsive to the central will, knowing no disobedience, and therefore no resultants of it in disease and death*. And unfortunately it seems to be hidden from them still. They are not yet out of the land of Maya or Illusion.

NOT PHYSICAL BUT SPIRITUAL

" The decease " to be accomplished was something infinitely

more profound, an experience unspeakably more pathetic, an event unimaginably more tragic, than such a death as the western world believes the Master passed through. It was a *real* decease ; that is, it was the decease or departure of the Christhood. It was the passing away from Him of all that He loved most, in order that He might enter into the work of the Sin-offering. To Him it was truly *spiritual or Soul death*, terrible beyond all that men and women could think of unto one who knew such a Christhood. It was as the passing from the fulness of day when the sun is most glorious, into the density of night when neither moon nor stars illumine the sky ; for the Light of the Eternal within Him was veiled, so that darkness environed Him. It was more, much more, than the departure of one whose life was crowned with royal dignity, and in whose hand was the sceptre of divine power, to the position of the very least in the realm, least in estate, least in spiritual realization. For He laid aside His royal diadem of Christhood, His regal robes of most beautiful purity, His rod of spiritual power, in order that He might descend into all the states necessary for the accomplishment of the Sin-offering.

Can any of our readers try to realize what it all meant to Him to lay down His life thus ; to exchange the estate of His wonderful Christhood for one that took Him into the places of the sinful, and made Him to sit down with them ? We know it is hard to believe it, and harder still to imagine what it was that He did. For, though the writer has been permitted to behold the way which He went, and to bear in some measure the burden with Him ; though He has had to witness again and again His Gethsemanes, and has anew beheld His anguish and heard His outbursts of pain and agony ; though he too has been overwhelmed by the awful tragedy as the sorrow of it has broken upon him ; yet he is unable to fully realize it all, or to express in adequate terms that which he has seen and felt.

F

THE CLOUD UPON THE SANCTUARY

THERE descended upon the little group a cloud, and there spake from out the cloud, a voice. *This is the Beloved One with whom I am well-pleased : hear ye Him.* It was like the cloud that was said to have descended upon the sanctuary, betokening the Divine Presence ; and the voice which spake from out the cloud on Sinai, Horeb, and Moriah, the messages of the Eternal One. It gathered the little group into itself for a time, an act which was significant of the divine exaltation of their whole being, and gave them moments of heavenly realization inexpressibly blessed—moments of the most supreme awe, when the sense of the Divine Presence was so great that the three disciples thus privileged bowed themselves to the earth in reverent adoration.

Thus it was with them ; and so it ever is when the Soul is so uplifted. The Mount of the Transfiguration is also the mount where the glory of the Lord is beheld. It is the wonderful spiritual condition of life in which the whole being is exalted ; when the inward powers rule the life, and the Soul is in a state to receive the vision of her Lord ; when the laws of life upon the heavens are the laws held sacred by the Soul, and applied to her own life ; when the worship of the Lord is her supreme thought, and the overthrow of the ways of Baal her supreme service ; when the laws of life given by Moses are realized in her vision and experience, and the purifying work of Elijah has touched her and caught her up in its " chariots of fire " ; when the Lord appears in the heavens of the Soul as her Sun, and His glory clothes her raiment and makes it glisten with His Radiance, and she henceforth knows through beautiful realization, the meaning of Christhood.

In such an hour the cloud is upon our sanctuary. We are

enveloped in that cloud, the sure testimony that His Presence is with us. It is an ecstatic hour, one in which the whole heavens are open unto us, and we behold the Lord our sun, Moses our lawgiver, and Elijah our energizing fire. And we hear the voice of the Eternal One speaking unto us even as He spake unto the three Initiates, saying, " *This is the Beloved One with whom I am well pleased : hear ye Him.*" For we are to hear and respond to the divine within us. We are to behold the Adonai, and hear His message. We are to see the Christhood, and know that it is the state of being with which the Eternal Father is well pleased. We are to understand that that is the Life which He seeks *within us*, and to have manifested *through us*.

For the message of Christhood is for all Souls and all times. It is the crown of the Soul's evolution, and the glory of her divine life. It is the realization of her own beautiful inherent divine powers, the consummation of her spiritual unfoldment. It is the perfect flower of the Tree of Life, "the rose of Sharon and the lily of the valley." Nay, it is " the vine " and " the fig-tree " conjointly ! the vine bearing the precious fruit whose juice is the wine of God—the Divine Love ; and the fig-tree bearing its ripe, rich figs whose flesh is food unto the Soul— the Divine Wisdom. *And thus it is the blossoming of the man of the Earth into the man of the heavens, the man crowned with the angelic life, and the angelic life crowned with the Son of God.*

The Realization for all Souls

Does the height and the splendour of it all appal and discourage you, reader, and make you feel it is too impossible to attain ? Does the realization of it appear so exalted that only the very few and very special Souls can ever hope to reach its sublime heights, and enter into its glory ? Yet it was the life lived by, and made manifest through, the blessed one whom we knew as the Master, and the attainment unto which He called us all when He spake unto us of the Father. It is the life which is inherent in all Souls, however lowly in estate they may now be ; the goal of all true Soul-evolution. It is for everyone, every man and every woman who feels that he and she would love to reach it and enter into its sublime realizations. In these days it is coming unto many who have been awakened into newness of life by the voice of the Son of Man, who have arisen out of the bondage to the sense-life and set their faces heavenwards, towards the pure life and service. For the Son of Man has risen from the dead, and the wonderful truth is now to be made known. The departure of the Christhood took place, as it was told upon the mount : " the decease " has been accomplished : the resurrection morning has more than broken. The Christhood is risen ; and it has been made manifest unto the disciples who beheld it in the manifestation given through the blessed Master.

G
THE THREE TENTS

L ORD *let us here make three tents to dwell in : one for Thee, one for Moses, and one for Elijah.* This was an hour of sublime ecstasy. The heavens had descended to meet the ascending heavens within them. The cloud had descended upon the sanctuary, the innermost court of their being, and from out the cloud the Divine One had spoken. The glorious vision was great within them. The spirit of the Divine Awe filled the sanctuary : they were bowed down before Him, even as the seraphim in Isaiah's vision. It was a blessed experience, a rare moment in the spiritual history of the group of Souls, prophetic of much for them all in the by and by. For the Master it was prophetic of the burden that awaited the bearing by Him, the accomplishment of the great work of the Sin-offering and the glory that should follow ; for the disciples it was prophetic of the blessed fellowship in the coming ages when the Sin-offering had been fully accomplished, a fellowship with the angelic heavens, and even the Divine Kingdom, transcending anything that men and women have since dreamt of or believed possible. It was an hour of supremest exaltation of Soul when everything of the earth-life was forgotten, when the things of the outer world were lost to the vision and only the things of the Soul were felt and beheld, when the Soul was so filled with the consciousness of the Divine Presence and the blessedness of angelic fellowship, that no desire remained within the disciples to come back to the conditions in the lower spheres of their earth-life.

How blessed the moments were may be gathered from the saying attributed to Peter. His whole Being spoke out from the fulness of the ecstasy which filled him. It is said of him by the evangelists that " He wist not what he said," implying that he did not understand the meaning of his own ecstatic expression. But in this commentary upon what he said we have another illustration of the fact that the writers did not understand the inner meaning of the stories which they recorded, and so they not only made most of them personal, but put their own interpretation upon them. It was not his own ecstatic utterance that Peter did not understand. What he said was not something spoken through him by another, and in a language which he knew not, such as is done through certain mediums under control. It was what he felt deeply at the time. And there was a meaning in his ecstatic saying far more profound than the ordinary reader of the narrative would grasp ; a significance for those who would sincerely and fully understand the vision and its meaning, surpassing in importance anything that has been given to it by any of the various schools of interpretation along traditional lines. It was not his own saying that he did not understand, but what had been said upon the mount concerning the things to be accomplished. It was what had been said unto the blessed one concerning *the departure* from the estate of Christhood. That he did not fully grasp. None of the disciples yet realized the stupendous nature of it, and the demands it would make upon the Master. Had Peter quite understood the meaning of the " decease to be accomplished," he very probably would have felt the saddening influence of it ; for he would then have seen how impossible it would be to realize the beautiful wish of his Soul, so far as the Master was concerned.

What were the Three Tents ?

O, there was a beautiful wealth of meaning in that ecstatic utterance. It was like a gold-mine full of the most precious unalloyed gold. It revealed the very Soul of the disciple, the innermost desire of his Being. It expressed so much that he would fain realize within himself, that he felt he *must* realize. It revealed what he thought of the Christhood. It expressed the wonderful effect of the sublime vision upon him. It was a manifestation of the divine Soul that he was. He would have had that hour prolonged indefinitely. He would have had the fellowship perpetuated. He would have had the Christhood vision within him to be continuous. The glory of the Lord he would have had shining for ever within himself. The blessed fellowship of Moses and Elijah he would have kept sacredly preserved on the mount. The laws of the Soul he would have had continually before him ; and in the Presence of the sacred flame of the divine energy he would have had his abode.

For what meant his strange request if it were not this ? Nay, what were the " tents " that were to be made in which the Lord, Moses, and Elijah were to dwell ? Were they not the threefold tabernacle of his own Being—the innermost court, the inner or middle court, and the open court ?—the Soul, the Heart or Spiritual Mind, and the mind with the body. Were not the three beheld by him in the vision the embodiments of all that he most desired—the Christhood, the law and the testimony of the Lord, and the flame of the Divine Spirit ? Was not that " trinity " of spiritual realization unto a divine fulness, the possession he most coveted?—the Jesus-life, the Christ-consciousness, and the Lord-consciousness?

AN AGE OF BEAUTIFUL HOPE

How very naturally it all appears to unfold step by step! And with what hope should it not fill every heart who truly desires after the divine vision? For the realization of the vision is for all, and unto that end is its meaning now made known. The hour has come when the vision must be told unto all who are able to hear it unto the receiving of its message. The wonderful truths which it contained have now to be revealed, and silence concerning them is no longer imposed upon those who beheld the blessed vision; for the Son of Man is risen again from the dead. The three days of His lying in the grave—the whole western world wherein the Divine Christhood has been buried during the three days or cycles of the Naros—have been fulfilled, and He has risen. In those days He descended into " the hells " to accomplish the Sin-offering and bring deliverance unto all who were bound; but now He has accomplished His *Soul-travail*, and has overthrown the powers that shut Him up within the grave, and set a seal upon His tomb. The meaning and nature of the decease accomplished may now be told, and the many things which He spake unto us in the days of the manifestation may now be unfolded. We are living in days when great blessing may be realized. We are living again in the days when a new age is dawning upon the world, an age in which the whole Planet has taken a move forward in the redemption of *all* her children, an age during which that redemption will not only be accomplished, but one in which the blessed and glorious life of the Christhood shall be restored. We are living in an age in which the vision of the Transfiguration may be interpreted in order that its glorious states may be entered into by all Souls who ascend the mount; for the vision awaits every one who seeks there for the divine communion.

H

AFTER THE TRANSFIGURATION

THE vision faded; the glory was withdrawn. We know what that would mean to them, for have we not passed through the like? Have we not been drawn upward to those heights where the vision glorious is beheld, to look upon the blessed One in manifestation, and then have had to descend to the lower reaches of the spiritual world to fulfil our mission to Souls? The Soul would fain have abode on the mount and retained the vision in its sublime reality; but each one had to descend once more to the earth-spheres. The Master must needs descend to go His way. *His Way!* Yea, the way He had chosen to go out of love for Souls, the way by which alone the astral kingdom could be purified, its " graven images " blotted out, the " middle wall " or " partition " which had been set up within it, broken down. He had to go His way through the hells where the fierce fires of passion burned, where the awful images made their dwelling amid the astral groves, where the altars of Baal were crowded with holocausts of victims, where the children of the Great Father-Mother were made to pass through the fires of Moloch, so that He might, in passing through with them, change the whole hell-conditions of the astral kingdom sufficiently to enable all to rise up out of them without let or hindrance from the evil images.

It was in that work that He saved others whilst Himself He could not save. The truism was one of the greatest ever uttered, though it has never been truly understood.

He had to go down from the mount of Transfiguration to the low-lying valleys of experience; from the blessed estate of Christhood to one in which all that His Christhood stood for would be laid aside so that His glorious raiment, so pure and lustrous, would become as the garments of those who made their dwelling in the various states through which He would have to pass ; from the blessed fellowship of the Highest, to the companionship of those who had forgotten Him and their own divine childhood.

Truly there is a pathos unspeakable in the saying, " *And when they were come down from the mount.*"

And what happened to the beloved Master, overtook, though in less degree, the three who went up with Him. They shared the glory of that hour ; and in some measure they shared the awful burden which He undertook to carry for the world. They went down to suffer also. They understood not fully the things spoken of on the mount, and so they questioned within themselves what could be meant by " the decease " and " the rising from the dead " ; but they soon were to see something of the meaning of *the departure*, and to be more fully instructed as to the event signified by the rising from the dead. And until that hour arrived they were to tell the vision to no one. Indeed they themselves were deprived of the blessedness of the vision when they had come down ; for they lost even the vision of the Christhood, *and saw no one save Jesus only*. The Eternal Christ, or Adonai, the Overshadowing One, was withdrawn, and they were overwhelmed soon after. Sorrow came to sit upon their brow and becloud their vision. For they also passed to bear their part in the divine tragedy. They were to drink of the cup given Him to drink and to be baptized with the baptism which became His lot. They were to remain with Him unto the end, and to tarry upon the outer spheres until He returned. They were thus to share not only the mystery of the blessed vision, but something of that other great mystery in the sorrow and poignancy of the suffering to be endured. Thus were they to know the glory of a Christhood as beheld in the vision ; and afterwards to share in the burden of Soul-travail expressed in the words " *The Passion of the Lord.*"

What the Three Symbolized

If only we could adequately portray all that it meant for the little group to descend from the mount of Transfiguration that those who read these pages might understand perfectly what it was that the Master had to accomplish, and the share which the three disciples bore in it ! But we find it impossible to express in any terms which we can command for writing, the profound experiences through which they all passed. They drank of His cup, or rather of the cup that was given Him to drink ; for they came to know the awful nature of *The Passion of the Divine Love* in the tragedy of the Sin-offering. Throughout the ages which have intervened since then, they have received the baptism with which He was baptized ; for they have known the awful bitterness of repudiation in every age in which they had to live, and crucifixion in one or other of its varied forms. For the West not only crucified the Lord, but likewise Peter, John and James. Western Christianity was built upon Paul and his views of the Mystery, and not upon the Teachings of these three who had known the Master so intimately. And throughout the era, the truths the three symbolized were inverted. For the West also turned the spiritual understanding (Peter), towards everything material ; the spiritual love-principle (John), away from its true manifestation ; and the spirit of fidelity to truth (James), into a path of unspeakable anguish. For in themselves the three disciples symbolized these three most precious Soul-principles, principles born of the divine within us. And thus, not only did these three suffer in their individual capacity ; but the principles for which they stood in their initiate names were likewise crucified. The spiritual understanding of things was accounted naught ; the love of the divine way in life was persecuted and slain ; and fidelity to the highest vision of the Soul was made the ground of the most painful and, sometimes, the most terrible repudiations. If the readers of these words are acquainted with the religious history of the West during the past eighteen centuries, they will see and understand how true our statement is concerning these things.

But we bless the Infinite Love that those days of oppression, persecution, spiritual crucifixion and repudiation will soon be of the past. The New Age has come with the arising of the Soul out of the grave of matter (materialism as expressed in the various religious systems of thought and worship), and the light streaming from afar will increase more and more as Souls are able to receive it, and the whole world shall become at last filled with the glory of it. The transfiguration of the Soul will be repeated. Many will ascend the mount full of the holy yearnings which bespeak true spiritual vision. For not only have the three who beheld that wonderful vision, come back from the past, and arisen with " the Son of Man " to make known the meaning of the vision ; but in not a few the divine principles which they also symbolized have been awakened to find beautiful manifestation in life and service. In them is the spiritual understanding open to receive of divine things ; the spiritual love-principle revealing how the Eternal One loves ; and the spirit of fidelity to truth making itself manifest under conditions the most trying, and often most painful.

The Christ and Simon Peter

*Being an allegory of the Soul when it has come at
the Vision of the Lord and is seeking unto a
Divine Christhood ; wherein is made manifest
what was meant by " Fishing on the Sea
of Galilee," and " Toiling all the night
without having taken anything," together with the esoteric sense of the
Great Draught of Fishes, Dining
with the Lord, and partaking
of the Holy Agapae : and
why the Soul shrank
from the Sin-offer-
ing Burden.*

A
THE NARRATIVE

THERE is a story told by the fourth Evangelist concerning the Christ and the inner group of disciples, whose profound meanings have been altogether hidden. It is found in the last chapter, where the Master is represented as having appealed to Simon Peter to know whether he truly loved Him. In the form in which it is now found in the narrative, its profound spiritual significance is lost, and its supreme divine import is obscured. Even its spiritual nature is changed through having been made personal. Yet it is one of the most Soul-searching and most wonderful appeals of the Divine Love to His children. It is a story whose whole atmosphere at once testifies to its impersonal and heavenly character, and whose meanings carry us away from the material spheres to those of the Soul, from the kingdom of physical things and events to that realm of spiritual experience within which the awakened Soul moves. How wonderful the appeal is ; how Soul-searching ; how spiritual in its purpose ; how unearthly in its nature ; how impersonal in its scope ; how utterly soulic and wholly divine is the vision intended, may be seen as we unfold the meaning.

The story begins with the opening incident in the chapter. It is connected with the Christhood manifestation unto the disciples ; and it must be noted that the manifestation is upon the shores of the Sea of Galilee. It comes to the disciples in an hour of dire extremity, when they have been toiling all the night of a most trying experience amid spiritual darkness, fishing for those spiritual meanings of their own history without which the life languishes. For the story of the seven disciples going afishing, led by Simon Peter, is a spiritual history and not a material event ; an inward rather than an outward experience. It is a narrative ; but the narrative is of the Soul. It is something which came to the Soul in its past experience, and is a process that many are going through at the present moment. It is real history both of the past and present.

The story was told by the Master in the form of an allegory unto the few who were able to receive it, and was embodied in the Logia of St. John.[1] And it was found by him who wrote the first public Record for the Churches—the Record upon which the four Gospels now in vogue were built up. Not knowing the spiritual and beautiful history to which it referred, he presented it as something that had outwardly occurred between the blessed Master and the disciples referred to. In this way were its meanings obscured and the force of the vision and the divine appeal lost to the Soul. For though there have been those who have felt that this and kindred allegories found in the Gospels could not have been literal narrative (as did some of the post-apostolic fathers),[2] yet none have discerned the inner spiritual significations, the profound truths presented, the deep soulic and divine experiences which are implied. And it is only in these latter days, the days of *the Regeneration*, when the Son of Man is once more making Himself manifest in the return of the Christhood through the restoration of the Soul by means of the Redemption or redeemed life, that the story is finding its true interpretation.

It is from the Divine Father-Mother alone that all heavenly wisdom proceedeth, and not from any man. Of ourselves we are nothing ; and from ourselves we know nothing of the inner meanings of the Soul's history. Whatever we have of that order of teaching is from above, and cometh from the Divine Love who alone illumines the understanding, and showeth unto us the sacred and beautiful things implied in the teachings of the beloved Master as these were given unto the inner group of disciples. From Heaven alone has the light broken upon our Soul. If we have seen the path of that history with all its sad

---

[1] See reference to this, pp. 39, 175, 283, 359, 468, 472, 486.
[2] Notably Clement of Alexandria, Origen, Augustine.

and wonderful experiences, and the still more wonderful works wrought by the Divine Love in order to recover all the Souls who went out from His Presence, and to regain for them the edenic life which was once lived upon this world, they have come to us from the divine kingdom. *The Lord within the Sanctuary of the Soul has been our illuminer.* It is of Him that we know these most wonderful Soul-truths. From the Lord alone have we received that light which maketh all things clear to the spiritual vision, and revealeth the meaning of all those precious teachings which the blessed Master gave.

O Light of life whose inshining dispelleth all darkness and maketh even the shadows to flee away at thine approach ! Light most blessed and glorious, whose Radiance lighteth up the hills and mountains of the Soul, those uplands of the divine dwelling, and maketh beautiful the lowlands of her outer spheres ! Light of the Eternal One, transcendent and ineffable, born of the Life of God within the Soul ! Make Thy Radiance to fill our whole being, that in all things we may show forth Thy glory, and be Thy humble servant through whom Thou dost re-interpret the wonderful Message which once Thou didst speak through Him who made Thy Wisdom and Thy Love manifest in the days of the manifestation of the Christhood and the exposition of Thy Love.

May the Light within our Lamp be Thine alone !

B
WHO WAS SIMON PETER ?

THE names of all the disciples of the Master were spiritual and symbolical. Often has the question been asked, What special value is there in a name ? Names have, however, often counted for much, not because they were names, but because of the things for which they stood. As we have seen in some of our other studies, the three names given to the Master by the writers of the Gospels were not personal, though they represented them as such ; but that they were wholly spiritual, representing the threefold life which they implied—the redeemed life, the Christhood, and the Lord consciousness. The spiritual states embodied in the Master and symbolized in the names which were applied to Him, were beautifully interpreted by Him.

And so it was with the various disciples. The names by which they are now known, were those of their Initiation, *i.e.*, the spiritual names given them by the Master. These names, therefore, stood for spiritual qualities, and were not personal.

The term Peter had a deep spiritual signification. It denoted a quality of Soul, a power of spiritual perception, the bed-rock upon which alone great and true spiritual experience and knowledge can be built up. It was the rock upon which alone the Church of the Living God was to be built, a foundation so firm and sure that the powers of evil would not be able to prevail against it. It had not the material and limited meaning in the mind of the Master which is given to it in a modern Greek translation, but referred to *the spiritual understanding*. It did not mean an earthly stone or rock, but a spiritual rock, one upon which the heavenly temple of Christhood could be reared. The name had, therefore, a profound meaning, and denoted the special spiritual faculty of the one unto whom it was given. Even in the Gospels it is stated that the Master gave the name to Simon after the latter had discerned the nature and meaning of the Christhood.[1]

PETER GOES AFISHING IN GALILEE

We are now in a position to explain the inner meaning of the narrative which states that Peter, and the disciples who were

[1] It was upon the foundation of that power within the Soul-system which was represented by the term Peter, that it is said the true Church of the Christhood is to be built up ; that means, that upon the Higher understanding alone is Truth established, through the recognition of which the life spoken of as the Jesus-life and then the Christhood-life is built up, until at last the Soul becomes absolutely one with her Divine Lord.

with him, went on to the Sea of Galilee to fish. In other studies we have explained the meaning of the Sea of Galilee, that it was *the spiritual mind*, and that to fish upon its waters was to seek for the meaning of hidden spiritual truths. Like the Sea, the spiritual mind takes on the conditions of the atmosphere. When peaceful and bright it reflects the conditions ; when storm-swept, it interprets them. Its depths are those of spiritual being ; its fish are Soul-truths. The fair hills of Galilee where the Master knelt to share the divine communion, are the blessed uplands of the Soul. Therefore, when it is said that Peter with other disciples went afishing, we are to understand that it was the Soul itself in the state represented by the term Simon Peter, seeking for the meaning of the Mysteries, the deeper Mystèries, which the Master had spoken of unto them.

Great and profound were the truths embodied in the first part of the narrative. It was indeed no ordinary fishing expedition, not even in an occult sense. It was an expedition of the Soul which issued in the most remarkable experiences. Night had fallen, that night which not infrequently overtakes the Soul when face to face with the more profound Mysteries. The Master had passed from the midst of the disciples ; the passing of the Christhood manifestation had taken place ; the work of the Sin-offering was about to begin. Though the blessed Master had said many things to the innermost group concerning that work, yet were they unable to fully apprehend the depth of meaning implied in what He had said. When the passing away from the outward manifestation had been accomplished, the inner group felt overwhelmed with the greatness of the experience which had befallen them, and the profound Mystery with which they stood face to face. It was as if the glorious sun had been withdrawn from them, and the darkness of night had fallen. He who had so wonderfully interpreted the Divine Love for them in a life of the most beautiful purity and goodness, had departed from their outward vision ; because the hour had come when He must needs take up the burden of ransom of which He had spoken—that burden in the bearing of which He was to be made as an offering for sin. He had brought to them the vision of true life for the Soul, even unto sublime fulness, in the redeemed life which He interpreted in His own life, and in the Christhood which He manifested in giving forth the Wisdom of the Divine Love in the remarkable teachings concerning the Soul and the purpose of the Divine Father-Mother towards this world. Often had He lifted them up in their thoughts and feelings far above the earth-life, even until their feet, as it were, touched the threshold of the angelic world. Nay, they had seen the divine glory breaking upon them as He unfolded the Divine Wisdom and spoke of the Divine Love.

What it was to be of that little group no one could possibly imagine unless they had been partakers of the hallowed communion, the joys and the sorrows which were experienced. O the hallowed hours, the blessed moments, when, withdrawn from the world without, the Soul was carried up and forward to the world of the Divine Presence within ! To understand them they had to be felt and realized. To know what these disciples missed when the Master passed from their midst one must have been of them. Is it any wonder then that they should have felt bereaved indeed, as those who had suddenly passed from the glory of day into the darkness of night ? Is there wonder that they felt themselves constrained in the night of that sad experience to go afishing that they might arrive at a clearer and fuller understanding of the wonderful mystery with which they found themselves confronted ? Or is it to be wondered at that they toiled all the night in vain ?

TOILING WITHOUT FINDING

O marvellous depths of meaning for the Souls of those who were plunged into such darkness as followed the passing of the

Christhood, as well as for those privileged ones of the inner group of disciples ! Who may be able to fathom these depths so as to reach unto the fulness of meaning implied in the spiritual narrative ? Who may bring up out of them the great draught of profound mysteries as a result of seeing and hearing the Blessed One, and the letting down of the net upon *the right side ?* Not only did the inner group of the disciples fish on the wrong side for a time, but ever since the Church Ecclesiastical was founded, has the fishing been upon the wrong side of the ship. And though the vision of the Blessed One came unto the Souls of the inner group of disciples to recall them from their error, yet the Church has toiled through the long night since her foundation as an outward kingdom even until now, without catching what should have come into the net, even the great fish of the profound mysteries embodied in the teaching of the Master. The Church has surely never had the true vision of the Blessed One, or she would not have toiled so in her rowing, and so largely in vain. She cannot have heard the true voice of the Blessed One, or she would also have heard His message to cast the net on the right side. Has she sought truly and earnestly, as she ought to have done and as she has sought other forms of power, to understand divine things ? If so, then surely even amid her toiling, the light would have broken, the morning as harbinger of the day would have come, the vision of the Lord walking on the shores of Galilee would have been seen, and the divine voice would have been heard in her midst as an actual experience, giving counsel, and calling all Souls into the most intimate and hallowed fellowship. For that vision has again been seen, and that voice has once more been heard even in these days.

But for those who are able and ready to see and hear from the Divine Love, the morning breaketh and the drawn out shadows of night flee away. Unto them shall the vision of the Blessed One come ; and they shall hear His voice, and regard His counsel, and *come into the divine fellowship of the agape* unto which they are called. They shall toil no more without finding those things of God for which the true ones ever seek ; and they shall no more let down their nets on the wrong side, but put them down on the right side and find all that they seek for, and far, far more.

C
THE VISION AT DAYBREAK

THE inner group had toiled all night but taken nothing. When morning broke they seemed no nearer the fulfilment of their desire. It had been a discouraging expedition. The darkness was not so great within them as it had been ; for they were beginning to realize that the passing from their midst of the blessed Master had been a necessity, and to recall what He had said unto them concerning it. And in that sense was the day breaking for them, and their darkness beginning to recede. *But as yet they had caught nothing of the innermost meanings of the profound mystery.*

But the Soul's extremity is the Divine opportunity. Never is the Divine Thoughtfulness so rich in provision as when the Soul finds itself alone and helpless without Him. And such is it here. Spiritually sad and weary the disciples turned their thoughts towards the shore from which they had set out, and behold a vision which astonished them, loomed out of the grey dawn ; for the shore from which they had departed on their expedition was that upon which the Divine One walked, the shore of the Sea of Galilee that looked inwards, that faced the Soul's Sanctuary where the Divine Presence dwelt. It was on that shore they had heard so much and learnt so many things from the beloved Master. There the very angels of God had walked and communed with them as the Master unfolded the Divine Love and Wisdom. And now in the midst of their disappointment and sorrow as they turned Eastward (Divinewards), the side of the rising sun, the spiritual locality whence

streameth the radiance of the heavenly Love and Wisdom—
the vision of the Lord rose before them, at first so dimly in the
grey dawn that they were uncertain that it was the Lord ; and
then more clearly, until all uncertainty gave way to confidence,
awe and joy. For it was not the personal Master, as has been
and still is believed, whom they saw, but the vision of the Lord
of Love. It was *an inward vision*, not something outward. It was
a spiritual vision, not a material form. It was *a divine vision*,
not one of a human and personal life. It was the Lord, the
Blessed One whom no man has ever beheld with the eyes of the
body, and whom Souls can behold only when they are able to
receive the vision. It was a vision of the Divine Presence within
the sanctuary of the Soul, the vision of the Soul herself through
looking inward toward the divine. For it is there the divine
vision breaks upon the spiritual mind. It is there alone that
man can find the Lord.

How beautiful and wonderful is the truth implied in the
narrative, and how full of meaning for all times, and ages, and
peoples ! Here indeed is a wealth of spiritual teaching little
dreamed of ; wealth like treasure buried in a heap of earth,
hidden from the eye of man and thus lost to him. Here indeed
are meanings of spiritual value for the Soul transcending all
outward experiences, only translatable unto such as have passed
through them, whose full interpretation must be found in
sublime realization. And the more the narrative is unfolded,
the more wonderful do the meanings seem. The depths grow
more and more profound as our way is trod, for the wealth of
the Divine Love becomes ever more and more manifest. The
shadows within us flee before the divine vision ; the night gives
place, not only to the day, but to such glory of noontide as
clothes the whole of life with the light of the divine radiance,
making perfectly clear and glorious all the uplands of the Soul.

*O most Holy and Ever Blessed One, we would bless Thee ! It
is of Thy Love for us that the Day breaketh and the night of our*

349

sorrowful toil cometh to an end. Long did we seek in vain for the fulfilment of our dearest hope ; but now have we once more beheld the blessed vision, and heard Thy gracious voice. At Thy command we will launch into the Deep, and let down our nets on the right side.

D

THE DIVINE INJUNCTION

"CHILDREN, *have ye naught to eat that ye may break your fast ?*" The question shows the divine thoughtfulness for the Soul, when its meaning is spiritually discerned. It had truly been a time of spiritual fasting with the disciples since the passing of the blessed Master. They had suffered much. In them the sense of loss was great. For " the bread of life " which He broke unto them, they hungered ; and there was none who could satisfy that hunger but the Divine Love. All through the long night had they fasted, though they toiled in the hope of finding some food for their Souls. In their dire spiritual extremity the Lord drew near. He showed Himself upon the shore that looked Eastward, and spake thus unto them—" *Children, have ye naught to eat that ye may break your fast ?* " " *We have toiled all the night and taken nothing,*" they said. They could find no sustenance in their toiling. " *Cast the net upon the right side, and ye shall find.*"

Such was the message that reached them from the shore where was beheld the Divine Presence. They had been fishing on the wrong side. Their failure was due to their mistake, not to the impoverishment of the waters of Galilee (spiritual truths in the mind) ; for in them were many fish (mysteries) waiting to be netted. The waters which had flowed down from the divine uplands, the spiritual truths which had come to them with the Master's teachings, contained many Mysteries, great and small fish for the nourishment of the Soul that only required to be rightly sought for by them. The spiritual mind was enriched with these treasures of the Soul for the very purpose that they might go afishing and find them. The Mysteries were meant for the spiritual man. They were of the Soul, and were meant to be understood by man. But they could be found and understood *only on the right side*. They could not be found and understood on the earthward side. There the vision was earthly, and the experiences were of an earthly order. Such of the Mysteries as had found their way to that side, had ceased to be Mysteries of the Soul; they had ceased to be living, palpitating, spiritual verities of deep Soul-experience, and had become mere earthly things, outward histories without potency, material incidents lacking in blessed spiritual and divine meaning. But on the right side, the side that looked Godward, the side of the Soul herself in her innermost noblest experiences, the Mysteries were preserved in their spiritual sense, and retained their divine meanings. There they were to be found as Divine Truths; and from that side alone could come their true interpretation.

It was this the inner group found when the dawn broke within their Souls, and they obeyed the divine injunction to let down their nets on the right side. For it is said in the story found in the fourth Gospel, that they caught a great many fish, yet their nets did not break; that they took in the nets one hundred and fifty-three fish, and found the catch almost too great for them, though their nets did not break.

FISHING ON THE WRONG SIDE

Here then we are face to face with a profound Soul-mystery; and we have given unto us a most beautiful interpretation of its meaning. How great the significance of it is for the Soul in a prophetic sense may be discovered by examining the history written by the Christian Church through all the long ages during which its leaders and teachers have professed to be " the fishermen " for the people, those who knew and understood the great mysteries of the Soul, the divine nature and purpose revealed in them, and who alone were able to rightly interpret them. What was done unto those who were dissatisfied with the earthward outlook, who felt that the nets were let down on the wrong side, and who sought for the meaning of heavenly things all through the long dark night of the era which has been so sadly misnamed Christian? They were suppressed by the ecclesiastical authorities. They were persecuted even by their brethren. Many of them, indeed, were cast out from the ecclesiastical ship as veritable Jonahs, to be drowned by the various agencies provided for getting rid of such mystical Souls.

The story of the true and pure Gnostics is interpretive of the action of the Church, and reveals the awful evils arising out of the wrong direction given to the spiritual mind. It shows how Souls suffered as they toiled throughout the long night, seeking for the true interpretation of the Soul's history, and the story of the manifestation of the Divine Love and Wisdom given by the blessed Master. Within the Church have been found many mystics, men and women who could find no satisfactory interpretation of that history and manifestation in the teachings given by the schools. And these as a rule have been *the saints* within her borders, though she rarely knew it at the time. These have been the men and women who have gone afishing on the Sea of Galilee to discover the inner meaning of the teachings wherein the Soul's Mystery was set forth. And, as a rule, they are those who have had to wear the crown of martyrdom—physical, national, ecclesiastical and spiritual. They are those of whom the world-systems showed themselves to be unworthy, whom the ecclesiastics could not understand, and whom the schools in various ways silenced.

The foundations of the world-systems are laid deep on the wrong side. They are the exposition of the evils gathered into the net cast furthest away from the divine side of life, with its beautiful ideals and spiritual aspirations. The whole machinery of the Church-ecclesiastical, and all her methods and ambitions have been such as are opposed to the very life which she has, through her leaders, professed to seek. They have been, and they yet very largely are, such, as obscure the truth and make the Soul seek on the wrong side for those things which can only be found on the right side. The various schools of religious thought have laid their foundations in traditions, and they have built up systems upon them which have *not* brought spiritual enlightenment, though they have often brought strife and persecution ; for they have all been and still are on the wrong side. And when Souls are constrained to go afishing on their own account ; when they feel the depression resulting from the spiritual darkness about them, and it dawns upon them that they must needs seek for the inner meaning of their own history elsewhere ; when they dare to launch out into the deep waters in the night of their spiritual travail, to there toil in the hope of finding such a catch of spiritual things as will satisfy their deepest longings, then do these systems not only prove inadequate for them, but they seek to oppress and even suppress them.

Such has it been in the past. Alas! that it should be so much so even in these latter days. *And still so now in 2001. Tiz a path of solitude to seek on the right side, though one is not alone.*

A Time of Blessed Hope

But blessed be God for His graciousness unto His children, the day breaketh and the darkness passeth away. The long night of fruitless labour is ended for all who turn to the eastern heavens, the right side where the dawn breaketh and the light of day sheddeth his beams ; for the Divine Presence draweth near, and the glory of the Lord may be beheld approaching. As it was for the anxious inner group of disciples, so is it now for all true mystics : to the Souls who desire the inner meanings of the profound teachings of the Blessed One, the Divine Vision cometh. The Lord walketh upon the sacred shores of Galilee, and is awaiting the weary children who are seeking for those things which He alone can give. He is looking for their approach to those shores, that He may speak with them. Some have, in these latter days, once more beheld the vision and heard His voice, and have let down their nets on the right side.

O the blessedness that is coming upon this age ; the glory that is being shed upon it from the divine arising within so many; the new and blessed interpretation of the Divine Love towards the Soul which is being sent forth here a little and there a little, in various parts of the earth ! Truly it is a most marvellous age, the most marvellous since the manifestation of the Christhood ; indeed, even more marvellous than that, since the Christhood has not only been re-interpreted, but the tragic Sin-offering has been accomplished, and now the Soul is able to rise up into the angelic heavens to see and hear divine things. It is the most wonderful and marvellous age since this world went away from the true path ; for now the astral kingdom, which through its elements losing their spiritual purity and magnetism brought about the fall of the Soul, has been so much changed by means of the work of the Sin-offering, that many are not only able to pass up through it to the angelic world when they leave these outer planes, but those who dwell upon the outer planes are also able to rise up through it to the angelic world, if they live lives of purity and goodness and love. And as men and women purify themselves, so will the astral world grow purer and purer until no evil remains in its elements, all its dwellers know the joy of Redemption complete and blessed, and all the children of this Earth be restored to the edenic life once more. It is, therefore, an age full of the most glorious hope for all Souls, and very specially for those who are ready for the divine vision. Who may declare its blessedness but those who have come into some measure of the divine realizations, who have beheld anew their Lord walking upon the shores of Galilee, who have once more heard His beloved voice calling unto them to let down their nets on the right side, who have obeyed His blessed injunction and have found a wealth of spiritual food, and who are now ready to follow Him still further whilst He gives unto them such food as only the inner group may eat of, *the higher initiates of the divine mysteries ?* For, if what has been done for us is marvellous, what has yet to come is still more wonderful. But the most wonderful of all is the inexhaustible fulness of the Divine Love and Wisdom.

E

THE GREAT DRAUGHT OF FISHES

WHEN the disciples heard the divine voice counselling them to let down their nets on the right side, they obeyed, and immediately did the net become filled with fish, even to the number of one hundred, fifty and three. Was there anything of special value in this number that it should have been remembered and recorded ? For emphasis does seem to be laid upon the fact that they caught one hundred, fifty and three. The importance of the taking surely could not be confined merely to the number of the fish, for the draught was not a great one viewed from the standpoint of seven fishermen. The numbers must have had some value other than the apparent one ; for, as we have seen, the fish were not creatures, but truths ; and the numbers referred to the spiritual value of the things which they had sought, and now were able to gather in. They indicated the spiritual state at which the disciples had arrived, the realizations of their own inherent divine potencies, the measure of the divine life which had become their possession. For the Soul can only find divine things to the extent that she is prepared. She can only apprehend those things which in the past she has known. When she goes afishing in order to find the inner spiritual meanings of her own history, of the divine purpose towards her, and the meaning of the wonderful manifestation, she can only gather out of the

Sea of Galilee (her own spiritual mind) such fish as are there to be caught and made use of for her nourishment. *Her real history is inward.* Whatever her outward manifestation has been in the eyes of the historian whose knowledge is gleaned from without, or in the judgment of science whose conclusions are all based on the outward and visible phenomena ; her real and true life has been inward, and the history and phenomena from which that life must be read are entirely spiritual. And they can be known and read only from the spiritual planes. And only in so far as that history has progressed in the direction of the fulfilment of the perfect evolution of her life, is the Soul able to receive from the Divine Love. Only that which she has learnt upon her path as she has moved along it and grown, can she immediately recognize as spiritual fact. And she can do that only when she is fishing on the right side. *Her history is within herself;* and her age or fullness of spiritual attainment is made manifest by means of that history. She cannot understand those things immediately of which she knoweth nothing within herself from her own past experience, much less speak or write of them. But when she is fishing on the right side, when she is turned towards the eastern shore—the divine kingdom within her, and the light from that kingdom is breaking upon her, then all that she has known gradually opens out to her vision, and she comes into the possession of her own inherent knowledge. When she turns to that shore and the eastern light is pouring its radiance within her, then does she understand from the divine within her all things of which she has known. When the truth is presented to her vision, she beholdeth its inner significance.

Mystic Meanings for the Soul

Thus it was with the seven disciples. They had toiled amid the darkness that had overtaken them through the passing of the Master, without discovering the meanings for which they sought, because they sought the meanings on the earthward side. But as soon as they turned to the eastern shore they beheld the divine vision ; and they heard the divine voice counselling them to seek in the right direction, and having followed its guidance, they were able to find all that they required and for which they had so long in vain sought. They let down their nets on the right side and took into them the great Mysteries the blessed Master had propounded to them and in part interpreted. These were the fish they caught, great fish whose taking was sure to try the net—the Intuition, the spiritual power within the Soul that nets all divine things. The net did not break in the taking of them. It was equal to the great strain put upon it. The Intuition was not disturbed by the remarkable discovery, showing that it was ready for such a service.

O the profound depth of the teaching given in the narrative, the wonderful nature of the unfoldment of Soul history, the testimony to the Divine Love and Wisdom ! How the wealth of sacred story increases as we proceed, and the depth and height of spiritual experience embodied in it stand unveiled ! The inherent wealth of the Soul is revealed as the numbers of fish taken are understood. She knows the meaning of the divine nature ; for that is symbolized by the first number, ONE. She knows the meaning of the divine trinity within herself, which is symbolized by the last number, THREE. She knows the four kingdoms which issue from the divine life within her, and which are to be her heritage—*the human, the angelic, the celestial, and the divine*—and which proceed from the divine and the Blessed One, and are bounded by the divine in trinity as expressed in the combination of the first and last numbers, One and Three. She knows the meaning of the *five senses* in their inwardness, the Soul signification of them, their origin and true function from the divine, and how they are encompassed by the life of the trinity ; for these are symbolized by the middle number, FIVE. And then, the combined numbers, making NINE, reveal to her the state at which she has again arrived in her return from the long night, the state of the Buddha or perfected Jesus-life, the entrance upon Christ-hood which she is henceforth to make manifest.

For in spiritual symbolism, One stands for the Divine. Three stands for the divine trinity—Fatherhood, Motherhood, Eternal Sonship ; the Eternal Spirit, the Eternal Substance, and the Creation : in the Soul system, the masculine and feminine modes, and the life ; *Joseph, Mary, Christ.* And Five symbolizes the five avenues of manifestation, the five true spiritual senses—the inward ear to hear ; the inward eye to see ; the inward sense to taste ; the power to feel from within all the powers which come through the other avenues, and the wonderful gift of power to think divinely as well as earthwardly. These five spiritual senses of hearing, seeing, feeling, tasting, and conceiving in thought, were all bounded by the One Life in the Three-fold manifestation in the Universe, the Planet, and the Soul of all creatures. And then, in the path of the Soul the number Nine—the sum of all the others when added together—represented the entrance of the Soul into the Christ-hood realization, not in sublime fulness, but in a large measure. For they took up that number into the understanding. It was Peter, the Understanding, who led the way. They understood the Divine Mystery. They arrived at a perception of the true meaning of the Christhood of the blessed Master. And they were on the path to follow *Him,* and to share His momentous work.

We may now behold what it was that was done when this wonderful Soul-story was materialized and brought down from its lofty realm to be regarded as only an ordinary incident in the lives of seven fishermen on an inland sea, and made extraordinary by an apparent divine interposition. We may behold how profound the teachings of the story were, and how they were changed from being inward divine things concerning the life of the Soul, to be outward and material things. And in so beholding them we may witness in a new and truer light the disaster which befell those who sought for the meanings on the wrong side ; how the story itself came to be made the foundation of a plea for the use of the creatures of the sea as food, and the taking of their lives as perfectly legitimate traffic, since the Divine Love sanctioned it through the Mastei.

O the terrible calamity which overtook these wonderful allegories told in the Logia of St. John, as well as the parabolic teachings given in the original Gospel Record of St. Matthew ! It has made the whole development of Christianity tragical, for that latter became historical rather than spiritual, a doctrinal and dogmatic system instead of a great new spirit and pure life. It marred the beautiful vision of the Master which was given in the Gospel of St. Matthew, and blighted the very fruit of His Soul-travail through changing the nature of His teachings. It left the world in darkness ; for the light which it gave to the West was false. It robbed the Soul of the vision of the true way, and sent men and women along a wrong one to their own bitterness and sorrow. It heaped dishonour upon the Divine Love, and set at naught the true interpretation of His compassion unto all Souls and all Creatures.

But now the veil is lifted. The touch of the Divine Love maketh all things new. " *He taketh away the letter that He may establish the spirit*." Blessed evermore be His Holy Name ; for His Goodness unto all His children is unspeakable !

F
THE MYSTERY OF THE FIRE

WHEN the seven disciples knew who it was who spake unto them, they not only soon found what they had been seeking for upon the Sea of Galilee, but they likewise found themselves upon *the eastern shore where the Lord was*. And when they reached that shore they found a fire with a fish laid upon it, and an invitation awaiting them to dine with the Lord. It was not one of the fish they had taken, but one provided by the Lord. It was, therefore, some new Mystery that was to be unfolded unto them. And that it was a profound Soul experience the sequel shows. For there is indeed a depth of meaning in the language of the Lord which has never been fathomed by those who have taught the people the supposed meaning of the story. It is indeed one of the most sacred experiences which can come to any Soul, far, far more sacred than any ordinary outward experience such as the story was reduced to.

The term " fish " as we have said, was the word that was used to symbolize a spiritual mystery ; and the term translated " fire " was made use of to express the Divine Energy. A " fish " was a deep or hidden thing ; and a " fire " was the coming into life of a new potency, a divine energy. " *He shall baptize with the Holy Spirit and with Fire.*" " *He shall baptize you with the Holy Spirit, and with Power from on High.*" Where it is said that " a fish was laid on a fire," as in the narrative which we are considering, we are to understand that there was about to be unfolded such a Mystery as would bring into the life of the recipient the consciousness of the Divine Presence, and, therefore, a divine power such as that consciousness gives. And the Mystery was that found unfolded in the narrative which follows. It was the Mystery concerning the nature of the Divine Love, and the quality of the Love which the Lord desires to see realized within and expressed by the Soul. It was the Mystery implied in that process by which the Soul passes from the state of *a personal* spiritual love, into the realization of *a universal divine love whose nature is wholly impersonal.* It was the call of the Soul to pass upward towards the divine realization, to evolve from the personal to the impersonal life ; from the attachments of the outward and earthly experience to those of the Soul ; from the loves which are generated of these earthly and outward attachments, to those which are the outcome of the divine indwelling.

It was, therefore, a Mystery of the most precious nature, containing such a truth for the Soul as would carry it further along the path of its true evolution. For the realization of it would close, as it were, one cycle of history, and open another wherein all experience would be upon a higher plane. In that sense the realization of the Mystery was a transition from one state to another ; but it was also a translation, an upward movement fraught with the most momentous issues. What it meant we shall see as we look into the " Sayings " of the Lord to Peter, and behold how the Understanding or higher mind shrank from confessing its preparedness to take such a step. We shall see how the Lord addresses the Soul, and how great is the burden of His meaning ; and we shall behold the Soul revealing her consciousness of the importance and depth of meaning in the question asked, and the step it invites her to take. We shall understand the reason for the question being asked three times, and the true meaning of the grief. And we shall also understand what it was that was implied in the saying that, when he was young he went whither he would, but that when he grew old others would carry him whither he would rather not go. Indeed we shall discover in these words a wealth of history which the Church and the Schools of systematic theology and christology have never dreamt of, a history momentous in its prophetic anticipations.

G

A MOMENTOUS QUESTION

THE question which it is said the Master addressed to Peter was part of the Mystery of the fish laid upon a fire. In the narrative it is made personal, though in the allegory it was impersonal. It was not a question asked of the man by the personal Master, but one asked of the Soul by the Divine Love. And it was asked at " the meal " when the Lord invited the disciples to dine with Him. For that " meal " was no ordinary one. It was not of an earthly order, and had naught to do with things material, except as the outward spheres were affected by it. The meal was altogether spiritual and soullic. It was of the Divine Love and the Soul. It had to do purely with the Soul in its attitude to the Divine Lord. It was a meal of the most profound nature ; sublime in its outcome, but unspeakably trying as an ordeal. How sacred it was those may understand who are able to follow us, and to enter into the deep significance of the thrice repeated question.

" *Simon, Son of John, lovest thou me more than these ?* " The address is to the Soul in that state of religious feeling in which it looks outward. Simon means the spiritual mind turned earthwards.[1] Our readers will remember another incident found in the Gospels in which the Master is represented as having made use of these words in His address to Simon Peter, "*Simon Simon, Satan hath desired to have thee that he may sift thee as wheat ; but I have prayed for thee that thy faith (spiritual vision) fail not, and that, when thou hast turned again, thou mayest strengthen thy brethren.*"

These words, which fortunately have been preserved for us, though in a personal setting, give a clue to the meaning of the term Simon, and what was coming to the Soul after the passing of the Christhood. They show the nature of the experience that was to be passed through when the burden of the Sin-offering was being borne. For the words were uttered in that connection as may be learnt from the context. We have, therefore, to understand that the supreme question asked by the Lord, was one relating to the state of the Soul, that state at which he had once more arrived after the accomplishment of the bearing of the

---

[1] *Vide* the Chapter on " In the House of Simon."

sin-offering burden. *It had relation, not to any man, but to the Soul of Him who bore that tragic burden.*

The Satan who desired to sift Simon as wheat (or the Soul with an outward aspect in experience) was none other than the materializing spirit, the king of the astral world, and so of that kingdom within which the Sin-offering had to be performed. For it is that kingdom which is and always has been since its formation, the great trier of man. It betrays, deceives and misleads him, making life's path difficult and sorrowful. It is that great trier of the children of men which was personified by the seer, that power which was to be thrown down or broken, and whose false prophet was to be overcome. That was the power which desired to possess the Soul ; the power which had to be met in the lives of the Sin-offering, and broken through changing its elements from a state of evil to one of good. It was the power that was to tempt and betray the Christ-Soul ; the very power which did tempt and betray Him in all those earth-lives lived by Him after the passing of the Christhood ; the power that turned His days into sorrow and anguish and His nights into weeping, that marred the beauty of His garments and stained them with the very life-blood of His Soul. It was that power for evil in this world which made Him " to tread the winepress alone," and red-dye his garments in sore travail.

SPOKEN CONCERNING THE SIN-OFFERING BURDEN

Now, the memorable words were spoken concerning the Soul ; and they were not spoken to a disciple of the Master, by Him. They were words spoken in profound soliloquy *through* the Master. They were words full of deep prophetic significance. They foretold what was about to happen. They anticipated the work of the Sin-offering. They indicated the nature of that work. Yea, they revealed the pathetic result unto the Soul who was to bear the burden. For there are implied in them the sad and tragic conditions to which that beautiful

Soul would be reduced as the outcome of bearing the burden and performing the stupendous task.

With these thoughts in our minds it will be more easy to understand the appeal as one made unto the Soul who bore the burden. It was an appeal unto Him, as well as to every Soul ; for He had to pass through all the experiences which come to all Souls, and to bear the like trials. He had to pass through all that they had endured, and know these things as they had known them, but with a depth and a fullness which had not been their portion. And so we may see a new meaning in the appeal ; indeed, a strange new meaning, one which may well make us pause and wonder at the greatness of the sacrifice which the sublime Master made. For the story was not just what is now found in the fourth Gospel. Originally it spoke of the future, as if wondering what would be the effect upon the bearer of the burden of all that He must needs pass through. What would be the issue unto that Soul ? Would He become so changed that no longer the Divine Love would prevail within the sanctuary ? Would He also become personal in attachments, and outward in vision and service ?

A Tragic Soliloquy

There is something so sacred, indeed almost too sacred for human eyes to witness even now, in the meaning of the profound and tragic soliloquy. For it was a soliloquy of the Master ; a prophetic outlook with its retrospective and introspective analysis ; a great sad history yet to be written, the results of which were already anticipated by Him, and viewed with certain falteringness and even dismay. He could see what the effect must be of such experiences ; and He dreaded them. He anticipated how terrible the issues would be ; and He was filled with fear. He knew what it was to love the divine with a perfect love ; and He dreaded the loss of that love. In sublime realization He knew the difference between *agapao* or divine love and *phileo* or friendship love. He knew how beautifully impersonal and universal the Αγαπη was, how rich in its manifestation, how blessed in its realizations ; and He had great inward dread lest He should fail in that love just as others had done. He had passed through the Gethsemane vision, and knew from that vision all that awaited Him in the path of the Sin-offering ; and He feared lest when He did return from His sore travail, His love would all be changed. And it was this feared change in Himself that was the subject of the profound and tragic soliloquy.

The pathos of what was said by Him concerning the future, the weary look in the Master's face, the sad wistful longing, the tragic grief in His voice, the awful Soul-yearning that was so manifest :—how unspeakable these were, and how impossible it is to portray them here ! Who of those who beheld Him in that hour apprehended the full measure of the work He was undertaking on behalf of the world, or the depth of feeling which then manifested itself in Him, and the meaning of the beloved one's fear ? It was a tragedy in anticipation ; but how tragic for Him the little group did not know. Had they done so, it would have overwhelmed them with the awful sorrow and anguish which they would have foreseen for Him. Had they ever dreamt that His anguish and sorrow would have been so great, and that He would have been so smitten with grief and spiritual loss, they would have been crushed, they could not have borne it. But the blessed Master hid from them all that it would mean of suffering to Himself, and only indicated sufficiently what was coming to enable them to apprehend the meaning of the Sin-offering as to its nature and purpose.

If our readers have thus far been able to follow us in our endeavour to make clear a most difficult presentation, we would now ask them to try and imagine for themselves what it must have cost the beautiful Soul to give utterance to the terms which form the question and the answer. Let them try to picture to themselves the sublime Master thus speaking in soliloquy. Let them change the story from the outward and personal to the inward and impersonal ; from the sayings of a teacher to a beloved disciple, to the sayings of the Soul in a divine consciousness to itself because soon that divine estate would have to be laid aside and a world-estate taken up in its stead. Let them try to understand how the Soul that had loved even as the divine, and who foresaw the meaning of the awful conditions into which He had to descend in the performance of the work given him to accomplish, could fear, lest, in the carrying out of the most difficult and most spiritually dangerous task, He should lose all that He held as most sacred, that His beautiful love should become changed in its nature, and that He should no more be able to respond to the high services of the Divine Love. In that way only will the profound significance of the sayings be opened up to them, and the mystery made known. They will then behold the mystery as one of the most wonderful acts of love.

WHICH : AGAPAO OR PHILEO ?

The question is an appeal to the Soul from the Lord within her sanctuary. The soliloquy of the Master is one that every Soul who is truly seeking the divine life will repeat for herself. The appeal is made to every one who passes into the state which the mystery of dining with the Lord upon a " fish " laid upon a " fire," represents. No Soul can escape it on the way of her true evolution. There comes to her an hour in her history when she must hear the divine voice within her sanctuary asking the all-important question, " *Simon, son of John, lovest*[1] *thou me more than these ?* " For the love of the Soul has to grow ; and it has to grow from an outward love to an inward, from a personal

---

[1] The two words made use of in the story of the Divine Appeal to the Soul have different degrees of meaning. Aγαπας refers to Divine Love, whilst Φιλω has only a personal application. Aγαπας was the word used by the Divine Lord, and Φιλω the term said to have been made use of by the Soul in the sorrowful soliloquy.

spiritual to an impersonal divine, from a local feeling to an universal, from the love of any man to that love which sees always the divine in man, and loves that only. For the Soul has to acquire, as a possession, the Divine Love. She has to come into the consciousness of that Love as a most sacred inheritance. She has to arrive at such a state of impersonal life that she is willing to become even as the Divine One in all her realizations and services. She must needs pass into the universal state of experience in which she not only feels herself to be one with all that lives, but to be even as the Divine One in the world. Her thoughts and feelings have to become the exposition of divine thoughts. Her love must be the interpretation of the Divine Love. By that Love she must needs be prepared to give even her very life in the divine service. She must thus be like the Master, ready to lay herself on the altar of the divine for the great service of the race. For when the Aγαπη is a beautiful realization within her Sanctuary, she will not shrink from laying down all the wealth of the glory of such a love at the feet of the Divine Father, to be used in His children's service.

We may now undertand how full of meaning the allegory is, and all that it calls to of devotion to the divine way. We may understand how very different the divine love is from that of mere personal love. We may see wherein the great difference lies between the love of the Soul and the love of the personal life, and behold how very limited the one is and how illimitable is the other. And so we may understand the nature of the question that is addressed from the Divine Lord to us, and how very diffident even the best of Souls must feel about answering the question.

PART IV.

Teachings of the Sin-Offering

The Temptations in the Wilderness

*Being a Picture of the Sin-offering States, and of the
nature and manner of the Soul's trial during the
accomplishment of the Sin-offering, and likewise of the reality of the Humiliation
of the Master, and the dire impoverishment of His Life as
the result of the supreme
Sacrifice which
was made.*

The Temptation in the Wilderness

A

THE EVANGELISTS' NARRATIVES

WE have now to consider some allegories relating directly to the Sin-offering, though their teaching is likewise for all Souls.

In the first three Gospels we have presented to us the remarkable experiences known as the Temptations, and these are made to follow immediately upon the Baptism of the Spirit. Indeed it is said in these Records that the Christ was led of the Spirit into the wilderness to be tempted of the devil. The Baptism in the river Jordan and the Temptations in the wilderness are thus brought into such close relationship that the one is made to follow the other as a natural sequence ; and the resultant is shown to be the astounding experiences which are embodied in the story. The rich gift of the Divine Spirit ; the attainment by the Soul of that blessed altitude when the vision of the glory of the Lord is beheld, and the voice of the Eternal One is heard speaking from amidst the glory ; the sublime realization by the Soul of the Divine Presence within its own sanctuary ; these are followed by the strange experiences implied in the Soul going away into " the wilderness " where there could be found no nourishment ; where only the wild beasts dwelt ; where the life would be sure to languish, suffering the pain of spiritual want, the extreme sadness of an unutterable loneliness, the dread arising from the awful environment, and the anguish imposed by the great Tempter as he tried the powers of the Soul whether they would not yield to him, obey his behests, and at last fall down and worship him.

It does seem on the surface as if the presentation were true, not only as an experience in the life of the beloved Master, but also in the order and nature of the events supposed to have taken place. By most of the Christian communities it is accepted as an historical fact ; and those who do not so accept it, seem also to have missed its inner meanings. For these meanings are concerned with the whole burden of the Sin-offering taken by the Master, and are so profound in their nature that one is constrained to stand in awe before the marvellous vision of the divine travail for the children of this world which they present to the Soul.

But our readers will witness, as we unfold the meaning of the picture presented, how purely spiritual it is. They will discover how far removed from the sphere of mere outward history are all the experiences narrated. They will learn how the story has had given to it an historical setting foreign to its meaning ; how it has become, through that false setting, misunderstood and wrongly interpreted ; how its significance was unrecognised by those who wrote the Gospels ; how they placed it, in their ignorance of its true meaning, at the commencement of the Christhood manifestation, and as an essential part of that manifestation, instead of recognising in it the embodiment of those profound experiences through which the Soul was to pass after the Christhood had been made manifest. For the story of the Temptations in the Wilderness was one told by the Master to the inner group of the disciples to illustrate, under the form of an allegory, how the Christhood would be laid aside in order that He might descend into the sad spiritual states represented by the wilderness of spiritual impoverishment ; and how He would there be tried through the very conditions by which all the children upon this fallen Planet have been tried and brought down to obey the behests of the power spoken of as the devil, and even to worship that power in the hope of possessing the world. It was a vista of the nature of the burden to be borne during the lives which were to be lived by the Soul in the Travail of the Sin-offering. It was a cameo of the nature of the temptations which were to assail Him in those lives, a vivid microscopic picture of the awful drama that was about to be enacted when the Christhood manifestation had been accomplished.

LIKE A MIRACLE PLAY

The presentation of the Temptations found in the Gospels is both strange and unreal. It is like the picture of a play in which the actors assume parts which have no reality in their experience. It is a drama in three acts, with a prologue and an epilogue. There are striking spectacular and wonderful scenic effects, yet over all there is the glamour of unreality. From the rise of the curtain, when it is said that the Master was led of the Spirit into the wilderness to be tempted by the devil, until it falls again as we are beholding angels ministering unto Him, there is such an atmosphere as we might expect to find in one of the old Miracle-plays—a mysterious feeling that whatever there was of reality in the original experiences represented by the actors and the spectacular, it is all nothing more than a moving shadow, unsubstantial and unreal.

And the effect upon the life of the spectators is exactly like that produced by a performance of some drama. The mind and the emotions may be moved for a moment as the drama proceeds ; wonderment at the astounding situations may be awakened ; but when the finale is reached and the play is concluded with all the garish trappings made use of to set off the representation, the spectators feel it is an unsubstantial pageant which has faded from their view, leaving not one wrack or great note behind it to sound forth the depths of meaning supposed to have been illustrated by the moving picture.

Is it any wonder that men and women have failed to understand how, and in what manner, and in how great a degree, the Christ was tempted and tried as they themselves have been ? Unto whom has the presentation of the Temptations given in the Gospels, brought the true vision and understanding of all that the Christ suffered in being tempted and tried like other

men and women ? Upon whom has that story impressed the
reality of the thing for which it purports to stand ? Who has
been enlightened through reading it as to the real nature of
the temptations which overtook the Master, how they came to
Him, when they came to Him, and how they were overcome
by Him ?

What was meant by Him being led of the Spirit into the
wilderness there to be the object of the most trying and terrible
experiences ? Who was the devil who came to Him there ?
What was the hunger which overtook Him, and what the
wonderful work which He was to perform in order to appease
it ? What was meant by the temptation to descend from the
pinnacle of the temple ? Where was the mountain from which
the vision of the kingdoms of this world and the glory of them,
was visible, and upon which the Master was asked by the
tempter to bow down and worship him, with the full assurance
that all these kingdoms would pass into His possession ? In
what way did He feel these awful temptations within Himself,
and overcome them by such strenuous efforts that He was well
nigh exhausted and had to be ministered unto by the angelic
world ?

Surely these questions are pertinent. They are indeed vital
to the clear understanding of the momentous experiences
implied. They arise out of the very needs of the Soul. They
must be capable of answers such as will unravel the tangled
threads of this most mysterious experience in the history of the
Christhood which is supposed to be truly set forth in the synoptic story. And in the following exposition we will endeavour
to present the *true meaning* of the Temptations of the beloved
who attained perfect Christhood, but who descended from that
estate in most wonderful humiliation in order to become like
His brethren, and help them up to that glorious realization.
We will show what the Temptations were, how they came to
Him, where they were borne, and the tragic purpose of them.

And so we ask our readers to follow us with reverent steps, and with earnest longings to know only the Truth at whatever cost it may come to them, fearing no man, but fearing only the Divine, having the true fear of the Lord, which is profound awe ; then the wonderment will become more and more, and the joyance within the Soul very great ; for the burden-bearing of the Divine Love will appear in a new light, and the Sin-offering in its reality be beheld.

B

DOES THE LORD CREATE EVIL ?

THE Master, it is said, was led of the Spirit into the Wilderness to be tempted. The thought seems almost inconceivable. God tempts no one with evil. He is the searcher of hearts and trier of the reins of the spirit of men and women, but He knows no evil in His way. Goodness, purity and truth mark all His actions. He doeth only good unto all His children. They are made strong through the conditions He creates for them ; not weakened in the way as they are by most of the conditions found in the life of this world to-day. They are all lifted up higher by the experiences through which He calls them to pass, and fitted for nobler service. It is not by His will, nor in accordance with His purpose, that they are brought down from spiritual altitudes in the way that they have been and still are through the evil in this world and the generators of evil. It was surely a terrible conception of the divine nature that led men to write concerning the Eternal Love that He created both good and evil, and to make it appear in the Sacred Books as if He affirmed Himself to be the creator of evil, even whilst He blamed His children for following the evil paths. The priesthoods of Jewry put into the Sacred Books which had come down to them from the ancient Hebrews, Books full of the Divine Love and Light, " *I the Lord am the Creator of good and evil* "; and, sad to relate, both Jews and Christians have believed that libel upon the character of the Divine. Judgments terrible and overwhelming sent forth upon both individuals and nations, were what the priesthoods of Jewry surrounded the divine name with, notwithstanding the fact that they also taught that He created the evil ; and thus they made the divine name to be dreaded and not loved, and covertly laid all the conditions in the world at the feet of the Eternal One.

THE DIVINE CHARACTER VINDICATED

The day has arrived when the divine character must be vindicated against the misrepresentations made by those priesthoods, and which were reproduced in another form under historical Christianity ; and also that representation of the presence of evil in this world found in certain modern philosophy. The hour has struck when the true cause of the presence of evil must be made known, and the nature of evil itself understood. A moment of momentous importance in the world's history is upon us, in which the meaning of the presence of evil is to be interpreted, and all its sad and most terrible consequences are to be explained ; when its effects upon the Soul will be clearly seen, and the way in which it brought about what is now spoken of and written about in the West in relation to the Christhood, as the Sin-offering. And it will be made obvious what was meant by the Master being led by the Spirit into the Wilderness to be tempted of the devil, the great purpose of it, and the awful experiences which came to Him as He confronted the forces personified as the devil, combatted and overcame them. And instead of the view given by the Jewish writers and the Hegelian philosophy, that the Divine Love was and is still the creator of all evil even as of the good, and that He created and still creates evil in order that through the experiences it brings to His children they might come into a truer knowledge of the good ; it will be seen what evil has meant unto that Love, the unspeakable burdens which it has imposed upon that Love, the grief which the effects of the evil have given that Love, the anguish of that Love in travail to blot out the evil, with all its effects, in the performing of the Sin-offering by means of which redemption was to be made possible for all Souls. The tragedy of evil will be understood as something very real, and not to have been a mere aspect and condition of the creation of Souls upon this world. It will be seen in its true light as a power which has militated against the true upwardness of all Souls, prevented the realizations which should have crowned all the children according to the degree of their unfoldment and the order to which they belonged, and imposed upon all, from the highest to the lowest, sufferings unspeakable and conditions unnameable.

A LABOUR OF DIVINE LOVE.

Now, when it is said that the Christ was " led of the Spirit into the wilderness," we have presented to us a truth whose profundity is indeed almost beyond the ordinary mind to conceive in all its fulness, though the truly spiritual mind may apprehend much of its significance. As we have already indicated, the experiences implied in the statement did not precede the manifestation of the Christhood, but followed it. To pass through them the Christhood had to be laid aside. They were those profound, painful and mysterious experiences which were foreseen in the Gethsemane, the very anticipation of which brought such anguish to the Master ; and which, notwithstanding His wonderful love and abandon to the divine will for service, caused Him to pray in His anguish to be delivered from the awful cup that He must needs drink of if He passed through these experiences. What those experiences were it is most difficult to relate, and we shall only be able to indicate them in the unfoldment of the Temptations. The one outstanding feature of them is that it was of the Spirit that the Master was led to undertake the awful burden which they implied. For the Divine Spirit to undertake any work is the testimony to the action of the Divine Love. When a Soul is led of the Spirit, it is the Divine Love who is operating through that Soul.

The work was, therefore, a work performed by the Divine Love through Him, following upon the wonderful Christhood which had been made manifest. It was a work taken up and carried through by the Divine Love for the sake of all the children. The Divine Spirit, as it is written in the synoptic Records, carried and led the Soul into the very conditions where the experiences were to be found, and amid which the work of the Sin-offering was to be accomplished. To be so led of the Spirit was the assurance that the work was one which the Divine Love found to be absolutely necessary for the accomplishment of the redemption of all Souls upon the Planet, human and creature. And the unspeakable anguish of the Master when it was given Him to see what it would imply, is the sure and certain testimony to the reality of evil, and its repugnant effects upon Him, showing how it is diametrically opposed to the divine ways. The picture of the anguish born within Him when He beheld all that it meant to perform such a labour, should suffice to impress all earnest Souls with the awful conditions into which He had to pass in the stupendous work given to Him to accomplish for this world. Alas, the multitudes of believers in the Sin-offering have no clear conception of its meaning, nor of the profound depths of most tragic experience into which it drew Him ; nor indeed do the leaders and teachers in the Churches seem to know. They think it was accomplished by the Master at the tragedy of the Roman Crucifixion, having no distinctively clear vision as to the true meaning of the Christhood made manifest through Him nor of the nature and function of the Soul as the Sin-bearer. From lack of insight they have confused the two offices and misapprehended the work of both. They have related both to the personal Master as if the *persona* were the Christhood, and as if a Soul in the life of manifestation of the Christhood could possibly be also the Sin-bearer. Not understanding what Christhood means, they have failed to interpret the beautiful meaning of the Christ-life, to the disaster of the Churches and the loss to the Soul of the most wonderful vision of purity, goodness, love, compassion and pity, lit up with the glory of the Light of the Divine Wisdom, ever beheld upon this World. They have made personal what was wholly spiritual and impersonal in the *persona* sense, though divine in the sense of *hypostasis*. And they have made entirely local what was in its very nature universal. They have revealed to the whole world that they have not rightly apprehended the meaning of the Master's Christhood, and in this way they have made that glorious and blessed manifestation of non-effect. And concerning the Sin-offering may we not truly say that they have shown that they were incapable of beholding and understanding its profound mystery, or surely they would not have strewn the western world with wounded and broken lives, many of whom were compelled to pass through prisons, dungeons and the stake because of the views they had of the mystery.

That which the Churches did not know at their foundation, and even through the ages have not yet discovered, it is now given us to make known unto them. And may the majesty of the Divine Love be made manifest, and the unspeakable pathos of its burden-bearing be deeply felt.

O, Man of Sorrows, can it be that all who pass by wag their heads, saying, " He saved others, Himself He cannot save ? "

Can it be that none knoweth of Thine awful anguish and Thy dire extremity, save he unto whom Thou has made it known through the travail of his own Soul ?

Can it be that all who should have known the meaning of Thy travail amid the wilderness, understand not how it was Thou didst undertake such a burden of pain and sorrow, and what it was that Thou didst for the race ?

381

O sorrow of sorrows that Thou shouldest have had to travail alone, and that there were none to understand the meaning of Thy travailing !

O grief unspeakable that those who ought to have known Thee in Thy travail should have been even as those who are children of the night !

O thought most sad that the Churches which arose in Thy name, should never have known Thee, nor the sacred purpose of Thy sublime humiliation and tragic work !

C

THE WILDERNESS

WHAT was the wilderness into which the Soul was led ? A mere place ? A locality of Judea ? It has been so presented in the narratives. Are men and women specially tempted when they have withdrawn from the world for meditation and prayer ? Is it not the experience of most of us that the great temptations of our life come to us from out the midst of the world-life by which we are environed ? Are they not fashioned for us out of the appeals which the world-life makes to our body-senses and mind ? How could any Soul be tempted where that world-life did not reach with its alluring and ensnaring appeals ? How could any one be blamed for turning some stones into bread, supposing that one to have the power to do so, if he hungered and no bread was to be found ? Would it be an act in which the Divine Love could be made manifest, for one to fast forty days in order to make a show of great powers of physical endurance ? Surely there must be meanings attached to the experiences through which the Master passed transcending anything of such a nature, meanings which will carry us away from the physical spheres to seek for the explanation upon that kingdom from which all temptations have come and now come. Surely the Master's experience in fasting was not of the order of those men who have sought to demonstrate to the world that it was possible to live upon these outer spheres for many days without food. Who witnessed the remarkable feat of endurance, the approach of the devil, and the great trial ? Was not He alone with the wild-beasts ? And what were the beasts that bore Him company, whose nature was of the desert or wilderness, and whose home was there ? How did the experience come to be known, since no one witnessed it but the beasts and the Heavens ?

How the Wilderness was Fashioned

The wilderness of Judea was such a place as readers of the story little dream of, though they have all been influenced by its life and powers. It was not a mere locality in Palestine, a strip of land belonging to that country. Indeed it was not on the physical spheres at all, though it influenced these spheres in a most evil way by its forces. Its wild beasts made incursions into these spheres and injured the life of the people. In its habitations were found every kind of evil thing—the lion and the bear, the tiger and the leopard, the wolf and the fiery serpent—that is the evil elements and influences which these wild creatures represent. It was what has come to be known as the astral kingdom, the kingdom that encircles the outer planes, difficult to understand, perhaps, by those who do not know that the very atmosphere influences them in their feelings and ways, but apprehendable by all who think seriously and deeply upon the mysteries of life. Men and women generally think of the heavens as being around the Planet, that they are indeed in the skies. And so they are, when we understand by them the angelic heavens. This world is encompassed by the Divine Love who ministers unto all Souls by means of the angelic heavens : had it not been so, the world and all its children would have been lost long years ago. But though the Divine Love has encompassed the world and ministered unto it through the angelic heavens, it is ages untold since this earth was the scene of direct angelic ministration until in these latter days. For its magnetic plane which once was truly beautiful in its function, was so greatly changed that it could not receive and communicate correctly the beautiful messages which were sent from the Divine Love unto His children. It was like a leaden atmosphere through which the glory of the Sun cannot break to give the earth true healing, invigoration and joy ; all the conditions were like such an atmosphere, heavy, dense, depressing to the Soul. The heavenly light thrown upon it was unable to reach those who longed for it. The density was so great that the light could not penetrate. The Souls of all creatures suffered. There was no " open vision " for the Soul : all the conditions were against such a blessed experience. The Life-forces poured in from the heavens were suspended in their operation. Spiritual life languished for want of nourishment, until all Souls entered into a state of spiritual death. Life became more and more material. As the spiritual sense grew weaker the body-senses became stronger, until life consisted wholly in ministering to these body-senses. As age after age rose and set only to find the growth of the outward sense-nature, men and women ceased to be truly human and became as beasts of prey. They had once known the fellowship of angels ; but now they only sought such fellowship as the senses of the body could give. And through the gratification of these, they descended from the human estate. By their conduct they brought into existence orders of life which should never have had any place in the heavenly Father's Household. As an outcome of their ways the whole of the heavy atmosphere or magnetic plane was filled with the most grotesque evil images, like a photographic plate receiving all the images exposed to it ; and these not only became permanent impressions upon the magnetic plane, but also magnetic in their action. They thus acted as living images whose action prevented any Souls from rising who would fain have done so, thus repeating the very history which brought

them into existence in the lives of men and women, and in-
tensifying the terrible conditions age by age, until the whole
Earth became, as it were, a pandemonium. The history of the
lives upon it being the history of unutterable shame, the
very heavens above were filled with grief inexpressible. And
at one time it did even seem as if this once glorious world were
irretrievably lost. No ministry could be given from the heavens.
No angel could descend upon its planes without losing the
angelic nature and life. The magnetic plane had long refused,
through its changed nature, to receive any spiritual magnetism,
and so it became the very " abyss," the home of every
conceivable evil. It was the age, or rather great epoch of ages,
which terminated in the Sodom and Gomorrah tragedy. It was
the time of Lot—the days of the most fearful living—days which
issued in the destruction of the wonderful plane of precious
gems which encompassed the Planet and acted as the reflector
of the divine glory ; for it threw that light upon the atmospheric
magnetic plane which broke up the light and distributed it over
all the Earth. For that plane had been fashioned after what has
come to be known as the flood, and was the wonderful " Bow
in the Heavens " which is said to have testified to the divine
goodness and love in their never-ceasing care for this world,
and their perpetual vigilance over all its interests.

The Beginnings of the Return

The atmospheric magnetic plane now known in eastern philosophy as the astral kingdom, lay between the physical planes
of the earth and the angelic kingdom. It became simply a
supersensuous elemental kingdom in which everything done
on the outer planes was adumbrated and repeated. And as no
angelic communications could penetrate it, it became absolutely
necessary to bring about a change in the conditions. But that
was not only a grave thing to accomplish, but one that required
untold ages. It was a process that went on from age to age, until
the elemental conditions were at last effected by the powerful

divine magnetism brought to bear upon them. The photosphere of the Sun, as that is now known, was fashioned for the specific purpose of acting upon these elemental conditions with a view to breaking them up, and changing all of them again into their original state, as in the days when they were all pure and beautiful, and perfectly performed their functions.

So age by age the process went on, until at last the outer planes were so affected by the divine magnetism that the Souls who had descended into such low states were touched and attracted towards higher things, and, ultimately, higher life. Then began again the expression of what is understood as *religious feeling*, which grew purer and stronger (comparatively speaking) as the ages passed, until some of the Souls were able to rise up high enough in the astral kingdom to receive angelic messages.

Thus came the ages when the underlying beautiful spiritual and divine truths contained in all the great Ancient Religions were communicated unto the Soul, truths which still underlie all these Religions notwithstanding their materialization and misrepresentation. But though so much was accomplished by the Divine Love for the world, yet the magnetic images remained near the outer planes, influencing both mind and body to such an extent, that, whilst the most spiritual desired to rise into the angelic conditions, these graven magnetic images prevented such a blessed realization. And it was to blot out these evil conditions that the Sin-offering was made. It was to attract and absorb these magnetic images and thus change their elements, that the lives of the Sin-offering were lived.

How this was done will now be partially unfolded.

O Love of the Father, how little men have understood Thy glorious manifestations! How impoverished must the Souls of men have been when they could think of Thy Love as something to be appeased in its anger against sin, or satisfied by other means

than the purification of all Souls, and their return into the true
Fold of the One Divine Life ! How terrible has been the darkness
within the Churches where the Light was supposed to brightly
shine, since they have never understood the meaning of Thy Nature,
nor the way of the Redemption accomplished by Thee ! What
shall be said of those who, all through the ages of Travail by the
Christ-Soul, have fashioned unto themselves other graven images
to worship, sacrificed upon their altars unto Baal, and bowed the
knee at the shrine of Mammon ! We know that the very Heavens
where Thy Love reigneth weep at the spectacle, and mourn that
the darkness is so great where the Light should ever have been so
glorious !

D

HOW THE WILDERNESS WAS CHANGED

WE have seen what it meant to effect sufficient change in
the elements of the astral kingdom so as to permit of
the divine magnetism again reaching the outer planes of the
Planet to find the Soul and draw it up out of the evil conditions,
so that it could receive communications from the angelic
kingdom. But the magnetic images were not destroyed in the
process. They continued to infest the astral kingdom, and affect
those who had not risen right up beyond the area of their
influence, filling growing sensitive Souls with the most awful
dread as they became magnetically affected by them, and were
made to repeat through their bodies the evil ways of those who
had caused these terrible images to come into existence ; with
the fearful results, that in essant conflict took place between
the Soul with its beautiful aspirations and feelings which had
been again awakened, and the feelings and desires of a low
personal life. Many desired earnestly to do good, but could
not because of the influence of these monstrous images of
iniquity. When they would do good, the evil overtook them.

THE MASTER

The magnetism of the Divine Love pouring into the astral
kingdom preserved the latent aspirations of the Soul, though
the graven images were not affected by its power. Nor could
they be overcome without the destruction altogether of the
astral kingdom, which destruction would also have involved
the withdrawal to the angelic heavens of all Souls who were
able to rise into that kingdom, and the loss of all those who
were unable to do so. Indeed it would have meant the dissipation
and loss of most of the human race. To save the human race,
and all creatures upon the Planet who were of that race though
not yet upon the human kingdom, another way had to be found
by which to destroy the evil images on the magnetic kingdom,
without injuring it ; and that way was by means of the Sin-
offering.

The infinite depth of the Divine Love has not been understood.
How unsearchable are His ways to the mind of man, will be
made manifest. That His Love could ever have been so grossly
misinterpreted by the interpretation given to the western
religion, is a tragedy. But the day hasteneth when the glory
of His Love shall flood the whole world, and all shall at last
come to know the wondrous doings of the Lord. The meaning
of the Sin-offering will be understood ; its profound mystery
will stand forth in the light of the new day ; its awful path will
be seen ; the cause of the unspeakable anguish will be beheld ;
Gethsemane will become a reality to the Soul's vision ; the
Temptation of the Master will no longer appear as an artificial
story ; the " identification " of the Christ with fallen humanity
will shine forth as the sublimest of realities ; the doctrine of
" commutation " will have found its true interpretation without
the terrible degradation of the Divine Love implied in the
interpretations the West has given to that doctrine ; the " handwritings " which were against the Soul will be understood,
and the manner in which they were all blotted out ; how " the
middle wall " or " partition " was broken down will be clear

unto the seeking Soul, who will see that it was no mere barrier between Jew and Gentile ; and then will the Divine Righteousness in all its beauty and glory shine forth as the noonday, and the Divine Judgments in their true light ; and men and women will marvel that they have not understood, neither apprehended, the true nature of the ever Blessed One ; and they will sorrow that they could ever have thought so ignobly of His Love, or so mistakenly of His purposes and ways.

E

TURNING STONES INTO BREAD

THE blessed Master passed from the manifestation of the beautiful Christhood to enter upon the work of destroying the evil magnetic images. He descended from the glory which He had with the Father, to enter the wilderness where the evil things had their habitations. Even in the *Creed* it is said that He descended into Hell, or as some read it, " into Hades," though what that meant the western world does not seem to understand. Swedenborg said that the Lord descended into the hells in order to bring them into such a measure of control as would prevent them from dominating the world; but there is no explanation of how this was done. Nor can it be conceived how the Lord could possibly enter the hells as such. To understand the divine nature is also to know that any such thing could not possibly have been done. The magnetic conditions of any state such as the term " hell " represents, would make it utterly impossible for the Lord, as the divine manifestation, to present Himself. The manifestation of the Lord can only be made where the spiritual conditions permit of it. If the magnetic conditions be opposed to the Divine Presence, there can be no manifestation. As well expect the vision of the Sun through an exceedingly dense atmosphere. The Lord through the photosphere of the Sun, and therefore as a Sun, operated upon the evil conditions which the human hells had set up in the astral kingdom, and continued to do so for vast epochs of ages, breaking up and changing the terrible conditions, and bringing the hellish abyss into purer states ; and so in that sense it is quite true that the Lord changed the hells. But there could be no real manifestation such as is understood by the vision of the Lord. Nor were the evil images which we have referred to destroyed.

Yet the Lord did approach the lower astral kingdom in order to destroy the evil magnetic images. And herein is the wonderful mystery of His descent. He nourished and sustained the Soul of the beloved Master as *He* descended into these awful states in human bodies fitted for the purpose. The Christ laid aside the glory of Christhood—glory which was even as the glory of the Father, so full of grace and truth was it, so pure and beautiful in every action, so loving, compassionate and pitiful unto all Souls and all Creatures—and entered into lives like the lives of those who were afflicted by these awful images, bore the burden with them, entered in a most real and tragic sense into identification with all who so suffered, was born into the outer planes time after time in bodies so constituted that the magnetic evil images were attracted to take up their dwelling in them, but only to be changed in their elements and passed off again. In each life so much of the work was accomplished ; and in these latter days that tragic Sin-offering has been completed. In each life so many of these terrible evil " hand-writings " were blotted out. They were attracted to the body, changed through its magnetism, and the elements passed off from the body. It was the Master who did it ; only one who had been in such a state of Christhood could have undertaken and accomplished it.

But in the process there was anguish unspeakable. For years in each life He hungered in His Soul. He was in a spiritual wilderness contending with the wild beasts fashioned out of human passion. Of the devil was He tempted ; for the devil is the negation of God and the Soul. He stands for spiritual darkness, for that state of experience in which it may be said, God is not. The devil is evil as opposed to good ; not a person, yet an influence. To make bread or true Soul-nourishment out of the stony conditions in which He found Himself, was the Master tempted. In each life did He suffer as one who endured trials of the most mysterious nature, as in different ways these images were attracted to Him to be destroyed ; ever longing to find the true way in life, the way back to Christhood, but never permitted to rise up out of the conditions which He had undertaken, until the hour came when the last of the magnetic evil images apportioned to that life had been destroyed. And then, as the portion of the burden allotted to each life had been borne, and He rose up out of the awful conditions to once more arrive at the consciousness of the Divine Love within Himself, there was such anguish as no man could possibly understand, unless as a Christ he also had passed that way. The heavens within Him were bowed down ; and the aura of the Heavens around Him revealed unspeakable grief.

And thus He put the devil behind Him in each life, however awful the conditions were, making manifest the beautiful and sublime truth that the Soul cannot subsist on any bread other than that which is the Word of God, that glorious divine Life-stream which proceedeth from God.

Herein then is part of the mystery of the Sin-offering. Who is able to gauge its depth of meaning ? Who would have dreamt of such a work on the part of the beautiful Soul whom we knew as the Master, filled and sustained by the Divine Love ? Who, reading the synoptic story of the Temptations, could have imagined that the *first act* contained so much of tragedy and anguish ? The work He came to accomplish was beyond all human imagination. None but the heavens knew its full extent.

The Church knew not at its formation ; and it seems not to know now. Those most sacred sayings spoken by the Blessed Master to the inner group of disciples, which indicated the forthcoming tragedy, were taken from the Logia of St. John. They were taken away when Paul visited " the brethren " (not the Church) in Jerusalem, and were changed in their significations and sent forth to the whole western world. No wonder there seemed to be two Pauls in the Epistles, one who was a Jew, and one who was a divine Seer. No wonder " the brethren " were moved to indignation when they knew the man, and discovered what he had done. No wonder the Churches have never arrived at the true meaning of Christhood and the work of the Sin-offering ; for they built up their heritage upon the Jewish conception of the Messiah and the Jewish doctrine of sacrifice. We need not marvel at the darkness within the sanctuaries of the West when we remember that " the hand-writings " on the " middle wall " or " partition " which were against the upwardness of the Soul, were related to the cere-monial laws of the Jews. and that that interpretation has always, with a few notable exceptions, prevailed.

Most lamentable it is to write such a history ; painful in the extreme because of those whom it concerns. Yet must the truth now be made manifest, though the burden of doing it sometimes seems more than we can well carry, *so profound is the mystery and so unspeakably great the Soul-Travail.* Only through the goodness and sustaining Love of the Divine Father, the healing and comfort of the Over-shadowing One, are we able to be sufficient for the work.

O, Eternal and ever Blessed One ! We would praise Thee within the Sanctuary of our being. We would adore Thee with the rising of the Sun of Thy Love to shine into our Souls the Light of Life. How glorious art Thou in Thy Majesty, how wonderful in all Thy ways ! Who is like unto Thee in the ways of Thy going, and in the works which Thy hands accomplish for Thy children ? Ever blessed be Thy Name, Thou hast wrought marvellous things for us whereof we are glad. Thou hast blotted out the graven images which were against us, overthrown the altars of Baal, and broken the power of his priests. Now may Thy children behold Thy wonderful works, and understand the wisdom in which they have all been wrought. May they stand within the House of the Lord to bless with Thy Blessing.

Amen and Amen.

F

THE PINNACLE OF THE TEMPLE

THE profound pathos so evident all through the unfoldment of the First Act, is continued with ever deepening mystery in the Second Act. The tragedy loses none of its poignancy, and the vision of the sublimity of the sacrifice grows more and more intense. The work of changing the evil magnetic elements through the body, not only brought suffering and pain to it, but anguish and agony unto the Soul. All the lives were filled with a strange inherent sorrow, even whilst the path was being followed by which " the handwritings " could be blotted out, a sorrow which no man could understand. Though the personal life went down into the ways of evil by following which the work could only be accomplished, and for a time seemed to enter into those ways in the spirit of those who sought them ; yet all the while was there present that mysterious plaintive sorrow as of one who did the things which had to be done on sufferance, as deeds which must needs be done however much the inner life loathed them.

The Second Act was indeed a temptation to descend from " the pinnacle of the temple," a temptation of the very Soul itself to yield in the way the story suggests, to descend as the Son of God to live the life as other men and women lived it, to make of the experiences bread for the life and pleasure for the Soul, to put away the sorrow of it all and strangle the feelings of loathing, to be as one who found such life to be the acme of the highest joys, the exposition and realization of life's supremest delights. For " the pinnacle of the temple " was the Christhood consciousness which, whilst vehicling through bodies adapted to each life, was under very painful limitations ; and the temptation came at times to descend altogether and be as those who had no such consciousness, and who knew not the unspeakable pain of such travail. For was He not ministered unto by Angels ? Had it not been promised that He should be upheld by their ministry during the accomplishment of the momentous work ? Was not the fiat of the Divine inviolable ? Why should He not just trust it and descend, and so know no more the awful agony and anguish begotten of the life because of His innermost consciousness of the Christhood nature ? How much easier it would be then to bear the awful load, to pass through all the lives He yet had to live without knowing those dread awakenings in each life after He had drunk the portion of the cup allotted to that life, awakenings which always came when the outer consciousness was purified through the purification of the life forces of both body and mind, and was able to receive the influences of the Christ consciousness ? For were not these awakenings terrible ? Every life had its own Gethsemane. The vision during the life of the Christhood manifestation, known unto readers of the evangelists as Gethsemane, and which was the vision unto Him of all He would have to pass through in these lives, was realized beyond all description or even imagination. Would it not be well for Him to escape from the travail which bore Him down and crowned the remaining days of each life with anguish born of the divine sorrow in His Soul ?

Verily, the Temptation to descend from the pinnacle of the Temple has a depth of meaning men and women wote not of. It has a significance beyond anything the various schools have ever dreamt of, and far-reaching in the scope of the experience signified. The profoundest mystery of it all is how He overcame the temptation, and vicariously bore His burden for the world.

G

THE EXCEEDING HIGH MOUNTAIN

IF the pathos deepens with the Second Act in the Divine Tragedy, it certainly does not grow less as the Third Act opens and unfolds. If the mystery of the Sin-offering has only grown more profound as we have withdrawn the vail to reveal the deep significance of the first and second temptations, assuredly it is greatly increased when we draw the vail which hides the meaning of the third. The mystery of the divine burden-bearing looms more and more out of the mists which arose to enshroud it and blot it out from the vision, and which left only a mirage for men and women to look upon, as we see the mists dispersed by the breaking upon them of the Divine Light. O the wonder and marvel of it all as the vista with its awful tragedy opens up to our view ! The undreamt-of dire extremity of the Soul ; the passionate longing for the Blessed Life and the consciousness of the Divine Presence within to be realized, only to understand that the burden must needs be borne unto the uttermost ; the deep mysterious sorrow flowing through His whole being as He yearned with unutterable desire for the exalted and beautiful vision which fills the Soul with the joy of God, only to know that all such blessedness had been laid aside by Him for many many ages, even until " the handwritings " were all blotted out and " the Regeneration " completed : who could look at these experiences unmoved ? O the depth of the hidden Wisdom of God revealed in the whole plan of the Redemption of all Souls, and the unspeakable love interpreted in the Soul's travail ! Who may with clarified vision behold its fulness of meaning for the Master, and the whole world of Souls, and see how the Divine Love opened up the way for the return of all unto the Divine Life, even as the Master went deeper and still deeper into the anguish born of it all ? May the lower mind—the mere outward intellect—of men and women be dumb before the sacred *mystery*, that they may look upon the spectacle with the most reverent feelings, and bow in *humility* that it should ever have been necessary, and in *praise* that the Divine Love conceived it and carried it through.

THE HOUR OF SUPREME TRIAL

In addition to turning stones into bread for the Soul, and the temptation to descend altogether from the inner Christ-consciousness so as to be saved from the burden of the travail and the repeated anguish in every fresh Gethsemane, there arose one other form of the terrible trial whose ordeal was even more fiery in that it brought into many of the lives He had to live, unspeakable oppression from many who loudly professed fealty to the Christ of the Pauline teachings concerning the Redemption and the way of its accomplishment. He passed under the bann of the Inquisitions of Roman Catholicism and English Episcopacy, not to speak of minor Inquisitions whose schools sought to hold and rule the inner consciousness and proscribe all who would not bow down to them. In many of His lives, after He had beautifully risen up out of the low state which it was necessary for Him to be in whilst the awful blotting-out work was being accomplished, He was made to pass through sufferings unnameable at the hands of those who created the various Inquisitions as instruments to compel obedience to the religious authorities, because He chose to follow the Divine Light that shone again within Him, rather than the ways of men whose light was as the darkness.

But amid all these He was tempted ; and though His inner consciousness never wavered amid the temptations, there were times when the outer life was sorely tempted to yield. On more than one occasion the offer of elevated ecclesiastical positions was the form in which the temptation came, provided He was prepared to bow down and worship the devil of earthly aggrandisement and power; and in this respect the height of the tempter was reached when there was held out to Him the prospect of reaching the Papal See if only He would yield to the wish of the Inquisition, renounce the new way of life upon which He had been travelling since He arose out of the low state in which He bore the Sin-offering burden, and cease to teach the way to the realization of that blessed Redeemed Life. That was the exceeding high mountain from which all the kingdoms of the world were beheld, that power which then sought, as it had for ages sought, and as it has ever sought since the foundation of the outward kingdom, to dominate the religious conscience and rule all nations.

THE MEANING OF THE VICTORY

But with the blessed Master it was always the same. He could not turn stones into bread for the Soul, but loved to know that the Soul can live alone upon the Word of God, the divine Life-stream flowing perpetually unto and into the Soul; that no evil in the world should ever be permitted to deaden the latent divine consciousness within; that however heavy the burden of earthly heritage, and however great the evils growing out of it, no one should compel the inner life to forget its divine childhood and pass down into spiritual unconsciousness, and in that sense try the divine tenderness, patience, and redeeming love; and, finally, that no one should ever yield up the inner light of the Soul to the voices and powers of the ecclesiastical and world-mind systems however severe the trial through which they were made to pass by such powers, but to persist at all cost in following that light, in the full assurance that it is not of man but of God, and that it will at last lead them back unto that glorious heritage when the full consciousness of the Christhood will have unfolded within them, and the Blessed Vision of the Divine Lord become a beautiful reality.

H

" MADE LIKE UNTO HIS BRETHREN "

IF the Temptations had been understood by the schools, the Churches would have been able to teach in what way the Master was " made like unto His brethren." They would have known the true meaning of the saying that He was tempted and tried like all Souls, but remained in Himself free from the guilt of sin. They would have seen and understood the difference between evil and sin, and known how it was possible for a life to have much evil in its personal experiences, whilst the Soul was inherently pure, loving only goodness. They would have been able to understand how these two apparently contradictory states could exist in the same life, the one opposing the other as if the actor were two different beings. And they would have known what evil was, and how it was caused ; and that sin was of a different order, having its seat in the spiritual nature itself and not in the personal life ; that whilst the outer is born of the elemental conditions, the inner and more subtle is born of the inner love principle of the Soul coming to love the things of the world-life as an end, and to seek its fulness in them.

For the two states are totally distinct. The outer represents the Soul in bondage by reason of the elemental conditions within and around the body and body-mind ; the inner represents the Soul in that spiritual state in which it is content to sacrifice all its highest divine aspirations and yearnings for the life which the elemental world gives through body and mind gratification. A true understanding of the difference between these two states of spiritual experience is absolutely necessary to the right interpretation of the lives of men and women about which the judgment of the world and the Churches is so frequently wrong. For judgment generally follows the path of phenomena ; and most of these phenomena are the outcome of elemental conditions in and around the body, and not the expression of the true inner life. But the Divine Love sees what is in men and women. He knoweth the way of the being within. He judgeth not from the phenomena, many of which are the expressions of very deep pain. He beholdeth the inward state. With Him there is no mistake in judgment. And He loveth all, and worketh out for all the redemption they need.

THE WAY OF HIS HUMILIATION

How like His " brethren " the Master was made, may be understood through understanding the temptations. Whilst He bore the burden of the Sin-offering lives, the phenomena were of an evil order. The judgment of the world upon Him then would have corresponded to the judgment of that world upon most things known as evil to-day. It would have judged from appearances. And then when He rose up out of the evil which was outward, and began to make manifest the inner life, the Church that professed to proclaim that inner life, and the way unto it, sat in judgment upon Him and condemned His way, just as it has always done unto any of His brethren who have sought to tell the world of the wonderful life of the divine *within* the Soul, and the glorious experiences born through its blessed realization. He bore the awful burden *with* them and *for* them as He blotted out " the handwritings " which were against them, thus removing " the middle-wall " which barred all their spiritual progress through changing its magnetic conditions as He drew the evil images to Himself ; and so He took upon Himself their infirmities and pains in a most real sense. He was made like unto His brethren in the sufferings which were involved in His lives on the outer spheres, and the anguish of Soul which followed the grievous afflictions. Like them He cried with bitter tears for deliverance from the fearful burden, yet bore the cross of shame with the obedience of a Son of the Highest. He was reviled and bowed down to the dust as He bore the burden, yet His beautiful love did not waver in its service for the Divine Love. His experiences may yet be found in these wonderful sayings worked up into the Pauline letter to the Romans—

" *O most wretched man that I shall be ! When I shall wish to do the good, evil shall ever be present ; and the good I would fain do I shall not be able to do, whilst the abhorred evil which will come to me, I will do. The messengers of Satan will buffet me in my way ; and only by the love of the Father, whose grace is great, shall I be prevented from being a castaway.*"

Love's Sublime Sacrifice

The sublimity of the love which ever moved Him in His stupendous sacrifice ; the depths of the terrible experiences into which it led Him ; the awful nature of the sufferings which arose out of it ; the un-utterable loneliness, anguish and agony which were His portion in each life, none but the heavens can know—those heavens whose watchers looked on in pro-foundest amazement and wonder. They veiled their faces sorrowfully at the tragedy, and bore to Him the cup of the Divine Love to sustain Him in the ordeal. By their hands the Chalice of Wine was placed to His lips to sustain Him in His dire extremity. But for that beautiful ministry He could never have endured the strain put upon Him.

How much the Churches have lost through not knowing these things. What wealth of love they have missed through the wrong vision of the Master which came to them as the result of the false portraiture presented in the Gospel Records, and the untrue interpretations put upon the Divine Nature and the ways of His Love. How very different the whole history of western Christianity would have been had the true light shone within the Churches and illumined all those who taught ; for then they would have taught with that Wisdom which cometh from God.

The Sin-offering was stupendous in its conception and accomplishment. It was not the Soul's Atonement, which each Soul must accomplish for itself through the unfolding of the divine life within it ; for Atonement means that the Soul has come into the realization of the One Divine Life. And, through the work of the Sin-offering in making purer the astral kingdom, all Souls may now rise up into the experience of that Blessed Life.

Nor was the Sin-offering the Forgiveness of Sins, nor the ground of the Divine Healing being vouchsafed to the Soul ; for the Forgiveness of Sin is the Divine Healing which flows into the life of the one who seeks divinely to rise out of all the evil conditions amid which he is held captive, and which fits the Soul to enter into the sublime realization of the One Divine Life. It was indeed because the human race as a whole could not rise up out of these conditions and have the glad experience of the Forgiveness of Sins, and consequent realization of the Atonement or One Divine Life, that the Sin-offering was purposed by the Divine Love and accomplished through the Soul of the beloved Master. And it is because of the beneficent effects of the Sin-offering through the changing of the astral kingdom, that this wonderful new age has broken upon us with its manifold healing ministries and spiritual light, when Souls all over the world are entering into the joy born of the divine healing or Forgiveness of Sins, and those who are able, into the realization of the One Divine Life, the Soul's AT-ONE-MENT.

The Logia of the Cross

*Being the Seven Profound Sayings spoken
in the Gethsemane concerning the Burden
of the Sin-offering and the Crucifixion of the Christhood which
had been made manifest, together with the true
interpretation
of the
Crucifixion.*

A

THE CRUCIFIXION

TO write of the crucifixion is indeed difficult ; for the presentation by the evangelists has come to be regarded by almost the whole of the western Churches as authentic. To many it will appear sacrilege to turn the historical narrative of the crucifixion into something different from that found in the Gospels. And yet it is just this thing that has to be done with the story of that sad and tragic event, and the precious Sayings which were reported as having been spoken by the blessed Master on the cross, if the crucifixion is to be understood and the profound meaning of the Logia realized. For the presentation in the accepted Records is misleading. In the first place it is not a correct account of what happened to the Master ; and in the second place the precious Logia of the Cross which were said to have been spoken during the crucifixion, were not of a personal nature. That the beloved Master suffered at the hands of the Sanhedrin, is quite true ; and that the Jewish leaders accomplished what they imagined to be His death through the Roman Judge, is likewise true. But what the Master passed through at the hands of the Jews is one thing, whilst His Crucifixion in bearing the burden of the Sin-offering is quite another. And in the Records the crucifixion of the Master and that of the Christhood are mixed up so effectually as to give a false impression of what took place in relation to the Master, and to hide from the vision of the Soul *the real crucifixion* as that was taught by Him—a crucifixion of another order to that of physical death, wherein was revealed the way of the Divine Love in bearing the awful burden of the tragic Sin-offering.

Elsewhere we have dealt more fully with the crucifixion of the Master and His resurrection. But it may be well here to remind our readers of these facts, namely :

That His body was in such a pure state that He could not die, for there was no element of corruption in Him ; though of course He could have withdrawn from the body ;

That He did not die on the Cross, but only swooned through the sufferings He was made to endure ;

That He had foretold to the inner group what would happen, and advised them what to do ;

That He was taken by them and cared for ;

That after many days the wounds healed, and He was so strengthened from the Divine World that He remained with them until *the real passing-over* took place and the Sin-offering began ;

That it was during those post-crucifixion days that all the profound teachings embraced in *The Stories of the Passover, The Gethsemane, and the Cross*, were spoken by Him to the inner group.

The real Crucifixion was not merely physical. It was spiritual in nature, for it was the crucifixion of the Soul. The event was not one whose spectacular was upon the outer spheres. No one beheld it upon these spheres as a crucifixion of a divine man ; its only intelligent witnesses were upon the divine kingdom. Nor was the event simply human ; rather was it one in which the Divine Love bore the burden, though the accomplishment of the work for which the burden was taken up was through Him whom we speak of as the Master ;—that is, through the beautiful Soul who was the vehicle of the glorious Christhood manifestation. It was, therefore, a spiritual event, a Soul experience, a divine tragedy whose scenes were many, whose several acts drove the nails more deeply into the hands and feet, and the sword into the side, of Him who was crucified, and which piled up the burden of pain and anguish upon the Soul until He passed through those awful experiences indicated in the anguish-cries of the Cross.

B

THE DIVINE CHARITY

THE Logia of the Cross are self-interpretive. It is true that they are profound, and that they have not been understood because they were made to relate to outward historical experiences on the part of the Master ; but, when read with the understanding opened, they are seen to contain their own meaning. That their meaning was spiritual will become more and more obvious as we unfold them in relation to the true Soul-history which they contain. They are most wonderful Logia ; beautiful in the divine charity which they express ; most gracious in their thoughtfulness and tenderness ; pathetic in the things that they reveal ; marvellous in the strength of devotion to the human race and endurance of suffering for its sake, of which they testify ; momentous in the sacrifice made manifest in them ; and, at last, over-whelming in the awful sublimity of the work accomplished in their utterance by the Soul. That they have been preserved for us is, indeed, a blessing for which our hearts should be fountains of gratitude. Who could have imagined that these Sayings on the Cross, associated as they have been for ages with history supposed to have been written upon the outermost spheres, were spoken by the Soul during the process of the crucifixion of the Divine Christhood consciousness within herself?

THE PRAYER OF LOVE

The first of the seven Logia said to have been spoken upon the Cross, was the prayer unto the Divine Father for the forgiveness of those who had accomplished the crucifixion. It was the prayer of love. Love suffereth long and is kind. Love forgiveth unto the uttermost. Hence this prayer of the Soul. For this prayer is true not only of the Christ-Soul, but of all Souls in a state of love. It was a request on behalf of those who had undertaken to present the spectacle to the western world of a Christ in whom some of the chief attributes of Christhood were lacking. It was a prayer on behalf of those who wrote the Gospel Records, wherein they betrayed and crucified the Christhood and heaped ignominy on the head of the Master. For they knew not what they did, or surely they would not have crucified the Lord of Glory, *the Divine Christ within the Soul*, by representing Him to be, in the ways of His life, even as most men and women were in their ways. The prayer was for all who misapprehended and misrepresented the meaning of the beautiful divine manifestation and the holy profound purpose of the Divine Love towards all His children. It was a prayer pulsing with the divine charity, sorrowing over the conduct of those who would send forth to the world a false Christ-vision which would mislead the Soul and prevent the West from arriving at a true understanding of the meaning of Life in the Divine ; grieving that any Souls should be so bereft of the true vision as to present the Christhood as personal, the Master Himself as the Adonai, and the one who should receive from all men and women that homage which ought to be rendered alone unto the Ever-Blessed One whom we think of as the Everlasting Father.

WHAT THE PRAYER ANTICIPATED

" *Father, forgive them, for they know not what they do.*" The sufferings and anguish of the crucifixion of the Soul began in what is known as The Gethsemane ; for it was there that the vision of what would be done with the Christhood vision and the Teachings, broke upon the Master. It was given to Him to foresee what would be written concerning His own ways of life ; how the glorious Christhood manifestation given through Him would be presented ; the representation and interpretation of the Sin-offering that would be given and sent forth throughout the West ; the kind of hierarchical kingdom that would arise in His name, claiming to be the kingdom of heaven and the gateway into the Eternal Life ; the false view of the nature and purpose of the Divine Love that would prevail, miraging all truth, misleading all Souls and preventing them from arriving at a true knowledge of the Redemption through the realization of the redeemed life, thus changing the Wisdom of God into the foolishness of men, until none could behold the glory of God in the face of Jesus Christ (that is, in the Redeemed Life and the Illumined State).

These things the Master beheld in that momentous vision whose burden weighed Him down and filled Him with a sorrow and an anguish which deepened until the hour of " the passing-over." And this beautiful prayer was the first utterance made by Him amid that vision. For whilst He was moved to anguish by the vision, His love never forsook Him. In the midst of His unspeakable sorrow, compassion was great towards those who would betray and crucify the Divine Love, and the vision and message which He had given.

When we look out upon the western world to-day and witness the religious condition of it ; when we behold the kind of priesthood that has taught it concerning the Divine Love made manifest in the Master, and the interpretation that priesthood has put upon the terms Jesus, the Christ, and the Lord ; when we realize what is the great aim of the ministry of that priesthood, how its teaching has prevented the growth of a truer spiritual consciousness, and given a wrong direction to the seeking Souls ; when we witness the sad limitations of the scribes of the modern religious schools, and their bondage to the traditional view of the Christhood, and to the letter of the Records which purport to portray Him ; when we understand the thing that stands for the Christhood in their vision, and the way they have continued to dethrone the Divine Father-Mother, and exalt to that throne to receive the divine honour and worship due only to the Eternal and ever Blessed One, Him who was only the vehicle of the Divine Love ; we then see the awful fruits of the Crucifixion of the Christhood, the results of the most mixed narratives which were sent out as true portraitures of the Life and Teachings of the Master. And the prayer of the Soul in its anguish will then have new point given to it, " *Father, forgive them ; they know not what they do.*"

CRUCIFIED BY THE WEST

The history of Christianity has not been a history of Christ-hood. It has rather been a history of crucifixion. The Christhood has been crucified. The Saints have been stretched on the cross. The Divine Love has been crowned with thorns, and wounded in hands and feet. Those who have desired to do honour to the Divine Love through the purity of their own lives, and in teaching to others the path of that purity, have been made to bear the burden of that cross which was fashioned by the various Christian Sanhedrins, and which was made the instrument of ignominious suffering for all such by the powers of the world. The Divine Love has been crucified by the very systems which have professed all through the history of Christianity to interpret and manifest that Love ; the left hand of the divine goodness has been pierced, and the right hand of the divine attributes has been nailed to the same cross through changing the meaning of the nature and operation of them. The feet of the Divine Wisdom have likewise been pierced and nailed to the materialism which has dominated the whole history of Christianity ; for the ways and purposes of the Divine Father-Mother have all been so changed that they have seemed to fail to effect the Redemption for which the Christhood was made manifest. The wonderfully beautiful and never failing *compassion* of the ever blessed One towards all Souls of whatsoever degree, and to whatsoever race, people or nation they belonged, has not been truly interpreted in historical Christianity, as the fearful conflicts of the ages make manifest to everyone who understandeth ; for the priesthood systems have had little real compassion even towards their own adherents, not to speak of the animus shown towards all who differed from them. And when we seek for the divine pity in that manifold historical development, where may we find its manifestations ? Where in that history is the manifestation of that sublime pity to be found ? Is not the western world which has been the theatre of the development of the new religious movement, the scene of the most astounding social and national conflicts whose very existence show how utterly absent from that historic development the gentle grace of pity has been ? How completely outside the operations of any pretence to a *real* pity, the subhuman creatures have been in that supposed most wonderful historic development ? Who can reconcile the conduct of the western world towards the subhuman races with the divine pity which their historic religion professes to teach and make manifest ? When any great religious movement is imbued with the Spirit to feel and make manifest the divine pity, surely it is not such an empty and meaningless sentiment as that which characterizes the development of historical Christianity, but an active spirit that covers with its protecting powers all weak creatures and all defenceless Souls.

New meaning verily may be read into the sorrowful prayer of the Master ; for He forsaw just what the West would do ; how it would profess the enlightenment, love and pity of the Christhood, yet betray in all its ways that Life for which the Christhood was to stand.

O Holy and ever Blessed One, Thou who dwellest between the Cherubim within the Holy of Holies, both in the Heavens and in the Soul of Thy servants, to show forth the Glory of Thy Love ; who is like unto Thee ? Marvellous are Thy ways towards us. Thou dost humble us in the dust by the greatness of Thy Love ; for its majesty in forgiveness makes us feel our own impoverishment. How little we must appear in Thy sight, Whose Presence filleth the Heavens, and Whose Love upholdeth all worlds and all Souls !

Yet are we Thy children, though of low degree in our present estate ; and we would rise into the fulness of life in Thee, to love as Thou lovest, yea to be even One with Thee in Thy Love, so that the Radiance of Thy Glory may pour through us for the healing and enlightenment of all Thy little ones. Unto this end do we pray Thee to make of us sacred vessels to bear unto all Souls the wine of the Divine Charity.

C

THE MOTHER AND HER SON

WE have now to consider some Logia of very special interest, containing as they do teachings distinctly beautiful concerning the relationship of the Soul to the Eternal Christ. For we have in them a glimpse of the Divine Motherhood and the Divine Sonship—that wonderful Motherhood which the Catholic Church has so greatly emphasized, though it has failed utterly to apprehend the gracious and profound meaning of it ; and that remarkable Sonship which the Reformed Churches have made the chief object in their religious vision and worship, but the nature of which they have not understood, nor the manner of its attainment. It is the apparent personal note struck in the Logia which has led to this misapprehension, as in so many other instances in the life of the Master found in the four Records. For, granted that the crucifixion of the Master was a reality, and such as is described in these four Records, there would appear to the general reader something very natural and beautifully pathetic in the Master so addressing His mother. There is little wonder that the suggested scene and saying has attracted devout Souls, especially in the Catholic Church, and filled their vision ; there is so much tenderness expressed in it, so much sorrow and disappointment, such poignancy born of the suffering being endured on the cross, and such overwhelming humiliation.

The Personal Element at Fault

But it is just this personal note which has to be eliminated from the history embodied, though no doubt unto many it will seem the removal from the Logia of all the true human elements. It is so very difficult for men and women to think impersonally, *to understand the difference between the Soul and the personality*, to realize that whatever is spoken concerning the Soul cannot be in any degree understood rightly if interpreted personally. When anything is postulated of the Divine and Universal Soul, it must be understood in an impersonal sense ; for it is spiritual and inward, not physical and outward. It is of the Soul, not of the body. It is even of the Universal, not of the mere unit or individual. It is, in a planetary sense, Macrocosmic, not Microcosmic.

It is here the teaching of the western churches has been so much at fault ; for throughout their history, ever since their foundation, they have emphasized the personal. It is the personal Virgin Mary and the personal Master who have loomed large in their thoughts, until these personal images have taken the place of the ever Blessed One, the Everlasting Father-Mother, in the vision and worship of the West. These are prayed to as Divine Beings. The image of them before the mind is not that of the divine principles and realizations for which they originally stood, but human and personal. They are simply that of a woman and her son unto whom divine attributes have been given. The profound meanings lying behind their names, and the soullic relationship in which they stand to one another, are not discerned. Concerning the momentous spiritual and divine history implied in their names and relationship, the Churches seem to have been in the dark all through their history. And this is surely an astounding thing, though it explains much in the historic development which the Churches represent.

The Virgin Mother

We have observed that the real Crucifixion was not personal

but spiritual. We have also explained the nature of the prayer which the Christ-Soul offered when, in the vision of Gethsemane, He foresaw coming events. Of like nature is the incident that represents the Christ as addressing the Virgin Mother. It is to be understood spiritually. The history of which it speaks is of the Soul. The terms in which it is expressed contain the hidden meaning. *Woman* was the word expressive of the feminine mode of the Soul. It was a term made use of in ancient symbolism to denote the divine motherhood, or the feminine principle in Deity from whom all things divine are born. In the individual or microcosm, it represented the intuitional side of the Soul's experience.

And how beautifully it expressed this great truth, namely, *that it is of the Soul in her feminine mode that all things spiritual are born within us ; that the Christhood comes to be apprehended and understood ; that the Christ consciousness awakens within the life and leads on to the yet larger consciousness of the divine indwelling—which consciousness continues to deepen until the Soul knows herself to be one with the divine, yea, to be also divine in her substance and attributes.* It is the *woman* in the human system who bears the child and brings it forth into the life of manifestation upon these outermost spheres ; and it is the *woman element* or feminine principle in every Soul-system, that bears the Christ-child and brings it forth into manifestation in the life of Christhood.

THE DIVINE SON

And the Son : He is also of the Mother, and from her. He is the fruit of the divine union, the outcome of the perfect Fatherhood and perfect Motherhood, the resultant of the projection of the Divine Spirit into Divine Substance. The Eternal Son is the Eternal Christ, the Adonai, the Beloved of the Father-Mother, the Only Begotten who is in the bosom of the Divine Duality, the Manifest of the Unmanifest Life, and the Manifestor of the Divine Will interpreted into purpose in all life and service. For He whom men and women worship as the Son (that is, in their intention ; though alas ! for the West that even yet the darkness is so great within it) is none other than the Adonai, the Only Begotten of the Divine Duality. And she whom so many in the West bow down before in worship (though alas ! the Church of Rome yet knows it not, having been deceived for ages, and blinded by the gods of this world) is none other that the Divine Feminine, the Divine Mother of all things pure and beautiful from whom the Eternal Christ, the Only Begotten One, is born in the Macrocosm and in the Microcosm. For, as it is in the Universal, so is it in the Individual. The Macrocosmic becomes Microcosmic in man. Of the Divine Duality within the Soul is the Christ born. He is generated from the Divine, and is brought forth by the Soul in her feminine mode. He is her Son, first as a little child, then as the Christ in the manifestation of Christhood. And of every human Soul-system is this true, whether it concerns the past, the present, or the future ; for only thus is our Sonship to the Divine Father-Mother realized, and divine Sonship at last attained. For, as we have shown elsewhere, Christhood is a state of spiritual realization by the Soul ; and Divine Sonship is the full realization of that state—a consciousness growing ever, more intense, more profound in its experiences, higher and more glorious in its visions, until it becomes perfected upon the Divine Kingdom, at which stage of Soul evolution the Soul becomes even as the Divine.

THE REASON FOR THE SAYING

It will now be possible to make clear these words said to have been uttered by the Master on the cross. The crucifixion having relation to all that was coming as the result of the betrayal of the Christhood manifestation by the writers of the Gospel Records,—this on the one hand ; and on the other, the betrayal by the astral kingdom of the Master when He went out from the kingdom of the Christhood to bear the burden of the Sin-offering ; and these things having been shown unto the Master during the Gethsemane vision, the words now under consideration were spoken by Him, namely, " *Woman, behold thy Son !* " It was a cry of surprise full of intense sorrow at the terrible misrepresentation of the Christhood made manifest in and through the Master, and the purpose for which the sublime Manifestation was made. For He saw how the Christhood was to be crucified by the Jews and the world-powers, first through the Records, and then through the hierarchical systems which grew out of these ; and it was to be crucified between the two thieves of spiritual negation and gross materialism—the one a denial of the divine manifestation, and the other a materialization which would be a perversion of the whole meaning of the Life and Teachings of the Christhood.

With such a picture before Him in the Gethsemane vision, is it any wonder that the Master should have thus spoken unto the Divine Mother (not the mother of the Master's vehicle, but the Divine who overshadowed Him), " *Woman behold thy Son !* " What a spectacle was coming, a spectacle that has continued all through the Era in which the Christhood has been professed ! Verily the crucifixion was too terribly real, and the thieves something more awful than two poor criminal children who had fallen under civil judgment ; for the powers all through the tragic ages have parted His Christhood garments amongst them, and for His Vesture have they cast lots ; and Mary has mourned with sorrow unspeakable, for she is the Soul whose beautiful Divine Son, the Christhood, has been so ignominiously crucified.

D

THE MOTHER AND THE DISCIPLE

IN connection with the foregoing there is given another saying attributed to the Master, the profoundness of whose meaning none could have guessed. It is the incident wherein it is said that in the midst of His own sufferings He was not unmindful of the sorrowing mother, and took thought for her future. Though one would have expected the Master, supposing that the history as recorded upon the outer spheres was true, to have arranged beforehand for that disciple to whose keeping He commended her, to take her into his own family, yet there is so much that is obviously beautiful and tender in the incident that it is not surprising to find it interpreted literally by the various schools of thought.

Yet however much of charm and tenderness there may be in this view of the incident, the material and historic interpretation has to be left behind if we would penetrate the veil and know the meaning of this wonderful Saying—" *Behold thy Mother !* " For here surely, as in the previous Saying, we transcend the outward spheres to enter the regions of the innermost. We pass from the objective picture to the subjective vision, from the historical sphere of the mind to the realm of Soul, from an outward historical event to a divine event in the Soul's history. Behind the veil of the letter we look not upon a man who was beloved of the Master, doing for Him whom he loved the deed of a true disciple and friend ; nor upon a mere woman who was the earthly mother of the Master, who is deeply smitten with sorrow and loss, and has to be provided for by that disciple. What we are permitted to behold within the veil, is transcendently greater. It is altogether spiritual, for it is of the realm of the Soul. It is in nature divine, for it is the vision by the Soul of the Divine Mother, the *real* Virgin Mary, and not one who is " the Mother of God " as Roman

417

Catholicism and some mystical writers would put it, but the *Motherhood of God*, the counterpart or complement of the Divine Fatherhood, and the Mother of Christhood or that spiritual estate of the Soul when it arrives at the divine consciousness.

Nor were the words spoken by the Master to one of the twelve, though in the fourth Record the Logia are so presented. They were addressed to Him who was then passing through such dire anguish in the vision of Gethsemane, known to the inner group as *the beloved one*, even the Master who was filled and overshadowed by *Him who is ever in the bosom of the Father*. It was He, as a Son of the Divine Mother, a Christ of God, who was to remember that the Divine Mother also suffered with Him, that the Divine Heart would bear the burden of the tragic Sin-offering ; that " the Heart of Mary," the Divine Motherhood, would be also pierced with the sword of sorrow ; for the Divine Love would travail through Him as He trod the winepress and red-dyed His garments.

Oh, what mystery unfolds itself to us here ! What depths of love are expressed in these Logia, obscured by the veil of materialism ! What transcendent visions of the nature of such a Christhood as that of the Master, as here revealed, and what is meant by the Divine Mother !

In the hour of His supreme anguish in the Gethsemane, when it was shown unto Him all that would befall His beautiful Christhood and the Divine Manifestation which had been accomplished through Him, and the nature of the crucifixion that would be His portion, the Master was heard to thus speak unto that Holy One who had overshadowed Him, saying—" Maria, behold Thy Son ! "

And as He anguished and beheld the low estates into which He would have to descend as He bore the agony of the crucifixion,

418

even into that of the magdalene, there came upon Him the over-shadowing of that One whom He so greatly loved, and there spake unto Him the Voice from out the clouds, saying " Son, behold Thy Mother." And the beloved one (the Master) took heart from that hour.

E
THE GREAT THIRST

A GREAT mystery now faces us as we turn to consider the meaning of these Logia which are reported as having also been spoken during the crucifixion,—" *I thirst.*" Who is equal to the fathoming of the depths of suffering expressed in them ? Not from the personal human standpoint can they be understood. They are beyond all that is personal in their meaning. The thirst that is said to have come upon all who were crucified in those times, can be understood. It was physical and the result of the injury done to the body of the crucified, intensified often by the duration of the crucifixion. So it was not an unnatural thing to associate such an experience with the sufferings of the Master. The words fitted the experience. Yet why record them, if the experience was universal in cruci-fixions ? Why show to the world that even He who was perfect in His life, and of whom it was said that He took the infirmities of the human race upon Himself, could not endure the brief sufferings of thirst ? What would there be precious in such a saying ? True, it would show that He suffered for a brief time as all who have endured crucifixion have suffered ; but the expression would not on that account contain any profound meaning. It could not have more than an ordinary significance given to it. Its value as an asset of the tragic Sin-offering would be *nil*.

Now the expression did contain a wealth of meaning. In the simple terms " *I thirst* " we find a depth of feeling and suffering beyond anything that could be conveyed in a personal sense, or endured of a personal order. For when we leave the personal and outward for the spiritual and inward, the words do not lose in value ; they increase. The burden of their meaning becomes greater, *the reality* of the Sin-offering is made obvious unto all who are able to pass through the evil of literalism into the realm of the spiritual. For the Saying—" *I thirst*," was spoken of and by the Soul. It was the awful thirst of the Soul for spiritual refreshing ; the growing consciousness of the withdrawal of the Divine Presence, the outcome of the loss of intimate heavenly fellowship ; the deepening sense of the lack of all those qualities associated with a divine Christhood. The thirst was for God, " for the living God." It was for the restoration of the consciousness of the Divine Overshadowing, the realization of the angelic fellowship, the inflowing to His Soul of the Divine Life stream. It was such a thirst as no man physically ever had, as no mere human Soul ever experienced, and such as could alone come to a divine Soul, *i.e.*, to one who had attained unto a divine Christhood, and who had descended from that sublime height to perform such a work as the Sin-offering implied.

THE WINE MINGLED WITH GALL

Here then we have a profound mystery, in which there is the revelation of a marvellous manifestation of love, a burden borne, the greatness of which no man could gauge, a divine drama, a Soul tragedy, a most marvellous vision of suffering and anguish by means of which the redemption of the race was to be accomplished, a work of such magnitude that it has taken all the ages since the blessed Christhood manifestation to accomplish. And that our interpretation of it is the true one, even the details, such as they are in the accepted Records, testify. For what was it that was given Him to drink ? Not pure water. One evangelist says they gave Him wine mingled with myrrh ; another, that they mixed the wine with gall ;

and that they put some vinegar upon a sponge and gave it unto Him ;—all which things, though apparent contradictions, are full of meaning. For amid the terrible anguish of the Christ-Soul in His travail, when His thirst for the lost vision of the Lord was greatest, those who ought to have been able to comfort and strengthen Him by assuaging in some degree the awful thirst, had only sour wine to offer Him, wine made bitter as gall with the terrible mixtures which they used to reduce the pure wine to suit the purposes which they had in hand. For these details have *spiritual* significance. The wine soured, mingled with gall, with a little myrrh mixed in it, yet withal only as vinegar, was none other than the kind of spiritual refreshment that the West had to offer as the result of the perversion of the beautiful vision of Christhood, the meaning of the Redemption, the nature of the Sin-offering, and the divine purpose towards all His children. The hierarchies had no help to offer to the Christ-Soul ; they only offered Him that which intensified His anguish. They did not and could not assuage the thirst ; what they gave only intensified the suffering. The outward historic development of what is known as Christianity speaks for itself to the unbiased student, and shows how the wine of the Divine Love was mixed with a little aromatic preserving myrrh, but mostly with gall. The angel who has ruled the West during that historic development, cannot be said to have been of the Divine Love ; for the gall of bitterness has played so large a part, that the thirsty Soul has many a time had to refuse to accept of the wine. What a picture of the Divine Love has been given during the era of that development ! And what a resultant we have had in the intellectual and priestly systems, all professed interpreters of the Christhood and the new divine covenant !

But the new glorious era has been born. The new day in which these awful wrongs done to the Divine Love and the Soul shall be swept away, has indeed broken. The real spiritual cycle of whose coming the Master spoke, is with us in its infancy.

The kingdoms of this world are *now* being so fashioned through the presence with us of divine potencies, that they may become the kingdoms of our God and His Christ. All the social and national conditions are undergoing change towards the Redemption. But these things are not being accomplished as the result of historic Christianity ; indeed all the new and blessed movements for the Redemption have begun, and still are largely kept, outside of its borders.

F

THE ANGUISH CRY

IN seeking for the full explanation of the anguish cry, we are conscious that the mystery of the Sin-offering deepens. There is a growing sense within us of its unutterably overwhelming nature. We find within the Logia such a revelation of the profundity of the depths of anguish passed through, that the Logia themselves cannot be adequately translated. The translation of the cry into the now familiar language—" *My God! My God! Why hast Thou forsaken me ?* " has *not* helped the student of the divine mystery to understand the meanings of the crucifixion and the burden which the Christ-Soul had to bear. Scholars have dealt with the terms, but seem to have failed to discover their meaning. Indeed it is not known whether they were originally Hebrew, Arabic, Aramaic or Greek.

Herein is another mystery. The Logia were not written in the language in which any of the Gospel Records were written. Could there have been purpose in this on the part of the writers of the present records ? We think not. Indeed it is they who give the rendering as " My God! My God! Why hast thou forsaken me ? " And therein they revealed how much they themselves were in the dark concerning the profound things contained in them.

THE TERMS OF THE CRY ARE CRYPTIC

The terms made use of themselves contain the meaning. In a very real sense are they cryptic. They are composed of terms from three different languages. They are in part Hebrew, Arabic and Greek. The expression " *Eli*," may readily be understood. It is Hebrew, and should be rendered " *My Lord.*" It denoted " the Angel of the Presence," spoken of as " the Angel of the Lord." It referred to the One who had overshadowed the Soul, and from whom the inward light of Christhood proceeded ; the One through whom the Master enjoyed the consciousness of the indwelling of God, and was enabled to function upon the divine kingdom ; that One by means of whose overshadowing He knew Himself to be one with the Father. As we shall see presently, it is a calling out by the Soul unto that Holy Presence ; an expression of great anxiety, even of dire anguish, on account of the awful conditions which, though as yet only present in vision, were nevertheless overwhelming Him. It was a cry of the Soul uttered in the midst of His Gethsemane visions when He foresaw the states of fearful spiritual darkness into which He must soon enter, and through which He must pass for many ages (three full Naronic Cycles) whilst He bore the burden of the Sin-offering by means of which the Redemption was to be brought nigh to every Soul. It was not addressed to the Ever-Blessed One, the All-Father, like the prayer of divine charity for those who were about to accomplish His crucifixion, or that of the committal of His Spirit. It is well to observe this, for it will aid the reader to understand what it was that happened unto Him.

A CELESTIAL SIGN

The term *Lama* is not so well-known as Eli. Indeed, scholars are divided as to its origin. It is not pure Hebrew, nor is it Aramaic. And the translation of it in the two Records is misleading. It was originally a term used to denote a Celestial Being, and was built up of four cryptic signs. Its meaning became known unto the ancient Hebrews, and was by them incorporated into the Hebrew tongue. For they knew the history of many Celestials, as their religious Mysteries testify. How the beautiful term came to have given to it only an earthly signification is not a matter we can now deal with. But suffice it to say that a Lama was one who ministered for the Divine Love unto the people. He was the Head and Teacher of a People.

And so, in the Logia of the Cross, the term has depths of meaning little imagined. It gives a glint of the high office occupied by the Soul who had given unto Him the sublime mission of the Manifestation, followed by the momentous work of bearing the burden of the Sin-offering. And it indicates when read in relation to the other terms of the anguish cry, the very nature of the sufferings into which He was going. For when so read it revealed the profound nature of the sacrifice to be made.

A PROFOUND CRYPTOGRAM

We have, then, these meanings in our thoughts when reading the Logia of the mysterious anguish ; and now we have to expound the meaning of the last term, *Sa-Bach-Thani*, and unfold the mystery which it conceals. It also continues to perplex scholars concerning its true and original form. Of this we have evidence in the recent scholastic pronouncements of both the " Higher Criticism " and the " Liberal Orthodoxy."[1] The expression is threefold ; and it is made up of three terms from different languages. The first was Arabic, the second ancient Hebrew, the third Greek. The first spoke of *It*—the Spirit ; the second of the loss of the spirit ; the third concerning the way of that loss. The first referred to the Light within the

---

[1] Readers will find it interesting to consult the latest views of the Higher Criticism upon these Logia expressed so ably in the ENCYCLOPEDIA BIBLICA ; and also the surprising statements in the Bible Dictionary by Dr. Hastings, which represents a Liberal Orthodoxy.

Soul ; for the Spirit is the Divine Flame who illumines the innermost Sanctuary. The second indicated what would happen unto that Light through the withdrawal of the Divine Overshadowing, and the consequent loss of the Spirit as a conscious Divine Flame. The third revealed the nature of the death the Soul would endure for a time—the time being the duration of the Sin-offering.

We have then in this marvellous expression—*Sa-Bach-Thani* —a cryptogram whose meanings are verily profound. The terms contain such a history as the Churches could never have supposed possible to befall the Master. They indicate a Sin-offering such as they have not even guessed at ; a Soul-travail that no mere man could have conceived for Him. Yet so was it with Him even as He Himself said ; and the history of the rise and development of historical Christianity, with all its warfare, strife, love of earthly dominion, persecution of the mystic Souls, and the perpetual crucifixion of the Christhood, is testimony to what happened.

The whole of the terms may now be understood as expressing what was awaiting the Master when the divine manifestation had passed, the Adonai who overshadowed Him had withdrawn from such beautiful and intimate association as had been His blessed experience, and the burden of the Sin-offering had fully come upon Him.

ELI ! ELI ! LAMA SA-BACH-THANI !

My Lord ! My Lord ! The Celestial Light is extinguished within my Spirit ; it is death to me.

THE WORK OF INTERPRETING

How difficult it has been to write of these most sacred Logia as the expression of the most profound experiences ever Soul passed through, none can know. Indeed, it is the most difficult task ever undertaken by us, or even appointed us to do. In the doing of it we have had to feel the adumbrations of the experiences passed through. And what these have meant as the vision of the Gethsemane has broken upon us in the process of the Soul-recovery, we can find no language to describe adequately. *The anguish was unspeakable*, and its effects are felt by us even now. We could never have imagined anything so terrible as His experiences of pain and sorrow—pain and sorrow so fearfully overwhelming as the agony in His anguish.

If only the West knew what it has done unto that Soul and the Christhood He made manifest, it would assuredly cease its boastings, its cravings for earthly dominion, its love of the spirit of material conquest, and, in the true spirit of the religion it has professed without understanding, it would bow itself in sorrow that its ways could have led it into such lovelessness, darkness and irreverence.

And if only all the Churches could be awakened to the consciousness of the truth as set forth in the Christhood of the Master, and the real meaning of the Redemption ; to apprehend the stupendous nature of the Sin-offering, and what that mighty sacrifice on His part has accomplished for the whole race ; and to behold how the Divine Love and Divine Wisdom have been beautifully and perfectly revealed in these things without doing violence to either—then they too would put away from them for evermore the ecclesiastical spirit that pervades them all, even those which are supposed to be non-priestly and non-ecclesiastical ; the craving for dominion in mere outward growth, which has made them appear as mere ecclesiastical propagandists ; the traditional spirit that extinguished such light as Jewry once had, and has prevented the growth of those who felt after the inner meanings of life and the Christhood ; the mind that has wrought such havoc in the Church's history and filled its pages with oppression in varied forms ;—then they also would at once cleanse their altars, and no longer offer upon them vain oblations ; they would put away from themselves the crying shame expressed in their habits and customs in eating and drinking, and bow in lowly reverence and true sorrow that they could ever have so misunderstood the Master in the Way of Life, and misinterpreted His manifestation of the Divine Love and Wisdom ; and they would prepare themselves to be true channels of blessing to the Souls of needy ones, interpreters of the Jesus-life in the purity of their own, and manifestors of His Christhood through being embodiments of the Love and Wisdom of the Divine Father-Mother.

G
THE ACCOMPLISHMENT

WE have now to speak of Logia which have not only been misunderstood through their having been related to the death of the Master on the Roman cross, but through the interpretation given to them by all the schools belonging to the various ecclesiastical bodies. Lying at the foundation of this misunderstanding and misinterpretation was the Jewish idea of sacrifice and atonement. For it was the influence of that conception which misled Paul and those who wrote the New Testament Records, especially the sacrificial teaching given in the Epistolary Letters. A Jewish interpretation was put upon the whole life of the Master, and the purpose of the Sin-offering. His death on the cross was viewed as the great sacrifice in which He bore, in some inexplicable way, the burden of the World's sin. His death was the " atoning act." And it was in this relationship that the Logia—" *It is Finished* "—were applied. They were understood to refer to the accomplishment of the Sin-offering by His death on the cross. The Churches have taught this all through their history. And though in these latter days some have sought to break away from the traditional view and find an interpretation more in harmony with the Divine Love and Wisdom, yet the Logia have remained undiscovered as to their true and innermost meaning. They have been, and still are, accepted without being understood. They are still made to relate to the Master personally, and to His supposed sacrificial death on the cross. And this most personal, local, and Jewish application of them, has hidden the true significance, even from those who have sought for the inner meaning.

But these Logia had no relation to the swooning Master upon the cross. They did not indicate, as is supposed, the termination of His earth-life as the Master. Rather did they refer to the awful anguish which arose out of the vision of Gethsemane ; and they spoke of the terrible nature of the burden that the Soul would have to bear. Their meaning was purely spiritual and soulic. Their reference was to the full accomplishment of the burden of the anguish ; to the tragic finale of the Gethsemane agony ; to the last act of the Passover ; and to the consummation of the descent from the Christhood estate, the completion (in the vision and anguish) of the path which had to be trod. They were uttered long after the outward crucifixion of the Master, and were the last words spoken by Him to the few members of the inner group who were with Him to the last.

THE MISTAKE OF THE SCHOOLS

Let us now look at the thing that was said to be finished. When read in the light of the anguished cry, as we have interpreted that cry, the meaning of the Logia becomes obvious. But what the western schools have meant is not so clear. They have contended that these Logia referred to the accomplishment of *a divine sacrifice* by means of which the world was redeemed. They have associated them with the idea of the consummation of *an atoning act* by which some great change was wrought in the attitude of the Divine Love towards all His children. And as the result of this supposed change in the

428

Divine attitude to man, the Redemption is said to have been accomplished.

But upon the face of it, and especially when the full history of the ages which have passed since that event, is known, it surely cannot be reasonably contended that the world is even now in a redeemed state after more than eighteen centuries of the profession of historical Christianity. For what are we to understand by redemption, if it be anything less than the restoration of the people to ways of purity and goodness ? And what are we to understand by purity of life and goodness of heart, if it be not the realization of purity in feeling, in acting, in all the ways of life, including eating and drinking ? And that goodness of heart is a quality covering and embracing in its compassion and pity, all Souls and all Creatures. What is the good of a redemption that is only intellectually objective and the belief in the accomplishment of an atonement for all Souls which in nature is not of the Soul, but remains nothing more than an objective intellectual affirmation ? Is there such a thing as redemption from evil and sin that is not truly *subjective*, whose motive and dynamic are not within the Soul, and whose process is not in the most real sense empirical ? What redemption will help a Soul to overcome all forms of passion, but the redeeming forces of the Divine Love within it by means of which evil is subdued and the whole life lifted into conditions of purity and goodness ?

It will readily be conceded (theoretically) that no mere beliefs or intellectual gymnastics can ever accomplish so much for the Soul as the redemption of life. Yet this is just what has been imposed upon the whole western world as the result of the unfortunate perversion of the doctrine of the Redemption. For the West has been taught to believe an illusion ; and, as a natural result, illusionary has been the redemption accomplished within its peoples. The western people have been taught concerning a redemption which was objective to themselves, with the natural corollary that their redemption has been a fiasco. It is now more than eighteen centuries since the redemption is supposed to have been accomplished; yet it is only in these latter days that the true meaning of redemption has dawned upon some Souls here and there, through whom new movements have been inaugurated with a view to bringing the truth home in a practical way to the minds and hearts of men and women. These Souls and their new movements have not even found room within the Churches. Both in the inception and outworking of the movements making for a *real* redemption, the leaders have had to be content to remain outside. There has been no room in the ecclesiastical inns to give birth to those forces which would bring the true redemption into the lives of all Souls.

To know how true this is we need only think of all the gracious movements of the present time having for their purpose the deliverance of the creatures from the tyranny of men and women, even of those professedly Christian, who, as a matter of course, eat their flesh, wear their coats, and oppress them in the name of science and necessity; the deliverance of the masses from the unjust laws of the land, and the unrighteous ways of those who have the power of wealth and position behind them; the deliverance of men and women from the darkness and ignorance of the ages whose barbarism still lives with them and oppresses and afflicts them, as is made manifest in their habits and customs; the deliverance of nations from their false visions of conquest, and peoples from their narrow sympathy, love and service, *to the recognition of the One Life, the One Humanity, the One Family, and the One Service for all by all.*

The Redemption which should have been begun eighteen centuries ago, and which should have continued spreading its influences everywhere and crystallizing its doctrine into the beautiful Jesushood or redeemed life, has only now begun in real earnest. That which the western world has believed to have been finished on the Roman Cross, has had no real existence ; and the real Redemption is now only inaugurated. It is as yet only in its first stages : when it is fully accomplished it will crown this distraught earth with a new glory. The peoples will be noble ; the nations will be righteous ; the societies will be just ; their families will be centres of pure love ; the individual citizens will be pure. The world's threshold will be the theatre of the most beautiful activities ; its cities will be communities of redeemed life. It will then be a world-beautiful in the manifestation of life everywhere. Within its gates there will be found no room for evil in the manifold forms in which we may behold it to-day. The shambles will no more desecrate its thoroughfares, nor the abattoirs witness the awful creature and human tragedies which are with us to-day ; for all the children of men will have risen out of their bondage to the fleshpots of Egypt, and have put away the cruelty involved in the system of flesh-eating which has with such glaring impunity proclaimed itself the right and divinely-appointed way of sustenance. Goodness, compassion, and gentleness will reign everywhere, and all creatures shall share in the blessing.

THINGS OF SUPREME IMPORTANCE

We have not made this detour without the need for it ; for it is of first importance that men and women should understand the meaning of *the redemption*. Until they do understand it and try to realize it, the highest and innermost realizations cannot be theirs. Even these profound things of which we now write will never be fully apprehended by the mind until the redemption is an accomplished fact within the life. Only through experience can they be beheld in their innermost significances. For the things of Christhood can only be entered into after the appropriation of the things of Jesus. The latter is the redeemed life ; the former is the transcendent glory that comes into the Soul as the natural outcome of the attainment of Jesushood. And we must understand, through realization, both the Jesus

431

life and the Christhood estate, ere we can hope to fully apprehend those things which belong unto the Lord. For the Lord
is the Over-shadowing One, the Adonai, the Eternal Son of the
Father-Mother.

Now, the Logia ascribed to the Master on the cross as having
noted the consummation of His supreme sacrifice on behalf
of the world, were really the expression of the Soul that the
Gethsemane vision was finished—that in the first place ; and in
the second place, that the divestment from the state of Christhood was accomplished. It was the last act of " the passing-
over " experiences, the words spoken when the beautiful
Soul changed places, passing from the glorious Christhood
realizations into those states in which He would for ages be
like His brethren, having their infirmities and spiritual sick-
nesses. *It was the real beginning of the Sin-offering, not its finish ;*
for the latter has only quite recently been accomplished. Since
His sublime act, when He laid aside His beautiful divine Christhood, it has continued until this age. And though the work
has been accomplished, the nature of which we have dealt
with elsewhere, *yet is it not finished.* For the redemption has
only begun, that *real redemption* unto whose realization by
all Souls He laid down His life that through Him the Divine
Love might cleanse the astral kingdom of its foul magnetic
images—the " handwritings " which were written against the
Soul on " the middle wall or partition," and so make it possible
for *all Souls* to rise out of the evil states in which they found
themselves, and reach unto Jesushood or the redeemed life.

H

THE SOUL'S BEQUEST

WE have now to consider the last saying of the cross. In doing so we find that the pathos grows more intense whilst the tragedy deepens. The sadness behind what is implied, is extremely great, but the action is sublime. The Saying reveals that beautiful confidence in the Divine Love which was so wonderfully manifested in the life of the Master, and confirms all that we have written concerning the loss unto Him of the Spirit so marvellously expressed in the Anguish Cry. The words are a remarkable testimony to the withdrawal of the Divine Overshadowing. And are they not startling evidence to the fact that He had to sacrifice the Light of the Spirit ? Does not the expression show how truly and fully He had to yield up unto the Father, the Divine Flame which burned within Him as a glorious divine consciousness ? " *He yielded up the Ghost,*" as one of the Records has it. To the keeping of the ever-Blessed One whom He always spake of as His Father, He commended His Spirit, " *Father, into Thy Hands I resign my Spirit.*"

To all who have carefully followed our presentation of the true meaning of the Logia of the Cross, it will be evident that these words could not refer simply to His passing-over from the earth spheres to those of the divine kingdom. A Soul who has the Spirit or Divine Flame by means of which it has not only spiritual consciousness, but that consciousness so intensified that the Divine Presence within its sanctuary is very real to it, does not part with that beautiful inheritance in the passing over from the outer spheres to the angelic world.

Yet it is just this very thing that is said to have happened in the case of the Master. He knew what had to be borne for the sake of the redemption of the race. He came into this world to bear it. And, as we have previously observed when dealing with the Logia of the Gethsemane, this was foreseen by Him in the awful vision of coming events. Nor can anyone understand so profound an experience who has not arrived at some measure of that spiritual consciousness. Nay, they must have known the blessedness of it, and then have been made to pass through the valley where the shadows of spiritual death are to be found, and in which the Light of the Spirit cannot shine. The most awful sorrow and anguish that could befall a Soul would be the loss of such an inheritance of light. To know it, as it has been our lot to know it in the recovery of these most sacred treasures associated with the Christhood manifestation and the Sin-offering, is verily to have to traverse paths of sorrow and anguish undreamt of, and to feel in reality as if the Divine Love had utterly forsaken the Life. For we have passed that way, knowing the heights and the depths of the whole tragedy, feeling not only our life but our very Soul to be pierced as with a sword.

To us the innermost meanings of these Logia of the Cross have been made very real. We have been made to witness the sorrow and anguish, and in large degree to be sharers of these. We have beheld the agony and heard anew the cries of anguish ; and we write of those things which we know. No world-learning has brought them to us. No world-wisdom could have imparted them. They are of the things of the Soul, and the knowledge of them is ours only through the goodness of the Divine Love. They are of the things which belong unto the Divine Wisdom, though unto many they may appear as foolishness ; for the wisdom of the various schools of religious thought, and of the Churches, is very largely only the wisdom of the world. They are of those things of the Wisdom of God which were hidden for ages before the manifestation, which the blessed One whom we know as the Master interpreted and made manifest, but which were veiled when the writers of the Gospel Records changed them in nearly all their relationships and meanings, when they applied them to events local, physical and personal, because they knew not that they were spiritual, universal, divine. They are of the innermost kingdom, of those most sacred Mysteries which dwellers on the angelic spheres desired earnestly to understand ; for they are the revelation of the Divine Love in its most practical manifestation, the interpretation, *par excellence*, of His beautiful and wonderful purpose for the redemption and perfecting of all His children. If they reveal transcendent love, it is because of the Divine Love. If they speak of profound sorrow, it is because the sorrow was borne by the Divine. If they make manifest unspeakable anguish, it is only because the anguish in all its intensity was known unto the Divine. And if they show how great the mystery was, it is surely because it was *the mystery of mysteries*, namely, how the Divine Love could stoop for the accomplishment of the redemption of all His children, even to their lowly estates.

The Lord's Passover

*Being an Account of the Last Hours of the Master
with the Inner Group, and His Passing Over
from the Christhood Estate to take up
the work of the Sin-offering, and
likewise an indication of the
nature of His Return in
the Days of the
Regeneration.*

A

THE STORY IN THE RECORDS

THE teachings found in the Logia of the Passover accentuate all that has been unveiled in the preceding chapter. But here also there has to be a discovering of the treasure. For the description given in the synoptics concerning the last Passover Supper partaken of by the beloved Master, reveals how the profoundest Sayings spoken through Him were materialized. What was a spiritual mystery of the deepest and most sacred nature, was made to relate to an outward and material event. What was related to Him in a purely soullic way, and to the divine work to be accomplished through Him, was brought down into the realm of Jewish ceremonial and the Passover meal. Things of a solely celestial nature which were embodied in allegory setting forth the mystery, were turned into merely personal actions. The deep mystery of the Lord's Passover was not only changed into a material supper, but all the profound things associated with it were also changed in a manner that prevented them from being understood. The great desire of the Lord to celebrate the Passover ; the inquiry of the disciples concerning where He would have it celebrated ; the sending of Peter and John to make preparation ; the sign that was to be to them as guide to the Guest Chamber ; the Guest Chamber in which the celebration took place ; the Celebration ; the astounding Sayings concerning the Fruit of the Vine, the Body broken as meat, the Blood poured out as drink for Souls, and the New Testimony of the Divine Love and Wisdom—all these precious things were made to relate to things and events which were material, personal, and outwardly historical.

What a treasure the writers buried beneath the Jewish ceremonial with its personal action and historical references, will be discovered as we unfold the wonderful event For all the actors and details will then become changed. The nature of everything will be transfigured. The glorious truths which have been so long hidden will once more be made manifest. The sublime action of the Christ-Soul will be understood by all who are able to enter into the meaning of it. The drama which took place will be beheld with a new understanding. The experiences which the disciples of the inner group then entered into, will assume new proportions and be impressed with new significances. The Lord's Passover will be unveiled to such Souls as are able to enter into its meaning. For the hour has come when it is to be once more made manifest.

A PROFOUND HISTORY

Little have the readers of the New Testament narratives imagined when the story of the Passover attributed to the Master has been read by them, the wealth of Soul history hidden within the material setting. Little have they dreamt that the fascinating story of that apparently natural Passover Supper, said to have been celebrated by the blessed Master and the inner group of His disciples, was one of the most profound histories in all the teachings attributed to Him, in which was revealed the nature of the Sin-offering, how the Soul was to bear it, and where and when it was to be completed.

The story, as it was originally set forth in the *Logia*, was very different from that found now in the four Evangelists. The writer who sent out the first Gospel Record to the Churches presented the story as an outward and personal event in the Master's life. And as that Record was the one made use of by those who wrote the synoptic Gospels, the materialized form of it is found in these Gospels with but slight variation. The original narrative, however, was greatly changed. It underwent considerable alteration at the hands of the writer of that Record. It was made to fit in with the Passover of the Jews, and to centre in the Master. The event became not only material and personal, but one which took only a brief hour to accomplish ; whereas the true event was non-Jewish, impersonal, and immaterial, being of the Soul, and covering all the ages of the era named after the Christhood.

To write of this profound experience is no light task, so sacred is it, so deep in its meaning, so wonderful in the Mystery of it ; for the vision of the Master is lost in that of the Adonai who stands before us as the Lord of Life. The voice we hear is that of the Adonai speaking through the Soul, telling of the wonderful mystery of the Divine Love in the process whereby redemption is to be accomplished for all Souls, and even the world itself. The whole scene changes, and we are carried away from merely material objects and actions to those of the Soul. The outward veil is drawn, and we look upon the divine mystery. We look into the sanctuary wherein the mystery has been concealed, and we behold the wonderful works of God. The shrine is beautiful with divine love, and the ministry performed is omnipotent. The altar is not of man's fashioning ; the sacrifice offered upon it is infinitely more than any man has ever imagined. We may well take off our shoes and uncover our feet, for the ground whereon we tread is most holy.

It was with " great desire " that the Lord desired to celebrate the Passover with the disciples who formed the inner group. And herein we have a revelation of the yearning of the Divine Love over Souls, which finds the way whereby their redemption can be accomplished. We behold at last the fulfilment of the Divine Love who purposed that redemption untold ages before, and who had been, all through those ages, preparing the way for its accomplishment. Every age that rose and set brought it nearer. The passing of the ages issued in " the fulness of time "—the time when the Christhood manifestations could be made, and the work of the Sin-offering begun. The Divine Wisdom had found a way whereby the " middle wall " or " partition " could be broken down, and the " handwritings " which were engraven upon it and which were against the Soul and inimical to the progress of the whole of the human races and the entire spiritual system of the Planet, could be blotted out. And now the Divine Love was about to begin the great work of accomplishing the removal of these obstacles to true spiritual growth. It was " *the mystery which had been hidden for ages,*" though it had been most clearly set forth and anticipated in the wonderful illuminations given unto those prophet Souls who were of the house of ancient Israel, now found scattered throughout the entire Hebrew Scriptures. It was the mystery concerning which the angels are said to have inquired, and which at last was to find its realization.

A Sublime Revelation

Many of the Psalms were portrayals of it ; many of the prophetic visions had relation to it. Those Psalms and prophetic writings in which it was portrayed, we will speak of when the hour comes for us to present the whole doctrine of the Sin-offering as foreshadowed before the Christhood and accomplished by the Christ-Soul. But we might here indicate that even in the Psalms the nature of the Sin-offering is clearly set forth ; the path of the Christ-Soul in the accomplishment of it is revealed in the most obvious way ; the suffering and the anguish endured by the Christ-Soul in bearing the burden, are portrayed ; even the nature of the Christ-Soul and His journeying into the remotest parts of the Soul experience, are unmistakably revealed, and are spoken of as the profoundest of all experiences. The height of His spiritual attainment, the depth of His humiliation whilst bearing the burden of the Sin-offering, the length to which the path would carry Him, and the breadth of its marvellous all-encompassing work, may be discerned.

The Lord's Passover was indeed something infinitely greater than any outward ceremonial such as the Records indicate, and which the Churches unfortunately have believed all through

442

their history. And the desire expressed was an unspeakably more profound experience than any desire to celebrate a feast such as that spoken of in the Gospels. It was the yearning of the Ever Blessed One towards all Souls, the longing for the hour of the redemption to begin for the world, the Divine Love praying for the hour of the accomplishment of all that had been purposed during the work of the Sin-offering, epitomized in that one Saying concerning the great desire to celebrate the Passover. The past ages are gathered up into it. All that the Divine Love had felt concerning the redemption of the whole planetary system with its manifold forms of spiritual life, finds expression in it. The beautiful devotion of that Love to the welfare of all Souls, is made manifest. It is, indeed, a sublime revelation of the divine purpose to accomplish this world's redemption.

B

THE CELEBRATION

THAT the words spoken through the Christ-Soul at the Passover celebration were momentous, every one will recognize who is able to enter into their meaning. The depth of feeling with which they were uttered cannot be conveyed in any language that we may use ; they had to be heard to realize that. But how beautifully spiritual they were in their significance will be obvious to the spiritually discerning. In them will be heard something more than an echo of the voice of the Divine Love ; indeed they will vibrate with the magnetism of Love, and reveal how the Ever Blessed One meets the needs of the human Soul. Here we have a picture of how the Divine pours out Life $(Z\omega\eta)$[1] upon all Souls, how He gives of Himself for their nourishment and redemption. In the fashioning of the Soul He gave of His fulness ; and in the redemption

---

[1] Zoe, as distinguished from Bios, the former denoting Soul-life and the latter the body-life.

of the Soul He gave without measure. But in the fashioning of the Soul the divine giving was full of great joy and blessedness ; whilst in the redemption the path lay through a veritable wilderness, the treading of which brought unspeakable pain, sorrow and anguish. For it was the way from Bozrah[1] to Edom, and back again ; the treading of the " winepress " alone by the Christ-Soul; the red-dyeing of the garments of Christhood, and the sore travailing of the Adonai through the Master as He bore the burden of His people.

THE MYSTERY OF THE PASSOVER

The celebration of the Passover was the profoundest mystery of the Divine Love ; for it was the passing over of the Soul from the wonderful manifestation of Christhood, to that state in which the burden could be borne, the Edom-path could be trod, and a highway opened up in and through the wilderness. It was the passing away of the Christhood of the Master—the descent from the Christhood state and consequent profound humiliation of that beautiful Soul who had risen from kingdom to kingdom until He was crowned a Son of God, and became even one with the Divine. It was the consummation of His beautiful purpose to be the vehicle through whom the Divine Love could work out the redemption for all Souls by means of the purification of the middle kingdom, known now as the astral world, " the middle wall or partition " which divided the heavens of the angelic world from the earth. He was the Soul who was the vehicle of the Adonai during the manifestation ; and so He had to pass from that most exalted and blessed state into one in which He could traverse the various hells which had been fashioned within the middle kingdom, in order to extinguish their fires, and bring the unruly elements into a state of obedience to the divine will. The Last Supper was the

---

[1] Bozrah was the ancient term which was used to denote the spiritual state known as Divine Christhood ; and Edom was the state of spiritual crucifixion, in which there was forgetfulness by the Soul of her past.

last spiritual fellowship the Master had with those who had learnt something of His secret ; and the Passover was the leaving of the blessed Christhood estate to take up the work of such a redeeming priesthood as had never before been known in this world. Little indeed does the universal Church dream of the true meaning of words such as these, " *Christ our passover is sacrificed for us* " ; for, in the passing over, the Christ-Soul sacrificed His wonderful Christhood in order to pour out His very Life upon the world unto its redemption.

A Long Separation

The event was one of the saddest in the history of this Planet, though it was born from a love which knew no limitations in its giving. It was the very saddest that ever befell those who had been of that inner group of disciples ; for to them it was the loss of such a love as they had never before realized to be possible in any Soul. For He not only went whither they then could not follow, but He went away from them in the sense that they never met again to know each other during the long ages of the performance of the sad and tragic Sin-offering, until in these latter days when two of them have been privileged to know Him again. His passing over was not such as the Records would seem to imply. It was not like that of a Christhood whose presence must still keep in touch with those in sympathy with the beautiful state. It was not a passing over into the wonderful angelic kingdom to manifest the Christhood there in a continued ministry unto all Souls. It was not a passing over that permitted, in even the least degree, any communication between Him and those He had drawn closely to Him. For Him the blessedness of such a continuation of beautiful fellowship was impossible because of the nature of the work which He had to do. The inner group could not then follow Him either on the outer planes of experience or in the heavens. It was essential that they should not again meet to know each other until the day arrived when *the fruit of the Vine could be drunk anew by*

445

them all in the Father's Kingdom. The Master would drink of
it no more until that day.

And very soon would they follow ; for they were to be sharers
of His Travail, to know His sufferings, to be baptized with the
baptism with which He was to be baptized, and to drink of the
cup of which He was to drink. They were to meet no more until
the work of the Lord's Passion had been accomplished ; until
the betrayal and crucifixion of the Christhood had taken place,
and the Christ-Soul had lain three days and three nights in
the grave. Then, when the resurrection morning broke, He
would rise again, and they would meet to know each other.

THE THREE NARONIC DAYS[1]

But it was not after the three earth-days as set forth in the
Records, that they were to meet ; nor after the crucifixion
by the Roman Judge ; nor after three days in the Palestinian
grave ; but it was after the three Naronic years, or celestial
planetary days of this Earth, during which the Soul of the
Master was travailing amid the hells, and the Christhood lay
asleep in the grave which was found in the West where the
chief priests and scribes, after crucifying His sublime Christhood, buried Him. Nor was it in the visions of the Lord which
have been confounded with His appearing unto the disciples
after the supposed resurrection, which we have explained
elsewhere. But it was to be after the tragic Sin-offering had been
fully accomplished. And now the Lord has arisen once more
from the grave wherein they laid Him. Unto Mary Magdalene
hath He appeared. Peter and John have beheld Him. All the
members of the innermost group have once more beheld the
vision. And now it is being proclaimed that the Christhood is
risen, and that the Christhood vision is being made manifest

---

[1] A Naronic Cycle or day is the time it takes the earth to pass from one
celestial sign to another. That covers about six hundred of our years ; so
that three such days embrace over eighteen hundred years.

unto many. For the *real Christhood* is being restored to the vision of the Soul.

And the Master through whom the Divine manifestation was made and the work of the Sin-offering accomplished, has likewise risen from the dead. He has finished the work which was given Him to do, and has ascended out of the hell-states into which He descended. He has now accomplished the work for which He passed over from His beautiful Christhood, and has become known unto the two who were to tarry until the day of His awakening.

O Love Infinite and Eternal, who could have dreamed of such an event as the Passover of the Lord ? Who could have thought out the way of the Lord's Passion ? Who could have foreseen its sad mystery and glorious issue ? Who could have anticipated the resurrection morning, and the discovery by Mary of Magdala of the risen Christhood ? Surely it is of God alone that these things have been accomplished, and the Christ-Soul who bore the awful burden, found again !

C
THE SENDING OF THE TWO DISCIPLES

IN the Records it is stated that Peter and John were sent to prepare for the celebration of the Passover. There is profound significance in the statement, though on the surface there seems really nothing of importance in it, because it has been understood as an outward event. But when the Passover is known to have been one of the most remarkable histories ever written by any Soul, and such as we have indicated, it will be seen that the sending of these two disciples had more than any outward significance attached to it, and that its meaning was far-reaching and divine. There are things implied in it which are not apparent, the real meanings being hidden through the historical setting.

Now, it was not to prepare any chamber in a house for the celebration, but to find again the Christhood vision which would be lost throughout the Naronic cycles, and the Christ-Soul, when the Passover was fully accomplished, that the two were sent. They were sent to prepare the way for the coming again of the Christhood manifestation through all those who once had known Christhood ; and to find the blessed Master after the accomplishment of the work of the Sin-offering. And in the doing of this they were to look out for the sign of a man who carried the water-pot ; for in him they would discover the owner of the guest-chamber in which the Divine Lord had wrought out the astounding and marvellous work by which the " middle wall " or " partition " was broken down, the " handwritings " were obliterated, and the principalities and powers in high-places which were inimical to the Soul, overthrown. It really meant that these two disciples who were of the most intimate friends of the Master, were to precede Him in the work of the awakening and the rising from the dead at the end of the time appointed for the coming again of the Son of Man. They were to precede Him in the work of proclaiming the coming of the New Avatar, to herald the dawn of the New Age, to point out the way unto the finding of Christhood. They were to find the Sign of the coming again of the Son of Man ; and when they had found it, they were to prepare the guest-chamber for the coming of the Lord. For they were to discern the meaning of the sign, and know that it was even as the Master had said.

THE APPEARING OF JOHN AND PETER

The two disciples have already appeared.[1] They came and

---

[1] Who these two were we are not yet permitted to tell, though it is just possible that a few Souls may discern. Their names are held back because it is so difficult to prevent personal worship ; and no name must stand between the Soul and the Divine. For the like reason the Master will never be again known as such, that there may be no repetition of the tragedy that overtook the beautiful impersonal Manifestation of Christhood, and His sublime teachings.

did their work. Discerning the sign and beholding the vision, they proclaimed the coming of the Son of Man. And since they proclaimed the message with prophetic voice, the awakening has been most wonderful everywhere. Marvellous indeed were the things given unto them to declare, and these are going out to all Souls who are able to hear with the spiritual understanding. They tarried upon the outer planes through all the ages of the Sin-offering, participating, in some measure, in the work of the Christ-Soul, though they never met the Master again to know Him from the hour of the Passover until in these latter days when they found Him, even as it was said they would.

John was to await the coming of the Christhood and the Master ; and that event Peter was also to await. But their tarrying was to be under different conditions, a truth which was verified in their experience. And whilst the two disciples referred to were to await the closing of the third Naronic Cycle and the opening of the New Naros, and to prepare the way for the coming of the Son of Man and the finding of the Eternal Christ, and through that finding, come into the consciousness of Christhood ; they likewise represented the two great divine principles of the spiritual system of every Soul, the love-principle and the spiritual understanding. The one represented that power within the Soul by means of which the spiritual life receives true nourishment from the divine—for it is through the love-principle that we are all spiritually nourished and made divinely strong ; whilst the other represented the vision-power of the Soul by means of which the Soul rises transcendently out of the earth influences into the heavenly conditions, and apprehends those things which are related to the Soul of the individual, the Planet, and the Universe.

SIGNIFYING TWO DIVINE PRINCIPLES

These two divine principles of the Soul whose true province within the Soul-system is to transcend all material objects, purposes and visions, had to remain on the earth-planes during the three Naros—the three Planetary days, long dark nights verily of the Sin-offering tragedy—and until the Son of Man had risen again and come into the Vision of the Divine Lord. For the Love-principle was compelled, by reason of the very conditions in the western world, to tarry upon the outer spheres, seeking its fulfilment in them, until the great awakening came with the breaking of the new day, the true resurrection morning, when it would set out to seek for that purer and higher fulfilment in true spiritual and divine realizations.

And the spiritual understanding also was to remain upon the outer spheres, seeking there for those things which were of the Soul and the Divine Father-Mother amid the earth-systems which would arise out of the conditions in which this cosmos was. It was foreseen that it would often be carried hither and thither whither it would fain not go ; would search much and long for that which it would not find ; would cry out for a light which broke not upon it, and have to rest satisfied with what the various systems were able to give unto it, until the day-break of the New Naros came, and the Christ-vision at last arose in the heavens, and grew ever clearer and brighter until the full vision of the Christhood stood out most beautifully —a vision obvious unto all who are able to behold with that true spiritual understanding. In many have these two divine principles of the Soul awakened again to go in search of the long lost Christhood experience, until, in the blessed realizations of life to-day, they have found the Lord once more.

THINGS THAT ARE FORGOTTEN

But whilst all this is being accomplished as the outcome of the glorious work of the tragic Sin-offering, the Soul who bore that awful burden has been almost forgotten. By many the wonderful new age is simply viewed as the outcome of a new departure in the process of the Soul's evolution. They look upon it as the crown of past ages, the resultant of the conflict of previous generations, the natural corollary of the solution of many of the life-problems dealt with to-day. They consider the Redemption to be nothing more than the arising of the Soul of the whole race through its best and eldest children, to a higher plane of consciousness. The very meaning of redemption is apparently forgotten in the new-found joy. These do not pause long enough to seriously consider by what wonderful process all this marvellous change has been wrought. They are content to know that the new age is with us. In the flush of the first joys of the new life, little room is found for such a sad and sorrowful subject as the way in which it has all been brought about.

Yet will the Churches of the West, and indeed all peoples, have to listen to this part of the message also, if they would understand the great divine Mysteries in which they all profess to believe in greater or less degree. And when the first child-soul joys of the new born Christ-life within all who have come into it, have found satisfaction, and they require more " wine," then will they turn unto the larger and truer conception of the whole Mystery to find still more joy in the new and larger vision which will fill the heavens of their Soul, in which they will be able to discern what a marvellous work was wrought out for them by the Divine Love through the Christ-Soul who was once known as the Master. They will see and understand when the Peter principle as well as the John principle is fully awakened within them, that the Divine Christ-Soul, in an universal sense, is the blessed Adonai, the Everlasting Son of the Father, the Manifest of the Unmanifest upon the Divine Kingdom, and that it was He who overshadowed and filled the Master with a fulness not hitherto known upon this Planet since the days of its descent into those conditions described by the Master as " this cosmos." They will then behold with an open understanding what it was that the Divine Love accomplished through that Soul in the process and burden of the

Sin-offering. The *real* redemption will appear as a glorious achievement by the divine within us lifting us all up into a life of beautiful purity and goodness ; and how that long delayed redemption is at last made possible for all, will be understood, and, when understood, will be beheld as the most marvellous of all. And in the new and fuller light will *all things become clear*.

D

THE SIGN OF THE AWAKENING

THE two disciples were to look out for the sign of the man carrying a water-pot ; and when they saw him they were to know that the work for which the Passover was celebrated had been accomplished. Nay, they were to know him as the Soul within whom and through whom the Lord had accomplished the great work of the purification of the astral hells, the overthrow of the false principalities and powers, the destruction of the graven images whose magnetic influence was so disastrous to the Soul—the terrible " handwritings " written long ages ago upon that kingdom by the human race. The sign was to have for them a double signification. It was to be celestial and spiritual ; universal and individual. They were to know it as the blessed sign of the coming again of the Son of Man, the Divine Christhood, in the overshadowing of the heavens and the awakening into newness of life of those who had fallen asleep in the Jesus-life or redeemed life, and the arising from the graves of an existence dominated by materialism, of many of those Souls who had once known the Christhood but who had also fallen asleep. And they were also to know it as the sign of the completion of that tragic work which began when the " passing over " took place, and continued all through the era until these latter days when it has been accomplished. They were to be guided by the sign for the finding of " the guest-chamber " where the Passover was celebrated, and the discovery of the Soul who became the vehicle of that most wonderful manifestation of the Christhood, and the yet more marvellous work of the planetary redemption wrought through the changing of the astral world or middle kingdom during His Soul-travail, the work which is known as the Sin-offering.

WHAT WAS THE SIGN?

The sign of the coming again of the Son of Man in the great awakening of Souls all over the world, is self-evident. The new joy born into the world as the result of this awakening is so real within the experience of many, that those who have felt it and beheld its manifestations, know indeed that the Lord is coming again, and that it is the awakening within the Soul of a spiritual consciousness and, in some Souls, of a divine consciousness. The sign coming into the Celestial Heavens is that of the Man carrying the water-pot: it is the Sign of Aquarius. Spiritually it is the precursor of the divine outpouring upon all Souls, the Zodiacal Sign upon the celestial planisphere of the Redemption and the Regeneration. For, in planetary evolution, the sign Aquarius (not in its annular sense, but in a celestial sense) is the sign of the attainment of the planetary spiritual system to the consciousness of the Divine Life when the whole household enters upon a new and yet higher phase of unfoldment before the Eternal and ever Blessed One.

But in the present instance it is less than that; and yet in a sense it is more. It is less than the attainment of spiritual consciousness by the whole household of the Planet, for many Souls upon the human kingdom are yet far from that state. But it is in another sense more than that, for it is the beginning of a *real* redemption for all Souls upon the Planet, and even of all the planes of the Planet; the genuine return of the Planet and its household to the conditions of the redeemed life; the attainment of the Redemption by all who are equal to entering into its realizations; the awakening within those who are in a condition to receive it, of the consciousness of the Divine Love as a living principle within them; and in some other older

Souls, the realization of that yet higher consciousness in which the Soul knows the Divine Presence, is always conscious of that Presence, has the experience of the Divine Over-shadowing, and is illumined from the Divine.

For such is the meaning of the present new age with its new born Light, Life and Joy.

THE PROJECTION OF THE SIN-OFFERING

But it also has another meaning. The Planet has often passed through the celestial sign of Aquarius. It passed through that sign upon the spiritual heavens, the celestial heavens, and the divine heavens long ages ago ere evil was known upon its planes or one Soul had fallen a prey to the betrayer—its astral or elemental kingdom. Since the descent known as " the fall," the Planet has passed through the sign of Aquarius many times without any apparent progress. Naros after Naros has risen and set, leaving the old conditions behind them. There were many movements which were apparently forward, but whose magnetic power was only temporary, so that they were followed by other movements distinctly retrogressive. With the birth of what have been spoken of as New Religions there have always appeared new phases of experience accompanied sometimes by strange and remarkable phenomena ; and with the appearance of these new phases there have seemed to be great upward movements towards the spiritual. But these have again been followed by seasons of astounding spiritual darkness and im-potence, not to speak of evils unnameable, so that the real progress of life towards spiritual realization was very greatly retarded. Indeed, so slow was the progress towards the re-attainment by the human races of the state of spiritual experience from which all fell through the planetary descent, that the Divine Love purposed to remove the cause of the sad hindrance. And it was *then* that the Sin-offering was projected by the Divine Love in order to remove the magnetic images within the astral kingdom whose presence was a perpetual obstacle to the Soul's progress. For only in this way could the Soul ever be perfectly redeemed from the influences of that kingdom, and rise up into the spiritual world to find the angelic life and realize the divine. And it was the accomplishment of that stupendous work which was appointed unto the Christ-Soul known as the Master; for through Him was the Divine Love to change the elemental or magnetic images, and rid the astral kingdom of them, so that the conditions of that kingdom might be purified, and that all Souls might be able to rise in spiritual estate higher and still higher until even the Divine Kingdom itself was attained.

Known to the Ancient Hebrews

That stupendous work was begun just after the Passover celebration; and it continued through the three Naronic Cycles which have come and gone again since then. It was anticipated in the Hebrew Scriptures alone, because only unto the ancient Hebrews was it revealed as something that would have to be accomplished ere the Redemption could come to the whole planetary household. The true ancient Hebrews were the most spiritual Souls upon the planet at that time. They had once known all the Divine Mysteries. Many ages prior to the planetary descent these Souls had been in the state of Christhood, and had been the teachers of the Planet's children. And it was through the schools which they founded for the teaching of the spiritual or " Lesser Mysteries," and the celestial and divine or " Greater Mysteries " to the more advanced Souls, that the Jews came into the possession of this most wonderful divine Mystery of the Sin-offering. But not understanding what was meant, they materialized everything; with the result that the Sin-offering became a priestly ceremonial, the victim a creature, the object being the removal of the Divine anger.

It was in this way that the beautiful Mystery became lost. The true doctrine of the Redemption was perverted; the Divine

Love was misinterpreted ; and the purpose of the Sin-offering was misrepresented. The wonderful allusions in the true Hebrew Scriptures to the Sin-offering ; the description of its nature ; the picture of its path ; and the portrayal of the sufferings of the Christ-Soul who was appointed to bear the burden—these were not understood by the priesthoods that arose out of the deteriorated schools. But the Scriptures containing these profound teachings were retained by the priests, and applied to their own religious ceremonial, their national experiences, individual histories of persons who were leaders and teachers amongst them. The remarkable Psalms wherein the *path* of the Sin-offering is most obviously pictured, and the terrible experiences of the Christ-Soul most clearly indicated, the Jews did not understand. Their spiritual significance was an unknown tongue to them. They made use of the Psalms in their services ; but most of the profound and sorrowful meanings in them they associated with experiences which were supposed to have been passed through by one of their own Kings.

And what happened to the beautiful Psalms also happened to the illuminations of the true prophets and seers concerning this stupendous Mystery. The priests were unable to discern the inner significance of them. They had not the power of true spiritual vision to do so. Between their teaching and that of the prophet-souls, the gulf was great. The one was of the lowlands of gross materialism, always cruel because of the sacrificial system of Jewry ; the other was of the heights of pure spiritual being, always merciful, and lit up with the glory of divine compassion. Throughout the Old Testament they are as two distinct voices uttering things irreconcilable ; two distinct systems in perpetual conflict with one another. For in the priesthood a purely materialistic system is found embodied ; whilst in the teachings of the prophet-souls, it is the spiritual system of the Soul or the Planet which is found.

The Sign of the Christhood

But there is a still further meaning couched in the Sign of Aquarius. It is the sign under which the Christhood was again to be made manifest in " the coming of the Son of Man upon the clouds of the Heavens." For the coming of the Son of Man is the return to the Planet of the Divine Overshadowing through the purification that has been effected upon the astral kingdom ; and the return of the Christ is the coming into the experience of all those Souls who once knew the Christhood estate, of the consciousness of the Divine Presence, the Divine Christ. The Water-carrier is the sign of the Redemption ; for water is the emblem of the great purifying power of the truth. Everywhere are the waters of purification being poured out upon all Souls through the purifying and rejuvenating influences that are at work. The Water-carrier is also the sign of the Regeneration ; for through the Redemption there will break upon those Souls who were once in a state of Christhood, visions of all the past, so that during this Sign there will be the recovery by Souls of past experiences. And these will ultimately add their volume of testimony to the profound things concerning which we have written. They will bear witness to the things of the Spirit—the Illuminations concerning the Soul, the Planet, the Christ-Soul, and the Divine, of which we have in part treated in these unfoldments.

But the sign of the Water-carrier was that sign in which the Christ-Soul was also to return from His long, lonely, sad and sorrowful journey. He was no more to partake of the fruit of the Vine until the hour arrived when they would all be brought together into the Kingdom of the Father, and then He would drink of it again. And that hour has come. The sign of the Water-bearer proclaims that He has once more arisen out of the grave wherein they laid Him ; for the Sin-offering is now accomplished, the astral kingdom is changed, the heavens of the divine are able at last to perform their

beautiful ministry to all Souls. And He will now be able to
" *see of the travail of His Soul.*"

E

THE GUEST-CHAMBER

FROM the foregoing interpretations it will be no surprise to
our readers to learn that the Guest-Chamber was no
ordinary room. They will indeed be prepared to hear that it
had an altogether spiritual signification, and was spoken
concerning the Soul. And they will understand how it was
that the expression " *the upper room* " or " guest-chamber "
came to have so sacred an association given unto it in the
portrayal of the Manifestation of the Christhood and the
Fellowship of the Master with the inner group of disciples.

What wealth of meaning has been lost to the Soul through
the materialization of this most beautiful truth ? What possible
experiences of the sublimest order have been denied to all
those who ought to have been able to enter into them ? Who is
able to appreciate the extent of the loss that befell the Souls
of all who once understood what the expression meant, and the
effect that the loss has had upon the thought of the entire
western world ?

Had the true meaning of " *The guest-chamber* " or " the
upper room " been known unto such Souls, the doctrine of
the Redemption which has filled and held the thought of the
western world, and caused its Schools to enter into strife
with one another, could never have been entertained and
accepted as the true interpretation of the divine purpose
towards this world, and of the Sin-offering as the expression
of that purpose. It was most unfortunate that the term had a
meaning given to it which has acted as a veil, hiding its true
signification, and leading the whole western world to associate
it with a room in some friend's home whither the blessed Master

resorted at times to hold fellowship with the inner group, and which was the scene of the Passover Celebration and the Supper of the Lord. The materialization of the idea embodied in the term, brought down from the spiritual world within Man to the outermost spheres of his experiences, one of the most beautiful and most sacred realities, changed the spiritual for the material, the Soullic for the earthly, the universal within the Soul for the local situation, the guest-chamber that was Divine in its relationships to something that was of the outermost.

THE NATURE OF THE GUEST-CHAMBER

The Guest-Chamber which the two disciples were sent to prepare, and which they were to find by means of the sign of the water-carrier, had, therefore, a purely spiritual signification. They were first to find the sign and then the Guest-Chamber ; and they were to prepare the latter for the return of the Lord. The sign was to be beheld and the Guest-Chamber found long after the " passing-over " was accomplished, and not before. They were to find it when the Lord's Passion was finished, the Sin-offering was made, and the return of the Lord was due. They were to find the Guest-Chamber in order to prepare it for the reception of the Lord. There was a real Guest-chamber ; and it required preparation for so Divine a Guest. There was an Upper Room set apart for the most sacred service ; and it had to be got ready for the reception. *Let these two spiritual facts be remembered. And this, also, that the mission of the two who were sent, was to carry out this work.*

We have said that the two sent were Peter and John ; that they were not only the two disciples of the blessed Master who were to tarry until the return of the Christ-Soul, but that they also represented the two great spiritual principles within the System of the Soul—the illumined Understanding or Higher Reason, and the Love-principle of the Soul. It is through the illumined understanding that the sign of the coming of the

459

Son of Man alone can be recognised ; and it is only through the application of the love-principle of the Soul that the Guest-Chamber can be got ready for the coming of the divine consciousness into it.

These were the two Apostles who first discovered the coming of the sign of Aquarius in a spiritual sense, and where the Guest-Chamber was to be found wherein the Lord would hold fellowship with His own. They made the discovery that a new day had dawned for this Planet and all her children, that the grey light which was breaking in the eastern heavens (the Divine Will in the Soul system) was the harbinger of the Christ age, and that it would grow brighter and brighter until the whole world was flooded with the glory of it. They it was who discovered in the yet early morning where the Guest-Chamber was to be found, and how that Upper Room was to be prepared ; for they beheld the Guest-Chamber to be none other than *the innermost Sanctuary of the Soul,* and that the way to prepare it for the coming of the Lord was to illumine it with the mystic light that was breaking, and to adorn it with the fruits of the Spirit. For within the Sanctuary or Guest-Chamber, is the Lamp of the Spirit and the Table of the Lord. Within the Lamp is the Oil of Life by means of which the Divine Light is able to communicate itself to illumine the whole Being ; and upon the Table of the Lord are the fruits of the Vine through which the Divine Love pours His Life into the Soul when the hour of the Fellowship returns.

These two blessed truths have been re-discovered, and are now being proclaimed unto all who are able to hear them. The doctrine of true spiritual illumination is being heralded through the voice of the Angel of the Lord within the Soul, and many are responding to the message. The meaning of true spiritual love is being interpreted from the angelic world unto all Souls who are in a state of spiritual development to enter into its meaning.

ITS PLANETARY SIGNIFICATION

But the preparation of the Guest-Chamber of the individual Soul able to enter into that most intimate fellowship with the Divine which is implied in the expression *The coming of the Lord into the Guest-Chamber*, has also the larger meaning for the whole planetary household. For, not only is the Redemption to be realized by the individual Soul, but even the Planet-Soul is to enter into the joys of that blessed state. The effect of the coming of the Lord into the individual Soul (which, as we have seen, means the awakening of the Soul to the consciousness of the Divine Presence within its own Sanctuary), is to be seen in the manifestations of the Redeemed life through all those who have entered into the blessed divine realization, with the result that many are being influenced towards that life in these days ; and more and yet more will turn unto its ways, until the entire human household is lifted up on to the spiritual planes. And through such a return of the Lord into the experience of all Souls, the spiritual conditions will be of such an order that the Planet-Soul will also be able to respond to the full magnetic attraction of the Divine Love, and gradually have all the planes of her once most beautiful sphere restored to their ancient glory.

That that glorious time is coming, is self-evident. The evidences are obvious unto those who are able to interpret aright the great Reform Movements, and the true spiritual awakening of our time ; and also to discern the inner meaning of the remarkable planetary changes which of late have been taking place, changes which baffle even the best students of scientific research in the domain of Physics, Astronomy, and Physiography. For the planetary conditions, those which are designated as purely physical, as well as those which are purely spiritual and social, are quickly changing, and, through the changes, *moving towards the grand consummation*. Concerning this movement we shall have more to say by and by ; but let our readers not forget the great and solemn fact that this Planet is a most wonderful living organism ; that the Planet-Soul is a glorious spiritual system ; and that the morning of the Redemption of that system has broken and is hastening to the glory of noon-day.

Its Relation to the Master

Yet once more must we refer to Him who bore the burden of the Sin-offering ; for the Saying had likewise reference to His return. In the stupendous task assigned to Him, it was necessary for Him to lay aside all His Christhood attributes *and become even as the very least of His brethren.* He had to descend into the various states in which they were ; to pass through the very conditions by which they were overcome ; to endure like trials and temptations ; to be buffeted by the opposing forces of the elemental world ; to be stung by the scorpions of the flesh ; to know the sore travail of the Soul passing through the bitter waters of spiritual death ; to arrive even at that awful state of Soul experience in which there is alive within the Soul the terrible consciousness of the withdrawal of the Divine Presence. What all such experiences meant to Him cannot even be imagined by any one who has not passed that way bearing within him the deep consciousness of the burden. And though in every life He rose out of the conditions amid which He found Himself and through which He was brought down and laid low in spiritual estate, yet it was only in the last life that the awful consciousness of all that He had passed through, and the treasure He had lost in His stupendous sacrifice, broke upon Him in the days of the Regeneration. Indeed, so terrible was the awakening to that consciousness, that the burden of all the past was again felt by Him with so great intensity, that it seemed as if He were passing through the conditions once more.

All this terrible awakening and realization was **anticipated.**

462

It was foreknown to the Master and it led Him to give utterance to some remarkable Sayings. In a new light we may recall these words spoken by Him, " *In the Regeneration, when the Son of Man cometh again, shall Faith be found in me upon the Earth ?* "

Whatever " Faith " has come to mean in these days, to Him it meant the vision of the Soul, the power to see and understand divinely, to penetrate all the veils of matter and behold the substance, to transcend all earthly things and reach the heavenly innermost. And He feared lest the effect of His Soul travail would be to deprive Him entirely of all spiritual power and vision, and to leave Him bereft of the inner vision by which the Divine Presence is apprehended and beautifully realized.

For Him also had the two disciples, Peter and John, a ministry to perform. They were to be His helpers in the Regeneration, when the whole burden of all the past would be felt as the sore travail of each life was adumbrated upon the mind.

How truly wonderful is the way of the Divine Love. His workings are too deep for the human understanding to discover of itself. That Holy Love which few seem yet to understand in its nature, doeth wondrous things for all His afflicted children ; and that Holy Wisdom which yet is but as foolishness unto so many, hath revealed the deep things of God.

The Washing of the Disciples' Feet

*Being an Allegory wherein is set forth the Manner
and Work of the Sin-offering, the laying aside
of the robes of Christhood and the pouring
out of the very Life in sublime Humiliation in order to accomplish the
Divine Will and make
possible the Re-
demption for
all Souls.*

A
AT THE LAST SUPPER

THE story of the Feetwashing recorded in the Fourth Gospel is one of peculiar interest. Its interest, however, does not lie in the supposed outward event, but in the inward spiritual experiences which are indicated. It was not an outward event, but an allegory of great and momentous experiences for the Master and the disciples.

The Feetwashing story is a precious gem. Its apparently insignificant details are invaluable assets. They are like the facets to the gem ; they are manifold reflectors of the light of heaven. In every one of them is the Divine Love revealed.

The allegory was one told by the Master near the close of the manifestation of the Christhood. It was spoken at what has come to be known as *The last supper in the upper room*. It was given under conditions the most sorrowful ; and it was addressed to the few friends who formed the innermost group. Those who heard the Master then could not fully enter into the complete understanding of the allegory, so profound were its meanings. But it impressed them deeply, and taught them much concerning the way of the Divine Love in accomplishing the redemption of all Souls.

How it is Misunderstood

" The last supper " was not any ordinary incident of religious import. It was an event such as the Churches have not even dimly perceived. Indeed, as yet, they have formed no true conception of it. They are under the impression that it was such a meal as the Jewish passover supper, and that the Holy Eucharist or Supper of the Lord was the concluding act. They associate it with things that were wholly outward and material, and attach to these a spiritual significance. But they have all been misled through the presentation of it in the synoptic Gospels. There the writers have made of it a meal taken by the Blessed Master and the disciples. And there is the like emphasis given to that view of it in the Corinthian Letters. The real Logia which were spoken through the blessed Master at the last supper, have been so broken up and changed by these writers, including Paul, that both Western and Eastern Churches have never known the nature of that last supper, nor the wonderful manifestation of the divine purpose contained in the whole event. Though they have had many of the precious Logia spoken in connection with the event, yet they have never read the Sayings with an understanding of their profound meaning ; for these have been applied to persons rather than to wonderful experiences into which the Soul of the Master was to enter—experiences through which He had passed in accomplishing the work which the Divine Father gave Him to do. They were applied in part to Peter the disciple ; in part to Judas, who was also a disciple, and who was represented as having betrayed the Master ; and there were other parts taken by Paul from the Logia of St. John and applied to his own experiences.

Thus it is that the last supper has *never* been understood by the Churches ; that the nature of " the feetwashing " has been misinterpreted ; that the character of the work by which the feetwashing was accomplished has been misunderstood ; and that the betrayal of the Master has been attributed to one who was not only a disciple of the Christhood, but a brother of the Master, and one who was beautiful in his love.

What was the Nature of it ?

The last supper was the most solemn of feasts. It was a service of the most sacred order. For was it not celebrated on the eve of the Lord's *passion* ? The little group of earnest longing Souls gathered together with a growing sense upon them of loss about to come, of great and poignant sorrows to be endured, of some deep mysterious anguish to be borne by the beloved one and shared by them, met as only Souls could meet who had known the Master, and who also knew that they were very soon to lose His presence from their midst. It was, therefore, no earthly feast in which they engaged, but one which was wholly spiritual. The hour was one of heavenly fellowship, though the things spoken of were of the saddest. Heaven overshadowed them with its glory; but the tragic Sin-offering cast its darkening shadow upon the group. The light divine threw its beautiful radiance within them all; yet they knew that the dark night would follow in which the shepherd of the sheep would be smitten. The glory of the Divine Love filled them; but they could not exult in the presence of the awful Mystery of the manifestation of that Love known as the Sin-offering. It was truly a feast of the Divine Love, one crowned with the light of the glory of God the Father-Mother; but the feast was within the Soul of each one present, and the bread and cup were those of the Life-Eternal and the Wine of Christ-hood. As the vehicle of the Divine Christ, the Master communicated these things to them; for they were to be sharers of the profound mystery, Souls who were indeed to drink of the same cup of whose full measure He had to partake, those who were prepared to receive a part of the baptism with which He was about to be baptized.

Oh, the sublimity of the vision of the Divine Love and Wisdom which then broke upon all who were present, and were made partakers of the supper!

The Wonderful Vision

The last supper was the last blessed spiritual feast which the disciples and the Master had together. Indeed it was the last spiritual feast which the beloved one was to enjoy before entering upon the Sin-offering work. The hour had come which called Him away to take up the work. The manifestation had been given of the sublime meaning of the Christhood ; but the manifestation was now about to pass with His own withdrawal. The transcendent vision had been revealed, and those who had beheld it with the " understanding " could never forget it. The way unto the realized consciousness of the Father-Mother had been made clear, and the process of the redemption obvious unto all who sought that blessed state in sincerity and truth. The inner meaning of the cross had been beautifully interpreted, from the first stage of self-denial to the last stage of the cross of Christhood. *The threefold path* had been portrayed and illustrated—purity, devotion, and love ; and all Souls might find their way back to the realization of the Presence within them.

But to accomplish this blessed work in its sublime fulness, more had yet to be done. The astral kingdom must needs be purified. The elemental world was full of principalities and powers whose dominion was great ; and these powers militated against the upwardness of all Souls. These were powers whose office was once beautiful, and whose ministry was intended to aid all Souls in the true evolution of their life ; but their nature had become changed when, in what is known as " the fall," the whole planetary system went wrong, and they ceased to obey the original divine laws. Through their changed condition they greatly oppressed all Souls. They so changed the inner impulse of the younger races of the children of the Planet that they came to follow paths which led them deeper and yet deeper into evil states, until they wrought upon the Planet such awful evil things as resulted in the terrible catastrophies indicated in the Old Testament stories of the Deluge, Sodom and Gomorrah. So tragic were the experiences through which they passed that the histories of them were written upon the astral kingdom of the Planet, and became " the handwritings " on " the middle wall or partition " of the planetary heavens, which were engraven against the Soul, and which prevented the Soul from rising up out of every evil thing to live the absolutely pure life and serve the divine. For, as we have elsewhere shown, these images or handwritings were all magnetic, and affected the spiritual magnetism of the individual life. And before the redemption could be an accomplished fact in the experience of every Soul, these conditions had to be changed, the images destroyed, " the handwritings " upon " the middle wall or partition " blotted out.

The Things which were Beheld

Now, it was this stupendous work which the Father had also given unto the Christ to do. And the wonderful vision that the disciples beheld on that memorable occasion was the way that such a momentous task was to be undertaken and accomplished. The Logia which were then spoken will best describe it. How burdened these were with a meaning whose nature was un-fathomable to all but those who were then called upon to drink of the cup of such Christhood, may be gathered from a prayerful perusal of them. Unfortunately for the whole world, and very specially for the religious communities which rose in the name of the Master, these most precious Logia were applied to an outward event, to persons, and to the Jewish Ceremonial Laws. The way of accomplishing the great work was changed from a divine drama enacted by the Christ-Soul through manifold lives whose action was upon the astral kingdom, into an event in the life of the Master during the divine manifestation. The Logia which revealed the nature of the betrayal, were also changed. They were made to apply to an outward event ; and the betrayer was made into a person who was also a disciple. Whereas, the betrayer was the astral kingdom, and the betrayal was through the power which that kingdom had over the various bodies into which the Soul of the Master had to be born for the work of the Sin-offering ; for the powers of that kingdom betrayed the Soul in every one of the lives that had to be lived, into the most terrible experiences of evil of every kind ; and it made these lives veritable burdens of sorrow and woe.

And likewise with those Logia which described *the nature of the work* upon " the middle wall or partition " of the planetary heavens ; they were taken by Paul from their setting in the Logia of St. John, and applied to the Jewish Ceremonial Law, the work accomplished being in Paul's view nothing more than the abolition of that Law as a binding ritual upon those who proclaimed themselves disciples of the Christ ; whereas it had relation to the changing of the middle heavens of the Planet by means of the destruction of the awful magnetic images upon them whose power was so great for evil, the overthrow of the unseen principalities whose rule had been so disastrous to the whole spiritual household of the Planet, and thus the blessed work whereby the astral kingdom was so changed for good that Souls could be approached from the heavens and ministered unto.

It is practically impossible for any one who was not of that inner group of Souls, to realize what the vision meant. For it was of such a nature that it made manifest at once the sublimity of the Christhood of the beloved one and the depth of *the divine passion* for Souls ; the glorious nature of Christhood, and the tragic character of the work of the redemption ; the wonderful exhibition of the Divine Love and Wisdom in the estates of Jesus and Christ, and in the process through which the whole spiritual system of the Planet was to be redeemed.

But in the " Sayings " that vision may be in some measure apprehended. The height and depth, the length and breadth of the Divine Love may be found expressed in them. The abounding riches of that Love, and the incomparable glory of the Divine Wisdom, will be obvious unto all who are able to spiritually discern. The true source of all Being, and the relation which all Souls sustain to that source, may be found most clearly revealed. The *Oneness* of all true life, and the unity of all Souls through that Oneness, may be perceived by the earnest seeker after divine realizations. The distinction which the Master drew between the world as a materialistic system, and the world from which He had come, will be most evident where there is the prayerful desire to know the inner meaning of the Sayings uttered by Him. It will be seen that this cosmos was a very different order from that kingdom whence He came. The experiences in this cosmos were also indicated in striking contrast to those experiences which came to the Soul who found the kingdom whence the Christ had come, showing that the present cosmos was not as the Divine Love and Wisdom had fashioned it, and that in its present state it imposed great tribulation upon the Soul. And (what is obvious throughout these Logia) it will be understood that the supreme purpose of the sublime manifestation was and is to gather Souls out of this cosmos or present order of things, into the kingdom of Christhood—the true kingdom of the Soul.

B

MAJESTIC STOOPING

IN the vision we behold the majesty of the Divine Love and the profound humiliation of the Christ-Soul. The allegory of the teacher stooping to bathe the feet of his disciples reveals these. The allegory illustrates what the Divine Love had purposed to do for all Souls. It made manifest unto those present what was required to be done, and how it was to be accomplished ; for all of them had been taught by the Master the inner meaning of the terms which He used. The unrobing, the girding of the loins, the pouring out of water into an empty laver ; the wonderful humility of the Soul in acting the part of a servant ; the cleansing of the feet ; the opposition of Simon Peter, with his subsequent desire to have not only his feet bathed, but likewise his hands and his head ; the remarkable saying of the Christ-Soul concerning His action—these are full of deep mystery, mystery whose unravelling has been impossible to the Soul until now.

So profound are the meanings set forth in these apparently simple details of what is supposed to have been a material event, that the Soul feels overwhelmed by the vision of them when they are rightly understood. Surely there never was such stooping to the dire needs of others as is here revealed ! There could not be a more profound manifestation of love in the whole of the universe, than this most wonderful voluntary humiliation. The depth of it, notwithstanding the awful darkness into which it took the Christ-Soul, is sublime. Those who here attain to the true vision of that most wonderful stooping, will be filled with the Divine Awe. Unto them will the Divine Love appear in a new and more glorious light ; and the hidden purposes of the Wisdom of God will stand out as gloriously as does the Sun in mid-heavens when the dark clouds have all passed, and his splendour is no longer intercepted and blotted out.

Verily, in relation to the wonderful vision of that glorious Love it has been even as the Winter of the Soul with all the heavens laden with dense clouds ; for the Lord as the Sun has been obscured, and His blessed purposes have been unknown. Men have guessed at them. The truly spiritual have felt that they were wonderful, though they could not understand them all. The mystic Souls have always sought for a meaning beyond anything the schools knew, and one which would not dishonour the Divine Love nor violate the innate sense of righteousness within them. They have tried to interpret *the passion of the Lord* in a larger way, a more divine and soullic way, than the schools have done. They have sensed the spiritual mystery ; though they have been unable to behold what it was. They have proclaimed that the Wisdom of God was not circumscribed in the way that the historical setting represented the sufferings of the Master, and that there were depths in the tragic Sin-offering surpassing anything portrayed in the outward history of the betrayal, trial and crucifixion. But who could have dreamed that there were such depths as are revealed in these recovered Logia? Who could have imagined the stupendous nature of the stooping of the Divine Love through the Christ Soul? None, unless it had been given them to behold it, *to know in very deed the Grace that was in the Lord Christ Jesus.*

It was of the Divine Love that the little inner group were privileged to witness the wonderful vision, and to hear the profound Logia concerning the accomplishment of the Divine Purpose by means of the Sin-offering; and it is alone through that same Love and Wisdom in all His graciousness toward us that we have been able to recover that past, and to present once more the most beautiful vision, to interpret anew those wonderful Logia which were spoken at that most eventful gathering, in order that *all may come to know the grace of the Lord Christ Jesus who, " though He was rich toward God," yet for this Planet's sake impoverished Himself that all Souls might be enriched.*

The Unrobing of the Christ

In the allegory the Teacher laid aside his garments and girt his loins with a towel. It was a picture of what the Master was about to do. He knew not only what was awaiting Him, but how He would have to receive it. The Gethsemane had revealed to Him the coming events, and He knew what was required of Him. He knew that He would have to descend from the high estate of His Christhood and enter into the low estates of this world; that He would have to lay aside His wonderful Christhood, and take up the lives represented by these low estates; that He would have to divest Himself of His glorious attributes in order to assume the life of all who had gone down even into the lowest hell-states. For the great work He had given Him to do could only be accomplished in this way.

The descent into " the lower parts of the earth " had, therefore, a significance more profound than that generally attributed to it. For " the lower parts " were the hell-states, and not the mere tomb. To lead " captivity " captive or into a new form of captivity, He had to descend to where the captivity was, and enter the states of the captives. In this way alone was He able to break up the conditions by which the captives were held, and make it possible for them to free themselves and rise out of the hell states. For it was in these acts of such wonderful humiliation that the graven images upon the astral kingdom or " middle wall or partition " were destroyed.

Thus the descent of the beloved one will be seen to have been very real. It will be understood in its true light. It will be beheld as something infinitely greater than the conception of that descent which the western world has held, and still holds. The impoverishment of the Christ will have new and deeper meaning given to it. The stooping will be seen and proclaimed majestic. The drama of the Sin-offering will henceforth be known to have been in every way worthy of God.

C

THE POURING OUT OF THE WATER

IF the unrobing or laying aside of the attributes of His Christhood meant so much, and the girding of His loins contained the mystery of His unspeakable limitations ; what shall be said of His pouring out the water for purification into the laver, and then lowly kneeling in great humiliation to wash the feet of the disciples ? Who is prepared to believe our report of all that the beloved Master said concerning the inner meaning of the action of the teacher portrayed in the allegory ? Unto whom will the arm of the Lord stand revealed in the vision which we are giving of that wonderful graciousness which led Him to take so lowly a position as to stoop to the needs of every one who needed aid to find the way back to the Father ? Who is prepared to believe our report of this marvellous transaction by which means were provided whereby the feet of those who were to be called His disciples, might be cleansed ? Unto whom may the vision we give reveal how mightily the arm of the Lord contended with all the evil conditions found upon " the middle wall or partition," how the Divine Love cleansed that part of the Planet's circulus from evil images, and prepared the way for the approach of heaven with its beautiful angelic ministry unto Souls ?

Our message is a sublime one. It bears within itself the Love and Wisdom of the Divine One. It is not of the nature of a phantasmagoria such as the theory is which is known as the Rectoral view of the Sin-offering, wherein the righteousness of the Eternal One becomes a mere display in order to overawe Souls and impress them with the Divine Awfulness, and His determination to punish sin. It is not like the ways of the buyer and seller of goods, the commutation of debts for an equivalent received, the forgiveness of human guilt because one most noble Son of the Father has loved the whole race unto the outpouring of His life even unto spiritual death, in order to cancel the indebtedness, as the vast majority of the Churches more or less believe. It is rather the vision of the Divine Love in and through the Master recognising the needs of all the fallen children of the Father, identifying Himself with the children and their needs, and carrying out the purpose of the Divine Wisdom in so fully identifying Himself as to enter into their very conditions. For the action of the Christ-Soul is the manifestation of the very real " identification " of the Divine Love with the low estate of all His children, and the performance of that great work by means of which the redemption of them all is to be effected.

How the inner group marvelled when the beloved one spake of the Divine purpose, and interpreted for them the meaning of the Logia! It seemed more than they could fully apprehend then, so great was the truth revealed, so stupendous was the work to be accomplished in realizing the divine purpose. But the water was poured out for them. The picture of the coming unrobing and girding of the loins was succeeded by that of the outpouring of the water into the laver for purification. For the water was the Divine Truth, the cleanser of life, the purifier of body and mind, the water of the redemption poured out from the sacred chalice of the Divine Love into the laver of the human mind, and applied to life by the Divine-Christ in every one, and especially to "the spiritual understanding" by which alone, when purified, the highest Love and Wisdom can be understood. The truth concerning the divine purpose was revealed. The truth about the way of the Divine Love was unveiled. The truth relating to the way of the Soul's return unto the Father was made manifest. The truth revealing the *oneness* of all true being was unfolded in the most beautiful way. The truth of the inter-relation of all Souls, and of all Souls unto the Divine Father, was made obvious in the awe-inspiring message which was then given. The truth concerning the very nature of the Soul as the sanctuary of the Divine Presence, and the regaining of the consciousness of that Holy Presence by the Soul when it would know itself to be one with the Father, was beautifully unfolded.

Such truth in its blessed manifoldness, and poured out with such a divine fulness, was to operate as a great purifier of the spiritual understanding, as the cleanser of the ways of life in all who would deign to follow the Nazarene into pure paths, who would seek out the Christ unto the finding of the Christ-hood life and service, and who would follow on to know the Lord as the most sublime inward realization of the Divine Presence. Within the sanctuary of the Soul the Divine Presence abides. The shekinah is there ; the overshadowing is found there ; there is the cloud of the Lord upon the innermost sanctuary. But in the more outward court of the mind is the laver, the receiver of truth from without when the light of the innermost sanctuary is grown dim, the sacred vessel which must be kept pure for the water of truth which the Divine Love is ever ready to pour into it through His Christ unto the purification of the whole of life.

D

THE REQUEST OF SIMON PETER

THE strong personal note in the fourth Record prevents the reader from grasping the wonderful meaning expressed in the request of Simon Peter. It is another striking instance of how the most sacred Logia have been lost, how their meanings have been changed from spiritual qualities and experiences into things material. For though there was a disciple of the Master named Peter, one greatly beloved and who loved the Master greatly, yet it was not unto him that the words were spoken by the beloved one ; nor was it he who made the strange request. The story, as we have pointed out to the reader, was an allegory told by the Master ; and the terms used in it were such as the disciples of the inner group understood.

The term which has been rendered Peter, meant the spiritual understanding, the cleansing of which was the last office in the work of purification on the part of the Christ. The allegory illustrated the process. The work of the Sin-offering had proceeded far ere that part was reached in which the purification of the understanding began. It will not be difficult for those who have been awakened in these latter days to high spiritual consciousness, who have left the graves of material bondage wherein they were entombed, and have risen into the glorious light and liberty of children of God, to now discern the inner meaning of the saying, " *Then cometh He to Simon Peter.*" For it is only in these latter days that the spiritual understanding is becoming purified in its visions of life and service. It is only in these latter days that the Christ-Soul reached that point in His great Office of Redeemer when the spiritual understanding could be approached for purposes of purification with any hope of success. We speak not only of individuals, but of the universal consciousness and spiritual mind of the whole of the Planet's spiritual system ; for that blessed work which is now in process of accomplishment as the outcome of the great work of the tragic Sin-offering, could only be wrought when the conditions of the astral kingdom were purified. The spiritual mind could not receive the sacred water from the chalice of the Divine Love, until the lower spheres of the astral world were cleansed of the fearful evil images which had been fashioned upon them long ages ago.

The Understanding of the West

The washing of the feet of Peter has, therefore, a deep significance. The cleansing of the spiritual understanding through the water of truth from the chalice of the Divine Love has a meaning of paramount importance, especially for the western world. That world long ages ago professed to discern and receive the Christ ; and it has continued to do so throughout what has been named the Christian Era, an era which should have been one of Christhood seeking by that world. It professed the Christhood without understanding its meaning ; and even yet it is hard to impress upon its consciousness that sad fact. It has shown by its religious history that it was quite unable to discern who and what the blessed Master was, and what was the meaning of the wonderful Christhood manifestation through Him. Its spiritual understanding has never been one to truly apprehend the meanings associated with the manifestation, or it would never have lived the life it has done and which it has taught others to do, nor have so ostentatiously gloried in the more outward aspects of the kingdom which it has reared in the name of the Master. Had it perceived who and what He was, it would have known that all its ways must be purified. It would have understood the redeemed life, have sought the beautiful ways of that Life, and shown to the whole world that Christianity was not only the crown of all other forms of religious expression, but that it gathered up into itself all the others, that its foundations were laid in purity of life, purity of love, and purity of action. It would have made manifest unto all peoples that Christhood meant compassion unto all Souls without distinction of race or nationality or country, and pity unto all the creatures. It would have revealed unto the whole world that the Christhood had its foundations in divine goodness and righteousness, that it knew but One Life in the heavens and on the earth, though the manifestations of that one life were infinitely varied; that the human races were all one great family, and that the divine Father loved them all and forgot none. Indeed had the Christhood been truly perceived and understood by the West, its countries would have been the scenes of the most beautiful Individual, Family, Social and National life; veritable homes where the paradisaical life was experienced once more; social centres where the people had no tragedies in the way, but where life's drama was angelic; nations whose God was the Lord, and not the Beelzebub of strife, the Mammon of Gold, and the Dragon of material power and dominion.

CHRISTIANITY MINUS REDEMPTION

But the western world could not perceive the meaning of the Christhood because its spiritual understanding was uncleansed. It could not perceive the meaning of the process of cleansing implied in the Sin-offering, because it had a false view given to it by Paul, an apostle who had not known the Master nor understood His teachings. And not until this age, indeed, not until these days, has it had presented to its vision who and what the Master was, and what was the meaning of the sublime manifestation through Him. As a result of the astral influences upon it, and the blindness of its teachers, that world has made of Christianity a new set of beliefs with ritual adapted to these, rather than the most beautiful of lives and the sublimest of all the sublime ideals the world has ever known. It has believed in a Christ whose Christhood it has never understood ; in a world-redemption which, however much of mystery was made to surround it, was hypothetical rather than real, theological more than a matter of life-realization. Purification has never been understood by it ; had it been so, the gross systems of eating and drinking, with the markets these have created with their attendant evils, could never have found the places which now they occupy, nor made their ramifications penetrate the whole of the States and Churches. With a true conception of the purification of life, such conditions as are implied in distilleries, breweries and wine-palaces, modern cattle traffic, abattoirs and shambles, vivisection and its laboratories with their persecuting high priests, the impoverishment of the weak and defenceless for the enrichment of the strong and fortunate, could have found no place in the various states, no encouragement or shelter from the various Churches, and no apologists in the name of the Divine Love.

PURIFYING THE CHURCHES

But it is now Simon Peter's turn. The spiritual understanding *must* be cleansed, otherwise there can be no true relationship to the Christhood. Whilst it remains uncleansed, there can be no true realization of the Christhood fellowship. To the western world the Christ has once more come, not as a person, but as a divine illumination and power restoring the vision of Christhood to the Soul, and interpreting anew the true laws of spiritual being ; and we can even now hear that world, as embodied in the various Churches, saying to the Christ, as the disciple is said to have spoken to the Teacher in the allegory, " *Dost thou wash my feet ?* " For it is with very great astonishment that the Churches hear the glorious message of the new process of cleansing which is now come to them all. The new light which is being so gloriously poured upon the world, and that from East to West and North to South, is revealing to the Churches by slow degrees the things they ought always to have known, and the life they always should have experienced. They have indeed been tardy to recognize how great the need was for a *real* cleansing of their life from the innermost to the outermost spheres. In their blindness they cannot behold what they should always have been, namely, communities through whose members the redeemed life was interpreted and the Christhood revealed ; for knowing neither they have failed in both.

Even now it is most difficult to impress the Churches with the true view of redemption, and to get them to understand the true meaning of purity, compassion and pity. They do profess these qualities ; yet they follow the ways of the barbaric and the carnivorous in their living, ignorant of the fact that the lives of the creatures are sacred unto Him who fashioned them, and that He cannot regard any one who does not think of them and shelter them from *every* form of cruelty, as truly pitiful and merciful. They would be merciful ; yet are they thoughtlessly unmerciful. They would be children of the All-pitying One ; yet do they fail to spread forth the wings of a true and beautiful pity. They would be sealed as followers of the Compassionate One ; yet understand they not how divinely full are the ways of compassion. They would be even as the One in whom they profess belief ; yet do they reject the ways of life by which alone any Soul can find its redemption, that way of life unto which the blessed Master called all Souls. Nay, they will not hear the message which comes from that past, because they are not yet able to see the true meaning of the Way of Life.

THE REQUEST OF AWAKENED SOULS

When a Soul is truly awake, it desires not only to have its feet cleansed, but, like the teacher's disciple, to have cleansed also the hands and the head. Its great yearning is to be purified from the innermost to the outermost spheres of life. To cleanse the hands is to make pure all life's actions. To bathe the head is to purify the thoughts of the mind. And to wash the feet of Simon Peter is to make the ways of the spiritual understanding pure. Some are willing to cleanse the outer without touching the inner. They are willing to go part of the way. And there are many who are willing to have inward purification if only they are allowed to follow the ways of life pursued by the world in their manner of living.

But when the spiritual understanding is made pure, all the spheres of life become pure as a natural sequence. When the feet of Simon Peter are bathed, the whole Soul-system is made clean. For when the understanding is purified and illumined, the Soul sees the meaning of her life upon every sphere, and brings all thoughts, feelings and actions upon these spheres into perfect harmony with the vision within. For the divine vision is restored unto the Soul. No longer is the mind like a veiled mirror unable to reflect, or a mirror whose surface is so affected by the elemental or astral kingdom that its reflections are untrue ; but it is a mirror so pure and true that it is able to reflect divine things correctly, even glories upon glories as they fall upon it from the Lord. When a man's understanding is purified, bathed in the water of truth poured out from the Divine Chalice, he sees to it that every power of life is also purified. He feels that he cannot pause anywhere until the work of purification upon the entire system is accomplished. He must needs obey the voice which then speaks to him from within the sanctuary of his Being.

O glorious and blessed vision of life from the divine kingdom ! Happy indeed are they who behold, and enter into realization !

Theirs is the kingdom, and the power, and the glory, which the Divine Love begetteth within the Soul and revealeth unto the Spirit.

E
THE ONE WHO BETRAYED

THE betrayal of the Christ is a subject that has provoked the profoundest interest. It is surrounded with incidents the most touching and pathetic. The story told in the four evangelists with their varying details, has awakened very real sorrow in many hearts, and dimmed with tears many eyes. Not a few are the Souls who have been moved by the picture portrayed in these Records, to have unbounded compassion for the Christ and unlimited condemnation for the betrayer. The vision of the betrayal is the most unhappy scene in the whole history of the Christ ; and upon the one who betrayed there is set a seal that fills the reader with the sense of an inexplicable mystery. For is it not written of the betrayal that it was divinely appointed ? and of the betrayer that he was chosen for the purpose ? Yet the full burden of responsibility is made to light upon the erring one, and the most awful woe is pronounced concerning him. He was selected to be the instrument, yet he was made the subject of the world's most scathing judgment and scorn.

If the presentation in the Records were correct, the man would have been one whose fate was the most appalling and the most pitiable, the most sad and the most unjust. If the story were historically true, it would be a blot upon the beautiful Divine Love and the wonderful Christhood. To have been fashioned for such a work as is therein set forth, would have been the most cruel ; and to have been chosen by the beloved Master in order to ultimately betray Him, would surely have been the most unlovely conduct on His part.

Did the writers of these Records understand what they were writing when they made such a presentation ? And did they know who Judas was whose name they found attached to this story in the first Gospel record written for the Churches.[1]

THINGS ARE NOT AS PRESENTED

The betrayal was not of the personal nature recorded in these Records, and the betrayer was not the disciple named Judas. The betrayal was something far more terrible than any mere betrayal of the Master to the Jews ; and the betrayer was a far more potent factor for evil than any one man. What was done was a stupendous thing which would have made any outward historical betrayer appear insignificant. There was a betrayal, but it was of the most overwhelming character ; there was a betrayer, but he was infinitely more powerful and subtle than any disciple.

It is quite true that the Master was betrayed to the Jews, and by the Jews to the world-powers, and that together they tried and condemned Him ; but the betrayal was not effected in the manner presented in the Records, nor were the condemnation and crucifixion such as are found and described there. The betrayal of the Master which is signified, was that accomplished by him who wrote the Record from which the materials for the four Gospels were taken, when the Logia were made to refer to outward instead of inward events ; and the betrayal of the Christ which is implied was accomplished when the false view of Christhood was presented to the Soul. But the betrayer was not even the writer of the Record which formed the basis of the four Gospels, nor the writer of the astounding Letters sent out in Paul's name. The betrayer was the astral kingdom.

---

[1] The first Gospel record written for the Churches was founded upon the Gospel written by St. Matthew and the Logia of St. John. That Gospel has also been recovered in these days, and is now known as *The Gospel of the Holy Twelve*. It was from this latter Gospel that the present received records were built up.

It was that kingdom which first betrayed the writers into ways of life that made spiritual illumination impossible, and prevented them from understanding the inner significance of the teachings found in the original Gospel by St. Matthew, and the Logia of St. John. The Christhood was betrayed to the vision of those Jews who wrote the historical life of the Master, because the astral kingdom dominated them and miraged the truth ; materializing what was entirely spiritual ; making personal those things which were individual, soullic, and divine ; turning universal soul-truths into local events, and destroying the vision of the Christhood so effectively that that vision has not been known again until these days, notwithstanding all the centuries of supposed Christian influence and teaching in the western world since the days of the manifestation.

The Betrayal a Momentous Thing

Thus will it be seen that, even from an historical point of view, the betrayal of the Master through the misrepresentation of His life, and the betrayal of the Christhood through the misuse of the Logia, was a much more momentous affair than selling the information of the whereabouts of the Master to the jealous and blind members of the Sanhedrin, an affair whose results have been tragically far reaching in that the whole western world was misled and deceived as to the meaning of the redemption which was to be accomplished for and in all Souls, the nature of the Christhood itself, and the Sin-offering to be accomplished.

Yet was the betrayal of the Soul of the beloved one still more momentous and tragic. These things were done to the vision of the redeemed life, which had been so beautifully interpreted, and to the Christhood, which had been so wonderfully manifested ; and the Souls of the Father's children who were to have been helped were deprived of those necessary visions, and in this way were impoverished.

But the yet deeper betrayal brought impoverishment to the Master. He who was rich in all things of the Divine nature, was made poor in His unique endeavours to aid the human races. For the astral kingdom depleted Him of all His divine attributes which He had acquired as He rose from sphere to sphere, kingdom to kingdom, and glory to glory. He had risen on to the divine kingdom to be one with the Father ; and the powers gained through that transcendent life He laid aside that He might become one with all the children of the Father who were lost amid the darkness of the spiritual wilderness. From the high estate of the divine kingdom which His Christhood represented, did He descend to the low estates in which all Human Souls were, that He might find for them a way of return unto the household of the Father.

It was through the astral world that the way lay through which He must needs pass. And it was as He passed from state to state, changing the astral conditions and purifying that kingdom, that He was depleted of His strength and impoverished in the way, because He had to give of His powers for the work which had to be accomplished. The betrayer pursued Him with remorseless ardour ; betrayed Him in every state into which He entered ; buffeted and scourged Him ; smote Him in railing mockery ; followed Him with relentless vigour from the hour of the laying aside of the Christhood garments (the divine raiment that adorned Him), until the Sin-offering was accomplished.

Through such a betrayal on the part of the astral kingdom, the Master had laid upon Him stupendous burdens, the weight and suffering of which were mightily increased through the betrayal of those who wrote the Records which the western world accepts as true portraitures of Him and His work, but in which His beautiful life is misrepresented, and the wonderful vision of the Christhood obscured. For had not those who were sincerely desirous of following the Christhood been so woefully deceived regarding the nature of the redeemed life which He so perfectly interpreted, there would have grown up communities of men and women who would have lived the life of true purity, compassion and pity, and have thus influenced the rest of the world ; the true vision of Christhood would have been understood and experienced by many ; the present semi-material religious communities would never have been called into existence ; the outward kingdom would not have been sought after ; nor would the beloved one have been left so absolutely bereft of aid from without when He arose out of the states in the various lives which He lived whilst performing the Office of the Cross in the awful Sin-offering.

The betrayal of the Christ-Soul strikes a deeper note than any one could have imagined who did not know the blessed Master, and who knew not the inner meaning of the profound " Sayings " concerning it. It sounded the very depths of His love for Souls and His devotion to the divine purpose. It tried Him unto the very uttermost, even until He would at times fain have sunk into utter unconsciousness in order to lose the awful sense of the spiritual impoverishment, suffering, sorrow and dire anguish, which were His portion in all the ages of this era since the days of the wonderful manifestation until these later days which have witnessed the completion of the stupendous task.

O ye who would truly understand this most wonderful of Mysteries, let true reverence fill your Souls ! Know that the arm of the Lord of Hosts is not shortened that He cannot save His children, but that He has, unto that end, accomplished through that One who bore the burden, great things for us, whereof we are glad.

F

ISCARIOT THE SON OF SIMON

IN the records it is stated with recurrent persistency that the betrayer was Judas Iscariot, the son of Simon. But, as we have already pointed out, there was only one Judas amongst the disciples, and He was of the Master's brethren. Why he should have been chosen by the writer of the first Record to be the butt and scorn of the world, may not be told here. But it was a great mistake, a cruel blunder which has had disastrous effects upon the whole western world, inasmuch as it misled all who accepted the statement as true, turned their thoughts towards a man who had been a disciple of the Master, causing them to think evilly of him, and to miss the deep meaning implied in the statement that the betrayer was Iscariot, Simon's son.

For poor Judas or Jude the day of rectification is come. The affliction which overtook him as the result of such blundering on the part of the writer of that Record, was terrible ; but the day of the restoration has come for him. He did go out in the night overwhelmed by the awful report which was spread abroad that he had betrayed the beloved one, and took away his earthly life. He could not bear the thought that he had had such dishonour heaped upon him. And so the Records have the truth in part, when they state that Judas went out into the night and took away his life. But they are wrong when they affirm that he was full of remorse, for he had none, having nothing over which to feel remorseful. But he was full of inexpressible anguish ; and that affected him so greatly that his mind gave way under the strain, with the result which we have named. The Record writer knew not what it was that he did when he wrote of Judas as the one who outwardly betrayed the Master to the Jews. For he not only misled the whole western world as to the meaning of the betrayal, but he caused a most precious life to pass through untold suffering.

WHAT ISCARIOT MEANT

What the writer of the Record found when " The Life " of the blessed Master, which was written by St. Matthew, fell into his hands, he did not understand. He took it to refer to an outward event. The coming of Iscariot, Simon's son, to betray, was the coming of no man amongst the group who had known the beloved one, but the coming of the new conditions into which the Soul had to enter. Those readers who have followed these unfoldments of the Master's Teachings, will be able to recall the explanation which we gave of the term Simon. *Iscariot the son of Simon is a state of the lower mind.* Simon means a mind turned towards material things. Simon (Peter), whom Satan desired to possess that he might sift as wheat, was the spiritual understanding turned unto the conditions represented by the term Simon ; and Peter was that understanding illumined. Iscariot represented that wholly worldly state born within the mind that has become enslaved to the outward and sense-life, the mind that calculates the outward value of any precious ointment of loving service rendered unto the Divine Love, and would turn it into a material value for other uses.

The mind of the first Sin-offering life into which the beloved one was born that He might carry the burden of the Sin-offering, was such a mind. It was a Simon mind giving birth to all those feelings implied in Iscariot. It represented a mind whose chief joy was to traffic in things sensuous. It was a mind full of the guile of the world, loving the night rather than the day, in a spiritual sense, because its deeds were of an evil order. Not that He ever came to love evil in any degree ; for there was no desire for wrong in Him even whilst the terrible lives in which the Sin-offering had to be made, were lived. He did no

491

sin, neither was there deceit found in Him, when the judgment of the heavens fell upon those lives ; for the Soul was ever yearning for the way of goodness and purity even whilst the outward personality sought the ways of the world. " He who knew no sin was made in the likeness of sinful flesh " that He might carry " the burden of the iniquity of the people," and through the flesh destroy him who had gained the dominion over the people, the astral power known as Satan, the great tempter and destroyer of the Soul. In a planetary sense the astral kingdom was Iscariot the betrayer and destroyer. In an individual sense it is the same. Iscariot, or the astral in any one when responding to the astral kingdom, becomes the Soul's betrayer and destroyer. And as in a planetary sense so in the individual ; only the Christ has power over it. Only the Christ within can destroy its power. Iscariot is the son of Simon within the individual system, just as he is within the planetary system. He is the creation of a mind turned so much outward that the polarity of the life is inverted or reversed. He was the son of perdition, being the offspring of our fallen state, individual and planetary. He first came into existence when the mind of the Planet went wrong, and all the elemental world was changed in its nature. That was the beginning of this cosmos concerning which the Master spake. And from the beginning of his career as a power in the Planet independent of the true spiritual forces which flowed into the system from the Divine Kingdom, he was a betrayer and deceiver, the father of lies and every evil thing.

It will now be obvious what was meant in the Logia by the betrayal and the betrayer. Iscariot will be seen and understood in his true light ; and no innocent disciple will be held up to the scorn and repudiation of the world—though verily that same world at the same time repudiates all that the Christhood meant. And it will likewise be apparent unto all who are equal to the study of those profound Logia, and to the discernment of their inner meanings, how it was that Satan entered into Iscariot on the eve of the Lord's Passion.

G

THE PROMISE OF A FULL UNDERSTANDING BY AND BY

IN the allegory it is stated that the Teacher said unto the disciple that what was done to him he could not understand then, but he would understand by and by; and herein was illustrated much that was spoken by the Master unto that consecrated and devoted circle. There were depths of meaning in the Logia which those who heard Him could not then sound, sayings whose full significance it was beyond them to grasp at the time. The Master knew this, and so He anticipated it. He prepared them for it, and filled them with the great hope that all things would at last be made clear. They were to understand by and by what things were about to happen unto Him, and the full extent of the betrayal that was even then at the doors awaiting Him; and awaiting them also. The Christhood was to be withdrawn. The Soul had to set out on a long lonely journey. The betrayer was already at work preparing to sell Him to the Jews that they might condemn His Christhood through their misrepresentation of it; and crucify Him in the sight of all the world by destroying the beautiful vision of the redeemed life which He had given to the Soul, and the true meaning of the Christhood. And for the second part of the tragedy the betrayer was likewise preparing; for all the forces of the astral kingdom were marshalled to smite Him in His own Soul-life as He performed the work of the Sin-offering.

But they were to come into the full knowledge of all these things by and by. The Holy Spirit was to bring all things to their remembrance, whatsoever He had said unto them. That Holy Spirit was the Paraclete who dwelt within the

Soul's sanctuary. He proceeded from the Father, and spoke not of Himself, but of the things of the Father ; and He would testify of the Christ. He would at last *show them all things*. He would enable them to understand those things which then were not clear because of the very profundity of their meaning.

Verily the Logia were rich in promise as well as in significance : promise whose fulfilment is now ; significance whose depths we have only of late been able to touch. Marvellous indeed are those Logia for the great wealth of their revelation concerning the Soul, and the Divine Presence within the sanctuary of every one. They are *the true Gnosis*, the very heart of all true knowledge concerning the way of the Divine Love. They are the true revelation of the nature of the Divine Love and Wisdom, and the inherent nature of the human Soul. They contain not only glints and gleanings of the Soul's historic past, but revelations of its relation to the Divine Father-Mother. In them the present cosmic conditions are shown to be other than those which the ever Blessed One purposed ; and it is obvious from them that these conditions have had much to do with the state of the human Soul all through the untold ages since the days of the descent of the whole planetary system in what is now regarded as " the fall." The cause of the deep tribulation of life was to be found in them. " *In this cosmos ye shall have tribulation ; but be of cheerful heart, for through the Christhood ye shall overcome.*" Between the conditions of the present cosmos and the true conditions of life for the Soul, there was obvious antagonism. The elements of the one were opposed to those of the other. The powers within the cosmos were at variance with those of the Soul. But through attaining to the Christhood they would overcome. To the Christhood the elements were submissive. The storm-spirits ceased their revelry, and the tumultuous waters became calm, when the power of Christhood was manifested. Over the Christhood state the enemy had no power. He had no power over the Christ until it was given from above. And it was given him from above only through the laying aside of the Christhood attributes that the Soul might be buffeted and scourged by the astral powers during the work of the Sin-offering.

So the way of victory, was the way of Christhood. In the Christ-hood state the Soul would find Life, even the abundant Life. In that holy estate the Soul would be one with the Father, even as He was one.

PART V.

Allegories of the Soul's Awakening

By Jacob's Well

Being an Account of the Soul's Journey through Samaria on the Way back to Galilee ; and having special relation to the burden of the Sin-offering, showing the Meaning of the Return of the Soul to the Consciousness of Christhood.

A

THE STORY IN THE FOURTH RECORD

THE story told in the Fourth Record, concerning the Woman of Samaria and the Master, is remarkable in many ways. There is in it so much truth that it appeals to the Soul. There is something fascinating in the pictures presented as, dioramically, they pass before the vision. There is first of all the picture of the beloved Master sitting by an historic well, resting Himself in the midst of Samaria through which it is said " He must needs " pass on His way to Galilee. That is followed by the setting forth of the disciples to find provision for themselves and Him. Then we have the coming of the woman to draw water, and the astounding revelations made to her. That is followed by the return of the disciples with food and the departure of the woman for the city, issuing in the woman's return with many others to hear the new message. And we have the interlude during which the Master said some deep things to the disciples.

The tableaux are wonderful ; the events are dramatic ; the dialogues are profound. There is pathos and there is majesty in the picture of the Master. The human element is emphasized in the conduct of the disciples who leave Him that they may go in search of food, and, upon their return, seem surprised that He could be sustained without having partaken of such food as they deemed necessary for sustenance. In the woman there is a wonderful display of feeling after the highest things, combined apparently with a low moral estate ; a remarkable candour in her answers and abandon in her attitude, and great strength of purpose made manifest in her questions and action. The whole drama is most picturesque and fascinating ; and in the subject-matter of the conversations we have given vistas of life under conditions both earthly and heavenly.

THE STORY TRANSFORMED

The whole story as told in the fourth Record is a remarkable one, and in some respects seems almost impossible. There is such a strange intermixture of the earthly and the heavenly, of the lowest and the highest, of the dominant outer sense-life and the latent sense of the divine life, on the part of the woman ; and on the part of the Master, a remarkable weariness of body combined with striking power of endurance which enabled Him to forego nourishment, an apparent lassitude in the body and mind which was superseded by inward strength and fitness for the work He was accomplishing.

All these things should impress the reader with the feeling that the story is not what it seems to be. And therein would the reader judge rightly ; for it is not such a story as the narrative would seem to indicate. It is no plain statement of things which occurred upon the physical planes, notwithstanding the very real human elements in the story. However profoundly interesting the narrative may appear, considered as an outward history of events in the life of the Master, the interest is deepened unspeakably when we behold the true meanings underlying the apparently outward events. For the history is spiritual. It is of the Soul. It concerns the travail of the Christ. *The events are related to the Sin-offering.* In no ordinary sense is it personal. When understood, the local environment gives place to great spiritual verities. The saying of the Christ becomes clear in its meaning, that *He must needs go through Samaria.* Jacob's well is no longer an earthly spring supplying water to assuage the body-thirst, but such a spring as the readers of the story have never even dreamed of. The awful weariness of the Christ has a new meaning given to it, and how it was that He came to seek rest by Jacob's well. The coming of the Samaritan woman to draw water from the well has new light shed upon it, so that its personal and outward history is superseded by its true inward impersonal and soulic meaning.

The whole story becomes like a transformation scene as the veil of its earthly elements is drawn aside, and its spiritual nature and divine significance are beheld.

The " Must-Needs " of the Christ

" *And He must needs go through Samaria.*" This is not the only instance in which it is stated that the Christ must needs do something. There was a " must needs " in His going to Jerusalem to be betrayed at the hands of the chief priests and scribes, to suffer many things through them, to be condemned and crucified. There was a " must needs " in His going away from the Christhood manifestation, and leaving the disciples for a time to pursue a path whither they could not then follow Him. There was a " must needs " for Him to keep the Feast before His " going hence," for which beautiful purpose He went up to the Temple of the Lord. There was a " must needs " for Him to partake of " the Passover " with His disciples in order that they might share the profound mystery which it signified.

The depths of meaning implied in all these things could never be fathomed by the human mind. No man of himself could know them. There are no materials at hand in the ordinary human life experience by means of which these depths could possibly be sounded. For these depths gathered into themselves the deep waters of experience through which all Souls passed upon this spiritual system. They contained not the experience of one Soul upon the Planet, but of all Souls. They contained the depth of *all the various states* into which those Souls had descended. For these " must needs " all relate to the tragic Sin-offering, to the descent of the Soul from the Christhood into the various states which had to be entered in the accomplishing of the work of the Sin-offering. And it is of the Divine Love and Wisdom that we now know these things. Of Him alone are we able to enter into the understanding of the marvellous things of which the Sin-offering speaks. From Him only does the light shine within us, that light which maketh all things clear, which causeth the night to pass and the day to break, which also maketh the long drawn out shadows to flee away as before a glorious dawn. In Him and through Him alone who is the light of life, have we arrived at the meaning of the profound mystery, at the sounding of those depths which no one of himself could fathom. It is marvellous in our eyes that He should have chosen us as His instrument to proclaim His way, to show forth *how* He accomplished salvation for us, and to make clear the way by which the Soul must return to her ancient inheritance. For His ways are indeed most wonderful, and are such as no man could understand unless it were given him from above. To see the inner meaning of such a story as we have now to expound, is to be overwhelmed with the wonder of it all that it could ever have taken place, that the beloved Master should have had such a work to perform, that the conditions upon this Planet could ever have been such as to make it necessary for Him or any divine Soul to enter into the awful states implied in the story.

To draw aside the veil that the truth may be now known, is no light task. It has made demands upon him who records these things from which he would fain have known some way of escape. The pain, the sorrow, the anguish of it all as its adumbrations fell upon him, were too terrible to be described, and too awful to be realized except by those who have in some measure shared the burden of travail. The joy of the wine of God with which the Soul was filled from the Divine Love when it awoke to the vision of Christhood and its powers, had to give place to the greater work of entering into the meaning of such a Christhood as that of the blessed Master's. The cup of the divine joy had to be replaced with the cup of the divine sorrow. The Marriage Festival had to be left after the first work was accomplished of turning the waters for purification into heavenly wine, so that *the passion of the Lord* might be both seen and felt. The blessed fellowship in Cana of Galilee had to be left for the aloneness, the sorrow, the anguish, the dire extremity of the Christ-Soul witnessed in Gethsemane. For these profound meanings which the Divine Love hath revealed unto him, and commanded him to give unto the Souls of all who are able to receive them, have been engraven upon the walls of his Soul.

The meaning of the Christ-Soul passing through Samaria must be found through understanding the term itself. For though the word came to be used to describe a part of the country inhabited by the Jews and the people who dwelt in that province, yet it originally was descriptive of a spiritual state. It was planetary in its signification. Originally it symbolized that spiritual experience in which it may be said that the Soul watches for the approach of the Divine Love. For the term signified a watch-tower, and those who became true Samaritans, were watchers for the breaking of the divine light.

But the term lost that high and blessed meaning during the ages which saw the very heavens of the Planet changed through the sad and terrible changes which took place in the elemental kingdoms. The watch-towers were all destroyed ; and those who watched were drawn down into the elemental kingdoms. But, if it be unspeakably sad to relate, yet it is true, the term was made use of to describe the very state into which the watchers fell, a state of experience wherein the sense-life in all its fullness was sought.. A Samaritan came to be thought of as one who was unfit to associate with ; and the term became one of opprobrium.

There are not wanting indications in the Gospels that it was so in the days of the Master. The Jews had no dealings with the Samaritans, it is said, though they shared and confessed the same religious beliefs. The Samaritans were a despised people ; though in the Records there are found several instances

505

in which they revealed a most wonderful religious feeling, beautiful devotion to the highest, and a humanitarianism which would have done credit to any true worshipper of the Divine. They were accounted by the Jews as unworthy to be included in Jewry ; yet it was the Samaritan leper who returned to the Divine Healer with gratitude and praise upon his lips, and another Samaritan who took up the wounded one found by the wayside, whom priest and scribe passed by. There is a wealth of pathos in these facts, for their meaning is deep. They reveal what was intended by the stories ; for they show how beneath the outward evil lives of some Souls there is a depth of real true religious feeling and nobility of spirit which from time to time find expression—a religious feeling and nobility of devotion far surpassing anything found in circles where the Samaritan would be despised and repudiated.

What it Meant for the Master

It was the state of the Samaritan that the Christ-Soul " must needs " go through, a state in which the sense-life dominated all the powers of the being. It was a state of sense-bondage in which the Soul was held captive, and made to endure the unnameable things which the perverted senses wrought upon the life. He had to pass through all that that state represented, to enter into the very conditions which were found amid those environments out of which such conditions grew, to bear the full burden of the evils they imposed upon the life, to know the depths of the degradation to which they led, to realize the power which the sense-life had over the sensitive Soul, to partake of the cup of bitterness which was given them to drink, to be known as one of them, to be despised as they were, to be accounted unworthy even as they were accounted unworthy to be spoken of as the children of the Divine Love, to awaken amid such awful conditions to the realization of their evil nature, to feel the sword of anguish pierce the whole being as the Soul strove to free herself from the influence of these

low conditions and rise into the pure air of a divine life:—
these were the things He " must needs " pass through in His
experiences as He journeyed through the land traversed by
the erring children of the Father.

And who shall say that beneath all the outward evils that came
to Him there was not a glorious and blessed purpose ? Who shall
say that that could not be possible, because the experiences
were so unlike those of a Christhood ? Who shall gainsay this
wonderful truth that " *He was made like unto His brethren* " *and*
" *was tempted and tried like as they are ?* " How long will those
who should know the truth, who believe that there was a Sin-
offering made by the Son of God, remain in the darkness concerning what that Sin-offering was, and how it was accomplished? How long will they refuse the Light of the Divine Spirit
which illumineth all things, and maketh clear unto the Soul
the meaning of this great Mystery ? How long will it be ere
they perceive the inner meaning of the things which they think
they believe, and behold *how* He was made " *sin* " on their
behalf, yet in His own Soul remained sinless ? Perhaps the
unfoldment of this wonderful allegory will help them to
understand.

B

THE SOUL'S GREAT WEARINESS

*I AM weary, even to the laying down of my burden, and would
fain find a place of rest.* These words reveal what it meant
for such a Soul to pass through Samaria. There is a depth of
meaning in them which the discerning may perceive. The
meaning of the rest which He sought will be obvious. The
Soul-travail was so great, the burden so heavy, the pain and
sorrow so deep, and the anguish so unspeakable, that He was
overwrought in His labours and would fain have withdrawn
from them. What a burden of pain it was that He so lovingly

bore ! What sorrow and sadness were His in the lives of His sore travail ! O, the awful Soul-weariness that overtook Him on the way ! How he longed for Soul-rest, and the blessedness of Christhood ! How pathetic and heartrending were His prayers as He cried out, when the burden was heaviest, to be delivered from it ! O, the unspeakable grief that was seen upon His countenance as He sat Him down by Jacob's Well ! What loneliness was present to Him as He rested Himself there ! Would that we could portray adequately for our readers the vision that comes to us of the sorrowful over-burdened beloved one as He sat beside the ancient halting place of refreshment for the Soul. It would be so different from the orthodox notion of what it all meant ; for it would mean so much more, infinitely more, than the ordinary interpretation of this story could show. It would surpass anything the interpreters have ever dreamt of.

What was the Patriarch's Well beside which the Christ-Soul sat Him down to rest His awful weariness ? The reader will have gathered from what we have said that even this part of the story is not to be understood literally. They will understand that it is not ordinary history, and that the events were not such as would seem to be indicated by a literal reading of the story. The apparently local relationships were really planetary, and those things which seem to have been material were spiritual in their nature. Through the materialization of them the beautiful terms lost their spiritual significations. And thus it came about that experiences which were born of the tragic Sin-offering were made to relate to persons and physical things. The One who was weary with His journey through the land was understood to be Jesus. The country wherein He journeyed was related to a little part of Palestine. The Well at which He sat was turned into an ancient spring of water. The parcel of ground on which the Well was situated, and which was believed to have been given by the Patriarch Jacob, was presented as a small portion of the country known as Samaria.

And so the material veil hid all the wonderful meanings. The outward took the place of the inward ; the physical was understood where only spiritual things were meant ; the local and personal colouring was made to obscure things that were planetary, and thus all the events were made to appear in the light of an ordinary experience in the life of the Master.

A WONDERFUL ILLUMINATION

So when we seek for the true meaning of the Patriarch's Well we have to seek in a region other than geographical ; and we have to seek for a Well whose waters are not those which are drunk of for physical refreshment. We have to pass from the domain of the physical to that of the spiritual, from the geographical situation to the planetary state when the land of Samaria, or the watch-tower, formed a part of its heavens. For the parcel of ground which is supposed to have been given by the Patriarch Jacob to his son Joseph was none other than the intermediary heavens between the more outward spheres of the Soul and the angelic kingdom. It was the first heaven into which the Soul entered on her way to the angelic world. It was the country of the Soul into which she entered first as she passed from the outer spheres upward towards the realization of the angelic life. Mount Gerizim was there—the mount of angelic worship, the mount or spiritual upland on which God was once truly worshipped. And the Patriarch's Well was there, that spring of true spiritual life whose waters were for refreshment, a well that was *deep* though its waters were only meant as aids by the way. For the Soul required such refreshing as this Well gave, as she performed her journey. The waters of the Well did not fully satisfy, though they assuaged the thirst. They were not the waters of Life Eternal, the which if the Soul drink she knoweth no more thirst ; but they led the Soul on to these. They refreshed her and made her long for more. It was the original purpose of those waters first to refresh the Soul, and then fill her with great longing for the waters which were unto Life Eternal.

For Jacob's Well contained the waters of the first realizations of angelic life, the life born of love. The House of Jacob was planetary, and was *the spiritual household*, the group of Souls who had attained to the angelic life.

Here then we have a most wonderful thing declared, a truth sublime and far-reaching in its significance, such an interpretation as explains not only the part of the story to which it belongs, but many other things besides. The ancient scriptures concerning Jacob and his Household radiate a new and more wonderful light. The God of Jacob is no longer the god of a man, but the head and crown of a glorious spiritual planetary system.

When the Christ-Soul sought rest for His extreme weariness at that Well, all things were changed. As we have already indicated, the whole land was changed and everything about it. Samaria had long been the land of the fallen. The elemental powers ruled over it. The waters of the well of Jacob did little more than slake the thirst of the weary Soul. They had lost their ancient power to lead on to the Life Eternal. This much is evident from the story itself. The land of Samaria was the land of the fallen of whom the woman may be taken as a type. And when the blessed Christ-Soul passed through it full of the awful weariness of one whose burden has been borne, though it has been far too great, it had fallen to its lowest. On Jacob's Well He sat full of very, very sad thoughts and great Soul longings, which none in that country could satisfy. He entered into the estate of the Samaritans, shared it with them, and knew the indescribable Soul-weariness where no refreshment for the spiritual life could be four d.

C

THE WOMAN OF SAMARIA

IT is a graphic and fascinating story that is told of the woman approaching the Well to draw water. She came for such replenishing water as she could get. The Well was not in the city where she dwelt, so she had to come out to fetch her store. The city of Sychar did not possess even such water as the Well was then able to supply. There is a profound significance in even these apparently accidental items in the story, for they show that the state of life found in the city of Sychar[1] was of a non-spiritual order. They reveal the conditions amid which the woman lived, for the term itself indicates a state of intoxication. We have seen that Samaria had come to mean the land of the sense-life ; to be a dweller in Sychar was therefore to be one who was intoxicated with the sense-life. And that is just what the woman is represented to have been. The picture drawn of her is such as may be found in any modern city of Samaria, meaning by that, spiritual states. She is said to have had five husbands, and that the one she now had was not her husband.

Now, we have clearly pointed out to the reader that nothing in the story is to be understood literally and personally, that it deals with history which is not ordinary, nor merely upon the outer spheres, but with the state of the Soul. Therefore it must be understood that the woman is only a symbol, representing the spiritual state of men and women who have been in the land of Samaria, many of whom are there still. The woman in her bondage to the sense-life (who, by the way, had a remarkable power of abandonment) was and is the Intuition held fast in the grip of the sense-life, forced to traffic with material desire in every form. Five husbands she had had, but these had been taken away ; and the one with whom she

---

[1] The City of Sychar was the spiritual state in which the Soul is drunken with the wines of the sense-life.

now lived was not her husband. And what could these husbands have been in the marrying of which the Intuition had had true union, but the five senses in their pure spiritual state as these were found within the Soul ? For the five senses whose outermost feelers are found in the body-life, were once absolutely pure and beautiful, and were the powers within the Soul through which the Intuition sensed, felt and perceived heavenly things. And what was it that the Intuition had taken unto itself to live with as a husband, though it could never truly occupy that relationship, since there could be no true union between them ? What could it be but the awful dominance of material things, the illicit traffic in everything of the sense-life, the degradation of the powers of the Soul to find their fulfilment through matter in its various forms.

People do not seem to realize what it all means, so blinded are they. They imagine that the sex aspect of this question is the only one. They do not seem to understand that whilst matter in any degree dominates the life and blinds the Intuition, so that it lives its life amid the things born of matter, and seeks fulfilment through them, they are living a false life in the sight of the Divine Love. Some are bound through the love principle to the feeling generated by it upon the outermost spheres, and these are they who come in for the condemnation meted out by men and women to each other, the judgment which the self-righteous world-spirit has to pass upon all who are supposed to be unworthy. These are accounted the magdalenes, both men and women, the fallen and outcast ones whose garments are specially soiled, and on whom opprobrium may be fittingly cast. These are as the poor publicans ; they have to stand in the outer courts, and be accounted the greatest sinners, to redeem whom the Sin-offering was specially made. These may stand apart from the self-righteous and pray, *God, be merciful unto me, the sinful one.* The pseudo-saints who are bound hand and foot to literalism and traffic with matter in every other degree, who tithe their mint and cummin and forget the weightier matters of the law, such as love, compassion and pity—these from afar off view these sinners, and too often superciliously thank God that they are not as they are.

How little men and women imagine what it all means, this awful traffic of the powers of the Soul in matter ? How slow they are to perceive its far-reaching ramifications ? How blind they are to its effect upon themselves ? The sex venue is not the only one through which the fearful ravages are made upon the life of the Soul. In very many the love-principle has found other outlets through which the traffic with the things of sense has been carried on—avenues of action whose results have been more disastrous to the Soul, though in the judgment of the world the effects are not seen to be so. Alas ! that so great darkness should have prevailed where light was supposed to shine ! Alas ! that men and women should have been taught to regard the love of the things of sense for the pleasure they gave as not only right, but a great goal in life to be sought for and pursued until gained ! O the sadness and the pity of it all that they should have had such destructive thoughts impressed upon them for ages and ages ! The love of money, the love of position, the love of dominion ; the love of everything that ministers to the body and the mind ; the love to reign upon the earth ; the love of power to rule all things material and to receive the homage of the world—these are traffickings with matter transcending in their power for evil the lower outward manifestations of the perverted love-principle, for they not only bring down the whole being to function upon the outer planes, but they dry up its spiritual vital forces, and take away all the beautiful spiritual magnetism which is generated from the activity of the love-principle within the Soul. They have the effect of encasing the Soul in a sheath of material armour from which she finds it most difficult to free herself. They gradually influence her to look at everything from the material standpoint, until all her once beautiful inward emotions born of the Divine Love within her have to seek for their fulfilment in material things. Her life is found in the objective world. Her visions are all visual. Her religious manifestation is only outward. And even her heavens are materialized. And so it happens, in process of time, that Ichabod is written upon the walls of her sanctuary ; for the glory has departed, and the Divine Presence can no longer be said to have His abode there.

D
THE SOUL QUESTIONING

THE supposed conversation between the woman of Samaria and the Master is striking in the extreme. It is striking because of the circumstances. The state of the woman is not such as to lead us to expect the remarkable questionings and profound discernment with which she is credited. The coming to the Well to draw such water as she could get there, in itself was a testimony to the spiritual thirst within. What a depth of inward perception there was present at that moment when she said unto the Christ, " *Give me of this water so that I thirst not again, neither come hither to draw !* "

Here we have, in the most incidental way, a Saying which reveals how unlike an ordinary story it was, and how spiritual its meaning. Those who came to Jacob's Well found only refreshment by the way ; but those who had the living waters of Christhood, had within themselves the Eternal Spring, and needed not to come to the Well of Jacob. And so the questioning of the woman reveals much more than is apparent.

And what a fulness of abandon there is in her conversation ! All reserve is cast to the winds as soon as the subject is of the Soul and concerning divine things. She seems to forget the purpose for which she came to the Well. Nor does she seem loath to repudiate any close relationship with the one whom she had chosen to husband her—all which is spiritually significant ; for few Souls would acknowledge readily, if at all, that they had illicit traffic in the things of the outward world. The supreme thoughts are, *What is this living water ? Whence may it be had ? Who is this who speaks as if He could give it ?* All else is forgotten in the quest—all that she has been and still is. The Jews had no dealings with the Samaritans, but what did that matter now when one who was evidently greater than Jacob was prepared to give to her the gift of an Eternal Well whose springs gave forth Divine Waters ? This stranger had discovered and unveiled her life to her, had probed her deepest thoughts and feelings, had read the secret of her very Being ; what after all did nationality matter in the light of these things, and if only the Messiah came ?

O the wealth of meaning for all Souls there is contained in this picture of the Soul! What depths of experience are revealed ! What glints and gleamings are given of the Soul's innermost yearnings for the coming of Christhood to her ! What a glimpse, so full of hope amid so much that is evil, of the Intuition of the Soul seeking for the light to break ! What a light it sheds upon the experiences of life, so full of spiritual pathos whilst the Soul is still held in bondage to the sense life !

In the same life the inner longings and the outer manifestations seem to be so very different. The dimmed vision has still something of the picture of Christhood before it, though it cannot behold Him. There is an anticipation of the coming of Christhood, though no clear perception of the meaning of that coming for the life. But there is a consciousness that the Christ will be greater than Jacob, and that He will tell the Soul of *all things*. The spiritual experiences of less degree will be superseded by those of greater degree. The life of the Soul represented by the waters of the Well of Jacob will grow more and more

515

intense in its realization as the whole Being drinks deeply, until the intensity of Soul-life known as Christhood is attained.

A Greater Than Jacob

" *Thou art then greater than our father Jacob who gave us this Well ?* " So much did the intuitive Soul discern. She discerned that the one who spake to her was more, much more, than anything Jewry had been able to furnish. She distinguished a deeper tone in the things that were said concerning the higher altitudes of Soul experience. She was able to differentiate between even the mere prophet and the Christ, showing how the process of illumination proceeded. She beheld the prophet in the divine teacher as the truth was unfolded ; but the vision grew clearer, until to her vision the prophet became the Christ, as her own past history was revealed unto her. There was no hesitation in her action when she heard the Christ-voice through the prophet. " *If thou knewest the gift of God, and who it is that speaketh unto thee, thou would'st have asked of Him, and He would have given unto thee the Waters of Life.*" Then was there most beautiful abandonment to the inrushing joys of the new and fuller life. " *Give me this water that I may not need to come hither to draw, and that I may not thirst any more.*" For when the Intuition truly beholds the inner meaning of life, everything must be contributive to the gaining of that life, and all those things which do not contribute to that sublime end must be superseded and even left behind. The earthen vessels which carried the water for the Soul's need are even forgotten in the great glad hope which springs eternal within the sanctuary. Though she came to draw water from Jacob's Well, yet even that fact was forgotten in the ecstasy born of the wonderful discovery that she was face to face with one greater than Jacob, one who was even more than a prophet since *He knew all things,* one who must be the Christ of God.

That is just the way of the Soul when the chains of her

bondage are broken, and she is free once more to rise. There can be no contentment for her in any form of captivity. She must again find for herself that beautiful spiritual liberty which is the heritage of the children of God. Even the springs from which she drew water in the earlier ages of her evolution must be forsaken for those springs whose waters are born of the Christhood, and which are essential to the realization by her of that most blessed estate. For is not that estate the great gift of God ? The gift is not in the form of a personal Christ, for there is and can be no such thing—*Christhood being always impersonal, though revealed through the personal life.* The gift is impersonal but individual, non-physical and wholly spiritual, transcending the ordinary human life because divine in nature, though finding its interpretation in and through the human life. For the gift of God is Eternal Life through the Jesus Life as that is realized to the fulness of Christhood. It is to know God in Christhood : " *For this is the Life Eternal, that ye may know the Father as He is made manifest in the holy estates of Jesus, Christ, and the Lord.*" It is a state of being, of high and holy spiritual realization of the Divine One who is ever within. It is the consummation of the growth of the consciousness of the Soul, the unfolding of her inherent powers, the enlargement and strengthening of her latent attributes, the crowning of her life with perfect childhood, the arriving at that stage in her history when she is crowned Son of God. For in that glorious experience she has Eternal Life within her. She has not only the vision of the Divine Lord before her, but the perfect inward realization of its sublime meaning. She needeth no more that any man should instruct her, because her Lamp is kindled from the Lord, and the flame of the Eternal Spirit illumines her. She knoweth all things from within, being instructed from the Lord whose dwelling-place she is. It is a gift indeed ; for the divine nature then becomes her possession, and the welling forth of the Waters of Life from all her springs is eternal. Her springs are everlasting ; her waters are divine.

THE SOUL'S ABANDONMENT

" *Come, see one who has told me all things, is not this the Christ ?*"
It was thus that the Christ was rediscovered by the Soul.
She intuitively perceived it. Who could know such wonderful
things concerning her own history but the Christ ? Who could
tell her of all her hidden past but the Christ ? Who could explain the story of Jacob's Well and the meaning of worshipping
upon Mount Gerizim, but one who knew all things even as the
Christ ? Who could discern the innermost meaning of worship
itself, that it was something infinitely higher and greater than
the limited view of it which Jewry had, or was implied in any
local, national or racial interpretation of it ? Who but the Christ
could have uttered so profound and sublime a truth—" *The
Spirit is of God ; and they who worship Him, must worship in
spirit ; for this is the true way to worship Him, and such as He
seeketh ?* " For it is through the Divine Presence within that
the Soul once more receives, discerns and knows the meaning
of Christhood, and reaches out to the fulfilment within herself
of that beautiful estate. To attain it she leaves everything of the
earth-life that has held her in bondage. Her abandon is complete ;
and it is beautiful in its spontaneity. Whatever her past may have
been, however sad the experiences and terrible the results,
she feels she must cry out for very joy, " *Come see the one who
has told me all things ; is not this the Christ ?* "

E

THE REVELATION OF THE CHRISTHOOD

IT is so difficult to perceive the inner meaning of the new
revelation of the Christhood, because of the form in which
the story was presented by the writer of the fourth Record.
It was told in a form at once so personal and geographically
local, that the spiritual meaning of the Christ-revelation to the
Soul has been completely obscured. Here, as in all the other
stories, the Christ is made personal. The personal life through

which the manifestation was made is represented as claiming to be the Christ. The expression " *I that speak unto thee, am He,*" has been entirely misunderstood. It has been represented as spoken by the beloved Master to a dweller in Palestine ; whereas it was an awakening of the Christ-consciousness within the Soul, and an appeal to the Soul from the Divine within her to recognise who and what the Christhood was.

As the outcome of the misinterpretation of this story and others like it, has not the whole western world gone astray in this very thing ? Has not historical Christianity shown itself to have been one vast blunder in this respect that it has failed to discern the impersonal character of the Christhood ? We know how difficult it is for men and women to think of historical Christianity as anything but a true development of the manifestation of the Christhood made through the Master, so influenced are they by traditions. It is not easy to impress them with the truth that the interpretation of the meaning of the Christhood which historical Christianity has followed, is a wrong one. They will not even approach the thought calmly, and seeking only the truth at all costs, that the Christhood was impersonal, and should not be confounded with any man, however good and noble ; that the man whom they worship was only the outward vehicle of the manifestation ; that the Christhood was entirely spiritual ; that the Christ Soul who made manifest the Christhood was the vehicle of the Divine, so that the manifestation was only the human expression of the Divine Life, Light and Love. It seems as if it were impossible for them to distinguish between things purely personal and those experiences which belong unto the Soul ; between the outer life and the great reality lying behind. In this way also are they unable to understand how it was with the Christhood of the Master. They confuse the personal and outward forms with inward spiritual life, the human with the divine. And they show that they do not understand the nature of the Christhood manifestation through the blessed Master, but confound the phenomenal life or historical personage with the Divine Presence of which He was the vehicle.

AN UNENLIGHTENED CHRISTIANITY

Such has been the effect upon the whole western world of the wrong interpretation of the Christhood given in the early days of historical Christianity. And the West has not yet awakened to see how disastrously the wrong view has affected the whole trend of thought and action which have so mistakenly come to be regarded as true Christianity, and also misinterpreted the experience of the Soul. For it barred the way to a true understanding of the nature of Christhood and the way in which the Soul arrived at the consciousness of her own inherent divine nature. It taught that the Christ was to be formed within ; but what that forming of the Christ within meant for the Soul was not explained, because it was not understood.

The same teaching has been given in greater or less degree all through the Christian era, yet the western religious communities have not come any nearer to the true conception of the profound truth implied in the expression. For they do not understand Christhood, and cannot arrive at the true vision of it for the Soul. When they speak of Christhood, it is of the personal Master ; and when they proclaim that the Christ is to be formed within, they think of the personal Master influencing in some mysterious way the life of the man or woman and even of that personal life taking up His abode in them. The idea of the impersonal nature of the Christhood, is lost to them. They see not the inherent glory of the Soul. They cannot apprehend the wonderful significance of the formation of the Christ within. They fail utterly to grasp the vital truth of the Soul's true evolution, namely, that the Christ who is to be formed within is the Christ who is already potentially present, and that it means for the Soul the unfolding of all her latent attributes. It is the growth of the seed into the plant, the unfolding of the powers of the plant in its foliage, the manifestation of the glory of the plant in its bloom, and the concentration of its life-forces in beautiful fruit. The true glory of life for the Soul is the Christhood estate ; the fruit of life is the sublime manifestation of all the transcendent attributes of Christhood. The growth of the Christ within is, therefore, the unfoldment of the divine life within us until we arrive at that consciousness of the Divine Love and the realization of the Divine Wisdom revealed in the Christhood of the beloved Master.

WHERE THE CHRIST IS REVEALED

The real manifestation of the Christhood to the Soul is and must ever be within her own sacred sanctuary. The true revelation of the Christ is there. The woman there discerns Him— *the Soul in her feminine mode.* It is the Intuition that discovers the Divine. It is through the Intuition, or the Soul in her feminine mode, that her own past can be made known unto her. And it is only when she is in a state to receive, that the truth can be revealed unto her. Until she is able to apprehend from within the meaning of all things, the hidden things of her own past are like so many things spoken in an unknown tongue. There is no understanding of them. Indeed, being yet in an unenlightened state, she may reject them as impossible. For it is the way of many amid the darkness ; they cannot receive the truth concerning their own past history and the history of this Planet. They are like those whose dwelling is always in the valley ; they have a most limited outlook. The altitudes are far above them whence the glorious visions are beheld. But like Gallio they care for none of these things, until the day breaks when they are prepared to hear of them and receive them, like the woman in the story. And then there is the like deep interest, the same wonderful abandonment, the deep spiritual feeling after the divine realization and a stretching forth towards the marvellous vision, the inward divine thrusting on to the glorious issue of Christhood realization.

G

THE COMING OF HARVEST

" SAY ye not, ' There are yet four months and then cometh the harvest ? ' Behold ! I say unto you that the harvest is come already." Was it even so in the days of the Christhood ? Did the harvest indeed come ? What was the ingathering ? These questions are not only relevant, they are essential to the understanding of the allegory. If the words were spoken by the Master, there must have been a very real meaning in them. And if He meant that the spiritual harvest had already come when the results of His Life and Teachings should be gathered in, then we ought to be able to find these results. It is quite true that we are pointed to the day of Pentecost for them, as that event is recorded in the Acts of the Apostles ; but when we turn to that Record we have to look in vain for a true conception of the meaning of the life and teachings of the Master. The Christhood is not portrayed in it, nor is there even a glimpse of the *true* meaning of the redeemed life. The Christhood there is only the personal life through which the Divine was made manifest ; and the Redemption is nothing more than a belief in that personal life. Nor can we find any other indication that the spiritual harvest had come. Few followed the Master in His way of life, and fewer understood the profound meaning of his Christhood manifestation. In other recorded " Sayings " of His which are supposed to have been much later than the one in this story, we are told that He spoke of the harvest as being " *at the end of the world*," whatever that may mean to the ordinary reader. But in this story it would seem as if the harvest were immediate, that its first-fruits had already appeared, and the full ingathering would be soon. What could it mean? For we know the Master's teachings had no contradictions; there were no failures in any of His predictions through lack of knowledge, for in Him in sublime fulness did the Divine Wisdom dwell.

A SCENE IN THE PASSION OF THE LORD

The allegory as it was told by the Master will in part explain the inner significance of the Saying. Bear in mind that though the allegory speaks of the Soul, her past history, her awakening to the Christhood, her new intuitive discernment of the meaning of Christhood, and her wonderful self-abandonment when she arrived at the vision; yet the whole allegory was a picture of a part of the history of the work of the Sin-offering. This latter was its original meaning. It spoke of the history of the Souls of all who went down into the spiritual state of fallen Samaria, but only as it showed the path which the Master had to pursue; for He had to become even as they had been. " *He must needs pass through Samaria.*" And in this passing through the conditions He revealed where those were in their spiritual life who had gone down into that spiritual state.

The allegory was, therefore, a picture of Himself as a dweller in Samaria, the sense-bound life; of the deep inward craving for the Waters of Life as the Soul bore the burden of evil; the anticipation of the coming of Messiah or the Christhood once more into His own experience, and the longing to be told all things in order that He might again understand the meaning of those events in His experience which were so mysterious; His great Soul weariness amid the work given Him to do and His desire to rest in the state known as Jacob's Well; the awakening of the Intuition once more to discern the Christhood and the self-revelation which followed; and then, the great joy of the coming of " harvest "—the full enlightenment once more as the result of arriving at the divine vision, the trooping back into the blessed and glorious Christ-service of all the attributes, powers and energies of the Life!

It was a picture, in part, of *the Passion of the Lord* through Him, and the return into the Christhood. And in the symbolism of the picture we have a vista of the blessed results of the tragic Sin-offering, in the Souls who left the City of Sychar in order to behold the Christ, the coming of " the harvest," truly men and women clothed in the white garments of purity, seeking to see and hear the divine within the sanctuary of the Soul.

It was, as we have said, an allegory of the work of the Christ ; but it revealed what was to be expected from the accomplishment of that work in the days when the Soul of the Master returned into the consciousness of His divine estate. It anticipated these days in which we live, the return of the Christ-Soul from Edom[1] into the land of Bozrah[2], the accomplishment of the great work of the Sin-offering which in these latter days has found its completion, and the awakening of all those who were ready to enter into the service. For we are in the days of " the harvest " now. The Christ has revealed Himself once more. For all who are able to drink of the Waters of the Divine Life, the waters of the Well of Jacob have been superseded. " *Say ye not that there are yet four months and then cometh the harvest. Behold, the fields are white already unto harvest.*" We are only at the beginning of this new Naros, the Naros in which the Christ was once more to appear ; yet are the fields whitening unto harvest. The Divine Christ has returned in the Divine Overshadowing, and the Christhood is being restored and Jesushood or the Redeemed Life made manifest. The Soul is being once more instructed concerning her real nature ; and her wonderful, if sad, past is even being revealed unto her. The Divine One has spoken, is indeed now speaking ; and a wonderful response is forthcoming. The work accomplished in Samaria has been stupendous, and the results are going to be glorious.

---

[1] The land of Soul-forgetfulness, or loss of the Christ-consciousness.
[2] The land or state of Christ-consciousness.

A BEAUTIFUL EPILOGUE

One soweth, another reapeth. Some are sent to reap that upon which they bestowed no labour. Others have laboured and ye have entered into the reaping of the fruits of their labour. And they who have laboured and they who now gather in the fruits, shall rejoice together. Such is the fitting conclusion to this most wonderful allegory of the work of the Christ-Soul. The tragic work has been accomplished. The Author (the Divine Love) and Finisher (perfecter) of our faith (spiritual vision) has wrought for us a work so stupendous in its nature that we could not have imagined it possible, even had we always understood its nature. And now the harvest is come when the glorious results are making themselves manifest in the awakening of Souls all over the world to seek out the divine meanings of life, some to arrive at the true vision of Christhood, and others to enter into the realization of that most blessed estate. The Christ-Soul is seeing of His Travail and He shall yet be satisfied. He shall behold how His profound labours were not in vain. For even as His labours were full of pain, sorrow and anguish, so shall the fruits be glorious with Soul-health, joy and praise. The reapers are rejoicing. Their work is resonant with Soul gladness.

But in the joy of the labours into which they have entered, let them not forget those who have laboured in sorrow and languished in sore travail. Let them remember what the Blessed One has done for them through the burden of the tragic Sin-offering. Let them not forget the sufferings of the Master, because of the glory which is now following. We are jealous for those who have verily laboured, toiling whilst the world rejoiced after its own way, bearing their heavy burden unseen and almost unknown by those who ought to have shared in the divine travail of their Souls. We are jealous for the momentous work of the beloved one, the Master, that it should be truly understood, and held in sacred memory by all who are entering into the joys of the divine life and service. *One soweth ;*

another reapeth. But let not the reaper forget the one who sowed. For what is it that is being reaped but the blessed results of the travail of the Christ-Soul, and of all who shared in His sufferings ?

A PROFOUND SAYING

But there is a saying recorded in the narrative which is burdened with profound meaning. It is this—*I have meat to eat that ye know not of. My meat is to do the will of Him who sent me, and to accomplish His work.* The disciples are said to have been surprised that He should talk with a woman of Samaria. They had left Him for a time that they might go to find fit nourishment for themselves ; and on their return they found Him still conversing with the woman. And they grew anxious concerning Him lest He should faint by the way from lack of fit nourishment. So they pressed Him to eat what they had provided. But He, for some reason not apparent to them, refused. He had meat to eat that they knew not of. Had some one given Him to eat ? No : it was His meat to do the will of the Father who had sent Him, and to accomplish His work.

How profound is the meaning of these sayings when viewed in the light of the Sin-offering ! Who could fathom their depth of meaning ? Only such as may have shared the burden, and unto whom it has been given to look into the depths of the divine offering ? the sea of *the divine passion.* The will of the Father was the Redemption of all Souls, even those who had gone away into the " far country," and beyond Jordan— beyond the land of spiritual consciousness. The redemption must include all Souls. Dark and terrible places had been passed through ere even Samaria had been reached. These were the experiences which had made the Christ-Soul so weary. He had eaten of the bread of those who had passed beyond the Jordan, not because it was fit nourishment for Him, but only because He came to seek and to save those who were lost, and to find them. He had to go down into their country. The bread of Samaria He had to break, and to do it all alone, no man regarding Him or His great need, in order that in the doing of it the dwellers of Samaria might find in Him their friend and helper. He had indeed meat to eat that they knew not of in order to accomplish for all souls what the Father purposed concerning them.

O blessed Christ-Soul! How few there are who are able to understand the mystery of the burden Thou didst bear, the full nature of the work which was given Thee to accomplish! How few are able to perceive the inner meaning of all Thou hadst to endure, and the nature of the lands through which Thou hadst to pass! How rare are the Souls who find themselves equal to the task of entering into the meaning of all that was accomplished by Thee as Thou didst " tread the winepress alone," even from Bozrah to Edom, and back again! It is with bated breath that the story of Thy travailing has to be spoken of, so few are able to hear it with the understanding. Even those who should have been able to share in some measure the burden with Thee, have themselves lost the power to realize what was the work which Thou hadst given to Thee to accomplish. But the glory of that work shall yet cover the earth, and all Souls shall be filled with the gladness and joy of its healing. For it was the will of the Father that not one of His little ones should perish, but that all should find their way back to Him.

O Mystery of Mysteries! O Love Divine and Triumphant! We bow in holy reverence before Thee, adoring Thy Name in wonder because of all that Thou hast wrought for us and the world through the beloved one.

The Raising of Lazarus

*Being the Recalling of the Soul from the Grave
wherein they laid Her, through the coming of
the Lord of Life ; with special reference to
the Impoverishment of the Christ, the
Sin-offering, Sickness and Death,
and the Reawakening of the
Soul in this Naros—
(Fourth Day).*

A

A STORY CONCERNING THE SOUL

THE story of Lazarus is full of beautiful meaning. It is often dwelt upon in times of sorrow, because it does seem at once to reveal the depth of the Christ-love and the greatness of the Christ-power within the Master. It seems to speak right to the heart concerning the divine compassion. Could there be a picture drawn more fully illustrating or showing forth the Divine Love in His tender solicitude for others, more full of thoughtfulness for human grief and loss ? Could a picture more effectively show how the Divine Love sorrows with all His children, and what His grief really means ? Is there not a wealth of love revealed in that part of the story which speaks of the Master having been so troubled in His Spirit as to have unutterable groanings whilst He laboured to restore the loss and banish the sorrow ?

The story is magnetic. There is a power of attraction in it that would be difficult for any one to define. It fascinates the imagination, and carries the reader into an atmosphere where the experiences are sorrowful and mysterious. It is a record of a miracle of grace, though the miracle was not of the order supposed to be described in the story of the fourth Evangelist ; for it was of the Soul, and because it was of that nature it holds the reader and fills the Soul with wonder. The secret of its power does not lie in any outward phenomena, but in *the divine breath* that breathes through it, the spiritual quality of the miracle and the divine-human revelation that lights up the story, transforming the incidents into histories of the Soul rather than of the body, an inward divine working for the accomplishment of a great work for the Soul by which *its sickness will not be unto death, but for the glory of God.*

The main incidents in the story were facts, but they were

facts upon the spiritual plane. They were not material events, but experiences wholly spiritual. For the story is not to be understood literally. It was originally an allegory which was told by the Master concerning the most profound spiritual history. From the wonder-working Christ to the greatly afflicted Lazarus, we have the vision of experiences transcendent and sorrowful. The disciples share in both, for the Soul's attributes have known the transcendent life also. But Mary and Martha are the chief mourners, for they feel the loss most intensely, it has come most nearly to them. For the Soul feels with great intensity any serious sickness that may overtake it, and the impoverished conditions of life which follow. For Mary, Martha and Lazarus are representative states of the Soul, and reveal certain experiences which have overtaken it during its history. The home at Bethany which contained them all, also contained a wealth of beautiful spiritual things. It was a home in which the Christ is said to have been greatly loved, and where there existed that beautiful spiritual intimacy expressed by the terms " The fellowship of Christ." It was a home to which the Christ frequently went, and within which it is said Mary and Martha entertained Him and His disciples. It was the home wherein the Christ was anointed by Mary with the most costly spikenard, a use unto which Iscariot said it should not have been put, but which the Christ said was *a gospel revelation to be told in due time to all the world*, a manifestation of the sublimest love, a deed of the most sacred order and containing the most profound meaning.

When we have interpreted the allegory it will be seen that the events embodied in it were not related to an ordinary and frequent illness and death of the body, and a marvellous resuscitation from an earthly grave, but to experiences much more sorrowful and more wonderful—more sorrowful as regards the sickness and death, more wonderful as a resurrection.

B

THE HOME AT BETHANY

THE stories associated with the home at Bethany have in them a charm which is all their own. In a remarkable degree they differ in this respect from many of the other stories which are recorded in the Gospels. Even the strong personal note and the setting in which they are now found, and which to most readers hide the mystic meanings of them, fail to prevent that indefinable something by which the reader is drawn to them, from exercising its beautiful spiritual influence upon the mind. Now and again the terms made use of cause rays of light to penetrate the material covering, and reveal " the world transcendent " and " the life immortal " as realities lying behind them. Even the strong personal note is changed at such times, and we find ourselves face to face with the world of the Soul. And when the reader is able to lose sight of the personal element introduced, and to penetrate the outer covering, there opens out to the vision of the Soul that world transcendent whose realizations are most glorious, and that life immortal whose fellowship is found with the highest. The whole group of figures in the stories are transfigured ; and the scenes are illumined with a glory which is at once impersonal and unearthly, is indeed of the Soul. The very names are significant ; and they tell in their own way the nature of the histories represented by them.

THE SIGNIFICANCE OF TERMS

The term Bethany, which in Biblical Dictionaries is transcribed as meaning " the House of Dates," had a most beautiful signification. It indicated that the Soul had reached a stage in its spiritual evolution when the consciousness of Christhood could be entered into. Bethany was, therefore, the house or state of the divine-consciousness within the Soul, and, in that sublime sense, was the house of Christhood. And the home at Bethany where the Christ was ever made welcome, and where there existed the most beautiful of heavenly fellowships, was the Soul in a state of Christhood as to its consciousness, and consequently in its love and fellowship. The very term thus gives to the home the most sacred meaning. It explains how it was that its fellowship was so wonderful, and why it happened that Mary sat at the feet of the Christ. It implies the reason for the great love made manifest in the home towards the Christ, the reverence revealed for the Christhood and the great confidence which the members of the home had in Him. For, when the Soul has once known the consciousness of that wonderful state which we speak of as Christhood, it for ever after knows that only in and through the indwelling divine Christ can the life eternal and immortal be regained, that alone through the divine ministry of Christhood will death to the Soul be banished and made impossible ; and that in Christhood only can there be found the true resurrection-life through the raising of the Soul from the grave of matter wherein it has been buried.

NAMES RICH IN MEANING

But the term Bethany was not all. It was the state of divine consciousness for the Soul, the house of the most heavenly fellowship ; but it was also the home of Mary and Martha. *And who was Mary, but the Soul ?* For the term Maria, as we observed in an earlier chapter, means the Soul. But it likewise means one who has arrived at the divine consciousness, and whose home or abiding-place is, therefore, at Bethany. And who was Martha the sister of Mary, whose service to the Christ was so beautiful if somewhat too anxious ? Was she not also the Soul in its outward look and action, just as Mary was the Soul in its inward and contemplative mode ? Were not these two representatives of one Soul-system, members of one another, the complementary modes of the Soul herself ?

In the Soul-system wherein the Christhood consciousness has been attained, the Soul is more than a single unit, though its beautiful system is in unity. It is more than one-fold, though its manifold life is one. It is expressed by the term *thirteen* in relation to its attainments,[1] and by the sacred term *seven* in relation to its nature.[2] In that state it is never alone. This is a profound mystery which can be understood only through entering into the state of divine consciousness implied in Christhood. And unto those who have " passed through," and again reached the beautiful consciousness of the divine indwelling and overshadowing, the knowledge of this mystery will enable them to understand the wonderful inner significance of such spiritual histories as those told of the home at Bethany. They will understand how a man can be one and yet many ; how his complex consciousness can be active upon all the kingdoms ; how he is one Soul-system, though he has two modes of manifestation—the inward and the outward, the contemplative and the active ; how he is one Soul, though his number in attainment is thirteen—the number representing the twelve Apostles or Gates of initiation passed through, and all that these have to teach the Soul on its way upward until they culminate in the Christhood ; how the man is one in nature though sevenfold in manifestation, having within himself all the elements of Elohim, elements which find their fulness in the realization of the sacred Seven Spirits of God, *the divine pleroma of such a Christhood.*

WHO WAS LAZARUS ?

But in the home at Bethany there was another member whose name is mentioned, though only in this connection. Lazarus

---

[1] The number thirteen which is considered to be so unfortunate for anyone, is a most beautiful number in sacred symbolism, since it represents the twelve attributes of the Soul attained and brought into service, the additional number, one, being the Christ within.

[2] Seven is the perfect number, denoting the intensity of the nature of the Soul in relation to Divine Realization.

is introduced into the tableau when the incident of his sickness has to be presented. Though he is only referred to in one other incident, and so is rarely heard of, yet it is evident that he was greatly beloved of the Christ. How full of meaning is that natural and simple expression, " *Lord, he whom Thou lovest is sick.*" Who then could Lazarus be in such a home ? He was said to be the brother of the sisters ; he was therefore of the same nature. The name implies the thing that is meant within the Soul-system. He was that element which had been most impoverished, and most required helping. As we unfold the subject this will become more obvious ; for Lazarus means one who is needy, one whose life has been impoverished, one who very specially requires the ministry of the Christ because of the sickness that has overtaken the life.[1] He too is a member of the wonderful Soul-system represented by Mary and Martha ; one who has known the Christhood, and has been and is still a beloved friend of the Christ. The term therefore represents a spiritual condition, a condition of great impoverishment, that can only be described as a spiritual sickness, which, if not healed, will lead to spiritual death.

Such then, were the elements in the home at Bethany. The spirit of contemplation and adoration of the ever Blessed One was there ; for the Soul Maria knew the blessedness of heavenly fellowship, and the glories to be beheld through the Christhood vision. The spirit of devotion and service was there, as illustrated in the service of Martha ; for the Soul entered into the joy of that service which is begotten in the heart that is consecrated to the highest, and was so full of devotion to the Christhood that it filled the whole vision of life at times to the exclusion of the spirit of contemplation and adoration. But the spirit of impoverishment had also been there, and it had increased until it became the awful sickness spoken of as *the fever*

---

[1] The meaning is to be found in another gospel story in which Dives and Lazarus figure, and also in the term Lazar-house, or house for the sick and impoverished.

of life. Within the Soul something had sickened until, at last, it fell asleep amid the suffering and anguish of spiritual death.

A SILENCE THAT IS REMARKABLE

The story is only given in the fourth Gospel Record. Though said to have been so greatly beloved by the Christ, a remarkable silence concerning Lazarus seems to prevail in the Records. He was not an Apostle ; yet was he one of the most intimate of the Lord's friends. He is not amongst those named as belonging to the inner group of disciples ; yet is he spoken of as the one whom the Lord specially or greatly loved. And in these apparent omissions, and in that one revelation of what he was to the Divine Lord, we have remarkable evidence of an internal order as to *who* he was, and what was the nature of the love of the Divine Lord towards him. It is quite true that the inner meaning of the allegory is lost in the material story, and that the unique purpose and the astounding Soul history implied in it, are lost to the reader because of the materialization. But though it was reduced to an account of an outward event in the history of a friend of the Master, and all the terms were changed into personal things, and the work of the divine grace into a miracle on the physical plane, yet glints and gleamings of its inner meaning are flashed upon the reader. In some of " the Sayings " attributed to Mary and the Master we have glimpses of the light of profound things hidden within the veil of the outward circumstances into which the allegory was changed by the writer of the fourth Gospel Record.

" *Lord, behold he whom Thou lovest is sick.*"
" *This sickness is not unto death, but for the glory of God.*"
" *Lazarus has fallen asleep, but we go down to awake him.*"
" *Lord, if Thou hadst been here, our brother had not died.*"
" *I am the resurrection unto life, saith the Lord ; and he who hath been in Me shall live again, though now he seem dead.*"

These are *sayings* whose meanings are not to be understood

by following the ordinary methods of interpretation ; *sayings* whose depths cannot be fathomed except by means of the divine sounding line. They speak the language of the Soul. The voice of deep waters is to be heard within them. No ordinary outward history can interpret them. Their utterance is of God ; and they reveal the potency of the Divine Love. Their message is of the Soul ; they express its great need of that Love. They reveal the Wisdom of that Love, and the mysterious purpose of the strange sickness which is said to have overtaken Lazarus. They make manifest that the illness was not physical, but spiritual ; that it was not of the body, but of the Soul. They obviously set forth that in the illness there was grave danger, but that the divine protection was vouchsafed so that no ultimate hurt would come to the Soul. Most clearly do they indicate that the sickness was divinely imposed, and that in the doing of it there was a high and holy purpose to be served. Indeed it is affirmed in unmistakable terms that, by means of it, the glory of the Eternal Father was to be made manifest.

The Mysterious Sickness

Surely if anywhere in the Gospel Records we are here confronted by a profound mystery ! Surely here the discerning Soul may get a glimpse of the meaning of the burden of the Sin-offering ! The sickness was not unto ultimate loss to Lazarus, but for the glory of God. Yet the sickness deepened until Lazarus slept as one who was dead. The Soul became more and more afflicted until the consciousness of the divine life was withdrawn. The path of the sickness ended in spiritual death. The burden of the world's fever pressed upon the Soul. The fever of human passion in its manifold forms, smote the Soul and bore down the life even unto spiritual death. It laid him low who had to bear the burden. It was an evil load, and grievous were the sufferings which accompanied it. Who could have imagined from the story found in the fourth Record, that it portrayed the going down of the Soul of the beloved Master into that sickness whose path ends in spiritual death ; that it could have indicated the meaning of the Sin-offering, and the distressing conditions which would accompany it ?

Yet such was the meaning of the story told in those eventful days in the Upper Room. To the inner group was it spoken as one of the deep *sayings* whose meaning would come to them with the coming of the Holy Spirit of Truth, the Paraclete, the Presence of the Divine One within the sanctuary of the Soul, the Remembrancer who was to recall to their remembrance the truths enunciated by the Christ. Like other allegories spoken by Him, this one has lain buried beneath the débris which the literalism of the writers of the Gospel Records threw over it. It has remained through all the ages of the Christian Era unknown except as an outward history, possessing remarkable spiritual magnetic attraction, a story that has not only appeared to reveal the human element in the love of the Master and his astounding occult power over the elemental world, but which has also filled the hearts of thousands of men and women with the great hope that their bodies would be raised out of the grave in an incorruptible state, and that such a rising from the dead was the true resurrection life. Its wonderful significance has never been suspected. Those who have been unable to accept the miracle recorded have nevertheless felt its charm, and have in consequence sought to explain away the miraculous element. But the magnetic power of it has lain in the divine history which it contained ; and to-day it is to be unfolded, and shown to be one of the most remarkable evidences of the reality of the tragic Sin-offering. Nay, it comes in an hour of deepest need for the whole of the western world when the question of the reality of the Christhood manifestation is to the front, and many are led, owing to the lack of spiritual vision within the Churches in these things, to the conclusion that the Master never lived, and that the Christhood manifestation never took place. It has been resurrected with the other profound teachings given in these studies, to testify to the reality of that appearing ; to confirm the truth and make manifest the nature of the Sin-offering ; to proclaim the awakening once more of the Soul who so impoverished Himself in bearing the burden that He was as Lazarus of Bethany, the calling of Him forth from the grave on the *fourth day*, the unbinding of Him and taking away of the grave-clothes, and His complete restoration to the blessed estate from which He went down when He took upon Himself the fever of the whole world.

That this is the true meaning of the story we will now make obvious by the yet fuller unfoldment of the significance of some of its details.

C
THE SICKNESS OF LAZARUS

" THIS *sickness is not unto death, but for the glory of God.*" These words contain a world of meaning. That they are fraught with mystery every thinking Soul will readily acknowledge. The mind, as a rule, is directed to the resuscitation of Lazarus as the explanation. The glory of God is supposed to have been very specially made manifest in that resuscitation. It is to be beheld, according to the interpretation given of the story by the schools, in the triumph of the Master over the elements ; the conquest of physical death by His divine power. A man sickens and dies ; he is recalled to life again as a manifestation of power. But there the glory of it all ends. For it is to the like life that the man is resuscitated. He is not raised to a life that will never-more know death. It is not *the immortal life* which follows the raising from the dead. It is not the introduction to that Soul, and to other Souls, of a new and deathless experience. It is not the beginning of a cycle of higher realizations for the human race. The triumph is only temporary. No great permanent good is accomplished. The glory is circumscribed by the local and personal element, and it fades away, leaving behind it nothing but the story, like a bright exhalation at night suddenly illumining the sky and as quickly subsiding into the surrounding darkness.

All true and good things are for the glory of God, even though they should happen to be personal and local ; but when a great divine work is performed, it is not, and cannot be, bounded by local and personal purpose. Like the magnetic rays of the Sun, the divine operation is universal, and is for the good of all. When the glory of the Lord is revealed, it is that *all Souls may behold it* and enter into the blessing which it brings. When the Lord operates for the comfort of His people, it is that *all* may know the healing of His Love. When He reveals the hidden wisdom of His Love, it is that *all*, in the degree in which they are able to behold it, may be enlightened and enriched.

What the Glory of God Means

Thus was it with the remarkable work wrought by means of the sickness of Lazarus. Its purpose was universal. Its objective was the human race. The ultimate glory of it was the redemption of all Souls. It was not a sickness unto ultimate Soul-death, but unto divine life. The mystery was of God. It was the secret of the Divine Love and Wisdom. The glory of the Divine Nature was to shine out of it. The glory of the Divine Love was to be shed abroad by means of it. In all that would be ultimately accomplished as the result of it, the glory of the Divine Wisdom was to be revealed in ever-increasing splendour. And in that day, the sublimity of the divine purpose would fill the thoughts of all men and women ; and they would marvel at the love which conceived so great a work, and the goodness that accomplished it. The very heavens were filled with wonder ; they were amazed at the stupendous undertaking.

It was enquired into by the angels as to the manner of its accomplishment ; the majesty of the Love that could purpose it filled them with awe. As the work was contemplated by them, Deep called unto Deep ; before them the Mystery grew in greatness as it was unveiled. The word went forth that Lazarus had fallen asleep, and they thought that it was well. But when they heard further that it was the sleep of spiritual death, they were filled with grief and dismay ; and their love for Lazarus gave vent to its sorrow in the saying, " *Let us also go, that we may die with Him.*" So beautiful was the angelic love that it sought to express itself in sharing the burden that had fallen upon the home at Bethany—the house of the Christhood. For when the awful burden of the Soul had borne it down even unto spiritual death, the whole heavens were bowed down in sorrow most profound.

THE GLORY MADE MANIFEST

The glory of God has been made manifest. The sickness was not unto ultimate Soul death, but for that glory. The Soul of Lazarus had to touch the border-land of spiritual death ($\theta\alpha\nu\alpha\tau\sigma\varsigma$) in the work that had to be wrought. But the return has been accomplished. The Soul has been raised from death. The grave wherein He was buried has had to yield again the sacred life which it contained. The voice of the Lord has spoken. Lazarus has been called forth. The glory of the Divine Love has been, and is being, revealed. The effect of Lazarus' sleep is showing itself. The world's fever is going down. It is less virulent. Its passion is changing. The delirium is less acute. Great are the forces at work for its healing. The whole spiritual system of the Planet is undergoing redemption. The elemental world is being brought into a state of harmony. Low-lying conditions are now feeling the action of the heavenly forces and are being raised. The righteousness of the Divine Love is revealing itself in making straight those ways that were crooked amongst

men and women, peoples and nations. The changed elemental
world has made it possible for the approach of the heavens
to the outer spheres of the earth, and the consequent outpouring
of the divine blessing.

The sleep of Lazarus was for the glory of God : the new age
is the fruit of that sleep.

D

THE WORK OF DIVINE GRACE

THERE is much that is deeply pathetic in the lines of the
poet, who in his most beautiful " In Memoriam " depicts
the raising of Lazarus. The language expresses not only the
poet's darkness concerning the inner meaning of this most
wonderful spiritual event set forth in the allegory, but likewise
that of the whole Christian world. For Tennyson's eager
question and unsatisfactory reply are representative. They
express exactly just where the Church has been, and is still,
alas ! in its vision of the inner meaning of things.

" Where wert thou, brother, those four days ?
    There lives no record of reply,
    Which, telling what it is to die,
Had surely added praise to praise.

" Behold a man raised up by Christ !
    The rest remaineth unrevealed ;
    He told it not ; or something sealed
The lips of that Evangelist."

Where was He during those days ? Performing the work
of the Sin-offering upon the earth, living lives full of the direst
sorrow. His very Soul was made an offering for Sin ; and He

543

languished amid the hell-states where were found the fever-stricken Souls who had gone down into such sad and terrible conditions. There are records of a reply to the question where He was ; but in the received Records these are obscured because they are mixed with material which does not belong to them. They were lost when they were changed. Many are the indications of what took place, but these have to be found and separated from the wrong associations which were made to surround them. In their present form the Gospels have not been contributory to a true understanding of the meaning of the Christhood as a manifestation, and the burden of the Sin-offering as a stupendous work of the divine grace wrought on behalf of the whole Planet. The Christhood has never been truly known since the days of the manifestation ; whilst the nature of the Sin-offering has been grossly misconceived and misrepresented.

THE RESULT OF THE GREAT WORK

We shall have to deal with the Sin-offering, as such, else-where ; here our chief purpose is to reveal wherein the wonderfully beautiful and pathetic allegory has found its fulfilment. For in that fulfilment only may its real meaning be made manifest. The " Work of Grace " may be recognized on every hand. Not only here and there amid scattered remnants, but all round the world, there is the evidence of a divine awakening of Souls. There has descended upon the Soul of the human race the Divine Breath which, like the breath of Spring, has quickened into newness of being the spirit in man. The wilder-ness-lives are now beginning to change and even blossom as the rose. The desert-lives are becoming pools of refreshment through the up-springing within them of the waters of living truth. The solitary lives are now discovering a new and blessed gladness in the higher ideals of life. Men and women are finding it less difficult to do good and to think purely. The true narrow way that leadeth unto Life is being found, for it is sought to-day with greater sincerity and earnestness. There is coming upon the earth the great spirit of love which makes for purity, peace and unity, and all are feeling its influence.

And all these things are the direct outcome of the work of divine grace wrought through the Soul who became Lazarus, the impoverished one, and went down into the sleep of spiritual death. It is the fruit of His Soul-travail during those weary days, the issue of the sublime giving of Himself; the resultant of the tragedy of the Sin-offering. That work of grace is beyond all language to portray adequately; words are poor vehicles for a theme so great.

Why was the Christhood manifestation so brief? How was it that the Overshadowing by Rā, the Divine Christhood, The Adonai, was so soon withdrawn? For what hidden purpose did the Christ pass from the outward and visible manifestation? Why in His consciousness was He forsaken of the Divine Love? If He whom the ever-blessed One loved in the very special way indicated, was permitted to go down into the sleep of spiritual death as one forsaken of the Lord, why was it? Unto what end? He who was said to have been most specially beloved fell sick, and the sickness was allowed to deepen unto death; could there be any sublime purpose in that? And could it be the way to make the glory of the Lord manifest?

These questions do arise; and they must be answered in a way that will at once reveal the purpose of the sickness, and the unfailing goodness of the Divine Love. They must appeal to the innermost of the reader as the truth; and they must appeal as reasonable to the mind. In them there must be no contradiction or violation of divine law.

THE FOURTH DAY MYSTERY

It was on *the fourth day* that the work of divine grace was made manifest. For three long days had Lazarus slept the sleep of spiritual death, and on the fourth the Divine One drew near. He who had been the beloved of Mary and Martha (the Divine Soul in its two-fold mode), and who was greatly loved of the Lord, had gone down as if He would never more rise again, had, indeed, passed into a state of spiritual death and been buried. For three long days the tomb had held Him. The three Naronic cycles since His passing, which had come and gone in the history of the Planet, still found Him asleep within the tomb where they had laid Him. For they were days of the Planet's movement through the celestial heavens, not mere brief days caused by the Planet's rotation. They were days of the Lord—the three Naros. And on the fourth day the Divine One drew near that He might awaken Lazarus out of His long sleep, and recall Him to the consciousness of the Divine Presence.

Surely the light will begin to dawn upon some who read these words ! For is not this the fourth day, the morning of the fourth Naros since the manifestation ? And has not the Divine One drawn near to perform the marvellous " work of grace " ? Has not the voice of the " Beloved of the Father " been heard in these days very specially calling, speaking to the mourning Soul words of comfort, telling over again in language of the Eternal Love that God would raise up the loved one who was so impoverished in His life that He went down into the sleep of spiritual death, proclaiming in unmistakable terms that the Christ within us all (the Divine Christ, The Adonai) is the resurrector unto Life, and that all who believe in that Christ and seek Him (in the Divine Presence within us) shall live even though they may have been dead ? Nay, may we not hear that voice calling forth from the grave the long-buried Christhood, commanding that Lazarus, the impoverished Christhood of the historical and traditional teachings, come forth out of the tomb, that He be unbound and the grave-clothes with which men adorned Him taken away, that He be loosened and set free from all the bondage, darkness and loneliness of the grave ? For has not the approach of the Divine Presence been the prophecy of the resurrection of all who were as Lazarus, all who have been dead ? Has it not spoken of the awakening of the Soul of the Planet ? the arising of the Christhood ? the recovery for the Soul of the divine vision ? Has not the new age beheld the coming of the divine afflatus, that overshadowing and filling of the Soul from the Highest with new and marvellous potencies, so that it rises as one raised from the dead ? Are we not living in days when the Christhood is being restored in human lives, when the true vision is being given back to many Souls, when the buried One who was so greatly beloved is being called forth from the tomb, and the grave-clothes removed with which He was buried, and which obscured His countenance and bound Him hand and foot ? Are we not living in the new Naros, the fourth day since the manifestation was made, and since the fever of the world was taken by the Christ-Soul in order that He might descend into the low-estates of life, even unto the uttermost known as spiritual or Soul-death ? the fourth great cycle since the Sin-offering was begun and the approach of the Lord of Life to seeking Souls, whose coming was to bring joy unto all who were mourning, to dry up their tears, and to demonstrate the power of the Highest in the resurrected life ?

WHAT OUGHT TO BE REALIZED BY US

Surely it is so ; and that it will be obvious to all our readers we have assurance. For they must know now the meaning of Christhood, and the sublime purpose of the manifestation. They must understand the nature of the Sin-offering, and the reason for the coming so gloriously of the new age. They must now realize why the Master went away, and how it was that He bore the awful burden of the world's mistake. They will understand what that burden was, and how He had to bear it. They will apprehend the nature of the sickness that

547

took Lazarus off, and how it was that the Soul became as Lazarus the impoverished one. Nay, they will behold the way in which the divine grace has conquered death itself, and overthrown him who possessed its power, even the devil and satan, the ruler of the outermost, the prince of the powers of the elemental world, the one who sat in the high places of the astral kingdom oppressing all Souls and preventing the saints from entering into their heritage ; and they will see that the Sin-offering was the means by which the astral world was purified, the process by which the evil images which filled it were destroyed, and, therefore, the most remarkable and astounding work of grace which was ever conceived even in the divine council, the manifestation of a love whose sublimity cannot be gauged and whose sacrificial labours no language can be found to adequately express. And along with all these things they will see and understand how it is that these most wonderful allegories which set forth the nature and work of the Christhood and the Sin-offering, and the nature and history of the Soul, have all been recovered through the return from the grave of that Soul through whom the Christhood was made manifest and who was the chosen vessel of the Lord to bear the awful burden of the Sin-offering lives by means of which the work of grace was wrought. And they will bless the All-Father-Mother for such a revelation of majestic and omnipotent Love. They will rejoice in the work of divine grace accomplished for them through the beloved one in having made it possible for them to rise out of the grave of matter, and for that work wrought within them as the result of the divine approach. They will remember when they sing their " Songs of Zion " that it is the fruit of great Soul-travail, and that through it alone has the consciousness of the Divine Overshadowing come into their own experience. This great and blessed truth must break upon them in the fulness of its meaning that they may understand how it is that in *this age* the new splendour of divine life has come into their vision and its supreme joy unto realization for them ; for the angelic world with its love and purity, its joy and beautiful service unto Souls, has always been as willing to bless as it now is, but could not minister as it now does, not even unto those whom we regard as the saints, because the astral kingdom was so impure and dense. And so the present wonderful approach of the angelic world to minister and bless, speaks of the great work of divine grace wrought for us all by the Divine Love through the Christ-Soul.

E

A VISION OF THE DIVINE SORROW

IN the story now found in the fourth Gospel it is stated that the Master wept. It is said that when He drew near the grave wherein Lazarus was buried He was filled with a great sorrow, and that His deep grief overflowed in tears. Nay, it is even affirmed of Him that when He beheld the grief of Mary, He groaned within His spirit and was deeply troubled. And this part of the story has always appealed to the heart. The tenderness implied in it, the identity of feeling, the sharing of the sorrow, the evident depth of grief, the mysterious agonizing within Himself, have drawn the heart into bonds of beautiful sympathy. And if this be true of the story as it is, how much greater in power must have been the true picture of the sorrow had that been preserved to us ! For in that picture the sorrow was unspeakable. It was not only the awful sorrow of the Master when He was drawing near the hour of His passing over to go down into the spiritual sleep through taking upon Himself the world's infirmity spoken of as a fever, but the profound grief of all the heavens at His going down.

And here we touch depths of sorrow which few can understand as possible. It was indeed a work of divine grace, the testimony of the most marvellous Love of God ; but it filled the whole heavens with grief. The Divine Love purposed the wonderful work of grace and carried it into effect by means of the Master ; but the divine kingdom mourned over the tragedy which came to the Soul in the way as He bore the burden by which alone that supreme grace could accomplish the work.

The blessed Master wept. He wept for very sorrow. He wept because the divine Soul within Him wept. His sorrow was the expression of divine sorrow. He groaned as He agonized. For was not the Soul within Him, Maria, one who had perfectly realized the divine within Himself ?[1] And was not He approaching the grave wherein He was to be buried ? Was He not on the threshold of the state known as Lazarus the impoverished one ? Were not the conditions of life known as the fever and spiritual death awaiting Him ? Can anyone fully realize all that it meant to Him to approach that state ; to see it in its terrible nakedness, and know that ere long the beautiful realizations of the Divine Presence would be withdrawn from Him, as He passed down into all that it meant ; to know that the consciousness of the riches of the Love and Wisdom of the Father, which was His continual heritage, would become lost to Him for ages, and that unspeakable spiritual impoverishment would be His lot with all the concomitant and terrible experiences of pain, anguish and loss which would flow from that impoverishment ? Is it any wonder that He wept when He saw the coming of these things to Him ?

---

[1] It is remarkable that the stories concerning *the three Marys* should so well illustrate the three degrees of the Soul in Christhood.

The Virgin Mary or Soul who arrives at that exalted spiritual estate in which not only Christhood is begotten and born, but also the Lord or consciousness of the Divine indwelling.

Mary of Bethany or the Soul in spiritual Christhood, that beautiful estate in which the consciousness of the Divine Love is great. It is the Angelic love-state, whose beautiful service is at the feet of the Lord.

Mary Magdalene or the Soul in her sorrowful state through the consciousness of her sad past, and her beautiful abandon in serving the Christ within.

CAN THE DIVINE SORROW?

But there is a still larger meaning in the story. The divine sorrow which is supposed to have been expressed through the most intense grief of the Master, was something transcendently beautiful. It was the sorrow awakened in the very heart of the heavens at the pain and anguish of the Christ-Soul. Can the heavens weep? Can the perfect Divine Love sorrow? Is it possible for the Highest to know grief? He who knoweth not what the Love of the Father is, would say that it is impossible. Not understanding that Love, he would not understand its feelings and ways.

But let such an one consider these things. Does human love, the more beautiful and perfect it grows, cease to sorrow and grieve over all its beloved ones when they are in trouble, pain, sorrow and anguish? Does human love, the more perfect it becomes within a Soul, also become more and more stoical, and so ever less responsive in its feelings to the conditions of other Souls? Is it not a fact that the more refined the love of the Soul is, the more sensitive it grows, and feels with ever-increasing intensity the conditions around it? Is not the very nature and atittude of true love expressed beautifully in that old-world story of David sorrowing over Absalom in language which is verily of the Soul, " *O Absalom, my son Absalom ; would God I had died for thee* " ? For is it not of the very essence of true love to take the sorrow, the anguish, the loss upon itself which may have come unto its dear ones ? And if this beautiful ministry be true of human love, how much more true must it be of that perfect love which fills the heavens, which is the very breath of angels and the life-stream of all their wonderful service ?

So may we understand the meaning of the sorrow that filled the Divine Father-Mother and the Logos who had over-shadowed and filled the Soul whom we now know as the Master, and the Master in whom that sorrow vibrated and through whom it expressed itself. The groaning within the Spirit was the sorrow of the Divine Kingdom over what was about to take place in the Soul who had so beautifully revealed the meaning of Christhood, and brought to those who could receive it the glorious truth of the indwelling Presence of the Divine Love. It was divine sorrow that was experienced when it is said that Mary remained at home overwhelmed with her grief; for it was the whole divine heavens sorrowing in the awful silence that followed the going down into spiritual death of the Christ-Soul. For until this day of the new Naros, sorrow and grief have been the portion of Maria. Bowed down have the heavens been since the fever of the world was taken as a burden and borne unto death, even the death of the Cross, *i.e.*, the crucifixion of the Divine Life, Light and Love within the Soul, and the consequent consciousness of unspeakable loss. The anguish of Him who bore the burden has been reflected and repeated through the heavens. The Logos has sorrowed: the Universal Christ has sorrowed: the Adonai, the Manifest of the Unmanifest and Ever-Blessed One, has sorrowed: for the work was that of the Father-Mother, and not of man. It was of Him and not of the human, except that the human lives lived by the Master after the Christhood Manifestation, were the instruments; for He it was who was chosen and sent by the Father to be the vehicle of the Divine Love for the accomplishment of the great work. And if all the ages of the three Naronic cycles through which we have passed since the days of the manifestation could speak, the story would be one full of the great divine sorrow endured whilst the Soul travailed.

LET US NOT FORGET THAT LOVE

And so, whatsoever of new life and the joy of that life has come to you, reader (for joy new and full is now breaking forth everywhere), do not forget that the joy which has come in this fourth day, in this morning of the new Naros, has come as the result of those things wrought through divine grace for all

Souls, the out-working of which filled the Soul with anguish and the very heavens with profound grief. Do not forget that the sorrow was borne for you, that your joy is the fruit of the travail of the Divine Love. You should know that the divine sorrow borne for you has been the cause of the joy of the Christ-love coming into your life as a realization. Henceforth remember in lowly love and reverence, that but for that *divine travail* you could never have entered into this heritage ; that but for the burdened sorrowing Christ-Soul you could not have reached those spheres whence all healing flows, and where the Christ-vision is beheld by you. To-day you have entered into the possession of that joy in great fulness for which the saints throughout the era have longed and only momentarily enjoyed ; for during all these long years the songs of the saints have nearly all been minor songs, full of the deep sorrow that filled them and the heavens of their encompassing.

How blessed a thing it is that is happening as the Soul of the race awakens, ye all will recognize. Of how much blessedness for the whole world it is the beautiful prophecy, ye who have entered into the joy of the new life will understand. And how well it presages the coming of the transcendent life for every Soul, and the divine glory (her former glory) for the Planet, ye will see who have passed through Bethany and arrived at a consciousness of the Overshadowing of the Highest.

O Love of the Father, the Eternal and Blessed One who is also our Mother, the Love whose Radiance is revealed through the manifest One who is our Lord and our Christ, the Love who is the Life stream of our Life, the breath and strength of our Being : out of the fulness of the love of our Souls, we would bless Thee. We are Thine alone. Thou didst fashion us in Thine Image, which once we bore ; and when we went down from our high estate, even unto the loss of our consciousness of childhood to Thee, Thou didst still love us, and in Thy love didst redeem us from our

*humiliation and lift us up again into the light of Thy Countenance.
Thou hast made us doubly Thine—Thine by creation and Thine
by redemption ; and so Thou art ours in this manifold way. We
are altogether Thine, and Thou hast become altogether ours.
Thou art in us, the Love of our Soul, the blessed Divine Consciousness that makes us one with Thee.*

*We would bless Thee ever more and more through the service
of our life : we would interpret Thy Love in all our ways.*

F
THE COMING OF THE LORD OF LIFE

" LORD, *if Thou hadst been here my brother had not died.*"
How great is the truth uttered in these words ? Spiritual
death is the result of the absence of the Divine Lord. Where
He is not, the Soul goeth down into spiritual death. The
elemental conditions smite it with their breath. They fill its
veins with their fire, and consume its strength. The grave of
matter becomes its prison home, and the grave-clothes of
material things its portion. It finds itself bound hand and foot
with the things of sense. The consciousness of true life dies
within it. The sense of the living Christ is gradually lost. The
Soul becomes Lazarus, an impoverished one, impoverished
even unto the loss of all those attributes which make life real,
the attributes of spiritual power and beauty.

But when the Lord of Life draws near there is a new awakening.
Where the Divine One fills the life, the Soul becomes alive
unto Him. The grave no longer is able to retain that Soul.
The grave-clothes fall away, for he is let loose from their
binding-power. Lazarus comes forth. The Lord of the Soul
speaks, and the Soul responds. He is the resurrection life, and
the Soul feels the inflowing of that wonderful rejuvenating
life-stream. The brother rises again. The Christ within is

quickened anew through the approach of the Divine Lord. The divine consciousness returns. The power to see and hear and feel divinely is restored. Once more the breath of the angelic love is felt, and its true sweetness and healing rejoiced in. Once more is the vision of the Lord beheld, and the joy of His fellowship realized. Gladness is restored to the home at Bethany; Lazarus is raised up into the richness of Life from the Lord, no more to know impoverishment and death through loss of Him ; and Mary and Martha are filled with holy joy. The Soul is now resonant with the joyance of the Lord. The songs of the Heavens fill her and make sweet melody. She can sit at her Lord's feet in sweet contemplation and communion ; and she can serve Him beautifully without over anxiety.

Such is the way of the Divine Love with the Soul full of sorrow, conscious of the loss, through spiritual impoverishment, of its brother the Christ-consciousness. It has been thus with many who will read these words of interpretation : it has been thus with him who writes them. The Divine Lord raises us up again. He maketh Bethany our home ; and he cometh with us to make His abode. He is again of us ; and He doth make us one with Him. No more death shall we ever know, nor the world's fever which brought us down to that impoverished state. For with Him is life in its sublime fulness found for us ; His guiding right hand holds all our pleasures. The gladness of the day is now ours ; the sorrow of the terrible night we shall know no more. Deep shall utter unto Deep within us as He breaks unto us the Mystery of His love. No longer will *Phileo* express our love for Him ; it shall be great and pure as *Agapeo*. The Universal, Soul-nourishing Divine Love will be realized. It will be even as the most precious and costly ointment for the anointing of His Christ. There will be no holding back in service. There will be no limitations to our devotion ; in our spirit there will be no giving unto Him. Our life will be all His, yielded up unto Him to be used as He willeth, where He willeth, how He willeth. For in the Beloved of the Father-Mother will our life be found.

He Calleth for us

O ye sorrowing and weary ones, children of the great Love, tenderly thought for by Him whose beautiful overshadowing is yours, He has come and calleth for you to comfort your sorrowful spirit, and restore within you the joy of His salvation. He has come to awaken again your brother and bring him back from the dead—your own innermost consciousness of Christhood which has been as one dead ; and the wonderful vision of your Beloved One which you had lost awhile—the vision of the Divine Presence within the sanctuary of your own Being. He has come to turn your sorrow into joy ; in place of your grief to give you the great gladness of His life ; to make the home of your Soul resonant with the music of the heavens, and your spirit to overflow with the milk and honey of His loving word. He is come that the Lazarus in you may be raised up and enriched ; that the Martha in you may find that true service born of immeasurable love ; and that the Mary in you may again sit at the feet of her Lord and learn from Him of the Divine Love and Wisdom.

He is come that you, O Soul whosoever ye be, may not any more know death and the grave—the loss of divine consciousness, the awful darkness which follows that loss, and the unspeakable spiritual impoverishment that overtakes the Soul. He is come that the grave may yield up what has been buried, that the lifeless one may be again restored, that the bonds may be broken with which your life has been bound. He is come that the one whom he loves may no more suffer, but know the boundless love of the Divine One, the holy and blessed Presence within the Soul. He is come to you, even to the feeblest of you all, to bring new strength and so clothe you with new life, that ye may exchange your feebleness for His power and your grave clothes for His beauteous garments of conscious love and purity and good. He calleth to all of you who

*are as Lazarus, impoverished in the way ; to those of you who love
to labour for the Blessed One in the more outward spheres of service,
and who are oft-times filled with undue anxiety in your labours
even to the exclusion of the real joy of your ministry and the
blessedness of quiet fellowship with Him ; and to those of you
whose service is of the innermost spheres, unseen by the world and
often misunderstood even by those who should understand, and
whose sorrow is thus intensified. For He bringeth unto you the
blessedness of His own Love, the joy of His own Life, and the
Light of His own beautiful spirit.*

The Woman that was a Sinner

*Being an Allegory of the Finding of the Christ by the
Soul after the accomplishment of the Sin-offering ;
the Office of Purification of the Christhood
entertained in the West ; together with
the Revelation of the Spiritual state
of the Western World, and
the manner in which it
has welcomed the
Christhood.*

The Woman that was a Sinner

A

THE BEAUTIFUL ALLEGORY

IN the third Gospel there is found the story of the woman who was said to be a sinner in the city, and who entered the house of Simon a Pharisee in order to reveal how great her sorrow was because of her past, and how greatly she loved the Christ. In the other Gospels there are references to this incident in the experience of the Soul, though they appear in relation to another incident which was quite distinct, and which did not take place in the house of Simon, but in that of Mary. The two stories were evidently not understood by the writers or they could never have confused them ; for they would have seen that the one referred to an experience of the Soul in her return from the path followed by the Sin-offering, whilst the other revealed the consecration to that stupendous work of the Soul who bore the burden of the Sin-offering. On this latter experience we have written elsewhere ; but here we would give a sufficient word to indicate what the gift of Mary was, and how the anointing was for the burial of the Christ. For it was the outpouring of the precious Life of the Soul, as the term Mary implies, upon the Christ, the con- secration of the One who was to bear the awful burden of the Sin-offering. The burial referred to was the burial of the Christ- hood. By and by we hope to unfold the meaning of the allegory more fully that the wealth of Soul-history may be beheld through which the Christ-Soul passed, and that all who are able to enter sympathetically into the meaning of the passing of the Christhood may have opened unto their vision the deep inner significance of that passing.

But the experience portrayed in that wonderful picture was long antecedent to the Soul-history revealed in the allegory of the woman who was a sinner. For this latter was a wonderful vista given by means of the beautiful allegory, of the return

561

of the Christ-Soul to the vision of Christhood ; the unspeakable sorrow that would break forth from the Soul as the result ; the inexpressible love towards the Divine Christ made manifest in the acts of sorrowful devotion ; and the profound yearning after perfect healing and restoration to the Christhood estate.

A Story of Soul Realities

It is one of the most remarkable stories given in the Records, remarkable alike for the pathos it reveals, the world of hope with which it should fill all Souls, the depths of Divine Love foretold, *the reality* of the Divine burden bearing on behalf of all His children, what it must have cost the Soul of the beloved one to awaken to such awful sorrow and anguish, the wonderful vision of divine goodness and gentleness, even towards such as are represented by Simon, the nature of the " forgiveness of sin," and the beautiful benediction of divine peace which falls upon the Soul after she has passed through her anguish.

It is only a vista that is given in the allegory ; but how much it reveals ! What a history it contains ! What depths of meaning are to be found when the foreground of the picture is left for the sombre background where meanings are only faintly yet quite distinctly outlined ! For many years have we found a magnetic influence in this picture beyond anything we could express. We have felt its appeal in the very depths of our Being. It has spoken to us as few other pictures have done. We have been conscious of much that we could not then articulate concerning the history which it portrays. The house of Simon ; the harsh judgment passed by Simon ; the pathetic picture of the overburdened sorrowing Soul ; the just judgment of the Divine Love expressed through the Christ ; the divine gentleness revealed towards him who was so harsh and unjust in his judgment ; the way of the Soul represented by the woman when her divine nature was quickened ; the way of the Divine

Love towards all Souls in their return ; how these have fascinated us and drawn us on to feel the reality of the divine goodness.

And now the picture stands out more luminously than ever, the fuller, stronger light bringing out more clearly defined than before, the interior meaning of the allegory. That which was then obscure in the background has now been illumined with light from on high.

THE HOUSE OF SIMON

The incident is said to have taken place in the house of Simon who is spoken of in the third Gospel Record, as one who was a Pharisee, and in two Gospels he is spoken of as one who was a Leper. Had it been an ordinary history of events upon the outer spheres of experience, the reception given to the Master by the host would have savoured of deep insult ; for the accustomed courtesies were refused to the chief guest. Nay, we could not even imagine such an one as Simon was said to have been, permitting for a moment the sorrowing fallen one to have crossed the threshold at any time, and especially upon such an occasion. For one who was a Pharisee was always careful about appearances, making clean the outside of the cup of life, even when the inside was full of all manner of evil. He would have viewed the coming of the sad and weary one, whatever her object was, as the polluting of his threshold. Indeed, she would never have been permitted to enter the outer courts of his dwelling.

When, however, we turn from the outer sense to the inward meaning, from the Jewish picture given in the Records to the true spiritual story, from the merely personal realm to that of the Soul, we find all the difficulties melting away and wonderful meanings taking their place. We behold no longer a Jewish house with so many Jewish actors ; but we find ourselves face to face with such a spiritual history as no one, since the days of the blessed manifestation until now, has imagined to be hidden within the story. The Pharisee remains in the picture ; but he is no longer a man, but a spirit, an attitude in life, a condition of mind. The Leper is not removed from the incident ; but he is not one who has been afflicted bodily with that fell disease, but is a spiritual condition of mind and heart. Simon is beheld in his true light, and his conduct to the Christ is understood. That he knew more of the woman whom he despised than he cared to have made known, will be evident ; and also, that he had much to do with bringing her into that pitiful and sorrowing state. His conduct all through the history embodied in the incident will be seen to be such as is there portrayed.

WHO IS SIMON ?

Simon represents the mind turned towards the outward world. All its concerns lie there when in the Simon state. It is wrapt in the things of sense in what we may speak of as a superfine sensualism. Its very religion is outward rather than inward, intellectual rather than spiritual. It will perform all manner of rites and ceremonies of a religious order, even whilst refusing the performance of the true rites of the spirit and the heavenly ceremonies of beautiful deeds of love, compassion and pity. It will glory in its narrowness, and doubt even the reality of such spiritual and divine realizations as come to the Soul in a state of Christhood, even whilst it invites the Christ to have meat with it in the house. Simon will repudiate the one whom he has caused to fall. He will bring her down, and then pass harsh and unjust judgment upon her. He will even offer insult to the Christ in refusing those spiritual courtesies which should accompany an invitation to so sublime a guest. For when the mind becomes as a Pharisee in attitude, Simon will do all these things and reckon nothing of them. They are ordinary events in his experience.

When Simon the Pharisee, who invited the Christ to dine with him, is understood, he will be beheld as something more

than a member of Jewry. He will be seen to rather represent
an attitude of mind characteristic of hosts of men and women
even in these days of supposed Christian enlightenment and
attainment. He will be recognized as the embodiment of a
certain type of mind found in the very heart of western civi-
lization ; of a spirit which prevails where the Christ is supposed
to be well known, reverenced and followed. Indeed, he was
not simply a Pharisee ; he was the type of the pharisaical spirit
which judges without knowledge, and passes condemnation
where it should manifest compassion. Nay, he was even more,
for he was the embodiment of the very spirit which condemned
the Christ and repudiated the Christhood, and so crucified the
Son of God ; for the spirit within him was that of the cynic,
the callous, the self-righteous, the oppressor ; the one who
within himself laughs to scorn the thought of such sublime
realizations as Christhood, such love towards the fallen as the
Christ revealed, such spiritual courtesies as the presence of
Christhood should draw forth from the mind. He was the very
embodiment of the fearful heritage which has come down to
humanity from past ages, that awful heritage given to the mind
as the outcome of its having turned its vision outward. His
self-righteousness, his spiritual blindness, his lovelessness, his
utter lack of tender pity towards the sinful, all reveal those
strange characteristics which are to be found prevailing where
the outwardness of religious belief is more than the true
inwardness of feeling and vision ; where the phenomenal
dominates, and the true spiritual finds little or no outlet ; where
the vision of life is circumscribed, local and material, and the
eyes of the Soul are veiled.

The spiritual impoverishment in Simon was appalling. His
very Soul seemed bereft of true human sympathy. He knew
who the woman was who sorrowed so much, and he despised
her. He knew that he had brought her low and covered her
with shame, yet he had no remorse within himself. He beheld

her anguish, but remained unmoved. He witnessed her profound grief because of her past, but could only judge her with condemnation. He was amazed at her devotion to the Christ ; and marvelled that the Christ could accept it. His whole attitude to both the Christ and the woman fills us with dismay, and constrains us to cry out in very Soul-agony, that we would far rather be Mary Magdalene than Simon the Pharisee ; that we would rather have the consciousness of her burden of the past and possess her wonderful abandon, her beautiful Christ-love, her unspeakable sorrow because her garments were so stained, and suffer all the scorn that the world could heap upon us, than possess that awful spirit of which Simon is the embodiment, that spirit which is the negation of Love, which blights all pure spiritual feeling within the Soul, dries up the very fountain of her life, and leaves her barren of those tender graces born within that one in whom is to be found the consciousness of the Divine Presence.

SIMON IN THE WEST

What a picture we may find in this character sketch of the very spirit whose triumph has been so marked in the whole of the western world right through the Christian era ! For what is the spirit that dominates that world, but the spirit manifest in Simon ? Let the centuries which have passed since the Christhood manifestation, speak ; then behold what a story it is they have to relate ! Where has Simon been during those ages ? Need we say that he has always been found where men and women have missed the inward spirit of the Divine Love, and vainly imagined that true religion consisted of outward respectability, the performance of mere rites and ceremonies, and the acquiescence in certain forms of belief ? He has been found in that Church which rose out of Jewry, a Church which professed to entertain the Christ, and which should have followed the ways of the Christ. O surely, if in one place more than another, all that Simon stands for should be unknown where the Christhood is present ! Surely in that house where the Christ has been asked to dine—the mind of the individual Soul, or the mind of the collective community, there should be absent all those callous feelings, those harsh and unjust judgments, those cynical thoughts, revealed in the character of Simon. When will men and women truly learn what true religion is ? When will they come to understand the meaning of the sad attitude of Simon the Pharisee ? How long will it be ere they discern the inner meaning of the Master's Sayings ? How long shall the day be delayed in the which they may arrive at a true understanding of the meaning of the Christhood, and all that it implies to entertain the Christ ? When will they arrive at that beautiful truth which is so obvious to those who have the power to spiritually discern ;—that no one can truly entertain the Christ who harbours the spirit of Simon the Phari-see ; that no one is able to discern who the Christ is, and what the Christhood means, except they be in a state of Soul-love ; that outward religious devotion and ritual observance accom-plish little for the life in which tenderness, compassion and pity have no place ; that Mary Magdalene who anguishes upon Simon's threshold has more power to discern the Christhood and serve the Divine Love, than the proud, the self-righteous, the cynic, the loveless mind has.

History repeats itself. The past is adumbrated into the present. Simon's house (the Pharisees) repudiated the Christ. The same is true to-day.

C

THE APPROACH OF THE CHRIST

THE entrance of the Christ into the house of Simon should have been the signal for such a preparation as would have proved the sincerity of the host, and shown how genuinely anxious he was to entertain the Christhood. With the approach of so divine a guest, all those spiritual courtesies implied in the providing of water for the purification of the feet, the kiss of welcome, and the anointing with precious ointment, should all have been awaiting Him. There should have been no hesitation, no lack, no failure to make manifest the welcome that was meant. Yet when the Christ entered the house of Simon, none of those Spiritual qualities so essential to the manifestation of true regard for the divine guest, greeted the Christ. They were not provided by Simon. He made his feast without them. He invited the Christ to his house, but it was very largely as he might have invited a complete stranger. He was curious to see and hear from him, though he understood not who and what He was. He would never have acted as he did had he known that the One whom he had invited, was none other than the Divine Love in manifestation. But he knew not. He was a Pharisee. His vision of life was compassed by the limits of pharisaical ritual. He knew no religious expression higher than pharisaism. The outworks of life were everything to him : he knew not the life within the Holy Place, the inner-most Sanctuary behind the veil. He was the personified state of the earthly mind ; the type of the conditions which prevailed upon the Planet ; the embodiment of the evil which had over-taken the magnetic plane ; the striking illustration of the Planet's reflective powers. No Christhood could be understood under such conditions. The Christ could not be discerned by the individual Soul or Planetary consciousness in such a state. The approach of the Divine Love could not be understood where all the spiritual elements were changed. There could be no true spiritual vision where the mind was so thoroughly inverted in its polarity, turned outward to seek for the fulfilment of life in things sensuous. For the true polarity is inward. To be in true equilibrium the mind must have its poles towards the Divine World. Only in this way can it receive true spiritual magnetism. Only in this way can those powers come to it by means of which spiritual vision becomes a reality. In this way only can it fit itself to reflect heavenly things.

How the West received the Christ

The meaning of Simon's conduct may now become more
apparent. He was not in a spiritual state to understand Christhood. His outlook was all earthwards, so it is not to be wondered
at that he knew not who the Christ was. He had not the power
to perceive any approach from the Divine Love. His condition
was such that he had lost the power to sense spiritual things ;
hence his cynicism, his utter callousness, his lovelessness, and
his unspeakable harshness in judgment and lack of tender
pity. He received the Christ as the Jewish world received Him
in the days of the manifestation, and as that world has received
Him ever since. He acted exactly as the western world has
acted since those days. For though the West, so to speak,
invited the Christhood, to dine with it, to be its friend and its
redeemer, yet has it never provided for the true reception of
the Christ, nor the coming of Christhood. Its water-pots
have never been truly filled with *the waters of purification*.
Nor even yet has it purified itself through cleansing its way
of living ; it has preferred to follow its own ritual. It has not
been able to discern that pharisaism could never even at its
best accomplish its redemption, and that it must learn the ways
of mercy and compassion. It has failed to discern the difference
between the value it has given to all life, and the intrinsic value
set upon all Life by the Divine Love. It has despised the little
children of the Father's household, and continued to oppress
them at will. It has professed to care for the creatures because
of their uses ; though in the use of them it has filled them with
untold suffering and anguish, and the world with antagonism.
It has always set its value upon them ; but the value has been
material, commercial and sensuous. The lives it could not in
its blindness understand, it has used as mere goods and chattels.
That wonderful *life* in them all, manifested in varying degrees,
it has taken away remorselessly. Its ministry unto them has
only had personal and selfish ends in view. It has not known
the true meaning of compassion, nor understood the nature of

the divine pity. When it invited the Christ to dine with it, to make its threshold the scene of His ministry, it invited Him as Simon the Pharisee did ; for it was barren of those attributes of love, compassion and pity which are always distinguishing features of the Soul.

ITS WAYS WERE NOT PURIFIED

When the Christ crossed the threshold of the western world, it was unable to discern any more meaning in His approach than Simon did, even though it did profess to regard Him as the supreme teacher, and come at last to deify Him. His Christhood it has never understood ; the meaning of His approach has been hidden from its vision through the veil of its pharisaism and the fact that it has been spiritually leprous. It has not loved the Christ any more than Simon loved Him (of course, we here speak of systems and not of individual Souls) ; and even whilst professing to entertain Him as the most desirable guest, it has shown how ignorant it was of His true nature and mission, and even cynically refused to regard with favour the Christhood-estate. Had it been truly sincere from the first, how very differently would all things have unfolded ; and what a different and much more noble history would have been written by the West since the blessed manifestation ! Had it meant to truly love and follow the Christ in the life of the Christhood, how very altered its conditions would have become. There would have been such a purification of every way of life, that evil would have found no place. The barbaric instincts, desires and tastes which for countless ages have dominated the West would all have been consumed in the fire of the Divine passion within the Soul. The feet would have been washed : Christhood would have been discerned to be *a cleansed life*. The truth of the Christhood manifestation would have been applied ; the water of purification would have accomplished its work. The Christhood would not have been entertained with unwashed feet. It would not have been left to this age to make so obvious a truth known.

The beautiful meaning of devotion to and love for the Christ-hood, would not have remained unknown until these days of the return of the Son of Man. Such a Christhood as the West believes in to-day, and has believed in all through the supposed Christian Era, could never have been ; and it would not have been but for the blindness, the callousness, the Soul lovelessness of Simon the Pharisee. The western world has believed in a Christ who ate the flesh of sentient creatures, and drank the wines of the earth in such fashion that during the wonderful manifestation the people said of Him, " Behold, a gluttonous man and a wine-bibber ! " And it has presented that view of the Christhood so effectually that, instead of the West having reared up a Kingdom of Christs to be the true interpreters of the Divine Love, it has made its threshold the scene of the most terrible blasphemy. It has been like a vast amphitheatre crowded with participators in the most shameless massacre of various orders of creatures whose helplessness has placed them in the power of their oppressors, whose cries of distress and anguish have been unheeded or brutally mocked, whose pain and sufferings have been accounted as naught, and whose precious God-given lives have been only valued for the sport or appetising pleasures which the afflicting and eating of them has given to the multi-tudes. The West has presented to the whole world the most awful anti-Christian drama which this distraught earth has ever known. Its ways have been those of anti-Christ. It has done for the Christ just what Simon the Pharisee is said to have done. It has invited Him to dine. But it has provided no water for purification of the feet ; no kiss of true abiding friendship has it given ; and it has had no precious ointment with which to anoint the Christhood.

D

THE SOUL'S SUPREME HOUR

WE now come to one of the most wonderful visions of
Soul experience in the whole of the recorded Sayings
of the blessed Master. Understood in its innermost history, there
is nothing like it in the whole literature of the world. For nobility
of purpose, for depth of divine passion, for mysterious awful
sorrow, for love and devotion, for absolute abandon to the
fulfilment of the noble purpose regardless of the place and the
conditions, as a Soul-experience it transcends all human thought.

It is a picture of the Soul in action when she once more
arrives at the vision of Christhood. The sorrow and anguish,
the sense of shame because of the past, the absolute abandon
to the hour, the flowing of her tears, her humiliation when
she stoops at the feet of the Christ that she may wash them
with her tears, the astounding tenderness of her feelings made
manifest when she takes her very hair to wipe the feet of the
Christ, the most beautiful devotion to the Christhood revealed
in her conduct as she kisses His feet, crowned with that act of
supreme love for the Christhood so wonderfully expressed by
her when she anoints the feet with precious ointment—all these
are born within her as the outcome of the Divine Overshadowing, for by means of it she arrives again at the consciousness
of her divine estate.

THE INNER VIEW OF THE STORY

With this view of the incident we are lifted above the merely
personal spheres to those which are impersonal ; from the
outer walks of life to the very innermost ; from the vision of
that kind of Mary Magdalene which has come to be associated
with the Story, to a region where physical sex is lost in spiritual
Estate ; from the vision of a poor woman whom callous men,
like Simon the Pharisee, have defiled, to a vision of Soul

history which is true of every Soul (whether of woman or of man) who has once known the Divine Life, Light and Love, and who has awakened from that spiritual stupor which is thrown over the Soul by the sense-life, to once more see and understand the true meaning of Christhood.

That it has an application to the personal life is quite true ; for it reveals the way of outward purification which must be followed if the Christhood is to be realized.

That it has an individual application is likewise true, for its message is for every Soul who is able to hear it with the Understanding.

But as a picture of the Soul it must not be interpreted as relating to a person, nor to one individual when applied humanly, but rather as showing the spiritual experience where the divine was once realized as a glorious *Presence within*, but lost through the sad conditions known as " the fall " of the Planet and the human race, and then recovered through the Christhood manifestation and the outcome of the work of the tragic Sin-offering.

Yet in its most inward signification it is more than all of these ; for it is the picture of the action of the Christ-Soul in His return from Edom, or the land of forgetfulness in which the Christhood was abandoned for the work of the Sin-offering, to the land of Bozrah in which the Christ-consciousness is regained, the Christhood vision once more beheld ; and the sense of the awful burden of the Sin-offering is so intense that it overwhelms the beloved one, fills him with dismay, and leads Him to such actions as are portrayed in the conduct of the woman.

A SAD BUT NECESSARY WORK

And herein is the Mystery of the Divine Love shown forth in its sublime fulness. *The divine passion revealed in the allegory*

*of the Woman of Samaria is here revealed as something which
has been completed :* but the memories of it are not yet dimmed,
so that the Soul is filled with anguish even in the presence of
the Divine Love ; and that, too, though the Christ-consciousness
has again returned, and the Christhood vision has once more
become clear. Nay, we have a revelation of the first thing
which the Master had to do when He awoke to the Christ-
consciousness and the vision of Christhood. He had to cross the
threshold of the house of Simon the Pharisee in order to wash
the feet of the Christ and cleanse them from every stain. For
He found that no water for purification had been provided at
the feast given by Simon the Pharisee. Simon had invited the
Christhood, but he wished to remain with unwashed feet. He
wanted the presence of the Christ, but without understanding
who and what He was, and the demands which such a blessed
presence would make upon him. So the West invited the Christ,
but understood not the meaning of the Christhood. The view
of that Christhood given by those who wrote and circulated the
New Testament Records was, that the Christhood manifestation
was such that He through whom that most glorious manifestation was given lived like those men and women who ate and
drank as those did who were called gluttonous and wine-
bibbers. They could make the man whom they portrayed
as a Messenger calling the Jewish nation to a life of righteousness, in preparation for the new life under the reign of the
Christ, an ascetic of the most extreme type, whilst they drew
a picture of Him who was to bring in that blessed reign, which
revealed Him to be less than the Messenger instead of greater,
as they said He was to be ; for they presented Him as following
ways of living which are the negation of purity, compassion and
pity, ways upon which the innocent and helpless creatures had
to lay down their lives to meet the needs of His body and His
sense-desires. They made Him to tread in the way of blood,
and thus stained the path of His Christhood, through their
ignorance of the beautiful meaning of that blessed estate, and

brought the picture of Him down to their own likeness or ways of living. They clothed Him with a purity which was nominal, and a goodness which was fatuous ; for their idea of purity was that of Simon the Pharisee, and they understood not the true significance of the terms compassion and pity.

Thus they ensnared and deceived the West by their mirage of *one whose ways were divinely pure and beautiful in everything.* Like Simon the Pharisee, they left Him with unwashed feet. And until now in these latter days when the Sin-offering has been accomplished and the Master has returned to the Christ-hood consciousness, did the West leave the feet of the Christ unwashen. Yea, until the beloved one Himself awoke to behold what had been done to the vision of the Christhood given in the days of the manifestation, and crossed the threshold of the house of Simon to wash away the stains from the feet of the Christhood, and thus show how wonderfully pure and good were all His ways, nothing was done to redress the awful wrong which the writers of the New Testament Records did to Him.

THE ORIGIN OF THE STORY

Upon the Souls of those who have prepared themselves to receive the wonderful vision of the truth herein set forth, a new light will have broken, a new glory will be seen by them in this wonderful allegory. To those who are not in a spiritual state to receive it, the exposition may seem fantastical. No doubt there are readers who will think that it is an anachronism to take what appears in the Records as an incident in the life of the beloved Master, and carry its true application into the present time. But there is no anachronism in what we have done. For we have shown that the incident covers the whole period from the time of the blessed manifestation until now. For more than eighteen centuries the feast of Simon the Pharisee con-tinued ; and only in these latter days has the Soul crossed the threshold to wash the feet of the Christhood from the stains found upon them within Simon's house.

The incident was originally an allegory told by the blessed Master some time after the awful Gethsemane vision. He was permitted to behold what would be done to the Christhood by those who could not understand it as a sublime spiritual state in which the Divine Life, Light and Love were realized, and the Redeemed Life was revealed. He beheld the conditions that would gather around the Christhood, and how it would be misrepresented. He was given to behold the impure Teachings that would be attributed to Himself, and the sad things that would be done in His name. He was allowed to witness the awful conditions that would prevail throughout the centuries during which the Sin-offering was being accomplished upon the astral kingdom, and what the state of the West where the Christhood was professed would be in the days of the return of " the Son of Man." And in the vision it was shown to Him what the first great work upon the return would have to be, even to enter the house of Simon the Pharisee who had invited the Christhood without understanding who and what He was ; to wash the feet of the Christ ; to shed tears of anguish whilst He purified the vision ; to wipe the very feet or ways of the beloved one with the glory of His own mind-powers (hair signifying the glory or powers of the mind), and to anoint those ways with the most precious ointment of Divine Love, to show how wonderfully pure and beautiful were all His acts as He trod the high-ways during the life of the blessed manifestation.

And so the Master set forth what would be done in the form of an allegory.

A Seasonable Word

Behold, ye who are able to perceive, the manner of the Love which the Father hath bestowed upon us ! Behold, and marvel at the wealth of the love of the beloved Master ! The cynics may scoff, and the unfaithful ones may jeer, at the work of the Soul who knows what the Christhood of the blessed Master was ; but the feet of the Christhood are being cleansed in the house of Simon the Pharisee, this too notwithstanding that the action has been condemned in quarters where it should have been gladly welcomed. Souls are coming to recognize the blessed fact that no Christhood could be possible where the lives of the creatures were slain for the gratification of the desires of the flesh, since Christhood is a holy spiritual estate in which the Divine Presence is realized and the Divine Love made manifest. The sublime work of the Master will yet be understood and rejoiced in when the meaning of His awful anguish breaks upon the Souls of all who could know Christhood, that anguish unspeakable witnessed in the house of Simon the Pharisee as He was bowed down in His humiliation with the awful sense of the past burden, and shed royal tears in His very Soul to wash away the stains from the feet of the Christhood vision, tears which were like the outflowing of the powers of His very Being, but full of purifying potency. Amid untold and indescribable pain, sorrow and grief has the washing of the feet of the Christhood been done. Under humiliation which no tongue could describe, have the feet of the blessed Christhood been washed, wiped, kissed and anointed.

Ye who are able to perceive the inner meaning of the story, let your gaze be reverent as ye behold what a love it was that so expressed itself, what a devotion it was which revealed itself through the Soul's wonderful abandon to the divine service. For *it is the supreme hour of the Soul,* the hour of her great sorrow through the vision of the past, the hour of her return into the consciousness of the Christhood, the hour of sublimest yearning for the realization of that most blessed estate.

E

SIMON'S VIEW OF THE SOUL'S ACTION

THE view which Simon the Pharisee is said to have taken of the woman's action and the attitude of the Christ towards that action, is characteristic of all those of whom Simon was and is the type. As is the Macrocosm so is the Microcosm. The house of Simon breathed the very atmosphere of the mind of Simon. The astral conditions upon the Planet were such at that time, and for ages after, that the minds of men and women were filled with the very spirit which Simon represented. For the individual reflected the universal astral conditions.

Nor have the evil effects of these influences upon the minds of the people been overcome, though the process of elimination, purification and perfect overcoming is now progressing. For the redemption has come. The trumpet of the Lord's Jubilee has been sounded, and the work of bringing every Soul into her own is now being accomplished. The bands of captivity to the sense-life are being broken, and the hour of deliverance for all captives is at hand.

But whilst this is being done, many are found in the state of mind typified by Simon the Pharisee. They have not risen out of the conditions which he represented. In their religious observances they are outward. Their tithes are those of sensuous things rather than those of the heart. They do not understand the nature of true religion ; and they repudiate its true manifestations when these are shown to them. They cannot enter into the deeper experiences of the Soul, knowing not yet its finer aspirations. They fail to discern the inner things of life, because just now they are as unable intuitively to perceive ; so they mistake the outward and sensuous things for them. They may profess to regard the Christhood favourably and invite Him to dine at their house, to become their special guest ;

but they cannot see beyond the outward to discern who He is, and what His teachings mean for all who would entertain Him as their guest. As their vision is of the outward world only, they are blind to the invisible. They see not, they hear not, they feel not the glorious spiritual universe. There may be such a world ; but who knows it ? Who has beheld with open eye the glories of the invisible heavens ? Who knoweth the nature of the Soul, what she is, what she was, and what she may become ? No one hath seen God the ever blessed One ; who then knoweth the Divine to interpret Him ? The ancients had visions and dreams of the beyond ; but the world has grown since those days, and the visions and dreams have grown dim and ceased to be realities. After this fashion do many reason.

Religious, yet Irreligious

Thus is it with all who are in the state of Simon the Pharisee. They are religious ; and yet in the best sense they know not what religion means, so that in their spirit they are truly ir-religious. They make a show of entertaining the Christ; but they question with an unsympathetic and even cynical spirit the things of Christhood. They know not the attributes of a Christ-hood ; and when these are interpreted for them, they reject them. They believe in no spiritual world within the Soul, a world so wonderfully built up that it corresponds to the great spiritual universe, and is able to reflect the life of that universe ; within them a veil is drawn which leaves them in the darkness. They cannot understand the office of a prophet, nor how the visions break upon the seer : for them these things are not realities. And so when they witness a Soul awakening to the Christhood consciousness, sorrowing over its own past, grieving at the conditions by which it is environed, pouring forth its sorrow and ministering unto the Christ in those things wherein they themselves have failed, they are unable to enter into sympathy with such an one. Their whole attitude is one of repudiation. Their pharisaism asserts itself. The cold soulless spirit that would judge unto condemnation, manifests itself. Within themselves do they say many things which, if articulated, would show that the spirit within is that of anti-Christ—the loveless, the compassionless, the pitiless spirit.

SIMON'S ATTITUDE TO GOD'S ILLUMINED ONES

Are not these things made manifest to-day in our midst ? Has not the West done these grievous things all through the ages of the era ? Has not the western mind treated the Christhood with scant respect ? How has it received the teachings of the Christhood ? What has it done to God's illumined ones ? Where has it sent the prophets ? And what has it done unto that Soul who dared to cross its threshold to wash the feet of the Christ with the very tears of life, to kiss them in glad devotion, and to pour out as an oblation in the divine service the precious ointment of the Soul's great love ?

As yet the whole work of cleansing the feet of the Christ is wrong to the western mind. Nay (alas, that this should have to be said !) there are many present in the house of Simon the Pharisee, who are not with him in his pharisaism, but who also think that the purification is altogether unnecessary. There are even disciples of the Christhood, aspirants after that sublime state, who are content that the Christhood-vision should remain with unwashed feet. They are influenced by the very atmosphere of Simon's house, and are led to view the work of cleansing as abortive. They do not seem able to understand the insult that has been offered to the Christ, and the sublimity of the service now being rendered by the beloved one in His return. They are not unlike the disciples in the story of the Transfiguration, as that is given in the accepted New Testament Records, who, though they must have heard what was said in the vision concerning the Sin-offering work of the Soul, yet were so carried away by what they felt, that they desired nothing more than to tent upon that Mount. They have failed to grasp the significance of the work which the Christ had to accomplish ; and they wist not or understand not what they say when they forget that work. Had they known the Master in those days they would also have known in these days what His beautiful Christhood was like ; what it must have been ; and what it must be shown to have been. *They would have known, had they sat at His feet, that there could be no such thing as Christhood realized by any Soul whose ways were not purified, whose heart did not breathe forth compassion unto all creatures, who knew not the meaning of the One Divine Life, and who failed to interpret the all-embracing, all-enfolding and all-sustaining nature of the Divine Love.* They would have likewise known that the blessed manifestation was twofold, and that only by means of its twofoldness could the divine purpose towards all His children (human and creature) be accomplished ; that the Christhood was essentially a redeemed life before it was one of divine illumination or anointing.

F

THE DIVINE JUDGMENT

AND now we are face to face with a profound heart-experience which should bring comfort, even the comfort of a great hope to many a weary outcast Soul who has had to share the burden of this Travail. For whatever Simon the Pharisee may think of the woman who has crossed the threshold of his house, the Divine Judgment upon her is such as any one may desire to have. Whatever view he may take of her action, certain it is that the Divine Love approves.

It is sometimes better to sorrow than to rejoice. There are hours in the Soul's experience, long weary hours, when to rejoice were impossible, and the Soul must needs sorrow. Those Souls who have not yet found these hours, have not fathomed the depths. There is sorrow that is not unto death

but unto life ; and it is divine sorrow. It is begotten through
the vision of life which breaks upon the Soul unto such fulness
that there follows the extended vision of her own past history.
And when that happens the floodgates are lifted, the waters
of sorrow flow swiftly and deeply, and in such fashion that
none may stay them in their flowing. In such sorrow there is a
mystery no one is able to interpret, unless that one " has passed
through." There is in it such a mystery as none can interpret
in all the wealth of its meaning, except it be given unto that
Soul to see and understand it. There is a mystery that men and
women wote not of and which seems to remain a mystery to
many who should by this time have come into its meaning,
found in the profound sorrow of the Soul when that awful
sorrow relates to her own experience. It is the mystery of the
sorrow and anguish revealed in the action of the woman in
the house of Simon the Pharisee. For such Soul-sorrow and
anguish before the divine reveal much. And what they reveal
God understands, though the world cannot appreciate its
profound meaning. That world which has torn and stained the
garments of the saints, sees only the outer state of those whom
it has cast down ; but to the inward world of the Soul where
the divine heavens are reflected, it has no power to penetrate.
Like Simon, it would have only scorn for that Soul ; it would
repudiate her sorrow and sore anguishing, and cast her out as
something unworthy of love and reverence.

But the Divine Love sees these things in a very different
light, and His judgment upon the Soul is not only just, it is
also beautiful. The wonderful devotion of the Soul who has
dared to cross Simon's threshold is approved of, and her
ministry to the Christhood is acceptable. That which Simon
looks upon with scorn, the Divine Love rejoices in. The tears
of the Soul are most precious ; the Lord preserveth them. He
putteth them in His bottle. The tears that wash away the stains
caused by Soul-travail are never lost. The tears shed in the

Valley of Baca (Weeping) become even as pools of refreshing ; for along that Valley lieth the path of the Redemption.

Nor is the action of the Soul in taking the outward glory of life represented by the hair (the outward powers of the mind), to wipe the feet of the Divine Christ, one whose results will be transitory ; for the washing will restore the vision of the Christhood to its perfect state.

Nor will the kiss of glad welcome and devotion to the Christhood fail to accomplish all that the Soul means by them. *For, however great the humiliation of the Soul in " her passing through " the supreme hour of her awakening to the divine consciousness, her beautiful purpose will be realized in noble ministry unto the Christ.* Her welcome to the Christhood will crown her with the perfect realization of that blessed estate. There will be nothing lost of the intrinsic value of the precious ointment with which she anoints the purified feet of the Christhood ; for its very aromatic powers will yet fill the house of Simon like sweet Breaths from the land of the Divine Love. For the anointing is precious in the sight of the heavens. The angels witness and rejoice in it, though so few on the earth planes yet behold its meaning. Such love truly is begotten of God ; for it is the Divine Spirit within the Soul revealing itself. There is no more precious unguent than such love ; there could be no more beautiful service in which to expend itself than that of the Christhood ministry.

O ye weary ones who have known the sorrow and anguish of such travail of Soul portrayed in the wonderful Mystery set forth in the allegory, behold how the Divine Love welcomes your return to the consciousness of the Christhood, and your beautiful ministry unto the Christ upon the threshold of the house of Simon !

The Forgiveness of sin

The divine judgment upon the action of the Soul is expressed in forceful and beautiful terms. There is in it no such spirit as men and women manifest towards each other in their judgment. *It is a judgment without condemnation. Its spirit is one of Blessing. Its Breaths are those of the Divine Love.*

There could be no more striking illustration of the way of that Love with the Soul than is furnished us in this allegory. If the terms are few, yet these few are pregnant with great meaning. If the picture shown us of the way of that Love with the Soul, appears a very small miniature, yet is the miniature perfect ; and it is like a storied urn containing the wealth of life bestowed by the ever Blessed One upon all His children who desire unto Him. The beauty of the miniature will be seen when it is understood what is meant by " the forgiveness of sin." It is essential to the true understanding of that way which the Divine Love takes with the Soul, that this also should first be understood. Men and women do not grasp the significance of its meaning. They think, because they have been taught so to think, that true forgiveness of sin means that He allows what they understand by judgment, to go by default, to pass by them. They imagine it is all accomplished when the Divine Love speaks to them, saying, " *Thy sins are all forgiven thee.*" They imagine it to be a mere attitude of the Divine Love towards them because of their sins, and that that attitude is changed when the word of forgiveness is spoken. They fail to apprehend the great truth, a truth which ought to be obvious unto all who try to understand the deeper things of life, that there is a human side as well as a divine side. To pronounce the word of forgiveness would be meaningless unless the Soul were redeemed from the influences of the evil.

The forgiveness of sin is a wonderful process in which the Soul is redeemed from the evils which have overtaken her. It is the " blotting out " of all life's transgressions, the removing from the life of the Soul of all those weaknesses and biases which have grown up during the long ages of her dwelling upon the outer planes, and have repeatedly taken her down from her inherent high estate to live the life of the world, a life of outwardness and sense-gratification. A true Soul would desire no other kind of forgiveness. The mere pronouncement of forgiveness would not be sufficient to bring her peace. She would not only desire the divine favours, to know that the blessing was hers ; but she would also desire pre-eminently that her own experiences were perfect in their purity, and in obedience to the divine will. She would never rest until there broke upon her that peace which is the outcome of such perfect healing as comes after the Soul has " passed through."

A BLESSED REALIZATION

Thus, a larger meaning breaks upon the sorrow and anguish of the Soul, represented by the woman in the allegory. There is no comforting her until the sorrow and anguish have had their way. They are born of the Soul's vision of her own past. She feels as if she could never forget that past ; hence her sorrow. For she beholds the Christ-vision once more, and yearns with all her Being for the perfect realization of the Divine Life, Light and Love. The woman's sins had all been forgiven. She had " passed through." The stains upon her were only nominal ; the evils which made them had all been taken away. The " good pleasure of the divine will " had been worked out in her ; she had passed through the waters of redemption, and even reached " the promised land " of the Christhood. The consciousness of the divine was now great within her ; but she could not rest. The vision of the Christ came to her, and it issued in her wonderful abandon amid her sorrow, her beautiful devotion in service to the Christhood. She dared to cross the threshold of the house of Simon the Pharisee where she found the Christ with feet unwashed and unwiped, unkissed and unanointed. For very sorrow did she weep that she herself had fallen so low, and that the beautiful Christhood of the Master had been left in such a state through the conduct of Simon.

For, whilst the allegory in this respect shows the way of the Divine Love and the meaning of the forgiveness of sin, yet our readers must see in it that deeper experience of the Master when He awoke to the divine consciousness again upon the completion of the Sin-offering, and saw what had happened unto Him as the result of that tragic work. *It was a vision of His own return. It was the state in which He would be when He returned. It was a forecast of what would await Him when He again awoke to the consciousness of the Christhood.* The awful sorrow and anguish in the house of Simon the Pharisee were His own anticipated. And the anticipation was even less than the realization. What the woman seemed to feel He felt with an intenseness no language can describe. He felt as if the past would never be blotted out, as if its influences upon Him could never be undone. He beheld once more the Christ-vision, but He felt as if He could never attain unto Christhood again.

So has He washed the feet of the Christhood of the Manifestation, with the tears of His sorrow and the pain of His anguish ; He has kissed the feet of the Divine Christ as only one could who had known Him of old ; He has anointed the purified feet with the most precious ointment of the whole love of His Being ; but He yearns ever more and more with unutterable desire for the perfect realization of that Divine Life, Light and Love once more.

There are depths in the vision which may not be spoken of. No sounding-line of ordinary human experience could reach them. There is a pathos beyond what is human in the fact that the beloved one who bore the burden of the Sin-offering, should have had such a consciousness of evil done by Him in the bearing of that burden, that, in His awakening again to the Christhood consciousness, He felt as if there could never more be any realization of all that complete forgiveness means for the Soul. Though the Divine Love was sustaining Him, and the divine judgment showed approval of the work He was doing, yet so profound was His sorrow and so poignant His anguish, that He felt as if He could not enter into the divine peace.

To know these things is to behold the story of the woman who washed the feet of the Christ in the house of Simon, in a transfigured light.

G
ENTERING INTO PEACE

THE Soul who passes through all the process known as " the forgiveness of sins," and has arrived at the restored vision of the Christhood, is on the royal road to the realization of the fulness of the divine life. She is on the highway to Zion, the state of perfect Christhood, when all her sorrow and her anguishing shall flee away, and her tears shall be dried by the Divine Love. She is like the woman in the story, though her sorrow, anguish and abandon may not be so full ; the supreme hour for her has come when realization of Christhood becomes a necessity, and she knows that she can have no peace until that greatly-to-be-desired estate comes in sublime fulness. For the peace which is meant is that of the eternal and ever Blessed One. It is the peace that is said to pass the understanding of man, because it transcends the earth-loves, the earth-visions, the earth-lives, and seeks only the Divine Presence. It is not mere contentment with the things of life as found around us. It is not even a state in which the ever changing conditions which environ us fail to disturb our spirit ; for there is nothing stoical in it. It is something far higher, a realization far more profound. It is that peace which the Christ-Soul once knew when He dwelt in the bosom of the Father—*in the consciousness of the Divine Presence within Him, when the Divine Love and the Divine Wisdom were His in blessed fulness.*

Experiences of the Christ-Soul

When He returned from the work of the Sin-offering, that tragic work for which His beautiful Christhood had to be laid aside so as to enable Him to do the Father's Will in changing the Astral Kingdom and making redemption possible for all Souls, He found the path back to the Christhood burdened with the most terrible memories of all that had happened to Him in the lives He had had to live as the Sin-offering. He found the way hard and bitter to tread. He awoke from the state of the Sin-offering lives to find healing for His Soul and peace for His mind in the state of the redeemed life and spiritual Christhood—a Christhood in which the chief realization is the Divine Love as a power within the Soul. But in the last life of the Sin-offering the whole of the past broke upon Him. When He had attained to the spiritual Christhood state in which He once more realized the divine healing and the peace of the Divine Love, there gradually broke upon His mind visions and voices of all the past. The burden of the Sin-offering came back upon Him in the most acute forms. The visions and voices were so terrible to Him that He felt as if He were living over again the awful things which He lived, beheld, and heard in those lives. So real were they unto Him that He felt all the evil influences intensely. The Gethsemane Vision was renewed with such intensity that the agony returned, and He cried out anew in anguish indescribable, *Eli! Eli! Lama Sabachthani!* The sorrow and anguish welled forth in Him as if there could be no more any true comfort, or divine healing for Him. He suffered more than any man or woman in the return. The path for Him was harder than for them. The sorrow of the way was greater than any others knew. The anguish was deeper than the deepest that other Souls passed through.

Hence the innermost meaning of our story. He found it most difficult to forget the past, to realize that all the evil that had come to him in the work of the Sin-offering had all been forgiven (cleansed away), and so to enter once more into that state which was once His beautiful heritage, even the realization of the Divine Christhood in which alone He could find again that perfect peace.

A Vision Full of Hope

But though the allegory pictured the return of the Master with the return of " the Son of Man," very specially, yet is the story one full of great hope for all Souls. *The Christ-Soul went the way of His brethren. He was made like unto them.* Their afflictions He knew. He shared the evils by which they were thrown down. He trod the path along which they went. And in His return to the vision of the Christhood, He had also to " pass through the great tribulation." And so the meaning of the story applies to them also. For them it is as the breath of the Divine Love. For them it has a meaning into which they may now enter. And if they do, then will they not only find the divine healing and peace, but they will give themselves with beautiful abandon to the service of the Divine Love. They will rejoice in the fact that the feet of the Christhood have been washed in the house of Simon the Pharisee, and that the anointing has taken place. They will be glad to have beheld the new vision of the meaning of Christhood. and to follow that vision whithersoever it leadeth them. They will not any longer be blind to the discourtesies of Simon, nor to the gracious work wrought by the Christ-Soul in doing for the Christhood what Simon refused or neglected to do. No more will they be content with a vision of the Christhood with unwashen and unanointed feet, knowing well that it is not the true vision, and that Simon is responsible for it ; for they will understand what the Christhood means.

O Eternal One, in whom we have our being ; the Ever Blessed in whom alone all blessing is to be found ; the All Good, from whom floweth all goodness ; the Pure and Holy One, in whom

*purity and holiness alone may be found ; the loving Father, full
of compassion unto all Souls and pity towards all creatures ; our
Healer ; our Redeemer ; our Sanctifier ; the Perfecter of our
lives :—Thee we would bless with our whole being.*

*O help us by the riches of Thy Grace to show forth the beauty
of that Life unto which Thou hast called us, and to make clear
its ways unto all Souls, that we may be Thy true children, the
Interpreters of Thy Holy Will. Amen and Amen.*

INDEX AND GLOSSARY

591

INDEX AND GLOSSARY

INDEX AND GLOSSARY

Page

593

INDEX AND GLOSSARY

594

INDEX AND GLOSSARY

595

INDEX AND GLOSSARY

INDEX AND GLOSSARY

QQ   597

INDEX AND GLOSSARY

INDEX AND GLOSSARY

INDEX AND GLOSSARY.

INDEX AND GLOSSARY

Page

601

INDEX AND GLOSSARY

INDEX AND GLOSSARY

INDEX AND GLOSSARY

INDEX AND GLOSSARY

The Order of the Cross

FOUNDED OCTOBER 1904

AIMS AND IDEALS
(FOUNDATION STATEMENT)

TO ATTAIN, by mutual helpfulness, the realization of the Christ-life, by the path of self-denial, self-sacrifice, and absolute self-abandonment to the Divine will and service:

It is of these things that the Cross as a symbol speaks. It stands for the Sign of the Order of the Cross, because its three steps are those which have to be taken in order to arrive at that Estate which it symbolizes. It speaks of the quest after the humble spirit and the pure heart. It speaks also of that further state of realization when the Soul gives itself in absolute abandonment for the Divine Service. The Three Steps are:—

PURITY OF LIVING
PURITY OF THE MIND
PURITY OF THE SOUL

Thus to endeavour by example and teaching to win all men to the love of Truth, Purity and Right-doing.

To proclaim the Brotherhood of Man, the essential one-ness of all religious aspirations, and the unity of all living creatures in the Divine.

To teach the moral necessity for humaneness towards all men and all creatures.

To protest against, and to work for the abolition of, all national and social customs which violate the teachings of the Christ, especially such as involve bloodshed, the oppression of the weak and defenceless, the perpetuation of the brutal mind, and the infliction of cruelty upon animals, *viz.:* war, vivisection, the slaughter of animals for food, fashion and sport, and kindred evils.

To advocate the universal adoption of a bloodless diet, and the return to simple and natural foods.

To proclaim a message of peace and happiness, health and purity, spirituality and Divine Love.

EXECUTIVE COUNCIL (1904)

J. TODD FERRIER, *Founder*, *Editor*, "The Herald of the Cross."
ROBERT H. PERKS, M.D., F.R.C.S. (Eng.), *Secretary.*

All Offices of the Order are Honorary

SYNOPSIS OF MAIN PUBLICATIONS

THE MASTER sets forth the Inner Meanings of the Master's Teachings and gives a true picture of Him as He was in His Life, public and private. The Birth Stories and the Allegories of the Soul are revealed in their true setting; with the Teachings on the profound Mystery of the Sin-offering, and the Allegories of the Soul's Awakening.

THE LOGIA contains the chief utterances of the Master, in the form in which they were spoken by Him. Here they are restored, including the real Mystic Sayings, found in the Synoptic Records, the Gnostic Record, the Pauline Letters, and the Apocalypse, containing remarkable histories of the Soul, the Planet, the Ancient Christhood Order, and the Oblation or Sin-offering.

LIFE'S MYSTERIES UNVEILED gives the Path of Discipleship and Aids to the Path of the Realization. It includes definitions of terms in their relation to these Teachings and many answers to questions asked at Healing and other Meetings. The principal theme of the volume is Initiations of the Soul.

THE DIVINE RENAISSANCE, Vol. I. i. The Message. The Divine Adept. The Superstructure of Man. ii. The Eternal Mystery. A Divine Apologia. The Seat of Authority. iii. The Path of the Recovery. The Redemption. The Divine Purpose of the Oblation. The Mass and the Oblation. Altars and Sacrifices. The Flame before the Altar.

THE DIVINE RENAISSANCE, Vol. II. i. Unto the Great Silence. Science and Religion. The Angelic Realms. Corpus Christi. The Sabbath of the Lord. ii. Beginnings of Historical Christianity. Pentecost. The Advent of Paul. The Stone the Builders Rejected. The Church of the Living Christ. The Seven Sacraments. iii. A Renascent Redemption. The Seven Thunders. The Healer, Manifestor, Redeemer. The Obedience of Christ. Our Lord and Our Lady. The Three Altars. iv. A Divine Oratorio. The Ministry of the Gods. The Divine Government. The Cosmic Consciousness. The Regnancy of Christ.

THE MESSAGE OF EZEKIEL. *A COSMIC DRAMA.* The Office of a Prophet. The Purport of the Book. The Divine World Unveiled. The Distinction given to Israel. The Mystery of Tyre and Zidon. The Pharaoh of Egypt. The Arising of Israel. The *Logia* of the Prophet Ezekiel: with extensive Notes to the *Logia. The Logia of Israel.* Vol. I.

ISAIAH. *A COSMIC AND MESSIANIC DRAMA.* i. The Unity of Divine Revelation. ii. The Prophecy. iii. The Word of the Lord. iv. A Divine Drama. v. The Mystery of the Sin-offering. vi. A Momentous Promise. vii. The Triumph of Adonai. viii. The Drama of Israel. ix. The Sign of the Cross. x. The Daysman of Israel. xi. The Appointed Redeemer. xii. The Five Cities of Egypt. xiii. The City of the Sun. xiv. The *Logia* of the Prophet Isaiah: with extensive Notes. *The Logia of Israel* Vol. II.

THE MYSTERY OF THE LIGHT WITHIN US. *With 17 coloured plates by Amy Wright Todd Ferrier.* i. The Luminous Cross and the Cross of the Elohim. ii. The Spectra of Souls and Stars. The Solar Fashion. iii. Auric Glimpses of the Master. iv. Celestial and Divine Estates. v. A Holy Convocation. Jacob's Ladder. The Adamic Race. The Secrets of God. The Girdle. The Blessing of Israel. A Divine Rhapsody.

PUBLICATIONS

By the REV. J. TODD FERRIER:

THE MASTER: *His Life and Teachings*	Large Crown 8vo		624 pp.
THE LOGIA: *or Sayings of The Master*	,,	,, ,,	436 pp.
LIFE'S MYSTERIES UNVEILED	,,	,, ,,	480 pp.
THE DIVINE RENAISSANCE, Vol. I	,,	,, ,,	402 pp.
THE DIVINE RENAISSANCE, Vol. II	,,	,, ,,	560 pp.
THE MESSAGE OF EZEKIEL: *A Cosmic Drama*	,,	,, ,,	280 pp.
THE MESSAGE OF ISAIAH: *A Cosmic and Messianic Drama*	,,	,, ,,	436 pp.

THE MYSTERY OF THE LIGHT WITHIN US
With 17 plates. Large Crown 4to 240 pp.

THE HERALD OF THE CROSS (Bound volumes)
Vols. VIII upwards. Large Crown 8vo

HANDBOOK OF EXTRACTS of the Teachings of The Order of the Cross, from the Writings of the Rev. J. Todd Ferrier.
Vol. I: Extracts A to D; Vol. II: Extracts E to J. Demy 8vo
Further volumes in preparation.

LETTERS TO THE CHILDREN With 5 plates	,,	,,	238 pp.
THE MESSAGE OF SOME OF THE MINOR PROPHETS	,,	,,	240 pp.
GUIDE AND INDEX-GLOSSARY to the Writings of the Rev. J. Todd Ferrier	,,	,,	432 pp.

SMALLER BOOKS (Paper Bound)

THE MYSTERY OF THE CITY UPON SEVEN HILLS	Demy 8vo		80 pp.
GREAT RECOVERIES	,,	,,	80 pp.
THE FESTIVAL OF THE MASS OF ISRAEL	,,	,,	72 pp.
THE STORY OF THE SHEPHERDS OF BETHLEHEM	,,	,,	72 pp.
SUBLIME AFFIRMATIONS	,,	,,	64 pp.
WHAT IS A CHRISTIAN?	,,	,,	64 pp.
THE SECOND COMING OF CHRIST	,,	,,	48 pp.
THE GREAT TRIBULATION . THE WORK	,,	,,	44 pp.
THE EVANGEL OF ST. JOHN	,,	,,	40 pp.
THE CHRIST FESTIVAL . THE WAYS OF GOD AND THE WAYS OF MEN	,,	,,	36 pp.
THE CROSS OF A CHRIST . THE RESURRECTION LIFE	,,	,,	36 pp.
THE PASSING OF SOULS	,,	,,	32 pp.
THE CONTINUITY OF CONSCIOUSNESS	,,	,,	32 pp.
THE SOUL'S JUBILEE	,,	,,	28 pp.
THE SEASON OF THE CHRIST-MASS	,,	,,	24 pp.
THE PATH OF DISCIPLESHIP	,,	,,	28 pp.
IF CHRIST CAME BACK?	,,	,,	28 pp.
A MEDITATION ON GOD	,,	,,	24 pp.
THE LIFE IMMORTAL	,,	,,	20 pp.
THE ORDER OF THE CROSS	,,	,,	16 pp.
THE MESSAGE AND THE WORK	,,	,,	16 pp.
THE INNER MEANING OF THE FOOD REFORM MOVEMENT	,,	,,	8 pp.
ON BEHALF OF THE CREATURES	Crown 8vo		128 pp.
THOUGHTS FOR THE DAY	,,	,,	52 pp.
THE ABRAHAMIC STORY	,,	,,	20 pp.

By E. MARY GORDON KEMMIS:

THE "GREATER WORKS" (Cloth bound)	Crown 8vo	64 pp.

FOR USE IN WORSHIP

PSALMS AND CANTICLES FOR WORSHIP	Demy 8vo		96 pp.
HYMNS FOR WORSHIP WITH TUNES	,,	,,	256 pp.

All prices on Application

Please address all communications regarding Literature, and make remittances payable, to THE LITERATURE SECRETARY, THE ORDER OF THE CROSS, 10 DE VERE GARDENS, LONDON, W8 5AE

Loan copies of any of the publications may be applied for to THE LIBRARIAN

MEETINGS

Regular meetings are held, at which all seekers after the Divine way of life are welcome, in the Sanctuary at the Headquarters of the Order of the Cross, as below, every Sunday at 11 a.m. and Wednesday at 7 p.m. throughout the year (except during the Summer Vacation); and there are Groups or Reading Circles for the study of the Teachings in many Centres in the United Kingdom, Australia, France, New Zealand and United States of America. Details will be sent on request, in writing, to the Trustees, at the address given below.

COMMUNICATIONS

Communications regarding the Literature of the Order should be addressed, and remittances made payable to, "The Literature Secretary", at the Head quarters.
Further information concerning the Order of the Cross and its activities will be gladly given to any inquirer, on application to:

THE TRUSTEES

THE ORDER OF THE CROSS
10 DE VERE GARDENS, KENSINGTON, LONDON, W8 5AE